Mass Communication Chronology

1960   Kennedy and Nixon meet in Great Debates

TV in 90% of all U.S. homes

Klapper's Effects of Mass Communication

1961   Key's Public Opinion and American Democracy

Kennedy makes nation's first live TV presidential press conference

Berelson's "Great Debate on Cultural Democracy"

Schramm team's Television in the Lives of Our Children published

1962   Festinger's cognitive dissonance article appears

Kraus's Great Debates

Air Force commissions Paul Baran to develop a national computer network

1963   JFK assassinated

Bandura's aggressive modeling experiments first appear

Networks begin one half-hour newscasts

1964   McLuhan's Understanding Media

1965   Color comes to all three commercial TV networks

Comsat satellite launched

1966   Mendelsohn's Mass Entertainment

Berger and Luckmann's Social Construction of Reality

1967   Merton's On Theoretical Sociology

1969   Blumer coins "symbolic interaction"

ARPANET, forerunner to Internet, goes online

1971   Bandura's Psychological Modeling

1972   Surgeon General's Report on Television and Social Behavior released

McCombs and Shaw introduce "agenda-setting"

Gerbner's Violence Profile initiated

FCC requires cable companies to provide "local access"

Ray Tomlinson develops email

1973   Watergate Hearings broadcast live

1974   Blumler and Katz's Uses of Mass Communication

Noelle-Neumann introduces "spiral of silence"

Goffman pioneers frame analysis

Home use of VCR introduced

Term "Internet" coined

1975   ASNE's Statement of Principles replaces Canons

Bill Gates and Paul Allen develop operating system for personal computers

1977   Steve Jobs and Stephen Wozniack perfect Apple II

1978   Digital audio and video recording adopted as media industry standard

1981   IBM introduces the PC

1983   Journal of Communication devotes entire issue to "Ferment in the Field"

1985   Meyrowitz's No Sense of Place

1987   Chaffee and Berger formalize "communication science"

1990   Signorielli and Morgan's Cultivation Analysis

1991   Gulf War explodes, CNN emerges as important news source

1992   ACT disbands, says work is complete

World Wide Web released

1993   Ten years after "Ferment," Journal of Communication tries again with special issue, "The Future of the Field"

1996   Telecommunications Act passes, relaxes broadcast ownership rules, deregulates cable television, mandates television content ratings

1998   Journal of Communication devotes entire issue to media literacy

2001   Terrorist at   D.C.

From the Wadsworth Series in Mass Communication & Journalism

General Mass Communication

Anokwa, Kwadwo, Lin, Carolyn, Salwen, Michael, *International Communication: Issues and Controversies*

Biagi, Shirley, *Media/Impact: An Introduction to Mass Media*, 6th Ed.

Bucy, Erik, *Living in the Information Age: A New Media Reader*

Craft, John, Frederic Leigh, and Donald Godfrey, *Electronic Media*

Day, Louis, *Ethics in Media Communications: Cases and Controversies*, 4th Ed.

Dennis, Everette E., and John C. Merrill, *Media Debates: Great Issues for the Digital Age*, 4th Ed.

Fortner, Robert S., *International Communications: History, Conflict, and Control of the Global Metropolis*

Gillmor, Donald, Jerome Barron, and Todd Simon, *Mass Communication Law: Cases and Comment*, 6th Ed.

Gillmor, Donald, Jerome Barron, Todd Simon, and Herbert Terry, *Fundamentals of Mass Communication Law*

Hilmes, Michele, *Only Connect: A Cultural History of Broadcasting in the United States*

Hilmes, Michele, *Connections: A Broadcast History Reader*

Jamieson, Kathleen Hall, and Karlyn Kohrs Campbell, *The Interplay of Influence*, 5th Ed.

Kamalipour, Yahya K., *Global Communication*

Lester, Paul, *Visual Communication*, 3rd Ed.

Overbeck, Wayne, *Major Principles of Media Law*, 2002 Edition

Sparks, Glenn G., *Media Effects Research: A Basic Overview*

Straubhaar, Joseph, and Robert LaRose, *Media Now: Communications Media in the Information Age*, 3rd Ed.

Whetmore, Edward Jay, *Mediamerica, Mediaworld: Form, Content, and Consequence of Mass Communication*, Updated 5th Ed.

Zelezny, John D., *Communications Law: Liberties, Restraints, and the Modern Media*, 3rd Ed.

Zelezny, John D., *Cases in Communications Law*, 3rd Ed.

Journalism

Adams, Paul, *Writing Right for Today's Mass Media: A Textbook and Workbook with Language Exercises*

Anderson, Douglas, *Contemporary Sports Reporting*, 2nd Ed.

Bowles, Dorothy, and Diane L. Borden, *Creative Editing*, 3rd Ed.

Chance, Jean, and William McKeen, *Literary Journalism: A Reader*

Dorn, Raymond, *How to Design and Improve Magazine Layouts*, 2nd Ed.

Fischer, Heintz-Dietrich, *Sports Journalism at Its Best: Pulitzer Prize(Winning Articles, Cartoons, and Photographs*

Fisher, Lionel, *The Craft of Corporate Journalism*

Gaines, William, *Investigative Reporting for Print and Broadcast*, 2nd Ed.

Hilliard, Robert L., *Writing for Television, Radio, and New Media*, 7th Ed.

Kessler, Lauren, and Duncan McDonald, *When Words Collide*, 5th Ed.

Klement, Alice M., and Carolyn Burrows Matalene, *Telling Stories/Taking Risks: Journalism Writing at the Century's Edge*

Laakaniemi, Ray, *Newswriting in Transition*

Miller, Lisa, *Power Journalism: Computer-Assisted Reporting*

Rich, Carole, *Writing and Reporting News: A Coaching Method*, 4th Ed.

Wilber, Rick, and Randy Miller, *Modern Media Writing*

Photojournalism and Photography

Parrish, Fred S., *Photojournalism: An Introduction*

Public Relations and Advertising

Hendrix, Jerry A., *Public Relations Cases*, 5th Ed.

Hunt, Todd, Grunig, James, *Public Relations Techniques*

Jewler, Jerome A., and Bonnie L. Drewniany, *Creative Strategy in Advertising*, 7th Ed.

Newsom, Doug, and Bob Carrell, *Public Relations Writing: Form and Style*, 6th Ed.

Newsom, Doug, Judy VanSlyke Turk, and Dean Kruckeberg, *This Is PR: The Realities of Public Relations*, 7th Ed.

Sivulka, Juliann, *Soap, Sex, and Cigarettes: A Cultural History of American Advertising*

Woods, Gail Baker, *Advertising and Marketing to the New Majority: A Case Study Approach*

Research and Theory

Babbie, Earl, *The Practice of Social Research*, 8th Ed.

Baran, Stanley, and Dennis Davis, *Mass Communication Theory: Foundations, Ferment, and Future*, 3rd Ed.

Rubenstein, Sondra, *Surveying Public Opinion*

Rubin, Rebecca B., Alan M. Rubin, and Linda J. Piele, *Communication Research: Strategies and Sources*, 5th Ed.

Wimmer, Roger D., and Joseph R. Dominick, *Mass Media Research: An Introduction*, 7th Ed.

Mass Communication Theory

Foundations, Ferment, and Future

Third Edition

Stanley J. Baran, Ph.D.
Bryant College

Dennis K. Davis, Ph.D.
Pennsylvania State University

THOMSON

WADSWORTH

Australia • Canada • Mexico • Singapore • Spain
United Kingdom • United States

Publisher: Holly J. Allen
Assistant Editor: Nicole George
Editorial Assistant: Amber Fawson
Technology Project Manager: Jeanette Wiseman
Marketing Manager: Kimberly Russell
Marketing Assistant: Neena Chandra
Advertising Project Manager: Shemika Britt
Project Manager, Editorial Production: Ritchie Durdin
Print/Media Buyer: Rebecca Cross

Permissions Editor: Joohee Lee
Production Service: Robin Gold / Forbes Mill Press
Text Designer: Robin Gold
Copy Editor: Robin Gold
Cover Designer: Ross Carron
Cover Printer: Webcom Limited
Compositor: Linda Weidemann, Wolf Creek Press
Printer: Webcom Limited

For more information about our products,
contact us at:
Thomson Learning Academic Resource Center
1-800-423-0563
For permission to use material from this text,
contact us by:
Phone: 1-800-730-2214 Fax: 1-800-730-2215
Web: http://www.thomsonrights.com

Library of Congress Control Number: 2002107738

ISBN 0-534-56163-2

Wadsworth/Thomson Learning
10 Davis Drive
Belmont, CA 94002-3098
USA

Asia
Thomson Learning
5 Shenton Way #01-01
UIC Building
Singapore 068808

Australia
Nelson Thomson Learning
102 Dodds Street
South Melbourne, Victoria 3205
Australia

Canada
Nelson Thomson Learning
1120 Birchmount Road
Toronto, Ontario M1K 5G4
Canada

Europe/Middle East/Africa
Thomson Learning
High Holborn House
50/51 Bedford Row
London WC1R 4LR
United Kingdom

Latin America
Thomson Learning
Seneca, 53
Colonia Polanco
11560 Mexico D.F.
Mexico

Spain
Paraninfo Thomson Learning
Calle/Magallanes, 25
28015 Madrid, Spain

Dedicated to Sidney Kraus

His words and actions in the years since the first edition of this book have
convinced us of the wisdom of our original decision to honor him
—our friend, mentor, and colleague

Contents

Section Three   The Rise and Fall of Limited Effects   124

Chapter 6 Limited Effects Theory Emerges   126

Chapter 7 Middle-Range Theory and the Consolidation of the Limited Effects Paradigm   156

Preface

We wrote the first and second editions of this textbook at a prosperous time in the life of our nation when U.S. media industries were undergoing rapid change. American corporations were spreading around the world. Dot com companies were thriving in a "New Economy" that some thought likely to prosper for decades. New media technology was evolving so rapidly and new media applications were proliferating so fast that a new scale of "Internet time" was created to measure change. "Brick and mortar" companies were distained in favor of virtual enterprises.

Change was also going on in media theory and research. Theory was in ferment as new perspectives challenged long-standing notions. Researchers struggled with questions flowing from the changes in media. They debated how best to understand the role of new media and chart their place among the well-established mass media. Considerable research focused on mass media entertainment and its effects. Researchers asked whether new media-based entertainment would displace established mass media. Would the Internet displace television or would the tube absorb the Internet? Would people pay the extra price to get HDTV? Did the protection of children from online smut require new laws? What would happen to face-to-face communication in the wake of the email onslaught? Virtual democracy? MP3? Web radio?

On September 11, 2001, everything changed. As we wrote the third edition to this textbook, the Western world was reeling from the terrorist attack on the World Trade Center in New York and on the Pentagon in Washington. A new type of war was declared on terrorism. Americans were told to make important sacrifices and to be vigilant, but at the same time to carry on our daily lives as though September 11 had never happened. As authors, we faced a serious challenge. When it comes to media theories, what is still relevant and what is unimportant? How can and should we understand the role that media now play in the world that has been radically altered? In our previous editions we argued, "the price to be paid for our failure to understand the role of media is dear." We pointed to controversies over the effects of media violence and the banning of rap music lyrics. We worried about growing dissatisfaction with modern election

xiii

campaigns and the role of an increasingly "bottom-line" focused press in our democracy. These questions remain important and will doubtlessly rise again on the media research agenda. But for a time these questions have been displaced by more pressing issues.

On September 11, we were eyewitnesses to an atrocity that will forever alter our experience of our social world. The power of media to mediate an event and bring it into our homes was never before demonstrated so dramatically. But how should we understand this power? Is it something we should embrace or fear? Is it a new form of media power or has it been seen before? In the weeks following the attack, our nation was swept by a wave of patriotism not seen since the Second World War. Support for government and the president rose to new heights. Did media play a role in fostering this transformation of public opinion? In a time of national crisis, what role can and should media play? These are new questions for this generation of media researchers, but they are also old questions— questions that the first generation of media researchers grappled with in the 1930s and 1940s.

This textbook uses an historical approach to presenting media theory. In previous editions, we argued that the value of this approach lay in its ability to reveal how social theory generally—and media theory specifically—develops in an ongoing effort to address pressing technological, social, and political problems. Often the most important eras for media theory development have been those of crisis and social turmoil. These are the times when the most important questions about media are asked and the search for their answers is most desperate. For half a century after the 1940s, we relied on media theories forged in the cauldron of economic depression and worldwide warfare. But by the 1990s, the concerns of earlier eras had faded. In our last edition, we asked whether an era of dramatic technological change might give rise to new media theories for a world whose problems were different from the 1940s. Did we need new media theories to fit a stable and orderly world with rising economic prosperity and startling but beneficent technological change?

Now we confront the challenges of a world in which many old questions about the role of media suddenly have an important new urgency. As you read this book, you will find that we devote considerable attention to propaganda. This attention is necessary because in the 1930s and 1940s, the most important questions concerning media centered on propaganda. Could media propaganda induce widespread conversions from one ideology to another? Was systematic censorship of media essential to the preservation of democracy as we faced the totalitarian threats of fascism and communism? How could propaganda be used to promote democracy at a time when the deficiencies of democracy were so evident and the fruits of totalitarianism so alluring to masses of people around the world? After September 11, similar questions are again being asked and answered in the highest circles of the

American government. Hollywood writers and executives were invited to meetings with the White House and military to win their aid and support for the war effort. Television networks were asked to voluntarily censor enemy video that could be sending coded messages. On television screens, we saw the faces of masses of angry people in cities across the Islamic world. Propaganda was clearly inflaming their passions. Could this propaganda kindle domestic unrest—could U.S. adherents to Islam be converted along with their counterparts around the world? We faced an enemy skilled at using propaganda to promote a religious ideology that most Americans find incomprehensible because it is so fundamentally opposed to their way of life. And yet, this ideology clearly had a strong appeal in many parts of the Islamic world. In the new war that we will be waging for years to come, media are likely to be among our most important weapons. A propaganda battle for the hearts and minds of people will again need to be waged. An understanding of media theory will provide crucial insights for this new war.

A Unique Approach

One unique feature of this book is the way we provide balanced, comprehensive introductions to the two major bodies of theory that currently dominate the field: the social/behavioral theories, which some have labeled communication science, and the cultural/critical theories. We need to know the strengths and the limitations of these two bodies of theory. We need to know how they developed in the past, how they are developing in the present, and what new conceptions they might produce because not only do these schools of thought represent the mass communication theory of today, they also promise to dominate our understanding of mass communication for some time to come.

Many texts emphasize social/behavioral theories and either ignore or denigrate cultural/critical theories. Instructors and students are then forced to supplement their texts with books that introduce critical/cultural theories—books that often express open hostility toward social/behavioral theories. To solve this problem (and we hope advance understanding of all mass communication theory), we systematically explain the legitimate differences that exist between researchers who use the different theories. We also consider possibilities for accommodation or collaboration between them.

The Use of History

In this book, we assume that it is important for those who study mass communication theory to have a strong grounding in the historical development of media theory. Therefore, in the pages that follow, we trace the history of theory in a clear, straightforward manner. We include discussions of historical events and people that students will find inherently interesting, especially if instructors use widely available videotapes and other materials to illustrate them (such as political propaganda, the *War of the Worlds* broadcast, Adolf Hitler, and so on).

The Use of Topics

It is important, too, that students realize that theories have been developed to address important questions about the role of media—enduring questions that will again become quite important as new media continue to be introduced and as we deal with a world reordered by September 11. We must be aware of how the radical changes in media that took place in the past are related to the changes taking place now. Examples can be found in discussion questions at the end of chapters.

We attempt this engagement with mass communication theory in several ways. Each chapter includes a section entitled "Exploring Mass Communication Theory," directing students to the Internet and World Wide Web where they can use **InfoTrac College Edition** to investigate hundreds of journals and magazines in search of supporting or enriching material, and where they are also directed to interesting Web sites relating to the chapter's content. The "Critical Thinking Questions" section serves two functions. First, students can review the chapters' important points and, second, students can use that information to think critically about their own values and assumptions. We believe that mass communication theory, if it is to have any meaning for students, must be used by them.

All chapters also provide lists of significant people and their writing; boxes that explain or illustrate important ideas, events, or theorists; definitions of important terms in the margins near where they first appear; and chapter summaries. At the end of the text is an extensive bibliography as well as a thorough index.

The Big Picture

This textbook provides a comprehensive, historically based, authoritative introduction to mass communication theory. We have provided clearly written examples, graphics, and other materials to illustrate key theories. We trace the emergence of two main bodies of mass communication theory—social/behavioral and critical/cultural—and conclude with a discussion of how these two traditions support the media literacy movement and might be combined to produce a new theory of mediated communication.

We offer many examples of social/behavioral and critical/cultural theory and an in-depth discussion of their strengths and limitations. We emphasize that media theories are human creations that typically are intended to address specific problems or issues. We believe that it is easier to learn theories when they are examined with contextual information about the motives of theorists and the problems and issues they addressed.

In the next few years, as mass media industries continue to experience rapid change and as we come to terms with the post–September 11 "new world order," it is quite likely that understanding media theory will become even more necessary and universal. All the old questions about the role of media in society and in people's lives will resurface with renewed relevance. This book traces how these questions have been addressed in the past, and we provide insights into how they might be addressed in the future.

The Supporting Philosophy of This Book

The philosophy of this book is relatively straightforward: Though today's media technologies might be new, their impact on daily life might not be so different from past influences. Changes in media have always posed challenges but have also created opportunities. We can use media to improve the quality of our lives or we can permit our lives to be seriously disrupted. As a society, we can use media wisely or foolishly. To make these choices, we need theories—theories that explain the role of media for us as individuals and guide the development of media industries for our society at large. This book should help us develop our understanding of theory so we can make better use of media and play a role in the development of new media industries.

Acknowledgments

In preparing this third edition, we have had the assistance of many people. Most important, we have drawn on the scholarly work of several generations of social and cultural theorists. Their ideas have inspired and guided contemporary work. It's an exciting time to be a communication scholar!

We work within a research community that might be in ferment but that is also both vibrant and supportive. In these pages, we acknowledge and explain the contributions that our many colleagues across the United States and around the world have made to mass communication theory. We regret the inevitable errors or omissions, and we take responsibility for them. We are grateful to our reviewers:

Daniel A. Panici, University of Southern Maine

John W. Owens, Western Carolina University

Dominic Lasorsa, University of Texas, Austin

Hong Cheng, Bradley University

Elizabeth M. Perse, University of Delaware

These reviewers helped us avoid some errors and omissions, but they bear no responsibility for those that remain. We also wish to thank our Wadsworth friends, whose encouragement and advice sustained us. Their task was made less difficult than it might otherwise have been by our first Wadsworth editor, Becky Hayden, and Chris Clerkin, the editor for the first edition of this text. These accomplished professionals taught us how to avoid many of the sins usually committed by novice textbook authors.

We must also thank our families. We admit that this has become something of a cliché. The truth, however, is that the families of authors must endure the authors' detachment, bad moods, and absences as the book is crafted. In State College, the Davis family—Nancy, Jeni, Kerry, Andy, Mike—and in Wakefield, the Baran family—Susan, Jordan, Matt, and Simmony—indeed suffered our detachment, bad moods, and absences. All did so with charm and love.

Finally, this book is the product of a collaboration that has gone on for nearly thirty years. We started our professional careers at Cleveland State University in 1973 in a communication department headed by Sidney Kraus. Sid inspired us, along with most other junior faculty, to become active, productive researchers. Today, a disproportionate number of active communication scholars have direct or indirect links to the Cleveland State program. Sid demonstrates the many ways that a single person can have a powerful impact on a discipline. Through his scholarship, his mentorship, and his friendship he has left a truly indelible mark.

Introduction to Mass Communication Theory

Chapter 1

Introduction

The distribution of TOPtext, a software program surreptitiously bundled with other programs freely downloaded from the World Wide Web, produced quite a bit of controversy in the online world, the advertising industry, and among many everyday citizens and media professionals in 2001. TOPtext was the latest in a long line of digital technologies supporting *contextual advertising;* that is, it instantly permitted advertising to appear on the screens of Web users whether they wanted it or not. Sure, Internet surfers were already aware of similar technologies. Cyber-advertising technologies such as *banners* (digital "billboards" sitting atop a Web page), *instititial ads* (images that appear and disappear when users move from one page to another), *pop-outs* (commercials appearing in a second, smaller window at the border of a Web page already being read), *extramercials* (columns of ad content that slide down over an existing Web page), *targeted keywords* (where an advertiser's commercials pop up on users' screens every time they type that sponsor's name), *pop-under ads* (commercials that suddenly appear, uninvited, as users move from site to site), and *transaction journalism* (the placement of hyperlinks directly in the text of a Web page), had served or annoyed users for years.

But TOPtext was something new. It gave advertisers the power to *buy the rights to specific words.* That is, every time users who had knowingly or otherwise downloaded this software onto their computers had a specific word or phrase appear on their screens—"cars," "home buying," or "music" for example—that word or phrase would appear, underlined in yellow. It did not matter what site was being visited or content viewed; if the purchased word or phrase showed up, it was highlighted. When users passed a cursor over the underlined word or phrase, an ad for the sponsor who now *owned* it would instantly appear over the text. If users clicked on it, they would be instantly sent to the advertiser's Web site, whether they wanted to or not. Many advertising executives saw TOPtext as "finally delivering the promise of advertising on the Internet," but others viewed it as "more of an intrusion on people's (Internet) behavior." Still other commentators objected to TOPtext on grounds of fairness. Said Scott Ross, new media director for the Web site of an independent record label, "These companies are preying on us people who are into using computers, but not so tech savvy that we know what we're doing. It's building a business model in a clandestine way. It's not kosher in my book. It's a covert operation" (Evangelista, 2001, p. D3).

But what's not kosher? Don't advertisers have a right to have their messages appear before the Web browsing public? Commercials appear in radio and television programming whether listeners and viewers want them or not. Increasingly, companies are paying for *product placements,* the insertion of their brands in movies and even books (Kirkpatrick, 2001). Nobody asks filmgoers and readers for *their* permission. Still, aren't the Internet and the Web different from those older, traditional media? Aren't they, or at least weren't they supposed to be freer, more under people's individual control, somehow more personal? For every newbie, a Web newcomer, there is a user turned off by the constant sponsor interruption and overall commercialization of cyberspace.

We are in the midst of a revolution in communication technology that is transforming social orders and cultures around the world. Each new technological device expands the possible uses of the existing technologies. New media can be combined to create media systems that span great distances but that can also serve a broad range of highly specific purposes. In retrospect, we now regard the first century of mass communication as one dominated by expensive, clumsy technologies that provided a limited array of services to gigantic audiences. We were forced to accommodate our needs to what the older media technologies could provide. Highly centralized media systems were established and controlled by large corporations located in the largest cities. For most of us, the term "mass media" still is synonymous with these "big media." Now, although we are caught up in a communications revolution, much of our attention is still riveted on the media dinosaurs. We are only beginning to understand the potential of alternative media to serve needs we didn't know we had. If this were not so, the Internet and World Wide Web would be neither as popular, nor as controversial as they are.

For many of us the immediate consequences of this revolution have been both pleasant and benign. The new media have greatly expanded our options for entertainment and information content. Instead of choosing from a handful of movies at local theaters or on three network television stations, we can select from thousands of titles available on cable channels, satellites, videotapes, and video discs. By exchanging copies of records, tapes, and discs with friends, we can create large home music libraries. At any given moment, we can tune to several different newscasts on television and radio. Using personal computers, we can access remote databases and scan endless reams of information on diverse, specialized topics. Rather than the handful of local radio stations available on our dials, we can hear ten thousand stations on the Web. We can use the Internet's interactive capabilities to experiment with and create new identities. An array of print media is available—many edited to suit the tastes of relatively small audiences. The old marketplace of ideas has become a gigantic supermarket. If you want it, you can get it somewhere.

In this textbook, we will examine how media scholars have conceptualized the role of media during this and the last century. Our purpose is to provide you with a broad and historically grounded perspective on what media can do *for* you and *to* you. We have reviewed some of the best (and worst) thinking concerning the role and potential of media. We ask that you join us in looking back to the origins of media and the early efforts to understand their influence and role. We will trace the challenge of new technology and the rise of various media industries, focusing on the theories that were developed to make sense of them. Finally, we will conclude with a review of current theory and assist you in developing a personally relevant perspective on media.

Keep in mind, though, that this is not a book about new media technology, although we will often use examples of new technology to illustrate our points and to demonstrate the relevance of various theories. Our purpose is to help you place new communication technology into historical and theoretical perspective. The challenges we face today as we move more deeply into the information age are similar in certain respects to those people faced during the era of the penny press or the Golden Age of Radio. We can learn much from examining how people have tried to understand media technology and anticipate its consequences for their lives. The theories of past generations can assist us as we face the challenges of today's new media.

This book is structured chronologically. This organizational scheme represents, in part, our support of Rogers, Dearing, and Bergman's belief that

> the most common means of investigating intellectual histories is the historical method, which seeks to understand paradigmatic change by identifying key instances of personal and impersonal influence, which are then interpreted as determining the parameters and directions of a particular field of study. A social scientific understanding of such histories, while acknowledging the importance of key instances of intellectual influence, must seek to identify patterns that represent influence over time. (1993, p. 69)

Our chronological structuring also reflects our view that most social theories, including media theory, are never completely innovative and are always the products of the particular era in which they are constructed. As geologist and zoologist Stephen Jay Gould writes of science in general, those who deal with theories "can work only within their social and psychological contexts. Such an assertion does not debase the institution of science, but rather enriches our view of the greatest dialectic in human history: the transformation of society by scientific progress, which can only arise within a matrix set, constrained, and facilitated by society" (2000, p. 31). Put more simply by historian Joan Jacobs Brumberg, and speaking specifically of those who traffic in social theory, "Science in and of itself has some culture embedded in it. How could it be otherwise?" (quoted in Belkin, 2000, p. 43). Present-day theories are mostly updated versions of old ideas, even when they provide seemingly radical revisions or sophisticated syntheses of earlier notions. To understand contemporary theories, it's important to understand the theories on which they are based. This does not mean, however, that mass communication theory developed in an orderly, chronologically stable way, with new, improved ideas supplanting older, disproved notions. Theories about media and violence, for example, have been around as long as there have been media (Ball-Rokeach, 2001; Wartella & Reeves, 1985). Concern about harmful media effects were voiced in this country as early as 1900 and were strongly articulated in the 1930s and again in the 1950s. The 1960s were the heyday of mass communication scholars' theoretical attention to the problem of media and subsequent viewer, listener, or reader aggression. One important component of the Telecommunications Act of 1996 was the requirement that television set manufacturers install an electronic violence-screening device, the V-chip. Still, Congress in every year since has held hearings on video and film violence.

This book is also based on the assumption that all social theory is a human construction—*an active effort by communities of scholars to make sense of their social world.* Individual theories often have many different objectives. Some forms of theory mainly guide the decision-making of political and social elites. These theories tend to focus on the *structure* of society and attempt to explain how it can best be preserved. Other forms seek transformation of the status quo. They explore the *dynamic processes* that underlie social change. Their purpose is to guide useful social change.

Scholarly communities differ in what they want to accomplish with the theories they create. From one decade to the next, there are important, qualitative shifts in theory construction as new groups of scholars emerge with new objectives and new ways of organizing older ideas. For example, during times of social turmoil or external threat, scholarly communities often become allied with powerful elites and work to preserve the status quo. At other times, scholarly communities spring up that are critical of the existing social order and work to reform or transform it. Still other communities have long-term, humanistic goals that include liberal education and cultural enlightenment.

We will consider five distinctive eras in the development of mass communication theories, beginning with the origin of media theory in the nineteenth century and ending with the emergence of an array of contemporary perspectives. As we explore each, we will describe the various types of mass communication theories that were constructed, consider their objectives, and illustrate both their strengths and their limitations. We will point out the purposes that these theories served and the reasons why they were replaced or ignored by later scholars. In most cases, these theories couldn't be validated by scientific research. Evidence directly contradicted many of their key notions. Eventually, proponents gave up trying to find evidence to support them, and interest in them faded.

We will tell the story of mass communication theory development. This story should help you better understand how past theories evolved and why current theories are considered important. Although many of the older theories have been rejected as unscientific or otherwise useless and are no longer used to guide our thinking, they remain important as milestones (Lowery & DeFleur, 1995), and some continue to enjoy contemporary acceptance by segments of the public and some media practitioners. Most important, though, you can't adequately appreciate existing theories without some knowledge of earlier perspectives.

In recent decades, the number and variety of mass communication theories have steadily increased. Media theory has emerged as a more or less independent body of thought in both the social science and humanistic literatures. This book is intended as a guide to this diverse and sometimes contradictory thinking. You will find ideas developed by scholars in every area of the social sciences, from history and anthropology to sociology and psychology. Ideas have also been drawn from the humanities, especially from philosophy and literary analysis. The resulting ferment of ideas is both challenging and heuristic. These theories provide the raw materials for constructing even more useful and powerful theoretical perspectives.

If you are looking for a concise, consistent definition of theory, you won't find it in this book. We have avoided narrow definitions of theory in favor of an inclusive approach that finds value in most systematic, scholarly efforts to make sense of media and their role in society. We have included recent theories that some contemporary researchers consider unscientific. Some of the theories reviewed are **grand**; they try to explain entire media systems and their effects on society. Others are very small and provide narrower insight into the use or role of media. Our selection of theories for inclusion in this book has been based partly on their enduring, historical importance and partly on their potential to contribute to future scholarship. This process is necessarily subjective and is based on our own understanding of mass communication. Our consideration of contemporary perspectives has been limited to those that illustrate enduring or innovative conceptualizations.

GRAND THEORY
Theory designed to describe and explain all aspects of a given phenomenon

Three Questions About Media

Throughout this book, we weave a discussion of three issues or questions provoked by mass media that have driven and continue to drive the development of mass communication theory:

- What potential is offered and what threats are posed by *new forms of media technology?*

- What forms of media bureaucracies or industries should be created to *control or regulate media technologies* so that their potential is realized and their threats minimized?

- How can media *serve democratic and culturally pluralistic societies?*

These issues have provoked ongoing debate and controversy during the past century. Most theories in this book address one or more of these questions. With the development of new forms of media technology—and with our national reassessment of our place in the world after the terrorist attacks of September 11—old questions have resurfaced and new answers are being sought. Today, the Internet and the World Wide Web inspire many of the same controversies sparked in earlier eras by the penny press, nickel movies, and dime novels. Cable television did the same, as did television before it and radio before that. The debates surrounding the Internet and Web—protection of children from indecency, control of offensive content, limits on hate speech, maintenance of personal privacy, protection of copyright, the threat of overcommercialization, the impact on our democracy of disparities in access to information and technology—have all raged more than once before. These controversies are not new. They recur routinely in predictable fashion.

In every era, proponents of new media technology would argue that it had the potential to interconnect people in powerful new ways, that technology could aid the formation of new communities by bridging cultural differences and dissolving barriers posed by space and time. New media advocates offer novel ways of structuring media industries to use this potential. Advocates look forward to the creation of ideal social orders in which media would serve as a bulwark for democracy, cultural pluralism, and dynamic yet stable social change. These, for example and as you are no doubt aware, constitute the oft-touted "promise of the Internet." Inevitably, media proponents were and are opposed by critics who charge that new technologies are inherently dangerous, that they will inevitably undermine the existing social orders, and precipitate widespread unrest and disorder. Again, for example and as you are no doubt aware, these make up the "threat of the Internet." Critics of emerging communication technologies support preservation of existing media industries and the status quo. For them, the risks associated with media experimentation are unwarranted. Critics regard new media proponents as idealistic dreamers and themselves as practical realists.

New media proponents also believe that media can be used to fundamentally alter our personal lives in useful, meaningful ways. They argue that new technology can expand each person's cultural and experiential horizons. They envision newly energized, *active audiences* in which people find ways of making media serve them so that their lives are more interesting and purposeful. Media opponents fear that average people will be overwhelmed by new technologies, paralyzed by the mesmerizing power of new media, and ultimately transformed into gigantic, *passive audiences*—a world of couch potatoes and cyberaddicts. Proponents foresee the rise of a responsible citizenry that uses new media to construct increasingly democratic forms of government, but opponents see the rise of demagogues whose power is based on the cynical manipulation of the public. Proponents envision ideal social orders in which new technology fosters cultural understanding so that people practicing many different cultures can live in harmony. Opponents argue that the same technology will sharpen and deepen cultural stereotypes and spread fears about other cultures. Thus, instead of creating harmony, new media will incite conflict or even open warfare.

It is impossible, for example, to discuss any aspect of the growing rancor and partisanship that characterize American political discourse, both in government and among people, without considering the impact of such media as traditional television and print journalism that insist on crafting simplistic, good versus evil, right versus wrong stories, talk (some say hate) radio, the Internet, fax machines, and desktop publishing facilitated by sophisticated, inexpensive computer technology. Can we say that media *caused* this phenomenon? Or did they simply reinforce an existing condition? To address these questions, we need to look at theory and the research based on it.

Within academia, many scholarly communities developed to investigate the role of media. Sometimes these scholars worked in close association with either proponents or opponents of media. Funding for the scholars' work came from groups, foundations, or corporations that lauded or feared media. These communities created a broad range of media theories—from the media paranoia found in some mass society notions to the global village community envisioned by Marshall McLuhan in the 1960s and reborn in the age of the Internet. Often theories began as little more than listings of media hopes or fears written by media proponents or critics. As theories evolved, research was conducted based on these ideas, and both the ideas and research they fueled were critically evaluated. Occasionally, theories excited widespread public interest, as when Marshall McLuhan declared that the "medium is the message (and massage)." But more often, interest in media theory has been limited to universities, government agencies, media industry researchers, and special interest groups like Fairness and Accuracy in Media (FAIR) and the now-disbanded Action for Children's Television (ACT).

For example, various theories of television violence inspire great controversy within the media industries and in academia by pitting industry researchers against university researchers and public interest groups. But these disputes tend to receive little attention from the general public, even when they are reported by the news media. Senator John Pastore became infamous among television network executives in the 1970s for his scathing criticisms of televised violence and inferior children's programming. Connecticut Senator Joseph Lieberman echoes Pastore's complaints today. Neither name is widely known even among the 80 percent of the public who, according to annual *New York Times* polls, consistently believes that there is too much violence on television.

Throughout this book, you will find boxes that feature our three questions about media. Some boxes focus attention on specific events that highlight or illustrate an issue. Others deal with debates between different groups over an issue. Some discuss how a theorist addressed an issue and tried to resolve it. Still others highlight and criticize important, issue-related examples of bad media theory. We hope that you will find these useful in developing your own thinking about these issues. You will be asked to relate material in these boxes to contemporary controversies, events, and theories. *Instant Access* boxes will present the advantages and disadvantages of the major theories we discuss. The advantages are those offered by the theories' proponents; the disadvantages are the views of their critics. These presentations are at best sketchy or partial presentations, and although they should give you a pretty good idea of the theories, you need to complete the picture with a full reading of the chapters and a great deal of reflection on the theories they present. In addition, each chapter will end with a section on exploring mass communication and one offering questions for critical thinking. The former will ask you to put yourself in the mass communication process. The latter will challenge you to examine your assumptions about that process and your role in it.

If we have learned anything about media over the past century, it is that they are not demonic forces that inevitably precipitate societal or personal disasters. Media alone don't create couch potatoes and cyberaddicts, or foster massive political demonstrations. But neither are they benign agents of a New Order ushering in the new Age of Enlightenment. People using media have the power to create either division or community. Media technology alone is powerless to initiate useful change. But technology can augment and amplify the actions of individuals and groups and, in so doing, facilitate rapid and widespread social change on an important scale.

Media technology does have certain inherent biases—it amplifies and encourages some ways of understanding the social world and some forms of action more than others. We must develop theories that explain these biases if we are to use media wisely. Rather than simply provoking fear or inspiring optimism, media theory should serve as a tool that guides our understanding and use of new technology. Media theory should enable us to shape media industries that serve our needs and minimize unplanned disruption to our personal lives and the society around us.

Defining and Redefining Mass Communication

MASS COMMUNI-
CATION *When a source, typically an organization, employs a technology as a medium to communicate with a large audience*

When an organization employs a technology as a medium to communicate with a large audience, **mass communication** is said to have occurred. The professionals at the *New York Times* (an organization) use printing presses and the newspaper (technology and medium) to reach their readers (a large audience). The writers, producers, filmmakers, and other professionals at Comedy Central use various audio and video technologies, satellites, cable television, and home receivers to communicate with their audience. Warner Brothers places ads in magazines to tell readers what movies it is releasing.

But as we saw at the beginning of this chapter, the mass communication environment is changing. When you receive a piece of direct mail advertising addressed by name to you, in which your name is used throughout, you are an audience of one—not the large audience envisioned in traditional notions of mass communication. When you sit at your computer and send an email to 20,000 people who have signed on to a **listserv** dedicated to a particular subject, you are obviously communicating with a large audience, but you are not an organization in the sense of a newspaper, cable television network, or movie studio. Light weight, portable, inexpensive video equipment makes it possible for an individual like you to profitably produce and distribute videos to quite small numbers of viewers. People attracted by many Web sites and cable channels can hardly be considered *mass* audiences when compared with the numbers that tune in to a network television program such as *Friends* or that go to a movie like *Harry Potter and the Sorcerer's Stone.*

LISTSERV *Software employed to manage online mailing lists, bulletin boards, or discussion groups that cover a variety of subjects*

MEDIATED COMMU-
NICATION *Communication between a few or many people that employs a technology as a medium*

INTERPERSONAL COMMUNICATION *Communication between two or a few people; typically face-to-face*

Most theories we will study in this text were developed before the modern communications revolution. This does not render them useless or outmoded, but it does require that we remember that much has changed in how people use technologies to communicate. One useful way to do this is to think of **mediated communication** as existing on a continuum that stretches from **interpersonal communication** at one end to traditional forms of mass communication at the other. Different media fall along this continuum depending on the amount of control and involvement that people have in the communication process. The telephone, for example, sits at one end. It is obviously a communication technology, but one that is most typical of interpersonal communication—at most, a very few people can be involved in communicating at any given time and they have a great deal of involvement and control over that communication—the conversation is theirs, they determine its content. A big budget Hollywood movie or a network television telecast of the Super Bowl sits at the opposite pole. Viewers have limited control over the communication that occurs. Certainly people can apply idiosyncratic interpretations to the content before them, and they can choose to direct however much attention they wish to the screen, but their control and involvement over the communication is largely limited to attending or not and viewing or not.

As you'll see when we examine the more contemporary mass communication theories, the new communication technologies have rendered this a crucial factor in understanding how individuals and societies use media and are affected by them. As communication theorists Steven Chaffee and Miriam Metzger explain, "contemporary media allow for a greater quantity of information transmission and retrieval, place more control over both content creation and selection in the hands of their users, and do so with less cost to the average consumer" (2001, p. 369). For example, the video technology DVD allows viewers not only to "re-edit" a film's scenes into whatever order they desire, but to insert alternative endings—that is, viewers can exercise more involvement and control over the outcome of the communication process than they have when watching the same film in a theater. This changes the relationship between audience members and content; it significantly affects meaning-making.

Five Eras of Media Theory

This book is divided into four sections. In the first (which you are now reading), we introduce you to this book, to mass communication theory, to the three media related issues, and to media research (Chapter 2). In the remaining three sections (Chapters 3 to 12), we trace specific eras in the development of media theory. Each section surveys key events, theorists, and theories. Individual chapters consider the most important theories in depth. In each section, we discuss how world events influenced thinking about media and show a timeline to help you relate important events in the development of media to the appearance of various theories and theorists.

Recommended class exercises encourage you to imagine how you might have regarded media had you lived in these eras. Chapters feature important theorists and their work, giving you insight into their concerns and motivations. Special attention is given to the three recurring media issues and to dominant perspectives on media in each era.

Within each era, the emergence of important conflicting perspectives can best be seen as the accomplishment of a research community working within the constraints imposed by its own values, preexisting ideas, and research standards.

Each research community was also constrained by competing theories, limited financial resources, externally imposed political restrictions, and values held in the larger society. Although isolated theorists can produce innovative conceptualizations, research communities give recognition to, develop, and then popularize these notions. We will consider how such communities have grown and functioned as we describe the theories they fostered or rejected.

As we move through the various eras of media theory, you will gain an understanding of how current thinking about media has evolved. You will learn why certain forms of theory are now considered obsolete even though they still appear interesting and potentially useful. Sometimes you will find that ideas that contemporary media scholars consider outdated are still discussed as valid in *TV Guide* or *Parent's Magazine.* You will learn why specific theories have enduring appeal to present-day researchers. You will learn about the discoveries that researchers hope to make as they work with current theories. In the last three chapters, we will discuss the perspectives on media that dominate current media research and offer an overview of some of the most interesting work being done today within these perspectives. The advantages and limitations of these perspectives will be outlined. You will be encouraged to apply ideas from these perspectives to your thinking about your own use of media and how new technologies might affect your life and your social world. We hope that some of you will seriously consider a career in media research. We hope that all of you will become more active, literate users of media, individuals who can take a leading role in shaping media to serve your needs and those of your community, nation, and world.

Now, we'll briefly summarize the five major eras in mass communication theory: the era of mass society theory, the emergence of a scientific perspective on mass communications, the era of limited effects, the era of cultural criticism, and the emergence of a belief in moderate effects. This summary should help you anticipate topics that will be discussed more fully in later chapters.

The Era of Mass Society and Mass Culture

Our description of mass communication theory begins with a review of some of the earliest notions about media. These ideas were initially developed in the latter half of the nineteenth century as new media technologies were invented and popularized. Although some theorists were optimistic about new technology, most were extremely pessimistic (Brantlinger, 1983). They blamed new industrial technology for disrupting peaceful, rural communities and forcing people to live in urban areas merely to serve as a convenient work force in large factories, mines, or bureaucracies. Theorists were fearful of cities because of their crime, cultural diversity, and unstable political systems.

For many social thinkers, mass media symbolized everything that was wrong with nineteenth century urban life. Media were singled out for virulent criticism and charged with pandering to lower class tastes, fomenting political unrest, or violating important cultural norms. Most theorists were educated members of dominant **elites** who feared what they couldn't understand. The old social order based on a landed aristocracy was crumbling and so was its culture and politics. Were media responsible for this, or did they simply accelerate these changes?

ELITES *People oc-cupying elevated or privileged positions in a social system*

MASS SOCIETY THE-ORY *Perspective on Western, industrial society that attrib-utes an influential but often negative role to media*

PENNY PRESS *Newspapers that sold for one penny and earned profits through the sale of increased numbers of readers to advertisers*

The dominant perspective that emerged during this period is referred to as **mass society theory**. It began as a collection of contradictory notions—some quite radical, others quite reactionary. Interpreting mass society notions is diffi-cult because they come from both ends of the political spectrum. These notions were developed by monarchists who wanted to maintain the old political order and by revolutionaries who wanted to impose radical changes. The same basic criticisms of media were therefore advanced by ideological foes. In general, mass society ideas held strong appeal for any social elites whose power was threatened by change. Media industries, such as the **penny press**, were a convenient target for elites' criticisms. These industries catered to socially inferior audiences using simple, often sensational content. The media of the time were easily attacked as symptomatic of a sick society—a society that either needed to return to old val-ues (monarchism) or be forced to adopt a set of totally new values (revolution). During this period, many intense political conflicts strongly affected thinking about the mass media.

The essential argument of mass society theory is that media undermine the traditional social order. To cope with this disruption, steps must be taken to either restore the old order or institute a new one. But who should do this? Should estab-lished authorities be trusted to take control of media? Should media entrepreneurs be allowed to operate freely? Should revolutionary groups be given access to media? At the end of the nineteenth century and the beginning of the twentieth century, fierce debate erupted over these questions. This conflict often pitted a landed aristocracy whose power was based on tradition against urban elites whose power was based on the industrial revolution. In time, the leaders of the industrial revolution gained enormous influence over social change. They strongly favored all forms of technological development, including mass media. In their view, tech-nology was inherently good since it facilitated control over the physical environ-ment, expanded human productivity, and generated new forms of material wealth. New technology would bring an end to social problems and lead to the develop-ment of an ideal social world. But in the short-term, industrialization brought with it enormous problems—exploitation of workers, pollution, and social unrest. Chapters 3, 4, and 5 present the thinking about media of this era.

Today, the fallacies of both the technology critics and advocates are easily ap-parent. Mass society notions greatly exaggerated the ability of media to quickly undermine social order. These ideas failed to consider that media's power ultimately resides in the freely chosen uses that audiences make of it. Mass society thinkers were unduly paternalistic and elitist in their criticism of average people and in their fear that media's corruption of the masses would inevitably bring social and cultural ruin. But technology advocates were also misguided and failed to acknowledge the many unnecessary, damaging consequences that resulted from applying technology without adequately considering its impact.

Emergence of a Scientific Perspective on Mass Communication

Mass society notions were especially dominant among media theorists through the 1930s and have enjoyed intermittent popularity since then whenever new technology poses a threat to the status quo. During the 1930s, world events seemed to continually confirm the truth of mass society ideas. In Europe, reactionary and revolutionary political movements used media in their struggles for political power. German Nazis introduced propaganda techniques that ruthlessly exploited the power of new media technology like motion pictures and radio. These practices seemed to permit political leaders to easily manipulate public attitudes and beliefs. All across Europe, totalitarian leaders like Hitler, Stalin, and Mussolini rose to political power and were able to exercise seemingly total control over vast populations. Private ownership of media, especially broadcast media, was replaced by direct government control in most European nations. The explicit purpose of all these efforts was to maximize the usefulness of media in the service of society. But the unintended outcome in most cases was to place enormous power in the hands of ruthless leaders who were convinced that they personally embodied what was best for all their citizens. An important exception occurred in Great Britain where an independent public corporation, the British Broadcasting Corporation (BBC), was established to operate broadcast media.

At the very peak of their popularity, mass society notions came under attack from a most unlikely source—an Austrian immigrant trained in psychological measurement who fled the Nazis on a Ford Foundation fellowship (Lazarsfeld, 1969). That immigrant was Paul Lazarsfeld, and for the field of mass communication research, he proved to be the right person in the right place at the right time. Like many of his academic colleagues, Lazarsfeld was interested in exploring the potential of newly developed social science methods, such as surveys and field experiments, to understand and solve social problems. He combined academic training with a high level of entrepreneurial skill. Within a few years after arriving in the United States, he had established a very active and successful social research center, the Bureau for Applied Social Research at Columbia University. Despite the generic name, the bureau conducted considerable amounts of media-related research throughout its early years.

Lazarsfeld provides a classic example of a transitional figure in theory development—someone well grounded in past theory but also innovative enough to consider other ideas and methods for evaluating theory. Though quite familiar with and very sympathetic to mass society notions (Lazarsfeld, 1941), Lazarsfeld was above all a scientist. He argued that it wasn't enough to merely speculate about the influence of media on society. Instead, he proposed conducting carefully designed, elaborate field experiments in which he would be able to observe media influence and measure its magnitude. It was not enough to assume that political propaganda is powerful—you needed hard evidence to prove the existence of such effects (Lazarsfeld, Berelson, & Gaudet, 1944). His most famous efforts, the Voter Studies, actually began as an attempt to demonstrate the media's power, yet proved, at least to him and his colleagues, just the opposite.

By the early 1950s, Lazarsfeld's work had generated an enormous amount of data (by pre-computer standards). Interpretation of these data led him to conclude that media were not nearly as powerful as previously imagined. Instead, he found that people had numerous ways of resisting media influence and were influenced by many competing factors. Rather than serving as a disruptive social force, media seemed to reinforce existing social trends and strengthen rather than threaten the status quo. He found little evidence to support the worst fears of mass society theorists. Though Lazarsfeld never labeled his theory, it is now referred to as the **limited effects perspective.**

LIMITED EFFECTS PERSPECTIVE *View of media as reinforcing existing social trends and strengthening rather than threatening the status quo*

Today, as you'll see in Chapters 6 and 7, the limited effects perspective encompasses numerous smaller media theories. These view media as playing a very limited role in the lives of individuals and the larger society. Many of these theories are widely used in guiding research even though their shortcomings are recognized. They are especially useful in explaining the short-term influence of routine media usage by various types of audiences. Several of these theories are referred to as **administrative theories** because they are used to guide practical decisions for various organizations. For example, these theories can guide television advertisers as they develop and evaluate campaign strategies to boost sales.

ADMINISTRATIVE THEORIES *Media theories used to guide practical decisions for various organizations*

The Limited Effects Paradigm Emerges

During the 1950s, limited effects notions about media continued to gain acceptance within academia. Several important clashes occurred between its adherents and those who supported mass society ideas (Bauer & Bauer, 1960). In 1960, several classic studies of media effects (Campbell, Converse, Miller, & Stokes, 1960;

Deutschmann & Danielson, 1960; Klapper, 1960) provided apparently definitive support for the limited effects notions. By 1961, V. O. Key had published *Public Opinion and American Democracy,* a theoretical and methodological *tour de force* that integrated limited effects notions with social and political theory to create a perspective that is now known as **elite pluralism.** Advocates of mass society notions came under increasing attack as "unscientific" or "irrational" because they questioned "hard scientific findings." Mass society notions were further discredited within academia because they became associated with the anti-Communist **Red Scare** promoted by Senator Joseph McCarthy in the early 1950s. McCarthy and his allies focused considerable attention on purging alleged Communists from the media. These purges were justified using mass society arguments—average people needed to be protected from media manipulation.

By the mid-1960s, the debate between mass society and limited effects notions appeared to be over—at least within the mass communication research community. The body of empirical research findings continued to grow, and almost all these findings were consistent with the latter view. Little or no empirical research supported mass society theory. This was not surprising because most empirical researchers trained at this time were warned against its fallacies. For example, in the 1960s, a time of growing concern about violence in the United States and the dissolution of respect for authority, researchers and theorists from psychology, rather than mass communication, were most active and prominent in examining television's contribution to these societal ills (we will examine their efforts in Chapter 8).

Many communication scientists stopped looking for powerful media effects and concentrated instead on documenting modest, limited effects, as you'll see in Chapter 8. Some of the original media researchers had become bored with media research and returned to work in political science or sociology. In a controversial essay, Bernard Berelson, one of the people who worked closely with Paul Lazarsfeld, declared the field of communication research to be dead (Berelson, 1959). There simply was nothing left to study. Berelson argued that it was time to move on to more important work. Ironically, he wrote his essay just before the field of media research underwent explosive growth. Throughout the late 1960s and the 1970s, students flooded into journalism schools and communication departments. As these grew, so did their faculty. As the number of faculty increased, so did the volume of research. But was there anything left to study? Chapters 10 and 11 help answer this question.

ELITE PLURALISM *Theory asserting that media use by sophisticated audiences enriches democracy*

RED SCARE *Period in U.S. history, late 1950s to early 1960s, in which basic freedoms were threatened by searches for "Reds," or communists, in media and government*

Cultural Criticism: A Challenge to the Limited Effects Paradigm

Though most mass communication researchers in the United States found limited effects notions and the empirical research findings on which they were based persuasive, researchers in other parts of the world, as you'll see in Chapter 9, were less convinced. Mass society notions continued to flourish in Europe where both left-wing and right-wing concerns about the power of media were deeply rooted in World War II experiences with propaganda. Europeans were also skeptical about the power of scientific, quantitative social research methods to verify and develop social theory. These methods were widely viewed as a distinctly American fetish. Some European academics were resentful of the influence enjoyed by Americans after World War II. They argued that American empiricism was both simplistic and intellectually sterile. Although some European academics welcomed and championed American ideas, others strongly resisted them and argued for maintaining approaches considered less biased or more traditionally European.

NEOMARXISM *Social theory asserting that media enable dominant social elites to maintain their power*

One group of European social theorists who vehemently resisted post-war U.S. influence are the **neomarxists** (Hall, 1982). These left-wing social theorists believe that media enable dominant social elites to maintain their power. Media provide the elite with a convenient, subtle, yet highly effective means of promoting worldviews favorable to their interests. Mass media can be viewed, they argue, as a public arena in which cultural battles are fought and a dominant or hegemonic culture is forged. Elites dominate these struggles because they start with important advantages. Opposition is marginalized and the status quo is presented as the only logical, rational way of structuring society. Within neomarxist theory, efforts to examine media institutions and interpret media content came to have high priority.

BRITISH CULTURAL STUDIES *Perspective focusing on mass media and their role in promoting a hegemonic worldview and a dominant culture among various subgroups in a society*

DETERMINISTIC ASSUMPTIONS *Assumption that media have powerful, direct effects*

During the 1960s, neomarxists in Britain developed a school of social theory widely referred to as **British cultural studies**. It focused heavily on mass media and their role in promoting a hegemonic worldview and a dominant culture among various subgroups in the society. Researchers studied how members of those groups used media and demonstrated how this use led people to develop ideas that supported dominant elites. Researchers discovered that people often resisted the hegemonic ideas and propagated alternative interpretations of the social world (Mosco & Herman, 1981). Although British cultural studies began with **deterministic assumptions** about the influence of media (that is, the media have powerful, direct effects), their work came to focus on audience reception studies that revived important questions about the potential power of media in certain types of situations and the ability of active audience members to resist media influence—questions that 1960s American media scholars ignored because they were skeptical about the power of media and assumed that audiences were passive.

During the 1970s, questions about the possibility of powerful media effects were again raised within U.S. universities. Initially, these questions were often advanced by scholars in the humanities who were unrestrained by the limited effects perspective and untrained in the scientific method. Their arguments were routinely ignored and marginalized by social scientists because they were

CULTURAL CRITICISM
Collection of perspectives concerned with the conflict of interests in society and the ways communication perpetuates domination of one group over another

unsupported by "scientific evidence." Some of these scholars were attracted to European-style cultural criticism. Others attempted to create an "authentic" American school of cultural studies—though they drew heavily on Canadian scholars like Harold Innis and Marshall McLuhan (Carey, 1977). This **cultural criticism**, although initially greeted with considerable skepticism by "mainstream" effects researchers, gradually established itself as a credible and valuable alternative to limited effects notions.

Emergence of a Moderate Effects Perspective

COMMUNICATION
SCIENCE *A perspective on research that integrates all research approaches grounded in quantitative, empirical, and behavioral research methods*

SOCIAL SEMIOTICS
THEORY *Integration of communication science and critical and cultural studies focusing on audience activity to understand how audience members make sense of media messages*

MEDIA LITERACY
The ability to access, analyze, evaluate, and communicate media messages

Limited effects notions have recently undergone important transformations, partially because of pressures from cultural studies but also because of the emergence of new communication technologies that have forced a rethinking of traditional assumptions about how people use (and are used by) media, as you'll see in Chapter 12. We are in the early stages, then, of what may well become the fifth era of mass communication theory. New perspectives that lend support to the idea of *moderate* media effects—for example **communication science**, **social semiotics theory**, and the **media literacy** movement—are emerging. Several factors forced this reexamination of old research questions concerning the power of media. New evidence specifies occasions when media influence can be strong (for example, Iyengar & Kinder, 1986; Wartella, 1997). This evidence is being collected using innovative research methods that make it easier to study long-term media effects. These methods also enable researchers to probe short-term effects in greater depth, assisting them in locating some forms of influence that eluded earlier studies (Berger & Chaffee, 1987a).

At the heart of these perspectives are notions about an *active audience that uses media content to create meaningful experiences* (Bryant & Street, 1988). The moderate effects perspective acknowledges that important media effects can occur over longer periods as a direct consequence of viewer or reader intent. People can make media serve certain purposes, such as using media to learn information and induce meaningful experiences.

This "meaning-making perspective" asserts that when people use media to make meaning—when they are able to intentionally induce desired experiences—there are significant results. Sometimes these consequences are intended by consumers, but sometimes results are unanticipated and not wanted. Factors that intrude into and disrupt this making of meaning can have unpredictable consequences. The perspective implies that future research should focus on people's success or failure in their efforts to make meaning using media. Both intended and unintended consequences of media use should be studied.

Theorists who develop moderate effects ideas have struggled with a critical deficiency in older limited effects notions. The limited effects perspective was unable to understand or make predictions about media's role in cultural change. By flatly rejecting the possibility that media can play an important role in such change, theorists were unable to make sense of striking instances where the power of media appears to be obvious. For example, limited effects theorists are forced to deny that media could have played a significant role in the Civil Rights, anti–Vietnam War, women's, and the 1960s counter-culture movements. Yet, leaders of these movements made significant use of media, both to recruit and communicate with members and as vehicles to express their views to the public. Moreover, a little common sense and a touch of historical reflection would argue that these movements were quite successful in their media use. One possible cause of the limited effects perspective's failure to account for these obvious examples of large-scale media influence rests in the notion of **levels of analysis.**

LEVELS OF ANALYSIS *The focus of a researcher's attention, ranging from individuals to social systems*

Social research problems can be studied at a number of levels, from the **macroscopic** to the **microscopic.** Researchers, for example, can study media impact on cultures, societies, or nations; organizations or groups; small groups; and individuals. It should be possible to approach the issue of media effects at any of these levels and discover comparable results. But the limited effects researchers tended to focus their attention on the microscopic level, especially on individuals, from whom they could easily and efficiently collect data. When they had difficulty consistently demonstrating effects at the micro level, they tended to dismiss the possibility of effects at the cultural, or macroscopic, level.

MACROSCOPIC THEORY *Attempts to explain effects at the cultural or societal level*

MICROSCOPIC THEORY *Attempts to explain effects at the personal or individual level*

For example, the limited effects perspective denied that advertising imagery could cause significant cultural changes. Instead, it argued that advertising merely reinforces existing social trends. At best (or worst), advertisers or politicians merely take advantage of these trends to serve their purposes. Thus, political candidates might be successful in seizing on patriotism and racial backlash to promote their campaigns in much the same way that product advertisers exploit what they think are attitude trends among Yuppies or the Baby Boom generation. But who would deny the effect on our democracy and our culture of political leaders' appeals to our baser tendencies?

These reinforcement arguments might be valid, but in their early forms, they were unnecessarily limited in scope. Moderate effects theorists developed reinforcement notions into a broader theory that identifies important new categories of media influence. These theorists argue that at any point in time, there will be many conflicting or opposing social trends. Some will be easier to reinforce using the marketing techniques available to advertisers. Potentially useful trends can be undermined as public attention is drawn toward opposing ones. From among the trends that can be easily reinforced by existing marketing techniques, advertisers and political consultants are free to base their promotional communication on those that are likely to best serve their short-term self-interests rather than the long-term public good. Thus, many potentially constructive social trends may fail to develop because existing techniques can't easily reinforce them or because opposing trends are reinforced by advertisers seeking immediate profits. The very same Saturday morning cartoons that promote the sale of sugared cereals might just as effectively encourage child viewers to consume healthier food. Or to return to this chapter's opening, the very same Internet that can lead to the creation of new and important intellectual, cultural, and social communities, the same Internet that can provide people with virtually unlimited control over their mediated communication, can be overwhelmed by more advertising, greater commercialization, and increasing sponsor control.

Ongoing Debate over Issues

The popularity of cultural studies and the rise of moderate effects notions have intensified discussion of our three media-related issues. No doubt you've been involved in arguments about violence and sexism on MTV, media influence in the electoral victory of George W. Bush over Al Gore, the propriety and impact of military control of U.S. journalists during the post–September 11 war on terrorism, and any of a number of media effects issues. Even though this debate can stimulate increased research and the development of better theories, it can also generate more heat than light. We must better understand why it has been so hard to come to a clear understanding of media influence and why it has been so easy to promote fallacious ideas about media.

The closing chapters of this book look at several emerging perspectives on media, how they address the three media related issues, and how they are translated into contemporary research efforts. You will be encouraged to use these theories to develop your own positions on the issues and to defend your views against alternate arguments. The theories in this book will remain abstract ideas until you incorporate them into your own views about media and their importance in your life. Ultimately, you are responsible for making media work for you and for guarding against negative consequences.

We are entering, in the first years of the twenty-first century, a period in history not unlike that at the close of the nineteenth—an era in which an array of innovative media technologies might be shaped into powerful new media institutions. Have we learned enough from the past to face this challenging and uncertain future? Will we merely watch as media entrepreneurs shape new media institutions to fill gaps created by the collapse of existing institutions? Or, will we be part of an effort to shape new institutions that better serve our own needs and the long-term needs of the communities in which we live? We invite you to address these questions as you read this book, and we will pose them again as a final challenge.

Exploring Mass Communication Theory

1   The contemporary media environment is increasingly crowded with new technologies seeking to exert themselves and traditional technologies looking to reinvent themselves. Visit these Web sites (or identify alternatives that might have more meaning for you) and compare how the "new kids," the "teenagers," and the "old lions" position themselves.

> *New kids*
>
> DBS (DirecTV)
> http://www.directv.com
>
> Tivo
> http://www.tivo.com
>
> *Teenagers*
>
> Fox Television
> http://fox.com/home.htm
>
> MTV
> http://www.mtv.com/
>
> CNN
> http://www.cnn.com
>
> Wired Magazine
> http://www.wired.com
>
> *Old lions*
>
> ABC
> http://www.abc.com
>
> NBC
> http://www.nbc.com
>
> CBS
> http://www.cbs.com
>
> Life Magazine
> http://pathfinder.com/Life/lifehome.html
>
> Newspaper Association of America
> http://www.naa.org/

2   The Internet offers several sites dealing with the controversies that surround this remarkable new medium. Here are some of the best. Access each and see if you can determine its philosophy on the power, value, and threat of the Internet.

The Center for Democracy and Technology
http://www.cdt.org/

Netscape's information about privacy protection
http://home.netscape.com/privacy/index.html

Links to Internet privacy issues
http://privacy.net/

The Electronic Frontier Foundation (Internet freedom issues)
http://www.eff.org

AC Nielsen Internet Advertising Marketing Research
http://www.nielsen.com

Internet parent guide
http://www.ed.gov/pubs/parents/internet

Internet definitions
http://www.whatis.com

 3 Use **InfoTrac® College Edition** to check a few of the contemporary popular magazines that you typically enjoy for their commentary on the Internet, World Wide Web, DVD, or other new communication technology. What is the general tone of that commentary?

 4 Examine the publications you found in your **InfoTrac College Edition** search for their predictions about coming technologies and their possible impact. What is the gist of their forecasting?

Critical Thinking Questions

1 Where do you stand on the fundamental issue of media impact? In other words, do you believe that media influence individuals, society, and the culture, and if you do, to what extent do they do so?

2 We make some strong claims about the power of the new communication technologies to reshape not only the media industries but also the world that relies on them. It is impossible to pick up a contemporary newspaper or magazine without seeing the same theme echoed. Are people making too much of the Internet and the World Wide Web? Are these technologies destined to become just "more TV" or another way to see ads and do your shopping?

3 The United States is a country that permits, even celebrates, its various differences. At the same time, it is a country with its own distinct culture—we know what it means when someone says he or she is "typically American." Do you see the fragmentation of the audience, as people search out and consume ever more

narrow forms of media content, enriching our diverse culture, or do you see it further dividing us and insulating us from one another?

4 In the aftermath of September 11, 2001, terrorist attacks on the World Trade Center and Pentagon, many media organizations engaged in serious self-reflection about, and analysis of, their performance during the first few days after the tragedies. What, if anything, did you learn about how the different media viewed their responsibilities to the public from that public soul-searching? Could you identify differences in approach between the different media, especially the old versus the new?

5 September 11 was a "fast breaking story" of the highest order. Did you turn to the net and Web for news and information in instant, Internet time, or were television's visuals and from-the-scene audio and visual more suited to your needs? Perhaps you favored the temporally removed reflection of newspapers and magazines? Can you explain your media choices during that difficult time?

Significant People and Their Writing

Crowley, D. J., and Paul Heyer (1991). *Communication in History: Technology, Culture, Society.* New York: Longman.

Delia, Jesse (1987). "Communication Research: A History." In C. Berger and S. Chaffee, eds., *Handbook of Communication Science.* Beverly Hills, CA: Sage.

Lazarsfeld, Paul F. (1969). "An Episode in the History of Social Research: A Memoir." In D. Flemming and B. Bailyn, eds., *The Intellectual Migration: Europe and America, 1930–1960.* Cambridge, MA: Belknap Press of Harvard University.

Lowery, Shearon, and Melvin DeFleur (1995). *Milestones in Mass Communication Research.* White Plains, NY: Longman.

Rogers, Everett M. (1986). "History of Communication Science." In E. M. Rogers, ed., *Communication Technology: The New Media in Society.* New York: Free Press.

Wartella, Ellen, and Byron Reeves (1985). "Historical Trends in Research on Children and the Media 1900–1960." *Journal of Communication,* 35: 118–133.

Chapter 2

Mass Communication Theory

Ours is a society that respects and believes its scientists. Science has given us an admirable standard of living and a deep understanding of the world around us. But not all scientists are revered equally. British astronomer and philosopher John D. Barrow opened his 1998 book, *Impossibility: The Limits of Science and the Science of Limits,* with this observation on the value of science and its practitioners:

> Bookshelves are stuffed with volumes that expound the successes of the mind and the silicon chip. We expect science to tell us what can be done and what is to be done. Governments look to scientists to improve the quality of life and safeguard us from earlier "improvements." Futurologists see no limit to human inquiry, while social scientists see no end to the raft of problems it spawns. (p. 1)

The *scientists* are the dreamers, the fixers, the guardians. They have sent us photos of stars a-borning, detailed the inner workings of the atom, and invented the microwave oven, the CD, and the World Wide Web. *Social scientists* are the naysayers, the Grinches of the world. They tell us that television is corrupting us, modern political campaigning has rendered us too cynical to participate meaningfully in our democracy, and parents are doing a dreadful job of raising their kids. Or, as technology writer David Brooks reminds us, "A survey of the social science of the past century shows it to be, by and large, an insanely pessimistic field" (2002, p. 22). As a result, we readily accept the good works of Barrow's *scientists*—The universe is continually expanding? Of course. The existence of quarks? Naturally—while we remain suspicious of those of the *social scientists*—

SOCIAL SCIENTISTS *Scientists who examine relationships among phenomena in the human or social world*

School uniforms improve pupil discipline? Not for my kid! Playing with Barbies destroys little girls' self-esteem? I don't think so!

Why does our society seem to have difficulty accepting the theories and findings of **social scientists**, those who apply logic and observation—that is, science—to the understanding of the social, rather than the physical world?

Overview

That's what we will look at in this chapter, questions about social science and the theories it spawns—specifically mass communication theories. We'll examine the difficulties faced by those who attempt to systematically study human behavior and the particular problems encountered when the issue is human behavior *and* the mass media. We'll define theory and offer several classifications of mass communication theory. Most important, we will try to convince you that the problems that seem to surround the development and study of mass communication theory aren't really problems at all: rather they are challenges that make the study of mass communication theory interesting and exciting. As Barrow wrote, "A world that (is) simple enough to be fully known would be too simple to contain conscious observers who might know it" (1998, p. 3).

Science and Human Behavior

CAUSALITY *When a given factor influences another, even by way of an intervening variable*

CAUSAL RELATIONSHIP *When the alterations in a particular variable under specific conditions always produces the same effect in another variable*

SCIENTIFIC METHOD *A search for truth through accurate observation and interpretation of fact*

At the center of our society's occasional reluctance to accept the theories of the social scientists is the *logic of* **causality**. We understand this logic. We'll use boiling water as a simple example. If we (or our representatives, the scientists) can manipulate an independent variable (heat) and produce the same effect (boiling at 100 degrees Centigrade) under the same conditions (sea level) every time, then a **causal relationship** has been established. Heating water at sea level to 100 degrees will cause water to boil. No matter how many times you heat beakers of water at sea level, they will all boil at 100 degrees. Lower the heat, the water does not boil. Heat it at the top of Mount Everest, it boils at lower temperatures. Go back to sea level (or alter the atmospheric pressure in a laboratory test), it boils at 100 degrees. Repeated observation under controlled conditions. We even have a name for this, the **scientific method**, and there are many definitions for it. Here is a small sample:

1 "A means whereby insight into an undiscovered truth is sought by (1) identifying the problem that defines the goal of the quest, (2) gathering data with the

HYPOTHESIS *A testable prediction about some event*

hope of resolving the problem, (3) positing a **hypothesis** both as a logical means of locating the data and as an aid to resolving the problem, and (4) empirically testing the hypothesis by processing and interpreting the data to see whether the interpretation of them will resolve the question that initiated the research" (Leedy, 1997, pp. 94–95)

2 "A set of interrelated constructs (concepts), definitions, and propositions that present a systematic view of phenomena by specifying relations among variables, with the purpose of explaining and predicting phenomena" (Kerlinger, 1986, p. 9)

3 "A method . . . by which our beliefs may be determined by nothing human, but by some external permanency—by something upon which our thinking has no effect . . . The method must be such that the ultimate conclusion of every man shall be the same. Such is the method of science. Its fundamental hypothesis . . . is this: There are real things whose characters are entirely independent of our opinions about them" (Peirce, 1955, p. 18)

Throughout this century, some social researchers have tried to apply the scientific method to the study of human behavior and society. As we noted in Chapter 1, Paul Lazarsfeld was one of the first to advocate applying social research methods to the study of mass media. We will consider the work of several other important pioneers in later chapters—Carl Hovland, Bernard Berelson, and Elihu Katz, to name only a few. Although the essential logic of the scientific method is quite simple, its application in the social sciences can be more complicated.

Take, for example, the much-discussed issue of press coverage of political campaigns and its impact on voter turnout. We know that more media attention is paid to elections than ever before. Today, television permits continual, eyewitness coverage of candidate activity. Mobile vans trail candidates and beam stories off satellites so that local television stations can air their own coverage. The Internet and Web offer instant access to candidates, their ideas, and those of their opponents. Yet, despite advances in media technology and innovations in campaign coverage, U.S. voter participation remains woefully low. The United States has one of the lowest rates of participation of all the democracies in the world. Can we assume that media campaign coverage has caused voting to decline? This is an assertion that mass society theorists would have been quick to make. Would they be right? How could or should we verify whether this assertion is valid?

As we shall see, the pioneers of mass communication research faced this situation during the 1930s. There were precious few scientific studies of, but many bold assertions about, the bad effects of mass media. Individuals like Lazarsfeld and Hovland, though, were reluctant to accept these claims without making observations that could either support the claims or permit them to be rejected.

These researchers faced many problems, however, in applying the scientific method to the study of mass communication. How can there be repeated observations? No two audiences, never mind any two individuals, who see political coverage are the same. No two elections are the same. Even if a scientist conducted the same experiment on the same people repeatedly (showing them, for example, the same excerpts of coverage and then asking them if and how they might vote), these people would now be different each additional time because they would have had a new set of experiences (participation in the study).

How can there be control over conditions that might influence observed effects? Who can control what people watch, read, or listen to, or to whom they talk, not to mention what they have learned about voting and civic responsibility in school, family, and church? One solution is to put them in a laboratory and limit what they watch and learn. But, people don't grow up in laboratories or watch television with the types of strangers that they meet in a laboratory experiment. They don't consume media messages hooked to galvanic skin response devices or scanned by machines that track their eye movements. And unlike atoms under study, people can and sometimes do change their behaviors as a result of the social scientists' findings, which further confounds claims of causality.

This implementation of the scientific method is difficult for social researchers for four reasons:

1 **Most of the significant and interesting forms of human behavior are quite difficult to measure.** We can easily measure the temperature at which water boils. With ingenious and complex technology, we can even measure the weight of an atom or the speed at which the universe is expanding. But how do we measure something like civic duty? Should we count the incidence of voting? Maybe a person's decision not to vote is her personal expression of that duty. Try something a little easier, like measuring aggression in a television violence study. Can aggression be measured by counting how many times a child hits a rubber doll? Is gossiping about a neighbor an aggressive act? How do we measure an attitude (a predisposition to do something rather than an observable action)? What is three pounds of tendency to hold conservative political views or sixteen point seven millimeters of patriotism?

2 **Human behavior is exceedingly complex.** Human behavior does not easily lend itself to causal description. It is easy to identify a single factor that causes water to boil. But it has proved impossible to isolate single factors that serve as the exclusive cause of important actions of human behavior. Human behavior may simply be too complex to allow scientists to ever fully untangle the different factors that combine to cause observable actions. We can easily control the heat and atmospheric pressure in our boiling experiment. We can relatively easily control the elements in a chemistry experiment. But if we want to develop a theory of the

influence of mediated communication on political campaigns, how do we control which forms of media people choose to use? How do we control the amount of attention they pay to specific types of news? How do we measure how well or poorly they comprehend what they consume? How do we take into account factors that influenced people long before we started our research? For example, how do we measure the type and amount of political socialization done by parents, schools, or peers? All these things (not to mention countless others) will influence the relationship between people's use of media and their behavior in an election. How can we be sure what *caused* what? Voting might have declined even more precipitously without media coverage. Remember the very same factors that led one person to vote might lead another to stay home.

3 **Humans have goals and are self-reflexive.** We do not always behave in response to something that has happened, but very often we act in response to something we hope or expect will happen. Moreover, we constantly revise our goals and make highly subjective determinations about their potential for success or failure. Water boils *after* the application of heat. It doesn't think about boiling. It doesn't begin to experience boiling and then decide that it doesn't like the experience. We think about our actions and inactions; we reflect on our values, beliefs, and attitudes. Water doesn't develop attitudes against boiling that lead it to misperceive the amount of heat it is experiencing. It stops boiling when the heat is removed. It doesn't think about stopping or have trouble making up its mind. It doesn't have friends who tell it that boiling is fun and should be continued even when there is insufficient heat. But people do think about their actions, and they frequently make these actions contingent on their expectations that something will happen. Do you generally go to a particular film only because you saw a single ad for it (simple causal relationship) or because, although never having seen any promotional material for it, you anticipate a good time—you go to the movie to make meaning, to create a specific kind of experience for yourself. For example, in one famous television violence study we'll discuss later (Chapter 8), young boys behaved aggressively, not because they had seen violent television shows, but because they *wanted* to see those programs. They were frustrated when experimenters denied them the ability to watch programs that they liked.

4 **The simple notion of causality is sometimes troubling when it is applied to ourselves.** We have no trouble accepting that heat causes water to boil at 100° Centigrade at sea level; we relish such causal statements in the physical world. We want to know how things work, what makes things happen. As much as we might like to be thrilled by horror movies or science fiction films where physical laws are continually violated, we trust the operation of these laws in our daily lives. But we often resent causal statements when they are applied to ourselves. We can't see the expanding universe or the breakup of the water molecule at the boiling point, so

Box 2a   Curiosity-Evidence-Knowledge:
The Communication Scientist as Social Detective

by Dr. John A. Courtright, who with communication researcher John Bowers, is co-author of Communication Research Methods. *Dr. Courtright is Professor of Communication at the University of Delaware.*

As you read the various chapters of this book, you will be exposed to (and hopefully learn) a good deal of information about mass communication and its widespread impact on our daily lives. Some of this knowledge will be straightforward and correspond to what your common sense tells you, but other parts of this knowledge base will be quite complex, highly theoretical, and could even run counter to your intuition.

Whether simple or complex, you may be surprised to learn that every bit of knowledge in this book represents the answer to one of several simple questions that scholars of communication routinely ask: Why? How come? What would happen if . . . ? Communication scientists are constantly displaying their endless curiosity by asking these basic questions and then systematically seeking their answers.

What makes the curiosity of the communication scientist—actually, any scientist—different from yours or some other nonscientist is not found in their superior intellects or charming personalities. What is different is the approach that communication scientists employ to satisfy their curiosity. What distinguishes this scientific approach to asking and answering questions is a never-ending emphasis on systematically seeking the answers. This "system," in turn, consists of the numerous procedures, techniques, approaches, and analytic devices that communication scientists learn during their formal university training. Just as a carpenter must

learn to use skillfully a hammer, saw, and level, the communication scientist is trained to use the tools of his or her trade.

Putting aside the idea of formal training for a moment, the best way to think about a communication scientist is not as a carpenter but, rather, to imagine her or him as a detective who is constantly obtaining evidence to prove a case. A detective may know that a person committed a crime, but unless he or she can obtain the evidence, a gut-instinct isn't good enough. Similarly, a communication scientist may "feel in her bones" that television has a certain impact on a particular group of people (say, children under the age of 12), but unless systematic and scientifically accepted procedures can produce convincing evidence of that impact, this scientist cannot persuade a jury of her peers (other trained communication scientists) of its existence.

Consequently, as you read the various sections in this book, remind yourself that what you are learning is the result of curiosity, followed by the systematic gathering of evidence. Even if a finding or theoretical assertion strikes you as nonsense ("I never behave like that!"), recall that the evidence has convinced knowledgeable scientists that the average person does behave like that (Maybe you're not average?). Finally, if you like the idea of being a social detective, you might consider pursuing a career as a communication scientist and scholar.

we readily accept the next best thing, the word of an objective expert, that is, a scientist. But we can see ourselves reading the paper and not voting and going to a movie and choosing a brand-name pair of slacks and learning about people from lands we've never visited. We don't need experts telling us about ourselves or explaining to us why we do things. We're not so easily influenced by media, we say. But most of us are convinced that other people are much more likely to be influenced by media (the **third-person effect**; Paul, Salwen, & Dupagne, 2000).

THIRD-PERSON
EFFECT *The idea
that "media affect
others, but not me"*

So although we don't need to be protected from media, *they* might. We are our own men and women, independent, freethinking individuals. We weren't affected by those McDonald's ads, we simply bought that Big Mac, fries, and a large Coke because, darn it, we deserved a break today. And after all, we did need to eat something and the McDonald's did happen to be right on the way back to the dorm.

Schizophrenic Social Science

Another reason that social scientists often don't get the respect accorded their physical science colleagues relates to the schizophrenic nature of social science itself. Kenneth Bailey (1982, p. 5) wrote, "To this day you will find within social science both those who think of themselves as scientists in the strictest sense of the word and those with a more subjective approach to the study of society, who see themselves more as humanists than as scientists." In other words, not all social scientists adhere to the same standards for conducting research or accepting evidence.

This book is about mass communication theory, so let's take an expressly mass communication example: televised violence. Do you believe that televised violence can lead viewers to increased levels of aggression? Surely this must be an easier thing to demonstrate than the existence of an ever-expanding universe. This link has been theorized ever since the first silent movie hero slugged the first silent movie villain. This link has been scientifically demonstrated in countless studies and has been articulated before the U.S. Congress by the government's top scientist, the Surgeon General. The U.S. Congress based its 1996 V-chip and content rating code demands on it. But you know very well that every viewer does not go out and hit his or her neighbor after watching *Lethal Weapon XIV*. In fact, most viewers don't. Some scientific evidence actually refutes the media and aggression link. But other survey, experimental, observational, and humanistic evidence argues that the connection does exist. Then, there is observational, humanistic, and experimental evidence that says it does not. So, the question remains: What is the most useful way to conceptualize the complex relationship that exists between specific forms of media content and individuals who use this content to induce experiences and to make meaning for themselves? To address such complex questions about the role of media, we must develop theories.

Defining Theory

THEORY *A concep-
tual representation
or explanation of
phenomena*

Scientists, physical or social, deal in **theory**. "Theories are stories about how and why events occur . . . Scientific theories begin with the assumption that the universe, including the social universe created by acting human beings, reveals certain basic and fundamental properties and processes that explain the ebb and flow of events in specific processes" (Turner, 1998, p. 1). Theory has numerous, more specific, definitions. Bowers and Courtright (1984, p. 13) offered a traditionally scientific definition: "Theories . . . are sets of statements asserting relationships among classes of variables." Bailey's (1982, p. 39) conception of theory accepts a wider array of ways to understand the social world: "explanations and predictions of social phenomena . . . relating the subject of interest . . . to some other phenomena."

Our definition, though, will be drawn from a synthesis of two, more generous views of theory. Assuming that there are a number of different ways to understand how communication functions in our complex world, Stephen Littlejohn (1996, p. 3) defined theory as a scholar's "best representation of some state of affairs" based on systematic observation. E. M. Griffin (1994) also takes this broader view, writing that a theory is an idea "that explains an event or behavior. It brings clarity to an otherwise jumbled situation; it draws order out of chaos . . . (It) synthesizes the data, focuses our attention on what's crucial, and helps us ignore that which makes little difference" (p. 34). These latter two writers are acknowledging an important reality of communication (Littlejohn) and mass communication (Griffin) theories: There are a lot of them, the hypotheses they produce are testable to varying degrees, they are situationally based, and they often seem contradictory and chaotic. As communication theorist Katherine Miller explained, "Different schools of thought will define *theory* in different ways depending on the needs of the theorist and on beliefs about the social world and the nature of knowledge" (2002, p. 19).

Denis McQuail (1994, pp. 4–6), for example, described "four kinds" of mass communication theory:

1   **Social scientific theory.** These theories are based on and guide empirical research. They permit statements about the nature, workings, and effects of mass communication. These statements or *hypotheses* are tested by making systematic and objective observations regarding mass media, media use, and media influence. For example, theories explaining the television and aggression link are typically social-scientifically based.

Box 2b   Questions, Questions . . .

by Joe Waterhouse, Associate Professor of Philosophy, San José State University

Thinking is asking questions. Thinking well is asking good questions.

Good questions aren't accidents; they occur only after the appropriate preparation. Preparation involves complete immersion in a field, immersion that can last several years and in some cases a lifetime. Preparation requires understanding what may be called the problem-situation; the array of background information for the problem, including the theories that offer competing solutions to the problem; and, the pros and cons of these theories. Typically, every problem has several main theories that have been proposed as solutions. Understanding a problem means understanding why each of these proposed theories is both attractive and unattractive. These attractive and unattractive features are the pros and cons of the theories.

But preparation is not, by itself, sufficient for asking good questions. Progress is made in science when someone with the appropriate preparation has the creative imagination to ask a new question. This new question does not have to be complicated. In fact, frequently it is viewed later

as an utterly simple one. Nonetheless, when first proposed, the question is new, provocative and fundamental—one that changes the field irreversibly.

And good questions produce an avalanche of questions.

You are a scientist. You ask questions, formulate various hypotheses as answers, evaluate these answers for yourself, and are led by this process to ask newer and deeper questions.

How are you going to be a good scientist? Ask questions! As you read a page, ask one hundred questions. For each of those questions propose one hundred answers. For each answer, ask one hundred new questions. Don't stop! Ever!

Texts are more than material to be learned: Texts are resources for asking questions. If a text says that something is true, ask if it is always true, or only true in some circumstances. If it is only true in some circumstances, ask what these circumstances are. And ask why these circumstances make a difference. Ask what the evidence is for the hypothesis, and

2 **Normative theory.** This form of theory explains how ideal media ought to operate within a specific system of social values. Theories of the press' role in a democracy would most likely fit here as would theories of media in an Islamic republic or an authoritarian state.

3 **Operational theory.** This type of theory is normative, but with a practical bent. It involves not only how media *should* ideally operate, but also how they *can* operate to meet specific ends. Theories of advertising and consumer behavior might fit here.

4 **Everyday theory.** This refers to the knowledge and ideas (theories) that all of us have by simple virtue of engaging in mediated communication. Each of us has our own theory about why the quality of contemporary television is as it is.

Box 2b   Questions, Questions . . . *(continued)*

why that evidence is regarded as relevant. Ask if other hypotheses can explain the evidence. If some hypothesis will not work, ask why not. And, above all, always ask why! Ask why about every part of an hypothesis! Ask why about everything!

Suppose, for example, you start with the question—why would someone want TOPtext on her or his computer? Many hypotheses could be proposed to answer this query; one offered by the authors of this text reported in Chapter 1 is that it finally delivers the promise of advertising on the Internet. But multiple questions now arise:

- Says who? One person's promise is another's threat.
- Does it work? If so, how well?
- Does it work better for some products and services than for others?
- Do people welcome or resent this intrusion in their Web use?
- What attributes characterize those who welcome it? Those who resent it?

- Do TOPtext's interruptions negatively influence people's evaluation of the interrupting advertiser? If so, how? Does it damage rather than help sales?
- Why would anybody want this constant commercial interruption?
- Does the surreptitious bundling of this software with other software violate people's rights?
- Is overcommercialization of the net damaging its appeal?
- Is the Internet overcommercialized?
- What kind of culture permits the selling of words and phrases?
- Isn't anything, not only our Web use, off limits for commercialization?

There is no end, no place to stop. Some answers to questions are better than others, but no answer is final. Not only does each question generate another question, but also it is closer to the truth to say that each question generates innumerable additional questions.

Or does it?

Other commentators on mass communication have suggested a fifth kind of mass communication theory. Many argue, for example, that the best way to theorize about the media is through *critical theory,* defined as "a loose confederation of ideas held together by a common interest in the quality of communication and human life. They are especially concerned with inequality and oppression. Critical theories do not merely observe; they also criticize. Most critical theories are concerned with the conflict of interests in society and the ways communication perpetuates domination of one group over another" (Littlejohn, 1996, p. 17). Communication theorist Katherine Miller adds that critical theorists "feel a responsibility not to simply represent the social world (though they would see representation as an important first step in the theoretical process) but to work as active agents of reform and radical change" (2002, p. 60).

SOCIAL SCIENTIFIC
THEORY *Theory
seeking prediction
and control*

CRITICAL THEORY
*Theory seeking
emancipation and
change in a domi-
nant social order*

HERMENEUTIC THE-
ORY *The study of
understanding,
especially by inter-
preting action and
text*

SOCIAL HERMENEU-
TICS *Theory seek-
ing to understand
how those in an
observed social
situation interpret
their own lot in
that situation*

Another way to classify mass communication theories is by their *goals*. The goal of **social scientific theory** is prediction and control. It measures phenomena or attributes of a situation to try to find measurable tendencies (ostensibly to better predict—and encourage or discourage—their occurrence). But there is social theory that is not *social scientific theory*. There is, as we've just seen, **critical theory**, the goal of which is emancipation from and change in a dominant social order (Jensen, 1990). Critical theorists strive to accomplish this through analyses of phenomena present in that social order from a specific set of values and perspectives. And there is **hermeneutic theory**, "the study of understanding, especially by interpreting action and text" (Littlejohn, 1996, p. 208). There are different forms of hermeneutic theory. For example, **social hermeneutics** has as its goal the understanding of how those in an observed social situation interpret their own lot in that situation. As ethnographer Michael Moerman (1992, p. 23) explained, social hermeneutic theory tries to explain how events "in the alien world make sense to the aliens, how their way of life coheres and has meaning and value for the people who live it." Another branch of hermeneutics looks for hidden or deep meaning in different symbol systems, for example in media texts.

What we see now is that much of our understanding of the mass media, and therefore many of our most useful theories, come, not only from social scientists but also from social critics and social observers as well. Mass communication theory springs from the ideas, work, and writing of people with different goals and decidedly different views of the world and the place of the media in it. Still, a good, useable theory should contain a *set* of statements that defines key concepts; specify the *relationships* between those concepts; *describe* some phenomenon using those concepts; offer *predictions* about the phenomenon; and suggest *explanations* for the phenomenon's occurrence.

Mass Communication and Theory

If we can agree on a very general definition of theory—something akin to Littlejohn's or Griffin's, not even demanding scientific proof, only reasonableness of our observations or explanations—why is there so little agreement about what constitutes a generally accepted theory of mass communication? One reason, as we've seen in Chapter 1, is that mass communication itself is being redefined. Englishman and keen observer of American media and American media theory, Jeremy Tunstall, gave another answer: "'Communication' itself carries many problems. Either the 'mass media' or 'communication' would cover a dozen disciplines and raise a thousand problems. When we put the two together, the problems are confounded. Even if the field is narrowed to 'mass media,' it gets split into many separate media, many separate disciplines, many separate stages in the flow, and

quickly you have several hundred subfields" (1983, pp. 92–93). Or to put it another way, several hundred theories.

Now it should be clear that mass communication theory is really mass communication *theories,* each more or less relevant to a given medium, audience, time, condition, and theorist. But this shouldn't be viewed as a problem. Mass communication
theory can be personalized, it is ever-evolving, it is dynamic. What we hope to do in
the following pages is provide you with the basics: the traditions that have given us
what we now view as classic theories of mass communication, some idea of the contexts in which they were developed and in which they flourished (if they did), the
knowledge to decide for yourself what does and does not make sense, and some def-
inite clues about where mass communication theory stands today.

Summary

Social science is often controversial because it suggests causal relationships between things in the environment and people's attitudes, values, and behaviors. In
the physical sciences, these relationships are often easily visible and measurable.
In the study of human behavior, however, they rarely are. Human behavior is
quite difficult to quantify, often very complex, and often goal-oriented. Social science and human behavior make a problematic fit. The situation is even further
complicated because social science itself is somewhat schizophrenic—it is many
different things to many different people.

Nonetheless, social science develops theories—conceptual representations or
explanations of phenomena—and tests the hypotheses those theories generate.
Mass communication theory can be divided into five categories: social scientific,
normative, operational, everyday, and critical theory. Another way to classify mass
communication theory is by its goals: social scientific theory seeks prediction and
control; critical theory seeks emancipation and freedom; hermeneutic theory tries
to understand how those in an observed social situation interpret that situation.
The explanatory power of mass communication theory, however, is constantly
challenged by the presence of many media, their many facets and characteristics,
their constant change, an always-developing audience, and the ever-evolving nature of the societies that use them.

Exploring Mass Communication Theory

1   You might not find discussions of mass communication theory, per se, on the
World Wide Web, but thousands of sites do deal with issues of importance to scientists who study mediated communication. Visit some sites devoted to children's

television, media violence, the effects of alcohol advertising, or other mediated communication issues. You can begin with those listed here, but you should search out your own. Once you have done so, see if you can determine the kind of theory that sustains these sites and the relationships they either assume or demonstrate. In addition, some of these sites are based in countries other than the United States. Can you detect differences in approach to theory among different lands?

Media violence

National Coalition on TV Violence
http://www.nctvv.org

Media Violence: Issues and Debates
http://www.screen.com/mnet/eng/issues/violence/issues/discuss.htm

Fighting Media Violence
http://www.families.com

Alcohol advertising

Center on Alcohol Advertising
http://www.tf.org/tf/alcohol.html

Children's media

Kids First
http://www.cqcm.org/kidsfirst/start.html

The Television Project
http://www.tvp.org

Center for the Study of Children, Youth, and Media
http://www.ccsonline.org.uk/mediacentre/main.html

2 Use **InfoTrac College Edition** to identify scholarly journals from social scientific fields that may interest you (for example, psychology, sociology, political science, consumer behavior, mass communication). Search their indexes for articles about or commentary on theory. What definitions of theory can you find? Can you see varying notions about what constitutes good theory among the different fields?

Critical Thinking Questions

1 Can you think of any examples of social science evidence from any field that you accept? Any that you reject? Can you think of any evidence of media influence that you have either accepted or rejected? If you are skeptical, can you explain why you are?

2   Can you develop your own definitions of the scientific method and theory that are more useful to you than what we've suggested? In other words, what kinds of ideas and evidence supporting them satisfy you?

3   Have you ever read or heard of any social scientific findings regarding media and aggressive behavior? If you have, do you believe what social science has told you about this controversial issue? Why or why not?

4   Think about the issue of the effects of media stereotypes of racial and cultural minorities. Do you believe that they can influence your attitudes toward members of those groups? Why or why not? What role did the media play in forming your attitudes about the presidential election imbroglio in Florida in 2000 and the apparently wide disparity in attitudes expressed by people of different political outlooks?

Significant People and Their Writing

Barrow, John D. (1998). *Impossibility: The Limits of Science and the Science of Limits.* New York: Oxford University Press.

Bowers, John W., and John A. Courtright (1984). *Communication Research Methods.* Glenview, IL: Scott, Foresman.

Daly, John A. "Colloquy: Getting Older and Getting Better: Challenges for Communication Research." *Human Communication Research,* 26: 331–338.

Littlejohn, Stephen W. (1996). *Theories of Human Communication.* Belmont, CA: Wadsworth.

McQuail, Denis (1994). *Mass Communication Theory: An Introduction.* Beverly Hills, CA: Sage.

Tunstall, Jeremy (1983). "The Trouble with U.S. Communication Research." *Journal of Communication,* 33: 2–95.

Section 2

Era of Mass Society and Mass Culture

1927 *Radio Act of 1927 creates FRC*

1933 *Payne Fund's* Movies, Delinquency and Crime

1934 *Communications Act passes, creates FCC*

1938 War of the Worlds *broadcast*

1939 *First public broadcast of television*
World War II erupts in Europe
Paperback book introduced to United States

1940 *Lazarsfeld's voter studies begin in Erie County*

1941 *United States enters WWII*
British develop first binary computer

1942 *Hovland conducts first war propaganda research*
British develop Colossus, the first electronic digital computer, to break
German war code

1945 *WWII ends*
Allport and Postman's rumor study published

1946 *John Mauchly and John Atanasoff introduce ENIAC, the first "full service"*
electronic digital computer

1947 *Hutchins Commission issues report on press freedom*
Hollywood 10 called before HUAC

Chapter 3

The Rise of Media Industries and Mass Society Theory

"Sophisticated" people giggled when conservative religious leaders recently condemned the children's television program *The Teletubbies* for "encouraging the homosexual lifestyle." The show's purple character carries a handbag and has a three-sided antenna on his head. Purple, you see, is "code" for homosexuality, the Nazis forced homosexuals to wear triangular badges in the prison camps—another gay symbol—and well, a purse *is* a purse. Author Brad Herzog smiled all the way to the bank as his book *States of Mind,* shot from number 122,040 to number 7 on Amazon.com's best seller list the day after he mentioned it while chatting with host Regis Philbin before competing in an April 2000 episode of the hit television series *Who Wants to Be a Millionaire* (Manners, 2000). No one in the television and film industries laughed when Congress called hearings in mid-2000 after four major public health groups—the American Medical Association, the American Academy of Pediatrics, the American Psychological Association, and the American Academy of Child & Adolescent Psychiatry—issued a joint statement definitively declaring that the effects of violent media "are measurable and long lasting . . . Moreover, prolonged viewing of media violence can lead to emotional desensitization toward violence in real life" (quoted in Albiniack, 2000, p. 14).

A kid's television show promoting homosexuality? Maybe not. One mention of an obscure book selling thousands of copies? It happened . . . you can look it up. Violent films and television making children more aggressive and less sensitive toward the pain and suffering of others? Some say yes; some say no.

For more than a century now, the role of media has been debated. Conservatives lament the decline of values sped by a liberal media elite. Liberals fear the power of a media system more in tune with the conservative values of its owners than its audiences. The school boards and city councils of hundreds of towns have debated installing filtering software on school and library computers, pitting advocates of free expression against proponents of child protection. Journalistic organizations willingly ceded much of their freedom to cover and report news of the war on terrorism to the military with very little public outcry. After all, we are at war! Controversial rapper Eminem is celebrated on MTV while his music is banned on scores of radio stations because it is considered racist and misogynistic. Congress convenes hearings in summer 2001 on the negative impact of hiphop. A blue ribbon panel recommends that the networks be forbidden from predicting the winners in political elections because those announcements keep people away from the polls. Media industries promise their sponsors significant impact for their advertising dollars but claim their fare has little or no influence when challenged on issues of violence, stereotyping, and drugs. Every company, government agency, and nonprofit group of any size maintains or retains a public relations operation. Why would anyone bother if media have little or no impact? Why would the First Amendment to our Constitution, our "First Freedom," protect the expression of media industries if they have no influence? Why do we grant media outlets and their personnel special protection if their contributions to our society are so insignificant?

Overview

MASS SOCIETY THEORY *Idea that media are corrupting influences that undermine the social order through their influence over defenseless "average" people*

Clearly, a lot is at stake when we debate the role of media. Controversy over media influence can have far-reaching consequences for society and for media institutions. In this chapter, we will trace the rise and fall of mass society theory. **Mass society theory** is an all-encompassing perspective on Western, industrial society that attributes an influential but often quite negative role to media. Media are viewed as having the power to profoundly shape our perceptions of the social world and to manipulate our actions in subtle but highly effective ways. This theory assumes that media influence must be controlled. The strategies for control, however, are as varied as are the theorists who offer them.

As we review the rise of mass society theory, we will highlight central assumptions and arguments, many of which have failed the test of time or of scientific study. We must be careful not to brand all forms of media criticism as necessarily naive forms of mass society theory. Some arguments first raised by mass society theorists still deserve attention. We will return to these arguments in later chapters and see how contemporary media critics have used them.

CULTURE WARS *Struggle to define the cultural foundation of the broader social order in which we live*

The debate over media that we trace in this chapter is in many respects a critical battleground in a larger **culture war**—a continuing struggle to define the cultural foundation of the broader social order in which we all live. The participants in this war are drawn from all segments of society. Central to the conflict are media entrepreneurs—the people who risk capital for the right to earn profits by producing and distributing media content. These individuals are inevitably opposed by other social elites who object to their actions and distrust the power that they wield. All sides claim the moral high ground in this struggle. Media entrepreneurs inevitably embrace the press freedom granted in the **First Amendment** to the Constitution. They argue, with considerable justification, that this freedom is fundamental to democracy. Nevertheless, critics charge that when press freedom is abused, when what they consider higher values are violated, then media must be restrained. But, just who determines which values are higher and who determines when they have been violated? These are issues for the Great Debate over media.

FIRST AMENDMENT
Guarantees freedom of speech, press, assembly, and religion

The Beginnings

In 1896, William Randolph Hearst, a prominent newspaper publisher, sent an illustrator to Cuba to cover the possible outbreak of war against Spain. Historian Frank Luther Mott (1941, pp. 527–537) reported that the artist, upon his arrival, sent this telegram:

HEARST, JOURNAL, NEW YORK

EVERYTHING IS QUIET. THERE IS NO TROUBLE HERE. THERE WILL BE NO WAR. WISH TO RETURN.

The publisher's reply was quick and to the point:

PLEASE REMAIN. YOU FURNISH THE PICTURES AND I'LL FURNISH THE WAR. HEARST.

At the time, Hearst was publisher of one of the largest newspapers in New York City as well as head of a chain of papers that stretched as far west as San Francisco. He was a leader in the dominant medium of his era—the mass newspaper. Every city on the U.S. East Coast had several large, highly competitive papers, as did major cities across the continent. Competition, unfortunately, encouraged irresponsibility. Most urban newspapers resembled weekly scandal sheets such as the *National Enquirer* that we find at today's supermarket checkout counters.

Hearst may well have sent an illustrator to Havana because he intended to make up war stories that would sell papers, and his irresponsibility triggered harsh critical response. The first theories of mass media developed as a reaction against practices such as this—in other words, against the excesses of a rapidly maturing, highly competitive media industry.

This was a turbulent period in world history, one characterized by enormous social change. Industrialization and urbanization reshaped both Europe and the

United States, initiating what is now referred to as the modern age. Most of this change was made possible by the invention and then rapid dissemination of new forms of technology. But technological change occurred with little consideration for its environmental, social, or psychological impact.

As with every instance of rapid social change, new social elites emerged and the power of old elites was challenged. In the late 1800s, increasing social control was wielded by a handful of industrial entrepreneurs—men who created vast monopolies based on factories, railroads, and the exploitation of natural resources. These men became known as the Robber Barons. The social change they wrought can be rationalized as progress, but a high price was paid—workers were brutalized, vast urban slums were created, and huge tracts of wilderness were ravaged.

Media were among the many technologies that shaped that modern era. An industrial social order had great need for fast and efficient distribution of information. The advantages of new media like the telegraph and telephone were soon recognized, and each new communication technology was quickly adopted—first by businesses and then by the public. During the 1860s, the telegraph was to the Civil War what CNN was to the 2001 war against terrorism in Afghanistan: It helped fuel and then satisfy widespread public interest in fast-breaking news coverage of the conflict. By the time the Civil War ended, the telegraph had spawned a number of **wire services** that supplied news to affiliated papers spread across the nation—the first electronically based media networks had been created.

In the mid and late nineteenth century, popular demand for cheap media content drove the development of several new media—the penny press, the nickel magazine, and the dime novel. High-speed printing presses and Linotype machines made it practical to mass-produce the printed word at very low cost. Urban newspapers boomed all along the East Coast and in major trading centers across the United States. Newspaper circulation wars broke out and led to development of **yellow journalism**, the irresponsible side of the penny press.

Intense competition swept aside many small-circulation and more-specialized print media. By increasing accessibility through lower prices, however, the new mass newspapers were able to serve people who had never before had easy access to print. Many papers succeeded because they attracted large numbers of readers in urban slums—first generation immigrants, barely literate in English, who wanted their piece of the American dream.

WIRE SERVICES
News organizations that provide content to subscribing media outlets

YELLOW JOURNALISM
Sensational, often irresponsible journalism

The Rise of Yellow Journalism

At the beginning of the twentieth century, every industry had its barons, and the most notorious—if not the greatest of the press lords—was Hearst. Hearst specialized in buying up failing newspapers and transforming them into profitable enterprises. He demonstrated that the news business could be as profitable as railroads, steel, or oil. One secret to his success was devising better strategies for luring low-income readers. His newspapers combined a low-selling price with innovative new forms of content that included lots of pictures, serialized stories, and comic strips. Some experts even say that yellow journalism got its name from one of the first comic strips—The Yellow Kid.

Like most yellow journalists, Hearst had little respect for reporting accuracy. Events were routinely overdramatized. Along with other New York newspaper publishers, Hearst was blamed for initiating the Spanish-American War in 1898 through inflammatory coverage that goaded Congress to declare war over an unexplained explosion on the battleship *Maine*. Hearst's telegram to his illustrator embodies much of what was wrong with yellow journalism. Reporters typically gathered only sketchy details about events and turned them over to editors who wrote exaggerated and largely fictitious accounts. Not surprisingly, during this period the public status of reporters was among the lowest for any profession or trade. By contrast, the printers who operated high-speed presses enjoyed greater respect as skilled technicians.

Cycles of Mass Media Development and Decline

The rise of mass media in the 1900s followed a pattern of industrial development that has been duplicated following every subsequent "revolution" in media technology. Whenever important new media technologies appear, they destabilize existing media industries—forcing large-scale and often very rapid restructuring. Large corporations based on old technologies go into precipitous decline while a handful of the upstart companies reap enormous profits. To survive, the large corporations are forced into cutthroat competition to gain control of new technology. Sometimes they succeed and sometimes they fail.

FUNCTIONAL DIS-PLACEMENT *When the functions of an existing medium are replaced by a newer technology, the older medium finds new functions*

This process is called **functional displacement**. For example, we are currently witnessing the rapid decline of network television viewership brought about by the growing popularity of cable and satellite television, VCR, and the Internet. At the same time, we are seeing the rise of new content providers such as the highly successful CNN cable channel and online news and entertainment magazines. The movie industry is experiencing a strong resurgence fueled by videocassette profits and suburban theater revenues. If network television is to survive amid all this change, it must find functions that it can serve better than any of the newer media can. Most corporations that control network television have already diversified their holdings and purchased companies that operate the new media. For example, where there was once NBC Television, there is now NBC Television, cable channel MSNBC (produced in conjunction with software giant Microsoft), all-news cable channel CNBC, World Wide Web sites parallel-ing all three, part ownership in cable channels American Movie Classics and Bravo, specialized NBC Web sites like *NBCi, CNET,* and *iVillage,* and cable and satellite companies in Europe and Asia.

The success of new media often brings a strong critical reaction—especially when media adopt questionable, competitive strategies to produce content or at-tract consumers. During the era of the penny press, mass newspapers quickly dis-placed small circulation, specialized papers, and many did so using highly suspect formulas for creating content. These strategies became even more questionable as competition increased for the attention of readers. In contrast to yellow journalism, current day "Trash TV" programs like *Cops, The Jerry Springer Show,* and *Inside Edi-tion* are as tame as kittens. But yellow journalists justified their practices by arguing that "everyone else is doing it" and "the public likes it or else they wouldn't buy it—we're only giving the people what they want."

New media industries often do specialize in giving people what they want—even if the long-term consequences might be negative. We see this in the current controversies over online indecency and hate speech. Unlike the "established" older media, new media lack the ties to other traditional social institutions that encourage or compel social responsibility. As each of the new media technologies developed, and as industries grew up around them to ensure stable supplies of at-tractive (if questionable) content, these technologies and industries necessarily displaced earlier industries and forms of communication. Often social roles and relationships were seriously disrupted as people adjusted to new media and their content. Most of these problems were impossible to anticipate. For example, dur-ing the 1950s, one of the first serious sociological studies of television's impact on American life found little evidence of disruption. The study noted that one of the most important changes brought about by television was that people spent less time playing cards with extended family members or friends. On the other hand, nuclear families actually spent more time together—mesmerized in front of the ghostly shadows on tiny television screens. Research by Schramm, Lyle, and Parker (1961) reported optimistically that towns with television actually had higher levels of library use and lower comic book sales than did those with only radio. Given widespread public distrust of comic books in the 1950s, these find-ings implied that television could be a positive force. We see this pattern mirrored today—those who argue that the Internet will eventually produce a return to greater participatory democracy counter critics of controversial online content.

As media industries mature, they often become more socially responsible—more willing to stop engaging in unethical tactics and more concerned about serving long-term public needs rather than pandering to short-term popular pas-sions. Cynics say that responsibility is achieved only when it will enhance rather than impede profit making; that is, responsibility is possible only when cutthroat

OLIGOPOLY *The concentration of increasing numbers of media businesses in the hands of a few large companies*

competition gives way to **oligopoly**—a handful of surviving companies stop competing and agree to carve up the market and the profits. In this situation, companies can turn their attention to public relations and eliminate the most offensive content production practices.

During the 1920s, two of the most powerful yellow journalists did just that, reforming so much that they succeeded in making their names synonymous with public service rather than bad journalism. The Pulitzer Prize and the work of the Hearst Foundation are widely (and properly) credited with advancing the professionalization of journalism and raising the ethical standards of the industry. Also during this decade, the American Society of Newspaper Editors was formed and pledged to "tell the truth about the news" in its famous "Canons of Journalism" (Schramm, 1960, pp. 623–625). A fledgling media industry had come of age. Again, we see this process in effect today. Most of the major Internet content providers willingly submit their sites to evaluation and coding tied to popular and freely distributed content rating software, touting their commitment to meeting public concern.

The history of mass media in the United States has been one of ebb and flow between periods dominated by mature, socially responsible media industries and competitive eras characterized by innovative and sometimes irresponsible practices. About the time that competition among mass newspapers was finally brought under control, publishers faced challenges from powerful new entertainment media—records, movies, and radio.

As these newer industries grew, they also experienced periods of intense competition that tested or crossed moral and ethical boundaries. Censorship of the movie industry was hotly debated throughout the 1930s. Government control of radio was widely and frequently advocated. In time, each industry matured and carved out a particular niche in the overall market for media content. Each developed codes of ethics and means of applying these codes. In almost every case, new industries chose to engage in self-censorship rather than accept external controls. The rapid spread of television in the 1950s brought another major restructuring of media. Today, yet another set of powerful communication technologies is transforming media. Personal computers are already delivering ever-increasing amounts of information into our homes via the Internet and World Wide Web. In less than a decade, the net and the Web have come to pose a threat to the survival of newspapers and broadcast media.

The most powerful forces influencing restructuring in American media industries are technological change, content innovation, and consumer demand. None of these operates independently. During eras of rapid change such as we are now experiencing, innovations in media technology force (or permit) rapid alterations in both the form and type of media content that we receive. Our demand for this content is also changing. Old media-use habits break down and new habits form as emerging media provide new choices in content. Some of us rent more and more videos, but others prefer cable television offerings or home computer services. Many of us get our news from television and radio, but growing numbers of us go online for our information about the doings of the world.

Mass Society Critics and the Great Debate over Media

With every change in the media industries, media critics have emerged to pose questions about unethical practices and to voice concern about long-term negative consequences, as you can read in Box 3a. These critics raise important and appropriate issues. During the early stages of development or restructuring, media industries are especially susceptible to criticism. Although this criticism is often warranted, we must recognize that many of the critics are not neutral observers with only the best interest of the public in mind. Most critics are not objective scientists or dispassionate humanists who rely on systematic observation or well-developed theory for their positions. Rather, their criticisms are to some extent rooted in their own self-interests.

Even when individual critics are selfless, they are increasingly likely to be paid by special interests for their work. Often their ideas would go unnoticed without promotion by special interests. For example, when television began to compete with newspapers, newspapers were filled with stories reporting the complaints of television critics. During the 1970s, much of the research critical of children's television would have gone unnoticed by the general public had it not been for the promotional work of Action for Children's Television.

Changes in media industries typically increase the pressure on other social institutions to change. Instability in the way we routinely communicate has unsettling consequences for all other institutions. Typically, the leaders of these institutions resent external pressures and are reluctant to change their way of doing things. In our society, critics have interpreted the rise of the media industries as threatening every other social institution, including political, religious, business, military, and educational institutions. The constant calls for overhauling political campaign financing are only one example. Media are even seen to have profoundly affected families—the most basic social institution of all.

It's hardly surprising, then, that leaders of these social institutions, and the special interest groups they sponsor, have raised a constant stream of concern about the power and harmful impact of media. As new media develop, critics fight to prevent the media's growth or to control their structure. For example, the development of television and later cable television were frozen for several years while the Federal Communications Commission listened to the arguments of industry critics. Although it is unfair to place all this criticism into a single category,

Box 3a   Fearful Reactions to New Media

The introduction of each new mass medium of the twentieth century was greeted with derision, skepticism, fear, and sometimes silliness. Here is a collection of the thought of the time that welcomed movies, talkies, radio, and television.

Movies and Talkies

When you first reflect that in New York City alone, on a Sunday, 500,000 people go to moving picture shows, a majority of them perhaps children, and that in the poorer quarters of town every teacher testifies that the children now save their pennies for picture shows instead of candy, you cannot dismiss canned drama with a shrug of contempt. It is a big factor in the lives of the masses, to be reckoned with, if possible to be made better, if used for good ends. Eighty percent of present day theatrical audiences in this country are canned drama audiences. Ten million people attended professional baseball games in America in 1908. Four million people attend moving pictures theaters, it is said, every day. $50,000,000 are invested in the industry. Chicago has over 300 theaters, New York 300, St. Louis 205, Philadel-

phia 186, even conservative Boston boasts more than 30. Almost 190 miles of film are unrolled on the screens of America's canned drama theaters every day in the year. Here is an industry to be controlled, an influence to be reckoned with.

American Magazine, September, 1909, p. 498

And if the speech recorded in the dialogue (of talking pictures) is vulgar or ugly, its potentialities for lowering the speech standard of the country are almost incalculable. The fact that it is likely to be heard by the less discriminating portion of the public operates to increase its evil effects; for among the regular attendants at moving picture theaters there are to be found large groups from among our foreign-born population, to whom it is really vitally important that they hear only the best speech.

Commonweal, April 10, 1929, p. 653

The version of life presented to him in the majority of moving pictures is false in fact, sickly in sentiment, and utterly foreign to the Anglo-Saxon ideals of our nation. In them we usually find this formula for a hero: He must commit a crime, repent of it, and be exonerated on the

---

many of the views expressed are consistent with mass society theory. This venerable theory has a long and checkered history. Mass society theory is actually many different theories that share some common assumptions about the role of media and society.

Mass Society Theory Assumptions

Mass society theory first appeared late in the nineteenth century as various social elites struggled to make sense of the disruptive consequences of modernization. Some (that is, the monarchy, the clergy, upper class politicians) lost power or were

Box 3a Fearful Reactions to New Media (*continued*)

ground that he "never had a mother" or "never had a chance"—or perhaps that he was born poor. The heroine is in most cases the familiar, passive, persecuted heroine of the melodrama.

Outlook, July 26, 1916, p. 695

Radio

In general one criterion must be kept in mind: the radio should do what the teacher cannot do; it ought not to do what the teacher can do better. However radio may develop, I cannot conceive of the time when a good teacher will not continue to be the most important object in any classroom.

Education, December, 1936, p. 217

Is radio to become a chief arm of education? Will the classroom be abolished, and the child of the future stuffed with facts as he sits at home or even as he walks about the streets with his portable receiving set in his pocket?

Century, June, 1924, p. 149

Television

Seeing constant brutality, viciousness and unsocial acts results in hardness, intense selfishness, even in mercilessness, proportionate to the amount of exposure and its play on the native temperament of the child. Some cease to show resentment to insults, to indignities, and even cruelty toward helpless old people, to women and other children.

New Republic, November 1, 1954, p. 12

Here, in concept at least, was the most magnificent all forms of communication. Here was the supreme triumph of invention, the dream of the ages—something that could bring directly into the home a moving image fused with sound-reproducing action, language, and thought without the loss of measurable time. Here was the magic eye that could bring the wonders of entertainment, information and education in to the living room. Here was a tool for the making of a more enlightened democracy than the world had ever seen. Yet out of the wizardry of the television tube has come such an assault against the human mind, such a mobilized attack on the imagination, such an invasion against good taste as no other communications medium has known, not excepting the motion picture or radio itself.

Saturday Review, December 24, 1949, p. 20

overwhelmed in their efforts to deal with social problems. For them, the mass media were symbolic of all that was wrong with modern society. Mass newspapers of the yellow journalism era were viewed as gigantic, monopolistic enterprises that employed unethical practices to pander to semiliterate mass audiences. Leaders in education and religion resented media's power to attract readers using content they considered highly objectionable, sinful, and Philistine (Brantlinger, 1983).

The rise of the mass press after 1840 posed a direct threat to the political and business establishment. Political newspapers were swept aside by the penny press in the 1840s and 1850s and then buried by the yellow journalism of the 1880s and 1890s. The political ambitions of the leading yellow journalist, Hearst, posed a very real threat to established politicians and businessmen. Hearst was a populist of his own devising—a man likely to pursue whatever cause would increase his personal popularity, even at the expense of the professional politicians around him. Hearst papers joined with other mass newspapers and magazines in producing sensational news stories that savagely attacked opponents in business and government. These accounts had strong reader appeal and came to be more feared by their targets than is the crew of *60 Minutes* today.

Envy, discontent, and outright fear were often at the roots of mass society theory. This theory makes several basic assumptions about individuals, the role of media, and the nature of social change. We list these assumptions, then discuss each in some detail.

1 The media are a malignant, cancerous force within society and must be purged or totally restructured.

2 Media have the power to reach out and directly influence the minds of average people.

3 Once people's minds are corrupted by media, all sorts of bad, long-term consequences result—bringing not only ruin to individual lives but also creating social problems on a vast scale.

4 Average people are vulnerable to media because they have been cut off and isolated from traditional social institutions that previously protected them from manipulation.

5 The social chaos initiated by media will inevitably be resolved by establishment of a totalitarian social order.

6 Mass media inevitably debase higher forms of culture, bringing about a general decline in civilization.

The first assumption is that the media are a malignant, cancerous force within society and must be purged or totally restructured (Marcuse, 1969, 1978). Although only the most extreme critics proposed dismantling media industries, some opponents of the new media proposed turning control of them over to other elites. In Europe, this argument won out during the 1920s and broadcast media were placed under the control of government agencies. Ironically, these efforts had disastrous consequences when the Nazis came to power in Germany. In the United States, many schemes that would have turned control of new media over to churches, schools, or government agencies were considered. Ultimately, a compromise was reached and a free enterprise broadcasting industry was created under the more-or-less watchful eye of a government agency—the Federal Radio Commission, which later evolved into the Federal Communications Commission (FCC).

But why are the media so dangerous to society? What makes them cancerous? A second assumption is that media have the power to reach out and directly

DIRECT EFFECTS
ASSUMPTION *The
media, in and of
themselves, can
produce direct
effects*

influence the minds of average people (Davis, 1976). This is also known as the **direct effects assumption** and has been hotly debated since the 1940s. Although each version of mass society theory has its own notions about the type of direct influence different media may have, all versions stress how negative this influence is and the extreme vulnerability of average people to immediate, media-induced changes. Average citizens are portrayed as being helpless before the manipulative power of media content. For several generations now, critics have envisioned innocent audiences of teenagers succumbing to gangster movies or hip-hop music, naive grade school children victimized by comic books or the *Teletubbies,* unsuspecting adults transformed magically into couch potatoes by the power of *Survivor* and *Ally McBeal,* gullible elderly folks handing over their last dime to televised insurance hucksters or greedy televangelists, and hate-filled misfits fueling social discord with racist online treatises.

Although it is not hard to locate isolated examples that illustrate every one of these conditions, it is misleading to regard any one of them as universal. When empirical researchers tried to measure the pervasiveness of similar effects in the 1940s and 1950s, they were surprised to discover how difficult it was to develop conclusive evidence. People simply were not as vulnerable to direct manipulation as critics wanted to assume. Often, other factors block direct influence or severely limit it.

The third assumption is that once media corrupt people's minds, all sorts of bad, long-term consequences result—not only bringing ruin to individual lives but also creating social problems on a vast scale (Marcuse, 1941). Over the years, virtually every major social problem we have confronted has been linked in some way to media—from prostitution and delinquency to urban violence and drug usage to the "defeat" in Vietnam and our loss of national pride. Tramps in the gutter have had their work ethic destroyed by reading trashy novels. Teenage delinquents have seen too many gangster movies. Disaffected housewives have seen too many soap operas, and drug addicts have taken too seriously the underlying message in most advertising—the good life is achieved through consumption of a product, not by hard work. There is some truth in these criticisms, but they are also highly misleading. Media are only one kind of institution that has shaped and continues to shape modern life. For such criticisms to be constructive, they must go beyond sweeping assertions. Unfortunately, most early mass society theory failed to do this.

Mass society theory's fourth assumption is that average people are vulnerable to media because they have been cut off and isolated from traditional social institutions that previously protected them from manipulation (Kreiling, 1984). The early mass society theorists idealized the past and had romantic visions of what life must have been like in medieval villages of Europe. Older social orders were thought to have nurtured and protected people from external manipulation. Although these views have some validity (every social order has some redeeming qualities), they neglect to consider the severe limitations of all previous social orders—including

Greek democracy. Most pre-modern social orders found it necessary to limit individual development and creativity. People were routinely compelled to do the jobs their parents and grandparents had done. People had to learn specific social roles based on the accident of being born in a certain place at a certain time. The personal freedom we value was unknown and unimportant. Folk communities were closed systems in which traditional culture structured social life from generation to generation. Even now, for example, we hear people speak longingly of the traditional values of pre-television America. But the America of the 1930s, 1940s, and 1950s afforded few opportunities to minorities, confined most women to homemaker roles, limited higher education access to a small elite, and imposed a host of other conditions that would cause rebellion today.

Yet the arguments that mass society theorists make about the vulnerability to manipulation of isolated individuals are compelling. These arguments have been restated in endless variations. They assert that when people are stripped of the protective cocoon provided by the traditional community, they necessarily believe everything that media communicate to them. Media are charged with gradually replacing many of the social institutions in a folk community. Media become the most trusted and valued source of messages about politics, entertainment, religion, education, and on and on. Thus, in the urban slums of nineteenth century America as in twenty-first century suburbia, news media compete to be friendly neighbors. It's like hearing it from a friend.

The disintegration of traditional communities has unquestionably provided many opportunities for media entrepreneurs. For example, story telling was an important form of entertainment in many folk communities. As these communities declined, a market opened up for different forms of mediated entertainment such as movies, television, and videos. Should mass media be blamed for luring people away from folk communities by offering more powerful forms of entertainment? Or, were media simply providing people with attractive content at a time when folk communities had lost their ability to control their members?

It is also useful to recognize that the influence of media can fluctuate sharply in relatively short periods. Certain media can indeed play more important roles during times of social instability or national crisis. But this doesn't mean that they are routinely or consistently dominant in comparison with other institutions or organizations.

The fifth assumption is that the social chaos initiated by media will inevitably be resolved by establishment of a totalitarian social order (Davis, 1976). This assumption was developed during the 1930s and reached its peak of popularity during the Red Scare of the 1950s. Mass society is envisioned as a chaotic, highly unstable form of social order that will inevitably collapse and then be replaced by totalitarianism. Mass society, with its teeming hordes of isolated individuals, must give way to an even worse form of society—highly regimented, centrally controlled, totalitarian society. Thus, to the extent that media promote the rise of mass society, they increase the likelihood of totalitarianism.

From 1930 to 1960, mass society theorists outlined a classic scenario for degeneration of mass society into totalitarianism. It describes rather accurately, for example, the rise of Hitler in Germany. In times of rapid and chaotic social change, demagogues arise who promise average people that important social problems can be solved by joining extremist political movements. These demagogues use media very effectively to manipulate average people and attract their support. As their movements gain strength, they place heavy political pressure on the traditional elites. Compromises place increasing power in the hands of demagogues. This power is exercised irresponsibly—political opposition is suppressed and democratic political institutions are undermined. Gradually, power is consolidated in the hands of the most ruthless demagogue and this person establishes a totalitarian state.

Fear of totalitarianism is a modern fear—a fear that only people who value individualism and democracy can experience. For such people, totalitarianism is a nightmare society—one in which everything they value most has low priority. All expression of individualism is outlawed. All forms of communication are severely limited and monitored by government.

A novelist, George Orwell, constructed a most enduring vision of this nightmare world in 1948. His novel, *1984,* effectively articulates the view of media inherent in mass society theory. In Orwell's world, Big Brother watches everyone through an eye on the top of their televisions. Televised propaganda is used to foment hatred against external enemies and promote love of Big Brother. The hero of the novel, Winston Smith, works at a job in which he literally rewrites history. He disposes of old newspaper stories, photographs, and other documents that are inconsistent with current propaganda. All records of dissidents and traitors are wiped out. Government engages in doublespeak—language whose meaning is so corrupted that it has become useless as a medium of expression. Peace means war. Freedom means enslavement. Justice means inequity and prejudice. Anyone who deviates from the dictates of the regime is imprisoned and "re-educated." Orwell describes the struggles and ultimate conversion of Winston Smith. At the conclusion of the novel, proof of Smith's loyalty to the Party is demonstrated by his spontaneous, emotional response to Big Brother on the telescreen (see Box 3b).

Throughout the twentieth century, awareness of the spread of totalitarianism grew. For many, it symbolized everything that was loathsome and evil, but others saw it as the "wave of the future." Totalitarians dismissed democracy as impossible because average people could never effectively govern themselves. Democracies were perceived as inherently weak, unable to resist the rise of charismatic, strong, determined leaders. Across Europe, in Latin America, and in Asia fledgling democracies faltered and collapsed as the economic Great Depression deepened. The United States was not immune. Radical political movements arose and their

Box 3b   Quotes from 1984

. . . He was alone. The past was dead, the future was unimaginable. What certainty had he that a single human creature now living was on his side? And what way of knowing that the dominion of the Party would not endure for ever? Like an answer, the three slogans on the white face of the Ministry of Truth came back at him:

WAR IS PEACE

FREEDOM IS SLAVERY

IGNORANCE IS STRENGTH

He took a twenty-five-cent piece out of his pocket. There, too, in tiny clear lettering, the same slogans were inscribed, and on the face of the coin the head of Big Brother. Even from the coin the eyes pursued you. On coins, on stamps, on the covers of books, on banners, on posters, and on the wrapping of a cigarette packet—everywhere. Always the eyes watching you and the voice enveloping you. Asleep or awake, working or eating, indoors or out of doors, in the bath or in bed—no escape. Nothing was your own except the few cubic centimeters inside your skull (Orwell, 1960, pp. 25–26).

. . . He gazed up at the enormous face. Forty years it had taken him to learn what kind of smile was hidden beneath the dark mustache . . . But it was all right, everything was all right, the struggle was finished. He had won the victory over himself. He loved Big Brother (Orwell, 1960, p. 245).

influence spread rapidly. In several states, right-wing extremists were elected to political office. Pro-Fascist groups held gigantic public rallies to demonstrate their support for Hitler. Radicals fought for control of labor unions. The thousand-year Reich envisioned by Hitler seemed more likely to endure than did democracy.

Why was totalitarianism so successful? Why was it sweeping the world just as the new mass media of radio and movies were becoming increasingly prominent? Was there a connection? Were radio and movies to blame? Many mass society theorists believed that they were. Without these media, theorists thought, dictators couldn't have gained popularity or consolidated their power. Broadcast media were said to be ideally suited to directly persuading average people and welding vast numbers of people into regimented, cohesive societies. Movies communicated powerful images that instilled the positive and negative associations desired by dictators.

What these critics failed to note is that when the Nazis or Communists were most successful, average people had strong reasons for wanting to believe the promises about jobs and personal security made by these extremists. Personal freedom has little value when you are starving and a wheelbarrow full of money won't buy a loaf of bread.

One of the profound ironies of the efforts to oppose the rise of totalitarianism is that these efforts often threatened to produce the very form of government they were intended to prevent. In the United States, an important example of this was provided by Joseph McCarthy, an obscure Republican U.S. Senator from Wisconsin who came to national prominence in the 1950s by claiming to oppose the spread of communism within the U.S. government. Just how far should one go in the defense of democracy? Are there times when you have to indefinitely suspend basic democratic principles in order to "save" it? McCarthy argued that communists were so close to gaining control in the United States that it was necessary to purge many people from government and the media. He claimed that if the rules of democracy were followed, these evil people would escape discovery and bring down our political system. McCarthy claimed to have a long list of names of communists that he dramatically displayed to journalists and newsreel cameras. Journalists cooperated by publishing his charges in front-page stories under banner headlines.

Media criticism of McCarthy was muted. Many journalists feared being labeled communists if they opposed him. Indeed, McCarthy followers were very successful in getting media practitioners fired from their jobs. Blacklists were circulated, and threats were made against media organizations that hired those named on them. Edward R. Murrow, the most prominent broadcast journalist of the 1950s, is credited with stopping McCarthy's rise with news reports and documentaries that questioned his tactics and the substance of his charges. Should media be blamed for causing McCarthy's rise—or credited with stopping him?

Totalitarianism was the biggest fear aroused by mass society theorists, but they also focused attention on a more subtle form of societal corruption—mass culture. The sixth and final assumption of mass society theory, then, is that mass media inevitably debase higher forms of culture, bringing about a general decline in civilization (Davis, 1976).

To understand this criticism, you must understand the perspective held by Western cultural and educational elites during the past two centuries. In the decades following the Enlightenment (an eighteenth century European social and philosophical movement that stressed rational thought), these elites saw themselves as responsible for nurturing and promulgating higher forms of culture, not only within their own societies but also around the world. In retrospect, their perspective suffers from some serious limitations. The literary canon promoted by these elites consisted mostly of white, male, Western, Anglo-Saxon, and Protestant literature. Too often, they believed that the white man's burden was to bring civilization and high culture to uncivilized parts of the world—even if this meant suppressing indigenous cultures and annihilating the people who practiced them. As we saw in 1992, the five-hundred-year anniversary of Christopher Columbus's arrival on the American continent, this event is no longer universally hailed as giant step in the march of civilization. Questions were openly asked about his and other explorers' brutality and destruction of otherwise competent cultures.

For defenders of high culture, mass media represented an insidious, corrosive force within society—one that threatened their influence by popularizing ideas and activities that they considered trivial or demeaning. Rather than glorify gangsters (as movies did in the 1930s), why not praise great educators or religious leaders? Why pander to popular taste—why not seek to raise it to higher levels? Why give people what they want instead of giving them what they need? Why trivialize great art by turning it into cartoons (as Disney did in the 1930s)? Mass society theorists raised these questions—and had long and overly abstract answers for them.

In Europe, these concerns justified government supervision of media through direct control or indirectly through public corporations like the British Broadcasting Corporation. Government there assumed responsibility for using media to advance high culture. Broadcasts of symphony concerts and Shakespearean drama were intended to enlighten the masses. Media were supposed to give people what they needed rather than what they wanted. This earned the BBC the nickname "Auntie Beebe."

Rise of the Great Debate over Media

The confrontation between mass society theorists and apologists for the media industries raged throughout the last century. The debate continues today in renewed and increasingly interesting variations, as we've seen briefly already and as we'll study in more detail as we trace the debate in its various forms in subsequent chapters. But in 1961, Bernard Berelson wrote an insightful summary that he entitled "The Great Debate on Cultural Democracy" that still stands as a classic. According to Berelson, the participants in this debate were **Practicus** (that is, media industry apologists), **Academicus** (that is, mass society theorists), and the emerging **Empiricus** (that is, mass communication researchers who used social science methods). For Berelson, resolution of the debate was simple—just listen to mass communication researchers like himself as they develop useful answers to the issues raised by the others. Berelson argued that both Practicus and Academicus had clear biases, but not so Empiricus. The Empiricus position was even more persuasive because it seemed to represent a moderate, compromise position located midway between the extremes represented by the other two positions.

Berelson's great debate didn't end in 1961. As we shall see in Chapters 6 and 7, the Empiricus position did become the **dominant paradigm** among mass communication researchers for about two decades. But it was widely ignored outside of academia. Media industry proponents and opponents have continued their struggle with seemingly studied ignorance of what Empiricus had to say. They paid attention to the findings of media researchers only when those results sup-

PRACTICUS *In the Great Debate over media, industry researchers*

ACADEMICUS *In the Great Debate over media, traditional elites*

EMPIRICUS *In the Great Debate over media, social science researchers*

DOMINANT PARADIGM *The prevailing thought or theory of the time in a scientific discipline*

ported their views. These findings documented "limited effects," thus Academicus routinely condemned them for underestimating the impact of media. On the other hand, even modest effects on specific audience subgroups were considered unlikely by Practicus (except, of course, by advertising and marketing researchers, but more on that later).

Early Examples of Mass Society Theory

Now we'll summarize several of the early examples of mass society theory. This set of theories is by no means complete. Rather, these perspectives combine ideas that were developed by others and represent how people in a given culture at a particular point in time thought about their social world. The examples described and discussed were influential at the time they were written and provided important reference points for later theorists. It is important to remember, too, that even where not specifically mentioned, the emerging mass media were clearly implicated in each example.

In subsequent chapters, we will deal with development of later theories that grew out of mass society theory. These continued to gain popularity until late into the 1950s. By 1965 however, mass society theory, in its classic formulation, was collapsing—inherent flaws had become obvious even to adamant supporters. Fear of totalitarianism had ebbed—at least within academia, and if mass culture was going to cause the end of civilization, it was already too late.

Although most assumptions of mass society theory have been challenged and discarded, the debate over mass culture endures. In the last chapters of this book, we will consider important new theories that articulate innovative ideas about popular culture. These inevitably draw on older notions about mass society and mass culture, but most reject the simplistic assumptions and criticisms of earlier eras. The newer theories no longer accept elite high culture as the standard against which all others must be measured. Totalitarianism is no longer feared as inevitable. Instead, attention is focused on the inherent biases of media when it comes to developing new forms of culture. Media are no longer seen as corrupting and degrading high culture. Rather, they are viewed as limiting or disrupting cultural development. Media don't subvert culture, but they do play a major and sometimes counterproductive role in cultural change.

Should current theories of popular culture be labeled as mass society theories? Or, should we officially declare mass society theory dead? Although some contemporary theorists clearly continue to draw on mass society notions, most are aware of their limitations. Our preference here is to limit use of the term "mass society theory" to formulations that (a) were developed before 1970 and (b) fail to account for the findings of media effects research.

Gemeinschaft and Gesellschaft

Gemeinschaft
In Tönnies' conception, traditional folk cultures

Gesellschaft
In Tönnies' conception, modern industrial society

Among the originators of mass society notions was a German sociologist, Ferdinand Tönnies. Tönnies sought to explain the critical difference between earlier forms of social organization and European society as it existed in the late nineteenth century. He proposed a simple dichotomy—**Gemeinschaft** or folk community and **Gesellschaft** or modern, industrial society. In folk communities, people were bound together by strong ties of family, by tradition, and by rigid social roles—basic social institutions were very powerful. Gemeinschaft "consisted of a dense network of personal relationships based heavily on kinship and the direct, face-to-face contact that occurs in a small, closed village. Norms were largely unwritten, and individuals were bound to one another in a web of mutual interdependence that touched all aspects of life" (Fukuyama, 1999, p. 57). In addition, "a collective has the character of a Gemeinschaft insofar as its members think of the group as a gift of nature created by a supernatural will" (Martindale, 1960, p. 83). Although folk communities had important strengths as well as serious limitations, Tönnies emphasized the former. He argued that most people yearn for the order and meaning provided by folk communities. They often find life in modern societies to be troublesome and without meaning. As far as mass society theorists were concerned, the emerging mass media not only disrupted kinship and direct face-to-face contact, they certainly were not gifts of nature.

In Gesellschaft, people are bound together by relatively weak social institutions based on rational choices rather than tradition. Gesellschaft represents "the framework of laws and other formal regulations that characterized large, urban industrial societies. Social relationships were more formalized and impersonal; individuals did not depend on one another for support . . . and were therefore much less morally obligated to one another" (Fukuyama, 1999, pp. 57–58). Naturally, it was the established elites (the traditional wielders of power and the most vocal champions of mass society theory) who stood to lose the most influence in the move from Gesellschaft to Gemeinschaft, as "average" people came to depend less on their influence and more on formalized and more objectively applied rules and laws. For example, when you take a job, you sign a formal contract based on your personal decision. You don't sign it because you are bound by family tradition to work for a certain employer. You make a more or less rational choice. You agree to perform a particular job in return for a salary. The contract lasts as long as you and your employer meet its conditions. If you fail to show up for work often enough, you'll be fired. If your employer goes broke and can't pay you, you'll stop working for him or her.

The marriage vow is another example of how important social institutions have been affected by the transition to modernity. In folk communities, these vows were defined as lifelong commitments that ended only with the death of spouses. Marriage partners were chosen by the heads of families using criteria determined by tradition and family needs. If you violated marriage vows, you were likely to be ostracized by everyone in the community. In these social orders, families endured crises and people found ways of surviving within them. In modern societies, families are much more fragile. Marriage vows are often violated, and though offenders can endure many negative consequences, they are not condemned by the society at large (a divorced man, Ronald Reagan, became President of the United States with almost no mention of that fact, and Bill Clinton enjoyed the highest public approval ratings of his presidency at the height of the sex scandal that led to his impeachment). Various factors have combined to make single-parent families common rather than the exception in our contemporary social order.

Over the years, media have been continually accused of breaking down folk communities (Gemeinschaft) and encouraging the development of amoral, weak social institutions (Gesellschaft). The Reverend Jerry Falwell, founder of the Moral Majority, and fellow televangelist Pat Robertson reflected this view in 2001 when they charged that the terrorist attacks on the World Trade Center and the Pentagon were the products, not of Islamic radicalism, but of the "American cultural elite's" systematic subversion of traditional family and social values.

Mechanical and Organic Solidarity

MECHANICAL SOLIDARITY *In Durkheim's conception, folk cultures bound by consensus and traditional social roles*

The French sociologist, Émile Durkheim, offered a theory with the same dichotomy as that of Tönnies but with a fundamentally different interpretation of modern social orders. Durkheim compared folk communities to machines in which people were little more than cogs. These machines were very ordered and durable, but people were forced by a collective consensus to perform traditional social roles. People were bound by this consensus to one another like the parts of a great engine—**mechanical solidarity.**

Durkheim compared modern social orders to animals rather than to machines. As they grow, animals undergo profound changes in their physical form. They begin life as babies and progress through several developmental stages on their way to adulthood and old age. The bodies of animals are made up of many different kinds of cells—skin, bone, blood—and these cells serve very different purposes. Similarly, modern social orders can undergo profound changes, and therefore the people in them can grow and change along with the society at large. In Durkheim's theory, people are like the specialized cells of a body rather than like the cogs of a machine. People perform specialized tasks and depend on the overall health of the body for their personal survival. Unlike machines, animals are subject to diseases and physical threats. But they are capable of using mental processes to anticipate threats and cope with them. Durkheim used the term **organic solidarity** to refer to the social ties that bind modern social orders together.

ORGANIC SOLIDARITY
In Durkheim's conception, modern social orders bound by culturally negotiated social ties

Social orders with organic solidarity are characterized by specialization, division of labor, and interdependence (Martindale, 1960, p. 87). Be warned, though, it is easy to confuse Durkheim's labeling of mechanical and organic solidarity because we naturally associate machines with modernity. Remember that he uses the metaphor of the machine to refer to folk cultures—not modern society.

Durkheim's praise for organic solidarity has been echoed in the many theories that have extolled the virtues of new media and new technology. Proponents of new media usually argue that communication technology will permit important new social bonds to be formed. Keep in mind the frequent allusions to an Internet-fueled "electronic democracy" in which the people can directly communicate with their leaders. There will be "electronic town halls" where the people will be able to decide what they want government to do for them. Politicians of all stripes promise to wire every classroom in the United States to the **Information Superhighway** to ensure all citizens access to their society. These arguments assume that these new mediated relationships would be an improvement over older forms of representative democracy.

INFORMATION SUPERHIGHWAY
The worldwide digital data network

It would be a mistake to view Durkheim as a naive optimist concerning the rise of modern society. His most enduring book, *Suicide* (1951), documented rising suicide rates in those countries where traditional religious and social institutions had lost their preeminence. In these nations, Durkheim argued, people experienced high levels of *anomie* or normlessness. In his later work, Durkheim showed growing concern for the declining strength of common morality (Ritzer, 1983, p. 99). People were no longer bound by traditional values but were free to follow their personal passions and needs. Durkheim believed that these problems were best viewed as social pathologies that could be diagnosed and cured by a social physician—in other words, a sociologist like himself (Ritzer, 1983, p. 110). Unlike conservatives who demanded a return to old social orders or radicals who called for revolution, Durkheim believed that scientifically chosen reforms would solve the problems inherent in modernity .

Mass Society Theory in Contemporary Times

Although mass society theory has very little support among contemporary mass communication researchers and theorists, its basic assumptions of a corrupting media and helpless audiences have never completely disappeared. Attacks on the pervasive, dysfunctional power of media have persisted and will persist as long as dominant elites find their power challenged by media. Two recent controversial books indicate modern articulations of mass society theory. In addition to firmly restating mass society notions, these books amply demonstrate mass society theory's many limitations (for example, distrust of "average people" and the presumption that the authors' values are the "right values"). Michael Medved in *Hollywood vs. America: Popular Culture and the War on Traditional Values* (1992) argues precisely what the title implies—American culture has declined because "the gatekeeper/cleric has wandered away and the carnival barker/programmer has taken his place" (p. 3). But mass society theory's most influential modern champion may well be British social critic and intellectual Roger Scruton. In *An Intelligent Person's Guide to Modern Culture* (2000), he makes clear mass society's elitism and support of elite culture:

> This book presents a theory of modern culture, and a defense of culture in its higher and more critical form. It is impossible to give a convincing defense of high culture to a person who has none. I shall therefore assume that you, the reader, are both intelligent and cultivated. You don't have to be familiar with the entire canon of Western literature, the full range of musical and artistic masterpieces or the critical reflections which all these things have prompted. Who is? But it would be useful to have read *Les fleurs du mal* by Baudelaire and T. S. Eliot's *Waste Land*. I shall also presume some familiarity with Mozart, Wagner, Manet, Poussin, Tennyson, Schoenberg, George Herbert, Goethe, Marx, and Nietzsche. (p. x)

Scruton also weighs in on the decline of traditional values: "Something new seems to be at work in the contemporary world—a process that is eating away the very heart of social life, not merely by putting salesmanship in place of moral virtue, but by putting everything—virtue included—on sale" (p. 55).

On popular entertainment:

> Fantasy replaces the real, resistant, objective world with a pliant surrogate. And it is important to see why this matters. Life in the actual world is difficult and embarrassing. Most of all it is difficult and embarrassing in our confrontation with other people who, by their very existence, make demands that we may be unwilling to meet. It requires a great force, a desire that fixes upon an individual, and sees that individual as unique and irreplaceable, if people are to make the sacrifices upon which the community depends for its longevity. It is far easier to take refuge in surrogates, which neither embarrass us nor resist our cravings. (p. 63)

On popular culture:

> Pop culture is . . . an attempt to provide easy-going forms of social cohesion, without the costly rites of passage that bring moral and emotional knowledge. It is a culture which has demoted the aesthetic object, and elevated the advert in its place; it has replaced imagination by fantasy and feeling by kitsch; and it has destroyed the old forms of music and dancing, so as to replace them

with a repetitive noise, whose invariant harmonic and rhythmic textures sound all about us, replacing the dialect of the tribe with the grammarless murmur of the species, and drowning out the unconfident stutterings of the fathers as they trudge away towards extinction. (p. 121)

And, finally, on the failings of higher education:

The gap between the culture acquired spontaneously by the young, and that which . . . should be imparted in the university, is so cavernously wide that the teacher is apt to look ridiculous, as he perches on his theatrical pinnacle and beckons the youth across to it. Indeed, it is easier to make the passage the other way, to join your young audience in the enchanted field of popular entertainment, and turn your intellectual guns on the stately ruin across the chasm. (pp. 121–122)

Beyond the ongoing concern of those who see "traditional values" and average people jeopardized by new communication technologies, two other factors have given new life, albeit weak, to current notions of mass society theory. The first is the phenomenally rapid diffusion of the Internet and the World Wide Web. New forms of media mean new forms of communication, which means the development of new relationships and the creation of new centers of power and influence. You'll recognize this as a near mirror image of the situation that faced our society at the turn of the twientieth century, the incubation period of mass society theory.

The second factor is related to the rise of these new technologies. We've already seen that media industries, when facing challenges from new technologies, undergo rapid restructuring. This is one of the reasons behind today's dazzling number and scope of media industry mergers. In July 1998, AT&T and British Telecommunications entered into a $10 billion merger to ensure their survival in the competitive telephone, cellular communication, cable television, and Internet markets. In that same month, and with the same goals, Bell Atlantic bought GTE Corporation for $53 billion. Just before these mega-deals, Westinghouse bought CBS, Disney bought Capital Cities/ABC, and Time Warner bought Turner Broadcasting. And in the wake of this round of mergermania, Seagram bought Polygram Music for $10.4 billion (1998); high-speed Internet access company @Home bought search engine Excite for $6.7 billion (1999); AT&T took over cable company TCI ($50 billion), bought another cable company, Media One, for $69 billion, and entered partnerships with two more cable providers, Time Warner and Comcast (1999); Clear Channel Communications purchased AM/FM for $16.6 billion, forming the world's biggest radio company (1999); and America Online swallowed giant media conglomerate Time Warner for $135 billion (2000). Each of these deals produced giant communication companies with holdings across many different forms of media reaching unimaginably large audiences across the globe. Rupert Murdoch's News Corporation is another example of concentration, also on a global scale. News Corporation is an Australian company that owns 789 different businesses in 52 countries and had

Instant Access	*Mass Society Theory*	
Strengths		**Weaknesses**
1 Speculates about important effects		1 Is unscientific
2 Highlights important structural changes and conflicts in modern cultures		2 Is unsystematic
3 Draws attention to issues of media ownership and ethics		3 Is promulgated by elites interested in preserving power
		4 Underestimates intelligence and competence of "average people"
		5 Underestimates personal, societal, and cultural barriers to direct media influence

CONCENTRATION
Ownership of different and numerous media companies concentrated in fewer and fewer hands

$1.32 billion in income in 1997 (World Class, 1998, p. 3). This **concentration** of ownership of media industries led journalist and media critic Ben Bagdikian to comment

> Left to their own devices, a small number of the most powerful firms have taken control of most of their countries' printed and broadcast news and entertainment. They have their own style of control, not by official edict or state terror, but by uniform economic and political goals. They have their own way of narrowing political and cultural diversity, not by promulgating official dogma, but by quietly emphasizing ideas and information congenial to their profits and political preferences. Although they are not their countries' official political authorities, they have a disproportionate private influence over the political authorities and over public policy. (1992, pp. 239–240)

Bagdikian, a strong proponent of media freedom, is no mass society theorist. But his concern is shared by many who hold mass society views of an ever-powerful media system wielding unassailable power over helpless people.

Summary

Criticism of media and new media technology is not a new phenomenon. For more than a century now, new media industries have inspired harsh criticism from a variety of sources. Berelson codified the antagonists as Practicus (media industry researchers), Academicus (traditional elites), and Empiricus (social scientists). Still, there has been much to criticize. The quality of much mass entertainment content has been lowered to satisfy audience's basest tastes and passions. Early news media (and today's supermarket tabloids) attracted huge audiences by printing speculative, overdramatized stories. The most important, continuing criticism of media took the form of mass society theory. Tönnies and Durkheim helped frame a debate over the fundamental nature of modernity that has not ended. For mass society theorists and media apologists, media were symbolic of modernity—representing either the worst or the best of modern life.

Early mass society theorists argued that media are malignant forces that have the power to directly reach, transform, and corrupt the minds of individuals so that their lives are ruined and vast social problems are created. Through media influence, people are atomized, cut off from the civilizing influences of other people or high culture. Totalitarianism inevitably results as ruthless, power-hungry dictators seize control of media to promote their ideology.

Initially, mass society theory gained wide acceptance. In time, however, people questioned its unqualified assertions about the media's power to corrupt and debase individuals. Mass society notions enjoyed longer acceptance in Europe where commitments to traditional ways of life and high culture have been stronger and where distrust of average people and democracy runs deeper. For the past fifty years, U.S. media researchers have been skeptical of the absolute power of media. In subsequent chapters, we will show how their skepticism was grounded in empirical observation. In study after study, researchers found it difficult to demonstrate that media could directly and routinely influence what people thought or did.

The debate about the role of media in modern life has not ended. Though many U.S. scholars were satisfied with the answers supplied by empirical research, European theorists were not. Many old questions about the power of media have recently been revived, especially because of the emergence of the Internet and the recent spate of giant communication industry mergers. Cogent new theories argue that media do play an important role in the development and maintenance of culture. The revival of this debate, as we'll see in later chapters, has reinvigorated media theory and research.

Exploring Mass Communication Theory

1   The ideas of Gesellschaft/Gemeinschaft and Organic and Mechanical Solidarity continue to intrigue social thinkers, even today. Visit the following sites to read a bit of contemporary writing on these venerable ideas. What do they add to your

understanding of Tönnies' and Durkheim's ideas? What do they add to your understanding of mass society theory?

Gesellschaft and Gemeinschaft
www.cchs.usyd.edu.au/bach/pub/community/g&g.htm

Organic and Mechanical Solidarity
www.sla.purdue.edu/people/soc/mdeflem/ztoen.htm

 2 Two arenas in which traditional elites and proponents of communication technology continue to do battle are the Internet and the recording industry. Go to these Web sites (or others of your choice) and examine the arguments and appeals of both camps.

Rock Out Censorship (against album labels)
http://www.theroc.org

The Electronic Frontier Foundation (Internet freedom issues)
http://www.eff.org

Internet Parent Guide (for control of Internet access)
http://www.ed.gov/pubs/parents/internet

The Blue Ribbon Campaign (Online freedom of expression)
http://www.eff.org/blueribbon.html

 3 Go to http://www.cjr.org/owners and check out the holdings of any of the companies mentioned in the section about concentration in the mass communication industry. Describe the holdings of these newly expanded corporations. Do the scope and reach of those holdings concern you as they do critic Bagdikian? Why or why not?

 4 Many public interest groups are expressing concern over concentration in the mass communication industries. Here are two that have taken their case to the Web. Find each and follow the links to their discussions of media ownership. What do you think of their arguments? Join the discussion groups they offer and present your views to others. Report your experience to your classmates.

The Virtual Institute of Information
http://www.vii.org

The Multinational Monitor
http://www.multinationalmonitor.org

 5 This chapter has included a lot of history. This is only natural because mass society theory is the first and oldest of the theories of mediated communication. Use

InfoTrac College Edition to search historical journals for articles about some of the times we've visited. For example, the 1840s saw the rise of the mass circulation newspapers. A host of new (and threatening) communication technologies appeared during the first decades of the twentieth century. Television and the Red Scare arrived fully on the scene in the 1950s. Rock n' roll is a product of the Fifties as well. What can you learn about individual, social, and cultural response to these events?

Critical Thinking Questions

1 Consider the current competition within the media industries, for example, network television versus cable television and newspapers versus online news. How will the outcome of this competition affect your life or your career choice? Do you fear the corrupting power of new communication technologies like the Internet and Web? Why or why not?

2 Do you expect that your life will be significantly better when emerging media technologies (for example, high definition television, virtual reality, improved multimedia, and the World Wide Web) become even more widely available? Will you be willing to pay more for these communication services? Will these services improve or degrade the quality of your life?

3 Why do you think the development of mass media aroused so much fear in the past? How justified were these fears? If you had lived in the 1930s, do you think you would have blamed media for causing the rise of Nazism or Communism? As you read the various criticisms of media, do any strike you as still being valid? Are there any you find ridiculous?

4 Do you agree with the view of the media articulated in Medved's *Hollywood vs. America* or Scruton's *An Intelligent Person's Guide to Modern Culture?* Why or why not?

5 Even the most severe critics of mass communication were forced to concede that the media's performance on September 11 and 12, 2001, was remarkable. In the 48 hours following the horrific events of the morning of the 11th, virtually all the major American media outlets offered responsible, measured, credible, ethical public service reporting. The question, then, in the current media era of OJ, missing Washington interns, and babies fallen into wells, is why don't the media perform at that level all the time, or at least more often?

6 Test your own position on the public service performance of the American mass media. Broadcasters lost millions of dollars in advertising revenue because of the

preemptions caused by coverage of the World Trade Center and Pentagon disasters of September 11. They did so willingly and in the spirit of serving the public. Many advertisers followed suit, refusing broadcasters' offers of "make goods" and other reimbursements for their missing commercials. Was this a once-in-a-lifetime example of broadcast and ad executives putting public service before profit, or little more than a particularly dramatic example of the service both industries perform on a regular, if less visible, basis? Explain and defend your position.

7   Were you aware of the Reverends Fallwell and Robertson's charge that the disasters of September 11, 2001, were the result of the excesses of the "cultural elite"? If you were, what was your reaction to that claim in that most horrible of times? Did you reconsider those words as time passed? Did your response change, and if so, how and why? What connection were they making between the terrorism of that day and "homosexuals and the ACLU"?

Significant People and Their Writing

Arato, **Andrew,** and **Eike Gebhardt,** eds. (1978). *The Essential Frankfurt School Reader.* New York: Urizen.

Bauer, **Raymond A.,** and **Alice H. Bauer** (1960). "America, Mass Society and Mass Media." *Journal of Social Issues,* 10: 3–66.

Kornhauser, **William** (1959). *The Politics of Mass Society.* New York: Free Press.

Scruton, **Roger** (2000). *An Intelligent Person's Guide to Modern Culture.* South Bend, IN: St. Augustine's Press.

Chapter 4

The Rise of Media Theory in the Age of Propaganda

Imagine that you have gone back in time to the beginning of the twentieth century. You live in a large, metropolitan area along the East Coast of the United States and you are a second or third generation American. You are a white, middle class, Anglo-Saxon Protestant. Your city is growing rapidly with new neighborhoods springing up daily to house waves of immigrants from poorer nations in Eastern Europe and the Far East. These people speak strange languages and practice strange cultures. Many claim to be Christians but they don't behave like any Christians you've ever met. Most keep to themselves in ghetto neighborhoods in which there are many social problems.

Most disturbing of all, these people seem to have no sense of what it means to live in a free and democratic nation. They are governed by political bosses who turn them out to vote for what you perceive to be corrupt, party machine candidates. If you pay attention to gossip (or read the right books or magazines), you hear about groups like the Mafia or Cosa Nostra. You also hear (or read in your newspaper) that various extremist political groups are active in these ghettos, spreading all sorts of discontent among these ignorant, irresponsible aliens. Many of these nefarious groups are playing upon the newcomers' loyalties to foreign nations. What would you do about this situation?

Well, you might want to start an America for Americans movement to purge these foreigners from the sacred soil of your homeland. If you are of a more liberal bent, you might be reluctant to do away with these people (even though they do represent a threat to your way of life). As a forward-thinking person, you want to convert these people away from their obviously misguided beliefs. You want them to adopt better forms of government as practiced by responsible officials, people similar to you demographically and culturally. You are aware that greedy employers are exploiting these people with 16-hour workdays and child labor, but you believe that's why they should join mainstream political parties and be responsible citizens. Perhaps, you figure, if they would only abstain from alcohol and adopt more rational forms of religion, that might help them see their problems more clearly.

Unfortunately, most of these recent arrivals don't seem to respond well to efforts designed to help them. Movements to eradicate them seem to make them only more determined to survive. Resistance grows ever more determined and is accompanied by violence on both sides. Now what do you do? You could become a Prohibitionist and successfully ban the sale of liquor. But this only creates a market for bootleggers. The power of organized crime is strengthened rather than reduced. Political party bosses flourish.

Or, you could become a political Progressive and work to break up gigantic interstate monopolies at the same time that you attempt to ban subversive labor unions. You might advocate the use of violence to break illegal strikes. But breaking up monopolies does little to help the poor immigrants. Labor unions grow ever larger and more militant. How will these people ever become true Americans and be absorbed into the American melting pot?

Now imagine that you are one of those aliens. How do you cope with life in the world's greatest democracy—you turn to your family and the friends of your family. Your cousin is a member of the political machine. He promises a patronage job—if you vote for his boss. You fight exploitation by joining labor unions that promise to correct bad working conditions. Above all, you practice the culture you grew up with and you stay within the confines of the ghetto where this culture is practiced. You resent Prohibition and see nothing wrong with consuming alcohol occasionally. You listen to family members and local political bosses who can do things for you and can be trusted to keep their promises.

Throughout that century, the United States was a nation of many cultures. At any given point in time, people in specific racial and ethnic groups were exploited and feared. Some of these groups escaped the ghettos and their children were absorbed into the amorphous American middle class. Other groups were less successful. Some members of dominant cultural groups attempted to assist these subordinate groups, but their efforts were only partially successful. Too often, their work was actually quite self-serving—not selfless. They sought to protect their way of life from the threats posed by other cultures and life styles. This led them to adopt solutions that only made problems worse. Put yourself back there in time. Take whichever role you choose. How comfortable would you be? What would you do? How would you feel about the changes around you?

Overview

MUCKRAKER
Crusading journalist, typically challenging the powerful on behalf of those less so

PROPAGANDA
No-holds-barred use of communication to propagate specific beliefs and expectations

The situation just described was an ideal breeding ground for violent social conflict. This battle was waged in the streets and through the ever-expanding mass media. Yellow journalists and **muckrakers** fought wars of words in the media; battle lines were drawn between defenders of immigrant groups and representatives of existing elites. The battle was not confined to polite newspaper editorials or human-interest feature stories. It was a struggle for the heart and soul of the nation (Altschull, 1990; Brownell, 1983). Nor was the struggle confined to the United States. In Europe, conflict across social class lines was even more intense and deadly.

In the United States, advocates on all sides were convinced of the Truth and Justice of their causes. Their way was the American way, the Right way, the only True way. They were opposed by the forces of Evil and Chaos. Mass-mediated **propaganda** spread throughout America, across Europe, and around the world. Everywhere it deeply affected politics and culture.

In this chapter, we will discuss how political propaganda was used and then survey some of the theories that were developed to understand and control it. Along with the normative theories discussed in the next chapter, these were the first true media theories. Within mass society theory, media were seen as only one of many disruptive forces. However, in propaganda theories, media became the focus of attention. Propaganda theorists specifically analyzed media content and speculated about its influence. They sought to understand and explain the ability of messages to persuade and convert thousands or even millions of individuals to extreme viewpoints.

Propaganda commanded the attention of early media theorists because it threatened to undermine the very foundation of the U.S. political system and of democratic governments everywhere. By the late 1930s, many if not most American leaders were convinced that democracy wouldn't survive if extremist propaganda was allowed to be freely distributed. But censorship of propaganda meant imposing significant limitations on that essential principle of Western democracy, communication freedom. This posed a terrible dilemma. If strict censorship was imposed, this might also undermine democracy. Propaganda theorists attempted to address and resolve this dilemma.

At first, some experts were optimistic that the American public could be educated to resist propaganda. After all, propaganda violates the most basic rules of fair, democratic political communication. Propaganda freely uses lies and deception to persuade. If people could be taught to critically evaluate propaganda messages, they could learn how to reject them as unfair and false. These experts believed that public education could save democracy. Nevertheless, optimism about the power of public education faded as both Nazism and Communism spread [America during the 1930s. More and more Americans, especially : immigrants from Europe, turned away from U.S.-style democracy an to listen to totalitarian leaders who promised social justice and jobs. They joined social movements based on propaganda imported more or less directly from Europe. In the United States, rallies were held to celebrate Adolf Hitler or Joseph Stalin and to denigrate inferior races and Wall Street bosses.

Propaganda experts became convinced that even if public education were a practical means of resisting propaganda, it would simply take too long. Time was running out as the Depression deepened. It appeared likely that a Nazi or Communist leader would seize power before public education had a chance to succeed. So propaganda theorists abandoned idealism in favor of strategies they regarded as realistic and based on scientific fact. Propaganda must be resisted by whatever means possible. Even though the threat of propaganda was great, there might be a silver lining to this cloud. If we could find a way to harness the power of propaganda to promote good and just ideals, then we would not only survive its threat but have a tool that could help build a better social order. This was the promise of what came to be called **white propaganda**—a strategy that used benign propaganda techniques to fight "bad" propaganda and promote objectives that elites considered good. After World War II ended, these white propaganda techniques provided a basis for the development of promotional communication methods that are widely used today in advertising and public relations. In fact, propaganda theory is experiencing a resurgence of interest precisely for this reason—the techniques used in these modern promotional efforts appear to many observers to be even more effective in the contemporary world of corporate media ownership (Laitinen & Rakos, 1997).

WHITE PROPAGANDA *Intentional suppression of potentially harmful information and ideas, combined with deliberate promotion of positive information or ideas to distract attention from problematic events*

The Origin of Propaganda

Propaganda was not an American invention. The term originated in the sixteenth century during the Counter-Reformation and was first used by the Society for the Propagation of the Faith—the Jesuits. The term *propaganda* has since come to refer to the no-holds-barred use of communication to propagate specific beliefs and expectations. The ultimate goal of propagandists is to change the way people act and to leave them believing that those actions are voluntary, that the newly adopted behaviors—and the opinions underlying them—are their own (Pratkanis & Aronson, 1992, p. 9). To accomplish this though, propagandists must first change the way people conceive of themselves and their social world. A variety of communication techniques is used to guide and transform those beliefs. During the 1930s, the new media of radio and movies provided propagandists with powerful new tools.

Fritz Hippler, head of Nazi Germany's film propaganda division, said that the secret to effective propaganda is to (a) simplify a complex issue and (b) repeat that simplification over and over again (*World War,* 1982). J. Michael Sproule (1994) argues that effective propaganda is covert—it "persuades people without seeming to do so" (p. 3); features "the massive orchestration of communication" (p. 4); and emphasizes, "tricky language designed to discourage reflective thought" (p. 5). The propagandist believes that the end justifies the means. Therefore, it is not only right but also necessary that half-truths and outright lies be used to convince people to abandon ideas that are "wrong" and to adopt those favored by the propagandist. Propagandists also rely on what is referred to as **disinformation** to discredit their opposition. False information is spread about opposition groups and their objectives. Often the source of this false information is concealed so that it can't be traced to the propagandist.

As U.S. theorists studied propaganda, they came to differentiate black, white, and gray propaganda. **Black propaganda** involved deliberate and strategic transmission of lies—its use was well illustrated by the Nazis (you can get an idea of the nature of that propaganda in Box 4a). White propaganda, as we've seen, involved intentional suppression of potentially harmful information and ideas, combined with deliberate promotion of positive information or ideas to distract attention from problematic events. **Gray propaganda** involved transmission of information or ideas that might or might not be false. The propagandist simply made no effort to determine their validity and actually avoided doing so—especially if dissemination of the content would serve his or her interest. Today we find the attribution of labels like "black" and "white" to the concepts of bad and good propaganda offensive. But remember one of this book's constant themes: These ideas are products of their times.

Propagandists then and now live in an either/or, good/evil world. Traditional elite propagandists at the beginning of the twentieth century had two clear alternatives. On one side were truth, justice, and freedom—in short, the American way—and on the other side were falsehood, evil, and slavery—Totalitarianism. Of course, Communist and Nazi propagandists had their own versions of truth, justice, and freedom. For them the American vision of utopia was at best naive and at worst likely to lead to racial pollution and cultural degradation. The Nazis used propaganda to cultivate extreme fear and hatred of minority groups. In *Mein Kampf* (1933) Hitler traced the problems of post–World War I Germany to the Jewish people and other ethnic or racial minorities. Unlike the American elites, he saw no reason to bother converting these groups—they were Evil Incarnate and therefore should be exterminated. Nazi propaganda films, of which filmmaker Hippler's hate-filled *The Eternal Jew* is a noted example, used powerful

DISINFORMATION
False information spread about the opposition to discredit it

BLACK PROPAGANDA
Deliberate and strategic transmission of lies

GRAY PROPAGANDA
Transmission of information or ideas that might or might not be false. No effort is made to determine their validity

Box 4a A Few Words from a Master Propagandist

In his book, *The War That Hitler Won,* Robert Herzstein described a speech made in 1928 by the Nazis' master propagandist, Joseph Goebbels. Herzstein wrote, "Goebbels started out from the premise that the aim of propaganda was political success, not intellectual depth. The role of the propagandist was to express in words what his audience felt in their hearts. The propagandist must feel the totality of the National Socialist idea in every aspect of his listeners . . . Goebbels believed that being in power gave a party or an idea the right to use that power . . . 'In politics power prevails, not

moral claims of justice,' Goebbels stated. He thus saw propaganda as a pragmatic art, the means to an end, the seizure of total power" (1978, p. 69).

And just how powerful an art was propaganda? Goebbels lectured his Nazi collaborators, "It would not be impossible to prove with sufficient repetition and psychological understanding of the people concerned that a square is in fact a circle. What after all are a square and a circle? They are mere words and words can be molded until they clothe ideas in disguise" (quoted in Thomson, 1977, p. 111).

negative imagery to equate Jews with rats and to associate mental illness with grotesque physical deformity, whereas positive images were associated with blond, blue-eyed people.

Thus, for the totalitarian propagandist, mass media were conceptualized as a very practical means of mass manipulation—an effective mechanism for controlling large populations so that the dominant majority came to have and act on certain beliefs and attitudes. If people came to share the views of the propagandist, they were said to be converted—they abandoned old views and took on those promoted by propaganda.

Propagandists typically held elitist and paternalistic views about their audiences. They believed that people needed to be converted for their "own good"—not just to serve the interest of the propagandist. Propagandists often blamed the people for the necessity of engaging in lies and manipulation. They thought people to be so irrational, so illiterate, or so inattentive that it was necessary to coerce, seduce, or trick them into learning bits of misinformation. The propagandists' argument was simple: If only people were more rational or intelligent, we could just sit down and explain things to them, person to person. But most aren't—especially the ones who need the most help. Most people are children when it comes to important affairs like politics. How can we expect them to listen to reason? It's just not possible. In the post–World War II United States, for example, this became known as the **engineering of consent**, a term coined by "the father of modern public relations," Edward L. Bernays. Sproule (1997, p. 213) quotes Bernays as wanting to expand freedom of press and speech to include the

ENGINEERING OF CONSENT *Official use of communication campaigns to reach "good" ends*

government's "freedom to persuade . . . Only by mastering the techniques of communication can leadership be exercised fruitfully in the vast complex that is modern democracy . . ." because in a democracy, results "do not just happen."

The propagandist also uses similar reasoning for suppressing opposition messages: Average people are just too gullible. They will be taken in by the lies and tricks of others. If opponents are allowed to freely communicate their messages, a standoff will result in which no one wins. Propagandists are convinced of the validity of their cause, so they must stop opponents from blocking their actions.

Propaganda Comes to the United States

From the viewpoint of old-line elites in the United States during the early years of the twentieth century, propaganda was a subversive form of communication invented by crazy Europeans who insisted on killing each other in endless, meaningless wars. There was widespread suspicion about propaganda. People in the United States were aware that modern propaganda techniques had been used with startling effectiveness to assemble massive armies during World War I. Never before had so many people been mobilized to fight a war. Never before had so many died so quickly under such harsh conditions. Early communication researcher Harold Lasswell expressed grudging respect for the propaganda efforts marshaled in the cause of the First World War, writing, "When all allowances have been made and all extravagant estimates pared to the bone, the fact remains that propaganda is one of the most powerful instrumentalities in the modern world . . . In the Great Society (modern industrial society) it is no longer possible to fuse the waywardness of individuals in the furnace of the war dance; a newer and subtler instrument must weld thousands and even millions of human beings into one amalgamated mass of hate and will and hope. A new flame must burn out the canker of dissent and temper the steel of bellicose enthusiasm. The name of this new hammer and anvil of social solidarity is propaganda" (1927, pp. 220–221).

After World War I, the propaganda battle continued, and it spread beyond Europe. During the 1920s, radio and movies provided powerful new media for propaganda messages. Hitler's rise to power in Germany was almost certainly aided by his total control over radio. Nations sought to spread their influence using propaganda. New political movements attracted members using propaganda. In the United States, the battle lines in the propaganda war were quickly drawn. On one side was the American Establishment, the traditional elites that dominated the major social institutions and organizations, including the major political parties and established social groups. On the other side were a broad range of social movements and small, extremist political groups. Many of these were local variants of groups that were much larger and more significant in Europe. From the point of view of the old-line elites, these groups were suspect. Foreign subversion was a constant fear. The elites believed the influence of these movements and groups had to be curbed before they ruined *our* way of life.

Extremist propagandists, whether foreign-based or domestically grown, found it increasingly easy to reach and persuade audiences during the 1930s. Only a part of this success, however, can be directly attributed to the rise of the powerful new media. In the United States, movies and radio were controlled by the existing elites. Extremists were often forced to rely on older media like pamphlets, handbills, and political rallies. When the social conditions were right and people were receptive to propaganda messages, however, even older, smaller media could be quite effective. And conditions were right. Remember the discussion of Gemeinschaft and Gesellschaft from the previous chapter: mass society theorists and the elites they supported believed that "average people" were particularly open to demagogic propaganda because those "unfortunates" lived in a rapidly industrializing world characterized by psychological and cultural isolation and freedom from the security of traditional, binding, and informal social rules and obligations.

American elites therefore watched with increasing horror as extremist political groups consolidated their power in Europe and proceeded to establish totalitarian governments. Fear grew that these groups could and would come to power in the United States. In several American universities, researchers began to systematically study both foreign and domestic propaganda—searching for clues to what made it effective. Money for this research came from a variety of government agencies and private foundations, most notably military intelligence agencies and the Rockefeller Foundation (Gary, 1996).

We will review the propaganda theories of three of the most prolific, imaginative, and complex thinkers of their time: Harold Lasswell, Walter Lippmann, and John Dewey. Given the number of books these men wrote, it is impossible to provide a complete presentation of their work. Instead, we will highlight some of their most influential and widely publicized ideas. In nearly every case, these men later refined or even rejected many of these ideas. Our objective in presenting their theories is to show how thinking about media evolved during a very critical period in world history—not to demean these individuals or to denigrate their work.

Most of the propaganda theories that developed during the 1930s were strongly influenced by two theories: behaviorism and Freudianism. Some combined both. Before presenting the ideas of the major propaganda theorists, we will first look at the two theories that influenced their thinking.

Behaviorism

BEHAVIORISM
The notion that all human action is a conditioned response to external, environmental stimuli

John B. Watson, an animal experimentalist who argued that all human action is merely a conditioned response to external, environmental stimuli, first popularized stimulus-response psychology. Watson's theory became known as **behaviorism** in recognition of its narrow focus on isolated human behaviors. Behaviorists rejected widely held views in psychology that assumed that higher mental processes (that is, conscious thought or reflection) ordinarily control human action. In contrast to such "mentalist" views, behaviorists argued that the only purpose served by consciousness was to rationalize behaviors *after* they are triggered by external stimuli. Behaviorists attempted to purge all mentalist terms from their theories and to deal strictly with observable variables—environmental stimuli on the one hand and behaviors on the other. By studying the associations that existed between specific stimuli and specific behaviors, behaviorists hoped to discover previously unknown causes for action.

Early media theorists, who saw the media as providing external stimuli that triggered immediate responses, frequently used behavioristic notions. For example, these ideas could be applied to the analysis of the Nazi propaganda films described earlier. The powerful, ugly images presented of Jews or the mentally ill could be expected to trigger negative responses.

Freudianism

FREUDIANISM
Freud's notion that human behavior is the product of the conflict between individuals' Id, Ego, and Superego

EGO *In Freudianism, the rational mind*

ID *In Freudianism, the egocentric, pleasure-seeking part of the mind*

SUPEREGO *In Freudianism, the internalized set of cultural rules*

Freudianism, on the other hand, was very different from behaviorism, though Sigmund Freud shared Watson's skepticism concerning people's ability to exercise effective conscious or rational control over their actions. Freud spent considerable time counseling middle-class women who suffered from hysteria. During hysterical fits, seemingly ordinary individuals would suddenly "break down" and display uncontrolled and highly emotional behavior. It was not uncommon for quiet and passive women to scream and become violent. Often these outbursts occurred in public places at times when the likelihood of embarrassment and trouble for themselves and others was maximized.

To explain this apparently irrational behavior, Freud decided that the self that guides action must be fragmented into conflicting parts. Normally, one part, the rational mind or **Ego**, is in control, but sometimes other parts become dominant. Freud speculated that human action often is the product of another, darker side of the self—the **Id**. This is the egocentric, pleasure-seeking part of ourselves that we, the Ego, must struggle to keep under control. The Ego relies on an internalized set of cultural rules (the **Superego**) for guidance. Caught between the primitive Id and the overly restrictive Superego, the Ego fights a losing battle. When the Ego loses control to the Id, hysteria or worse results. When the Superego becomes dominant and the Id is completely suppressed, people turn into unemotional, depressed social automatons who simply do what others demand.

Propaganda theorists used Freudian theory to develop very pessimistic interpretations of media influence. For example, propaganda would be most effective if it could appeal directly to the Id and stimulate it to overwhelm the Ego. Alternatively, if through effective propaganda efforts the cultural rules (the Superego) moved the self in the direction of the Id, people's darker impulses would become normal—a strategy skillfully used by the Nazis. Behaviorism and Freudianism were often combined to create theories that viewed the individual as incapable of rational self-control. People were seen as highly vulnerable to media manipulation; media stimuli and the Id could trigger actions that the Ego and the Superego were powerless to stop. Afterwards, the Ego merely rationalizes actions that it couldn't control and experiences guilt about them. Accordingly, media could have society-wide, instantaneous influence on even the most educated, thoughtful people.

Magic Bullet Theory

By the 1920s, Freudianism and behaviorism were combined to produce a simplistic propaganda theory. In it, media stimuli were assumed to operate like magic bullets that penetrated people's minds and instantly created associations between strong emotions and specific concepts. By carefully controlling these magic bullets, propagandists felt that they could condition people to associate good emotions, such as loyalty and reverence, with their own country and associate bad emotions, such as fear and loathing, with their enemies. The propagandists saw average people as powerless to resist this influence.

MAGIC BULLET THEORY *Media penetrate people's minds and instantly create effects*

Magic bullet theory assumed what behaviorism was never able to adequately demonstrate: External stimuli, like those conveyed through mass media, can condition anyone to behave in whatever way a master propagandist wanted. People were viewed as powerless to consciously resist manipulation. No matter what their social status or how well educated people are, the magic bullets of propaganda penetrate their defenses and transform their thoughts and actions. In magic bullet theory, the rational mind was a mere façade, incapable of resisting powerful messages. People have no ability to screen out or criticize these messages. The messages penetrate to their subconscious minds and transform how they think and feel.

If magic bullet theory was valid, we would indeed live in a scary world. Imagine a nationwide audience of typical people listening to their favorite radio program. Suddenly a master propagandist breaks in with a message, "Everyone paint your faces purple!" The next day, riots break out as people demand that the government make available purple paint distribution centers. The price of a paintbrush skyrockets to sixty dollars. Havoc reigns! Sounds like an old science fiction movie, doesn't it? Nevertheless, from the early 1900s through the 1950s, similar tales of mass conversion were taken seriously. After all, it happened in Germany, Russia, Japan, and Italy, didn't it?

The advocates of magic bullet theory cited numerous examples of the apparent power of media. Although many of these were from Europe, some were from the United States. One of the most frequently cited examples occurred in October 1938, when Orson Welles, the producer of a weekly CBS radio network program, played a not-so-funny Halloween joke on his listeners. The show was to be a dramatization of an H. G. Wells novel about an invasion from Mars. It began, however, with an elaborate ruse, simulating a live dance music show from a New York hotel. The show was repeatedly interrupted by phony news bulletins: A spaceship had been observed. It had landed in New Jersey. Strange creatures were emerging from it. Then, the fictitious reports ceased and real life panic broke out in several cities, especially those that were near the fake landing site. Critics of the power of radio interpreted this as proof of the validity of magic bullet notions. We will return to this example in Chapter 6 and discuss why it might not provide conclusive proof about the power of media.

Lasswell's Propaganda Theory

Lasswell's theory of propaganda combined behaviorism and Freudianism into a particularly pessimistic vision of media and their role. The power of propaganda was not so much the result of the substance or appeal of specific messages but, rather, the result of the vulnerable state of mind of average people. Lasswell argued that the economic depression and escalating political conflict had induced widespread psychosis and this made people susceptible to even crude forms of propaganda. According to Floyd Matson (1964, pp. 90–93), Lasswell concluded that even relatively benign forms of political conflict were inherently pathological (Lasswell, 1934). When conflict escalates to the level it did in Germany during the Depression, an entire nation could become psychologically unbalanced and vulnerable to manipulation. Lasswell argued that the solution was for social researchers to find ways to "obviate conflict." This necessitates controlling those forms of political communication that lead to conflict. Matson stated, "In short, according to Lasswell's psychopathology of politics, the presumption in any individual case must be that political action is maladjustive, political participation is irrational, and political expression is irrelevant" (1964, p. 91).

Lasswell himself rejected the simplistic magic bullet theory. He argued that propaganda was more than merely using media to lie to people to control them.

People need to be slowly prepared to accept radically different ideas and actions. Communicators need a well-developed, long-term campaign strategy in which new ideas and images are carefully introduced and then cultivated. Symbols must be created and people must be gradually taught to associate specific emotions with these symbols. If these cultivation strategies are successful, they create what Lasswell referred to as **master** or **collective symbols** (Lasswell, 1934). Master symbols are associated with strong emotions and possess the power to stimulate beneficial large-scale, mass action if they are used wisely. In contrast with magic bullet notions, Lasswell's theory envisioned a long and quite sophisticated conditioning process. Exposure to one or two extremist messages would not likely have significant effects.

Lasswell argued that successful social movements gain power by propagating master symbols over a period of months and years using a variety of media. For example, the emotions we experience when we see the American flag are not the result of a single, previous exposure to it. Rather, we have observed the flag in countless past situations in which a limited range of emotions were induced and experienced. The flag has acquired emotional meaning because of all these previous experiences. When we see the flag on television with patriotic music in the background, some of these emotions may be aroused and reinforced.

Lasswell believed that past propagation of most master symbols had been more or less haphazard. For every successful propagandist, there were hundreds who failed. Although he respected the cunning way that the Nazis used propaganda, he was not convinced that they really understood what they were doing. He regarded Hitler as a mad genius who benefited from the psychoses induced in the German people by economic depression and political conflict. When it came to using media, Hitler was an evil artist but not a scientist. Lasswell proposed combating Hitler with a new science of propaganda. Power to control delivery of propaganda through the mass media would be placed in the hands of a new elite, a **scientific technocracy** that would be pledged to using its knowledge for good rather than evil.

In a world where rational political debate is impossible because average people are prisoners of their own psychoses (remember behaviorism and Freudianism) and therefore subject to manipulation by propagandists, Lasswell argued, the only hope for us as a nation rested with social scientists who could harness the power of propaganda for Good rather than Evil. It is not surprising, then, that many of the early media researchers took their task very seriously. They believed that nothing less than the fate of the world lay in their hands. As a result, Lasswell's propaganda-for-good became the foundation for numerous official efforts to "improve" and spread democracy at agencies such as the Voice of America, the United States Information Agency, the Office of International Information and Educational Exchange, and the State Department (Sproule, 1997, pp. 213–215). Not

MASTER (OR COLLECTIVE) SYMBOLS *Symbols that are associated with strong emotions and possess the power to stimulate large-scale, mass action*

SCIENTIFIC TECHNOCRACY *An educated, social science-based elite charged with protecting vulnerable average people from harmful propaganda*

all of Lasswell's contemporaries were taken by his call for elite control of media, however. Matson, a severe critic of Lasswell's theory, complained that Lasswell's "contemplative analysis of 'skill politics and skill revolution' has disclosed to Lasswell that in our own time the most potent of all skills is that of propaganda, of symbolic manipulation and myth-making—and hence that the dominant elite must be the one which possesses or can capture this skill" (Matson, 1964, p. 87).

Lippmann's Theory of Public Opinion Formation

Despite Matson's critique, many other members of the social elite, especially within major universities, shared Lasswell's vision of a benevolent social science-led technocracy. Although Lasswell's work was never widely read, his views were shared by leading academics and opinion leaders, including one of the most powerful opinion makers of the time—Walter Lippmann, a nationally syndicated columnist for the *New York Times*.

Lippmann shared Lasswell's skepticism about the ability of average people to make sense of their social world and make rational decisions about their actions. In *Public Opinion* (Lippmann, 1922), he pointed out the discrepancies that necessarily exist between "the world outside and the pictures in our heads." Because these discrepancies were inevitable, Lippmann doubted that average people could govern themselves as classic democratic theory assumed they could. The world of the 1930s was an especially complex place and the political forces were very dangerous. People simply couldn't learn enough from media to help them understand it all. Even if journalists took their responsibility seriously, they couldn't overcome the psychological and social barriers that prevented average people from developing useful pictures in their heads. Eric Alterman, political essayist for *The Nation*, quoted and summarized Lippmann's position:

> Writing in the early twenties, Lippmann famously compared the average citizen to a deaf spectator sitting in the back row. He does not know what is happening, why it is happening, what ought to happen. "He lives in a world he cannot see, does not understand and is unable to direct." Journalism, with its weakness for sensationalism, made things worse. Governance was better left to a "specialized class of men" with inside information. No one expects a steelworker to understand physics, so why should he be expected to understand politics? (1998, p. 10)

These ideas raised serious questions about the viability of democracy and the role of a free press in it. What do you do in a democracy if you can't trust the people to cast informed votes? What good is a free press if it is literally impossible to effectively transmit the most vital forms of information to the public? The fact that Lippmann made his living working as a newspaper columnist lent credibility to his pessimism. In advancing these arguments, he directly contradicted the libertarian assumptions (see Chapter 5) that were the intellectual foundation of the U.S. media system.

Like Lasswell, Lippmann believed that propaganda posed such a severe challenge that drastic changes in our political system were required. The public was vulnerable to propaganda, so some mechanism or agency was needed to protect them from it. A benign but enormously potent form of media control was necessary. Self-censorship by media probably wouldn't be sufficient. Lippmann shared Lasswell's conclusion that the best solution to these problems was to place control of information gathering and distribution in the hands of a benevolent technocracy—a scientific elite—that could be trusted to use scientific methods to sort fact from fiction and make good decisions about who should receive various messages. To accomplish this, Lippmann proposed the establishment of a quasi-governmental intelligence bureau that would carefully evaluate information and supply it to other elites for decision-making. This bureau could also determine which information should be transmitted through the mass media and which information people were better off not knowing.

Reaction Against Early Propaganda Theory

The propaganda theories of Lasswell and Lippmann seemed to carry the weight of real-world proof—the globe had been engulfed by two devastating World Wars in a 30-year span and the Cold War was raging. Sophisticated and apparently successful propaganda characterized these conflicts. Yet, there was opposition. One prominent critic of this early propaganda theory was the philosopher, John Dewey. In a series of lectures (Dewey, 1927), he outlined his objections to Lippmann's views. Throughout his long career, Dewey was a tireless and prolific defender of public education as the most effective means of defending democracy against totalitarianism. He refused to accept the need for a technocracy that would use scientific methods to protect people from themselves. Rather, he argued that people could learn to defend themselves if they were only taught the correct defenses. He rejected simplistic magic bullet notions and asserted that even rudimentary public education could enable people to resist propaganda methods. Dewey "took violent issue" with Lippmann's "trust in the beneficence of elites." "'A class of experts,' Dewey argued, 'is inevitably too removed from common interests as to become a class of private interests and private knowledge' . . . He saw democracy as less about information than conversation. The media's job, in Dewey's conception, was 'to interest the public in the public interest'" (Alterman, 1998, p. 10).

Dewey's critics saw him as an idealist who talked a lot about reforming education without actually doing much himself to implement concrete reforms

(Altschull, 1990, p. 230). Dewey did no better when it came to reforming the media. He argued that newspapers needed to do more than simply serve as a bulletin board for information about current happenings. They should serve as vehicles for public education and debate. They should focus more on ideas and philosophy and less on descriptions of isolated actions. They should teach critical thinking skills and structure public discussion of important issues. His efforts to found such a paper never got very far, however.

James Carey (1989, pp. 83–84) contends that Dewey's ideas have continuing value. Carey argues that Dewey anticipated many of the concerns now being raised by cultural studies theories (see Chapter 11). And as you'll read in Chapter 12, Dewey's belief that educating people to think critically about media content and how they use it is at the heart of the growing media literacy movement.

In one very important respect, Dewey's ideas about the relationship between communities and media were quite innovative. Lasswell and Lippmann saw media as external agencies, as conveyor belts that deliver quantities of information to isolated audience members. In Chapter 8, we will discuss Lasswell's classic linear model of mass communication: Who says what to whom through what medium with what effect. Dewey believed such models were far too simplistic. They ignored the fact that effective media must be well integrated into the communities they serve; media are at the center of the complex network of relationships that define a community. Media should be understood not as external agents but as servants that facilitate public discussion and debate, as guardians and facilitators of the public forum in which democratic politics are conducted.

Dewey believed that communities, not isolated individuals, use communication (and the media of communication) to create and maintain the culture that bonds and sustains them. When media assume the role of external agents and work to manipulate the "pictures in people's heads," they lose the power to serve as credible facilitators and guardians of public debate; they become just another competitor for our attention. The potentially productive interdependence between the community and media is disrupted and the public forum itself is likely to be destroyed. This argument concerning the disconnection of media from communities is now of considerable interest (see Chapters 10 and 11) and foreshadows contemporary debate over the proper role of media within communities.

Modern Propaganda Theory

Consider the Hippler and Sproule characterizations of propaganda from page 72—simplify a complex issue and repeat that simplification; use covert, massively orchestrated communication, use tricky language to discourage reflective thought. Some contemporary critical theorists argue that propaganda conforming to these rules is alive and well today and that it is practiced with a stealth, sophistication, and effectiveness unparalleled in history. These theorists point to a number of "natural beliefs" that have been so well propagandized that meaningful public discourse about them has become difficult if not impossible. Political discourse and advertising are frequent areas of modern propaganda study, and the central argument of this modern propaganda theory is that powerful elites so thoroughly control the mass media and their content that they have little trouble imposing their Truth on the culture.

Close your eyes and think *welfare.* Did you envision large corporations accepting government handouts, special tax breaks for businesses, companies building ships and planes that the military does not want? Or did you picture a single mother, a woman of color, cheating the taxpayers so she can stay home and watch *Jerry Springer?* This narrowing of public discourse and debate is examined in works such as historian Herb Schiller's *Culture, Inc.: The Corporate Takeover of Public Expression* (1989), communication theorist Robert McChesney's *Corporate Media and the Threat to Democracy* (1997), and linguist Noam Chomsky's *American Power and the New Mandarins* (1969), *Deterring Democracy* (1991) and, with Edward S. Herman, *Manufacturing Consent* (1988).

All offer a common perspective. Take advertising as an example. Different ads may tout one product over another, but all presume the logic and rightness of consumption and capitalism. Our need for "more stuff" is rarely questioned, the connection between wealth/consumption and success/acceptance is never challenged, and concern about damage to the environment caused by, first, the manufacture of products and, second, their disposal, are excluded from the debate. The point is not that consumption and capitalism are innately bad, but that, as in all successful propaganda efforts, the alternatives are rarely considered. When alternatives *are* considered, those who raise them are viewed as out of the mainstream, or peculiar. By extension, this failure to consider alternatives benefits those same economic elites most responsible for limiting that consideration and reflection. Sproule has written thoughtfully and persuasively on advertising as propaganda in *Channels of Propaganda* (1994) and *Propaganda and Democracy: The American Experience of Media and Mass Persuasion* (1997) (see Box 4b for some of his ideas).

This current reconsideration of propaganda theory comes primarily from critical theorists and, as a result, its orientation tends to be from the political left (Chapter 2). For example, economist and media analyst Herman (1996) identified five *filters* that ensure the "multi-leveled capability of powerful business and government entities and collectives (for example, the Business Roundtable; U.S. Chamber of Commerce; industry lobbies and front groups) to exert power over the flow of information" (p. 117). These filters enable powerful business and government elites "to mobilize an elite consensus, to give the appearance of

Box 4b   Propagandizing Drugs

In 1998, political rivals Speaker of the House Newt Gingrich and President Bill Clinton joined to announce a $1 billion advertising campaign to fight drugs. At the same time, the U.S. House of Representatives passed Section 484(r), The Suspension of Eligibility for Drug-Related Offenses, an amendment to its Higher Education Funding bill that canceled the financial aid of a college student convicted of even misdemeanor possession of drugs, including marijuana. The United States had embarked on a "War on Drugs" and entrusted its command to a "Drug Czar." In time of war, it is only logical to direct great resources to the cause and to pass restrictive legislation.

Yet, these efforts are a part of what J. Michael Sproule (1994) calls the "perverted debate over drugs." The drug debate in the United States proceeds "as if there were only one legitimate position to be expressed—total prohibition of mood-altering drugs. Since pleasure drugs had to be illegal, the only significant body of national discussion centered on the penalties to be assigned to lawbreakers, the various methods for speedily detecting violators, and the pace of constructing prisons to house drug criminals" (p. 303).

Because of the perverted debate, the public, fearing the soft-on-drugs label, shies away from consideration of potentially valuable solutions like decriminalization, intervention and treatment, and other strategies that treat drug users as people in need of help rather than as criminals or—what every war needs—enemies. This has occurred despite the fact that "every dollar invested in drug treatment saves taxpayers $5. Drug treatment cuts criminal activity by as much as two-thirds . . . (and) the Federal Bureau of Prisons found that inmates who got drug treatment were 73% less likely to be re-arrested than those who did not" (Drug war . . . , 1998, p. 6B).

Sproule (p. 307) concludes that the propagandizing of drugs (simplify and repeat) has "encouraged government agencies, schools, and other channels of public communication to outdo themselves in disseminating an essentially unexamined conclusion—that making drugs illegal was the only way to handle their use and abuse."

What else is left unexamined? What questions go unasked? Consider the withdrawal of financial aid from college students. College students on financial aid can spend their money to get thoroughly drunk, get in their cars, and cause a serious accident. But even if convicted of drunk driving and grievous bodily harm, those students would not lose their aid. In fact, "no other felony or misdemeanor conviction—including rape, murder, and armed robbery—results in the loss of aid to pay for higher education" (O'Leary, 2001, p. B7).

The amendment's sponsor, Indiana Republican Mark Souder, said in defense of his plan, "Drugs can mess you up for life" (Jacobs, 1998, p. 9B). But isn't alcohol a drug? Don't 44 percent of all college students admit to binge drinking—five drinks at one sitting—in any given two-week period (Jacobs, 1998, p. 9B)? Didn't students at Michigan State University, Washington State University, the University of Connecticut, and Ohio University engage in violent mass riots in the spring of 1998 when their campuses attempted to crack down on drinking? Hasn't alcohol messed up many lives?

Consider Viagra, the so-called "potency pill." It, like marijuana, LSD, heroin, and cocaine, is mood altering, consumed to enhance pleasure, has negative side effects (for example, 69 deaths in the first five months of its 1998 release), and is psychologically addictive. Yet, not only is it legal, insurance companies, including the federal government, even pay for it. It can be argued that Viagra has medicinal use, but this argument can be raised about illegal drugs as well.

The issue is not "drugs: good or bad?" The argument made by contemporary propaganda theorists is that there is no meaningful public debate beyond this question and, as our prisons become increasingly overcrowded with nonviolent drug offenders, the society suffers.

democratic consent, and to create enough confusion, misunderstanding, and apathy in the general population to allow elite programs to go forward" (p. 118). The first two of Herman's elite-supporting filters are *ownership* and *advertising,* which "have made bottom line considerations more controlling . . . (T)he professional autonomy of journalists has been reduced" (p. 124). The next two are *sourcing* and *flack,* increasingly effective because "a reduction in the resources devoted to journalism means that those who subsidize the media by providing sources for copy gain greater leverage" (p. 125). Here, he is specifically speaking of the power of corporate and government public relations. Finally, the fifth filter motivating media toward propagandistic support of the status quo is the media's "belief in the 'miracle of the market.' There is now an almost religious faith in the market, at least among the elite, so that regardless of the evidence, markets are assumed benevolent and non-market mechanisms are suspect" (p. 125). These themes, as you will see in Chapter 11, accurately mirror many of the core assumptions of critical cultural theory.

Behaviorists Richard Laitinen and Richard Rakos (1997) offer another critical view of contemporary propaganda. They argue that modern propaganda, by their definition "the control of behavior by media manipulation," (p. 237) is facilitated by three factors—an audience "that is enmeshed and engulfed in a harried lifestyle, less well-informed, and less politically involved, . . . the use of sophisticated polling and survey procedures, whose results are used by the propagandists to increase their influence, . . . (and) the incorporation of media companies into megaconglomerates" (pp. 238–239). These factors combine to put untold power in the hands of powerful business and governmental elites without the public's awareness. Laitinen and Rakos wrote,

> In contemporary democracies, the absence of oppressive government control of information is typically considered a fundamental characteristic of a "free society." However, the lack of aversive control does not mean that information is "free" of controlling functions. On the contrary, current mechanisms of influence, through direct economic and indirect political contingencies, pose an even greater threat to behavioral diversity than do historically tyrannical forms. Information today is more systematic, continuous, consistent, unobtrusive, and ultimately powerful. (1997, p. 237)

There is also renewed interest in propaganda theory from the political right. This conservative interest in propaganda takes the form of a critique of liberal media bias. Other than surveys indicating that a majority of journalists vote Democratic, there is little serious scholarship behind this assertion. In fact, what research there is tends to negate the liberal media bias thesis, as the large majority of media outlet managers and owners tend to vote Republican. McChesney commented, "The fundamental error in the conservative notion of the 'liberal' media (is) it posits that editors and journalists have almost complete control over what goes into news . . . In conservative 'analysis,' the institutional factors of corporate ownership, profit-motivation, and advertising support have no effect on media content . . . The notion that journalism can regularly produce a product that violates the fundamental interests of media owners and advertisers and do so with impunity simply has no evidence behind it" (1997, p. 60).

Libertarianism Reborn

By the end of the 1930s, pessimism about the future of democracy was widespread. Most members of the old-line elites were convinced that totalitarianism couldn't be stopped. They pointed to theories like those of Lasswell and Lippmann as proof that average people could not be trusted. The only hope for the future lay with technocracy and science.

In the next chapter, we will trace the development of theories that arose in opposition to these technocratic views. Advocates of these emerging ideas didn't base their views of media on social science; rather, they wanted to revive older notions of democracy and media. If modern democracy was being threatened, then maybe the threat was the result of having strayed too far from old values and ideals. Perhaps these could be restored and modern social institutions could somehow be purified and renewed. Theorists sought to make the libertarianism of the Founding Fathers once again relevant to democracy. In doing so, they created views of media that are still widely held.

Summary

The first half of the twentieth century was a highly traumatic period in which the basic principles of democracy were tested. The power of mass media was demonstrated by totalitarian propagandists who used media to convert millions to their ideas. Though Nazi and Communist propagandists wielded media with apparent effectiveness, the basis for their power over mass audiences was not well understood. Early theorists combined Freudianism and behaviorism to argue that propaganda messages were like magic bullets that could easily and instantly penetrate even the strongest defenses. No one was safe from their power to convert. Later theorists like Harold Lasswell held that propaganda typically influenced people in slow and subtle ways. It created new master symbols that could be used to induce new forms of thought and action. Both magic bullet and Lasswell's theories assumed that media could operate as external agents and be used as tools to manipulate essentially passive mass audiences. Also believing in the propaganda power of mass media was columnist Walter Lippmann, whose skep-

Instant Access

Propaganda Theory

Strengths	Weaknesses
1 Is first *systematic* theory of mass communication	1 Underestimates abilities of average people to evaluate messages
2 Focuses attention on why media might have powerful effects	2 Ignores personal, social, and cultural factors that limit media effects
3 Identifies personal, social, and cultural factors that can enhance media's power to have effects	3 Overestimates the speed and range of media effects
4 Focuses attention on the use of campaigns to cultivate symbols	

ticism with the self-governance abilities of average people and distrust of lazy media professionals brought him to the conclusion that the "pictures in people's heads" posed a threat to democracy.

Opposition to these early theories of propaganda came primarily from thinkers like John Dewey. Relying on traditional notions of democracy, their idea was that people were, in fact, good and rational, and the counter to propaganda was not control of media by a technocratic elite, but more education of the public.

Contemporary propaganda theory, centered in critical theory, argues that public discourse is shaped and limited by powerful elites to serve their own ends. Advertising's underlying theme that consumption and capitalism are beneficial is another area of interest to propaganda theorists.

Exploring Mass Communication Theory

1   Several places on the Internet support the contemporary propaganda theory view that propaganda is alive and well. Four, in particular, are noteworthy. Visit these and other, similar sites, both pro and con, and determine for yourself if the claims of contemporary propaganda theorists are valid, that is, are we being propagandized, what is the effect of this propaganda, are the solutions suggested reasonable?

Advertising and consumerism
Media Foundation
http://www.adbusters.org

Narrowing public discourse
Cultural Environment Project
http://www.cemnet.org

Concentration
http://www.cjr.org/owners

Corporate censorship of news
http://www.sonoma.edu/ProjectCensored/

 2 The ideas of Dewey and by extension, Lippmann, are presented online on the Web site of the Center for Dewey Studies. Visit this site to determine for yourself who is more correct in his assumptions about typical people and their abilities to govern themselves.

Center for Dewey Studies
http://www.siu.edu/~deweyctr/

 3 Use **InfoTrac College Edition** to scan the tables of contents of advertising and marketing journals like the *Journal of Advertising* and the *Journal of Advertising Research*. Identify "how-to" articles, that is, those that offer instructions on how to undertake effective advertising and marketing campaigns. Can you identify techniques that conform to either older or more contemporary conceptions of propaganda?

 4 Use **InfoTrac College Edition** to find the tables of contents of public opinion publications like *Public Interest, Political Science Quarterly,* and the *American Political Science Review.* Is propaganda, by whatever name, examined or discussed in these publications? If so, what is the tenor of that discussion?

Critical Thinking Questions

1 Explain what you think is meant by propaganda. Give some examples from your own experience. Is a bit of official propaganda necessary to maintain order in a society? If you think it is, how much is enough? If you think it isn't, why not?

2 Is the use of propaganda ever justified? If so, should limitations be placed on it? Is deliberate lying or deception ever justified?

3 Discuss the dilemma that propaganda created during the 1930s. Which was worse—censorship by our own elites or the threat posed by subversive totalitarian propaganda? Is censorship of communication always a threat to democracy? Can you envision a contemporary scenario similar to that of the early propaganda period that would justify official propaganda efforts? For example, the contemporary German government is working diligently to prevent Nazi material from entering Germany by means of the Internet. If you do not favor this overt censorship, would you advocate official government propaganda as an alternative?

4 Recall Lasswell's view that people can be conditioned to associate strong emotions with master symbols. Think of a symbol that you find very powerful and consider the emotion that it arouses in you. How did this symbol come to have this meaning for you? Did media messages or interactions with other people influence you?

5 After the terrorist attack on America on September 11, 2001, images of the World Trade Center's Twin Towers—both in flames and intact—were ubiquitous. Can you make an argument that the Twin Towers became a master symbol? If so, what meanings did they convey? To what end was this master symbol used? By whom?

6 Both independent investigations and the military's own analyses have conclusively demonstrated that military press briefings in both the Vietnam and Gulf wars were often composed of intentional lies and obfuscations. And as in those conflicts, Pentagon spokespeople in the war on terrorism that follwed the attacks on the World Trade Towers and the Pentagon continued to see their jobs as spinning the conflict for maximum benefit of the military. Are you troubled by this "manufacturing of consent"? Should government employees intentionally lie to the press and public? Don't we have the right to know precisely how the war is being conducted so we can make a reasoned judgment to support or not support the government's actions? Doesn't this smack of old-fashioned elitist notions that the people don't know what's good for them?

7 In early 2002, during the war on terrorism, Secretary of Defense Donald Rumsfeld announced that a new division was to be set up in the Pentagon, the purpose of which was to provide information to foreign governments and journalists. In a moment of candor, he admitted that intentional lying—disinformation—would be a significant tool in the arsenal of this office. Reaction, both at home and abroad, was instant and negative. The greatest democracy in the world, one that has enshrined in its Constitution the importance of a free press to its people, the argument went, should not be lying to that press. It's war, countered the office's supporters, disinformation has important strategic and propaganda value. Still, plans for the new office were quickly scrapped in the face of the controversy. What do you think? Is lying to the press ever proper? If so, how much? Where do you draw the line?

8 Dewey argued that public education was the best means of resisting propaganda. Why did so many propaganda experts reject his views as idealistic and impractical? Do you think that average people can be educated to resist the influence of propaganda? Why or why not? How about yourself, are you able to resist propaganda?

Significant People and Their Writing

Chomsky, Noam (1969). *American Power and the New Mandarins.* New York: Pantheon.

Dewey, John (1927). *The Public and Its Problems.* New York: Holt.

Herman, Edward S. and Noam Chomsky (1988). *Manufacturing Consent.* New York: Pantheon.

Lasswell, Harold D. (1927). *Propaganda Technique in the World War.* New York: Knopf.

Lippmann, Walter (1922). *Public Opinion.* New York: Macmillan.

McChesney, Robert (1997). *Corporate Media and the Threat to Democracy.* New York: Seven Stories.

Schiller, Herb (1973). *The Mind Managers.* Boston: Beacon.

Sproule, J. Michael (1994). *Channels of Propaganda.* Bloomington, IN: EDINFO.

——— (1997). *Propaganda and Democracy: The American Experience of Media and Mass Persuasion.* New York: Cambridge University Press.

Chapter 5

Normative Theories of Mass Communication

When Michael Powell assumed the Chairmanship of the FCC in 2001, he promised a Commission that would "tread lightly" when it came to regulating broadcast content (McConnell, 2001, p. 28). "I don't want the government as my nanny. I still have never understood why something as simple as turning it off is not part of the answer" (quoted in Hart & Naureckas, 2001, p. 4). But almost immediately, his FCC began cracking down on what it saw as indecent content, and its target was rap and hip-hop.

Powell's FCC fined two stations $7,000 each for violating its indecency rules. The Commission defines indecent content as material that depicts sexual or excretory activities or organs in a way patently offensive by community standards, and it prohibits broadcast of this material between 6 A.M. and 10 P.M. when children are presumably in the radio and television audience. The first case involved commercial station KKMG in Colorado Springs, Colorado. The popular FM station had aired the "cleaned up" version of controversial rapper Eminem's *The Real Slim Shady*, an edited-for-broadcast rendition of Eminem's expletive filled album cut. The song—admittedly sexist, misogynistic, and homophobic—had already been aired 125,071 times nationally in the time between its release and the FCC's action, complained the station's attorney, and rather than indecent, *The Real Slim Shady* was "a caustic commentary on social inequality and hypocrisy" (McConnell, 2001, p. 28).

The second case involved the airing of feminist rapper Sarah Jones' *Your Revolution*. Community station KBOO in Portland, Oregon, played the song, which denounces the sexual degradation of women in hip-hop, during a two-hour public affairs program. KBOO's lawyers informed the FCC that the song parodies popular music that encourages sexism and casual sexual behavior, that Jones had been invited to perform her song at numerous high schools across the country, and that the Commission was punishing an attempt to respond to offensive speech with more speech, the basic assumption of the First Amendment to the Constitution and therefore, of our democracy. The Commission remained unconvinced. Lyrics such as "Your (women's) revolution will not happen between these thighs," however well meant, were still "unmistakable patently offensive sexual references that appear to be designed to pander and shock" (quoted in Hart & Naureckas, 2001, p. 4). The noncommercial FM appealed the fine, telling the FCC that it had no right to punish it "solely on *its* views of offensiveness and *its* view of merit . . . To punish a station for the broadcast of officially disfavored subject matter is the essence of governmental censorship" (emphasis theirs; quoted in "Fear Factor," 2001, p. 54).

SAFE HARBOR
Government sanctioned times, typically very late at night, when controversial content may be broadcast

But is it censorship? If these tunes had been aired during the **safe harbor**, the hours after 10 P.M. and before 6 A.M., the Commission would not have objected. And don't we, as a nation, have an obligation to protect our children from filth such as this? But, is it filth? One person's filth is another's caustic commentary; isn't that what freedom and democracy are all about? Still sexist, misogynistic, homophobic rap like Eminem's *The Real Slim Shady* debases our culture and promotes harmful attitudes and possibly behaviors among impressionable young people. Yet if this is true, doesn't anti-sexist, anti-misogynistic, anti-homophobic rap like Sarah Jones' *Your Revolution* have just the opposite effect? So who should decide? Maybe a little bit of censorship makes sense; after all, these are only two rap songs in a world of limitless media options. But, is there really such a thing as a little bit of censorship?

Modern media-saturated society is rife with conflicts such as these. Should there be Web filters on school and library computers? Should newspapers publish the names of sex-offenders who have served their time? Why do the broadcast networks bleep out curse words but air scenes of decapitation and mutilation? Should advertisers be allowed to buy commercial space on grammar and secondary school lunch menus? Should reporters from all media be allowed to publish stories based on information provided by people unwilling to be identified? When our nation is at war, are reporters journalists first and Americans second, or are they Americans first and journalists second? None of these questions is easily answered, and perhaps they should not be. Each houses the conflict between our basic belief in freedom of press and expression and our desire to build a humane, meaningful society in which all people can live safely and with dignity.

As we saw in Chapter 3, this conflict is not new, nor is the question of whose values should prevail in its resolution. This is precisely why we value our First Freedom; it protects (or should protect) the resolving debate. As we saw in Chapter 4, many people inside and outside the media industries were so mistrustful of the people and the press that curtailment of our freedom of press and expression had significant support among many elites. Who could blame them?

Overview

During the yellow journalism era, most media professionals cared very little for the niceties of accuracy, objectivity, and public sensitivities. But in the first decades of the twentieth century, a crusade began among some media industry people and various social elites to clean up the media and make them more respectable and credible. The watchword of this crusade was *professionalism* and its goal was elimination of shoddy and irresponsible content.

Some sort of theory was needed to guide this task of media reform. This theory should answer questions such as these:

- Should media do something more than merely distribute whatever content will earn them the greatest profits in the shortest time?

- Are there some essential public services that media should provide even if no immediate profits can be earned?

- Should media become involved in identifying and solving social problems?

- Is it necessary or advisable that media serve as watchdogs and protect consumers against business fraud and corrupt bureaucrats?

- What should we expect media to do for us in times of crisis?

These broad questions about the role of media are linked to issues concerning the day-to-day operation of media. How should media management and production jobs be structured? What moral and ethical standards should guide media professionals? Exactly what constitutes being a "journalist?" Are there any circumstances when it is appropriate or even necessary to invade people's privacy or risk ruining their reputations? If someone threatens to commit suicide in front of a television camera, what should a reporter do—get it on tape or try to stop it? Should a newspaper print a story about unethical business practices even if the company involved is one of its biggest advertisers? Should television networks broadcast a highly rated program even if it routinely contains high levels of violence?

NORMATIVE THEORY
A type of theory that describes an ideal way for media systems to be structured and operated

Answers to questions like these are found in **normative theory**—a type of theory that describes an ideal way for a media system to be structured and operated. Normative theories are different from most of the theories we will study in this book. They don't describe things as they are nor do they provide scientific explanations or predictions. Instead, they describe the way things should be if some ideal values or principles are to be realized. Normative theories come from many sources. Sometimes media practitioners themselves develop theories. Sometimes social critics or academics develop them. Most normative theories develop over time and contain elements drawn from previous theories. This is especially true of the normative theory that currently guides mass media in the United States: It is a synthesis of ideas developed over the past three centuries.

This chapter examines a variety of normative theories of media including some that are questionable or even objectionable. We proceed from earlier forms of normative theory to more recent examples. Our attention is on the normative theory that is predominantly used to guide and legitimize most large media in the United States—**social responsibility theory**. For some time now, the debate about normative theory has been muted in the United States. Social responsibility theory has seemingly provided such an ideal standard for media that further debate was considered unnecessary. The past thirty years have seen unprecedented growth and consolidation of control in the media industries, and, as a result, gigantic conglomerates dominate the production and distribution of media content. Yet, even these conglomerates have found that social responsibility theory provides practical guidelines for their operations and legitimizes what they do.

We will assess why social responsibility theory has enduring appeal for American media practitioners. We contrast it with theories popular in other parts of the world. Then we speculate about its future. As new industries based on new media technologies emerge, will social responsibility theory continue to guide them or will alternatives develop? Social responsibility theory is suited to a particular era of national development and to specific types of media. As the media industries change, this guiding theory might have to be substantially revised or replaced.

Take a few minutes now, before you read the remainder of this chapter, to think about your views concerning the role of media for yourself, your community, your state, your nation, and your world. What are the most important things that media should and shouldn't do? What standards of behavior should media practitioners follow as they perform these tasks? Is it permissible to do beneficial things but use questionable or unethical practices? For example, should reporters deliberately lie or engage in burglary to expose corrupt business practices? What about using a hidden camera to catch a corrupt politician taking a bribe? What about the high percentage of entertainment programming on television? Should there be less entertainment and more content that informs and educates? Should reporters accept official Pentagon statements about the success of its military missions? If you were a Commissioner on Michael Powell's FCC, how would you have voted on the punishment of KKMG and KBOO? How would you defend your position? Knowingly or not, your decision would be based in normative theory.

SOCIAL RESPONSI-
BILITY THEORY
A normative theory that substitutes media industry and public responsibility for total media freedom on the one hand and for external control on the other

The Origin of Normative Theories of Media

RADICAL LIBERTARI-
ANISM *The absolute
belief in Libertari-
anism's faith in a
good and rational
public and totally
unregulated media*

FIRST AMENDMENT
ABSOLUTIST *Those
who believe in the
strictest sense that
media should be
completely un-
regulated*

TECHNOCRATIC
CONTROL *Direct
regulation of
media, most often
by government
agency or com-
mission*

Since the beginning of the twentieth century, the role of mass media in American society, as we've already seen, has been hotly debated. Sharply conflicting
views have been expressed. At one extreme are people who argue for what we
will term **radical libertarian** ideals. These people believe that there should be no
laws governing media operations. They are **First Amendment absolutists** who
take the notion of "free press" quite literally to mean that all forms of media
must be totally unregulated. These people accept as gospel that the First Amendment dictate—Congress shall make no law . . . abridging the freedom of speech
or of the press—means exactly what it says. As Supreme Court Justice Hugo
Black succinctly stated, "No law means no law."

At the other extreme are people who believe in direct regulation of media,
most often by a government agency or commission. These include advocates of
technocratic control, people like Harold Lasswell and Walter Lippmann. They
argue that media practitioners can't be trusted to communicate responsibly or to
use media to serve vital public needs. Some sort of oversight or control is necessary to ensure that important needs are satisfied. The views of these advocates are
considered most seriously during times of crisis when we need media to serve
specific needs.

As we saw in Chapter 4, these advocates of control based their arguments on
propaganda theories. The threat posed by propaganda was so great that they believed information gathering and transmission had to be placed under the control
of wise people—technocrats who could be trusted to act in the public interest.
These technocrats would be highly trained and have professional values and skills
that guaranteed that media content would serve socially valuable purposes, for
example, stopping the spread of terrorism or informing people about natural disasters or a disease like AIDS.

Other proponents of regulation based their views on mass society theory
(Chapter 3). They were troubled by the power of media content to undermine
high culture with trivial forms of entertainment. Their complaints often centered
around the way that sex and violence were presented by media. These regulation
proponents also objected to the trivialization of what they consider important
moral values.

Thus, both propaganda and mass society theories can be used to lobby for
media regulation. In both perspectives, media are viewed as powerful, subversive
forces that must be brought under the control of wise people, those who can be
trusted to act in the public interest. But, who should be trusted to censor media?
Social scientists? Religious leaders? The military? The police? Congress? The
Federal Communications Commission? Although many powerful people believed
in the necessity of controlling media, they couldn't reach consensus about who

should do it. Media practitioners were able to negotiate compromises by pointing out the dangers of regulation and by offering to engage in self-regulation—to become more socially responsible.

LIBERTARIANISM
A normative theory that sees people as good and rational and able to judge good ideas from bad

The advocates of regulation were opposed by people who favored various forms of **libertarianism**. Eventually, social responsibility theory emerged from this debate. Social responsibility theory represents a compromise between views favoring government control of media and those favoring total press freedom. This didn't satisfy everyone, but it did have broad appeal, especially within the media industries. Even today, most media practitioners use some variant of social responsibility theory to justify their actions. To fully understand social responsibility theory we must review the ideas and events that led to its development.

The Origin of Libertarian Thought

Modern libertarian thought can be traced back to sixteenth century Europe—an era when feudal aristocracies exercised arbitrary power over the lives of most people. This era was also rocked by major social changes. International trade and urbanization undermined the power of a rural aristocracy. A variety of social movements arose, including the Protestant Reformation, that demanded greater freedom for individuals over their own lives and thoughts (Altschull, 1990).

AUTHORITARIAN
THEORY *A normative theory that places all forms of communication under the control of a governing elite or authorities*

Libertarian theory arose in opposition to **authoritarian theory**—an idea that placed all forms of communication under the control of a governing elite or authorities (Siebert, Peterson, & Schramm, 1956). Authorities justified their control as a means to protect and preserve a divinely ordained social order. In most countries, this control rested in the hands of a king who, in turn, granted royal charters or licenses to media practitioners. These practitioners could be jailed for violating charters, and charters or licenses could be revoked. Censorship of all types, therefore, was easily possible. Authoritarian control tended to be exercised in arbitrary, erratic ways. Sometimes, considerable freedom might exist to publicize minority viewpoints and culture as long as authorities didn't perceive a direct threat to their power. Unlike totalitarianism, authoritarian theory doesn't prioritize cultivation of a homogeneous, national culture. It only requires acquiescence to a governing elite.

In rebelling against authoritarian theory, early libertarians argued that if individuals could be freed from the arbitrary limits on communication imposed by Church and State, they would "naturally" follow the dictates of their conscience, seek truth, engage in public debate, and ultimately create a better life for themselves and others (McQuail, 1987; Siebert, Peterson, & Schramm, 1956). Libertarians blamed authorities for preserving unnatural, arbitrary social orders. They believed strongly in the power of unrestricted public debate and discussion to create more natural ways of structuring society.

In *Aeropagetica,* a powerful libertarian tract published in 1644, John Milton asserted that in a fair debate good and truthful arguments will always win out over lies and deceit. If this were true, it followed, then a new and better social order could be forged using public debate. This idea came to be referred to as Milton's **self-righting principle**, and it continues to be widely cited by contemporary media professionals as a rationale for preserving media freedom (Altschull, 1990). It is a fundamental principle within social responsibility theory.

Unfortunately, most early libertarians had a rather unrealistic view of how long it would take to find the "truth" and establish an ideal social order. This ideal order was not necessarily a democracy and it might not always permit communication freedom. Milton, for example, came to argue that the "truth" had been found by Oliver Cromwell and its validity had been demonstrated by his battlefield victories. Because he was convinced that Cromwell had created the ideal social order, Milton was willing to serve as the chief censor in Cromwell's regime. He expressed few regrets about limiting what Catholic leaders could communicate (Altschull, 1990).

When it became clear during the eighteenth century that definitive forms of "truth" couldn't be quickly or easily established, some libertarians became discouraged. Occasionally, they drifted back and forth between libertarian and authoritarian views. Even Thomas Jefferson, author of the Declaration of Independence, wavered in his commitment to press freedom and his faith in the self-righting principle. He voiced his deep frustration with scurrilous newspaper criticism during the second term of his presidency. Nevertheless, he reaffirmed Milton's self-righting principle in a letter to a friend written in 1787, "Were it left to me to decide whether we should have a government without newspapers or newspapers without government, I should not hesitate to prefer the latter" (Altschull, 1990, p. 117).

Libertarian ideals are at the heart of the United States' long-term experiment with democratic self-government. The revolution of the American Colonies against Britain was legitimized by libertarian ideals—recall Patrick Henry's famous statement, "Give me liberty or give me death." The newly formed United States was one of the first nations to explicitly adopt libertarian principles in the Declaration of Independence and the **Bill of Rights.** The latter asserts that all individuals have natural rights that no government, community, or group can unduly infringe upon or take away. Various forms of communication freedom—speech, press, and assembly—are listed as among the most important of these rights. The ability to express dissent, to band together with others to resist laws that people find to be wrong, to print or broadcast ideas, opinions, and beliefs—all of these rights are proclaimed as central to democratic self government, as you can see in Box 5a.

SELF-RIGHTING PRINCIPLE *Milton's idea that in a fair debate, good and truthful arguments will win out over lies and deceit*

BILL OF RIGHTS *The first ten amendments to the U.S. Constitution*

Box 5a   A Stirring Defense of Free Expression

Concurring with the majority in the 1927 Supreme Court decision in *Whitney v. California*, Justice Louis Brandeis penned this stunning defense for freedom of expression:

> Those who won our independence believed that the final end of the State was to make men free to develop their faculties; and that in its government the deliberative forces should prevail over the arbitrary. They valued liberty both as an end and as a means. They believed liberty to be the secret of happiness and courage to be the secret of liberty. They believed that freedom to think as you will and speak as you think are means indispensable to the discovery and spread of political truth; that without free speech and assembly discussion would be futile; that with them, discussion affords ordinarily adequate protection against the dissemination of noxious doctrine; that the greatest menace to freedom is an inert people; that public discussion is a political duty; and that this should be a fundamental principle of the American government. They recognized the risks to which all human institutions are subject. But they knew that order cannot be secured merely through fear of punishment for its infraction; that it is hazardous to discourage thought, hope, and imagination; that fear breeds repression; that repression breeds hate; that hate menaces stable government; that the path of safety lies in the opportunity to discuss freely supposed grievances and proposed remedies; and that the fitting remedy for evil counsels is good ones. Believing in the power of reason as applied through public discussion, they eschewed silence coerced by law—the argument of force in its worst form. Recognizing the occasional tyrannies of governing majorities, they amended the Constitution so that free speech and assembly should be guaranteed. (Gillmor & Barron, 1974, pp. 21–22)

Despite the priority given to communication freedom, however, it is important to recognize that many restrictions—accepted by media practitioners and media consumers alike—have been placed on communication. Libel laws protect against the publication of information that will damage reputations. Judges can issue gag orders to stop the publication of information that they think will interfere with a defendant's right to a fair trial. Other laws and regulations protect against false advertising, child pornography, and offensive language. As we saw at the chapter's outset, the airing of "offensive" content can be prohibited. The limits to communication freedom are being constantly renegotiated. In some eras, the balance shifts toward expanding freedom, but at other times, freedom is curtailed. Whenever new media technologies are invented, it is necessary to decide how they should be regulated. The debate over communication freedom never ends, as we see today in the ongoing and heated debates over Internet freedom and press access to military activities.

Why is it necessary to place limits on communication freedom? The most common reason for limiting communication freedom is a conflict over basic rights. For example, where do the rights guaranteed to you by the Constitution end and those of another person begin? Do you have the right to shout "Fire" in a crowded movie theater if there is no fire? If you did, many other people would be hurt—don't they have a right to be protected against your irresponsible behavior? Similar questions arise when groups attempt to stir up hatred and resentment against racial or ethnic minorities. Does a group opposing abortion have the right to place the names, addresses, and photographs of doctors who perform the procedure on its Web site, calling them murderers, all in the format of a wanted poster, complete with "reward?" Does it have the right to publish the names, ages, and school addresses of those doctors' children? Does a Klansman have the right to tell lies about African Americans or gays? Shouldn't such irresponsible forms of communication be controlled? The larger issue, the one that goes beyond that of communication freedom, is the question of fundamental human rights and how best to maximize them at a given point in history.

But what about freedom of the press and expression? Just how far can producers and media outlets go in exercising their rights? Should they be allowed to invade your home, publish erroneous information about you, or deceive you with false advertising? Do media professionals have the right to produce and distribute anything that will earn profits, or should some limits be placed on them? If so, who should place and enforce those limits? If laws are written to protect individuals from irresponsible media, can these laws become a means of censoring the media?

The Marketplace of Ideas: A New Form of Radical Libertarianism

Though libertarian thought in the United States dates from the country's founding, it has undergone many transformations. An important variant emerged in the 1800s during the penny press and yellow journalism eras. Throughout this period, public confidence in both business and government was shaken by recurring depressions, widespread corruption, and injustice. Large companies, most notably in the oil, railroad, and steel industries, created nationwide monopolies to charge unfair prices and reap enormous profits. Workers were paid low salaries and forced to labor under difficult or hazardous conditions. Public respect for newspapers also ebbed as publishers pursued profits and created news to sell papers. Several social movements, especially the Progressive (liberal) and Populist (champion of average folks) movements, sprang up to call for new laws and greater government regulation (Brownell, 1983; Altschull, 1990). Anti-trust legislation was enacted to break up the big monopolies. Libertarians feared that these laws and regulations would go too far. They sought to rekindle public support for libertarian ideals.

Some media practitioners developed a cogent response to Progressive and Populist criticisms. They argued that media should be regarded as a *self-regulating* **marketplace of ideas.** This idea is a variation of a fundamental principle of capitalism—the notion of a self-regulating market. In classical capitalist theory as formulated by Adam Smith, there is little need for the government to regulate markets. An open and competitive marketplace should regulate itself. If a product is in high demand, prices will "naturally" rise as consumers compete to buy it. This encourages other manufacturers to produce the product. Once demand is met by increased manufacturing, the price falls. If one manufacturer charges too much for a product, then competitors will cut their prices to attract buyers. No government interference is necessary to protect consumers or to force manufacturers to meet consumer needs. Another term used to refer to these ideas is the **laissez-faire doctrine.**

According to marketplace of ideas theory, the laissez-faire doctrine should be applied to mass media; that is, if ideas are "traded" freely among people, the correct or best ideas will prevail. The *ideas* compete and the best will be "bought." But there are some difficulties in applying this logic to our large, contemporary media. Media content is far less tangible than other consumer products. The meaning of individual messages can vary tremendously from one person to the next. Just what is being traded when news stories or television dramas are "bought" and "sold"? When we buy a newspaper, we don't buy individual stories, we buy packages of them bundled with features like comics and horoscopes. We can choose to ignore anything in the package that we find offensive. When we watch television, we don't pay a fee to the networks. Yet, buying and selling are clearly involved with network programs. Advertisers buy time on these shows and then use the programs as vehicles for their messages. When they buy time, they buy access to the audience for the show; they do not necessarily buy the rightness or correctness of the program's ideas. Sponsors pay more to advertise on programs with large audiences. Clearly, the media marketplace is a bit more complicated than the marketplace for refrigerators or toothpaste, as shown in Box 5b.

In the American media system, the marketplace of ideas was supposed to work like this: Someone comes up with a good idea and then transmits it through some form of mass communication. If other people like it, then they buy the message. When people buy the message, they pay for its production and distribution costs. Once these costs are covered, the message producer earns a profit. If people don't like the message, then they don't buy it and the producer goes broke trying

MARKETPLACE OF IDEAS *In Libertarianism, the notion that all ideas should be put before the public, and the public will choose the best from that "marketplace"*

LAISSEZ-FAIRE DOCTRINE *The idea that government shall allow business to operate freely and without official intrusion*

Box 5b Which Model of the Marketplace?

The Market Place of Ideas sees the operation of the mass media system as analogous to that of the self-regulating product market. Take this example and judge for yourself the goodness-of-fit.

Product Producer	Product	Consumer
Model 1		
A product producer	produces a product as efficiently and inexpensively as possible	for its consumers who wield the ultimate power, to buy or not to buy.
Model 2		
Hersheys	produces candy efficiently and inexpensively on a production line	for people like us. If we buy the candy, Hersheys continues to make similar candy in a similar way.

Product Producer	Product	Consumer
Model 3		
NBC	produces people using programs— their production line—	for advertisers. If they buy NBC's product, NBC continues to produce similar audiences in similar ways.

What do these models imply about the quality of candy in the United States? What do they say about the quality of television?

to produce and distribute it. If people are wise message consumers, then the producers of the best and most useful messages will become rich and develop large media enterprises, and the producers of bad messages will fail. Useless media will go out of business. If the purveyors of good ideas succeed, then these ideas should become more easily available at lower cost. Producers will compete to supply them. Similarly, the cost of bad ideas should rise and access to them should lessen. Eventually, truth should win out in the marketplace of ideas just as it should triumph in the public forum envisioned by the early libertarians. According to marketplace of ideas theory, the self-righting principle should apply to mass media content as well as to public debate.

The marketplace of ideas is self-regulating, so there is no need for a government agency to censor messages. Audiences won't buy bad messages and therefore irresponsible producers will go broke. But what if advertiser support permits bad messages to be distributed for free—maybe people will be less discriminating if they don't have to directly pay to receive these messages? What if the bad messages are distributed as part of a large bundle of messages (that is, a newspaper or television news program)? If you want the good messages, you also pay to subsidize the bad messages. What is bad for you might be good for someone else. You might not like horoscopes or soap operas but you have friends who do.

Just how useful is marketplace of ideas theory? After all, government regulation of the consumer marketplace is now generally accepted as necessary. Few people question the need for consumer protection laws or laws regulating unfair business practices. The consumer marketplace benefited from regulation, so why not regulate the marketplace of ideas? Since 1930, media critics have asked this question more and more frequently, and the recent rampant concentration of media companies has added new urgency to the call for government intervention. Even so, marketplace of ideas theory enjoys significant support within the media industries.

That media industry support resides in the "duality" inherent in the marketplace of ideas philosophy, one that "has allowed widely divergent interpretations of the metaphor to develop" (Napoli, 1999, p. 151). Media policy researcher Philip Napoli identified two interpretations of the marketplace of ideas. "Economic theory-based interpretations of the marketplace of ideas emphasize efficiency, consumer satisfaction, and competition," he wrote, "Whereas democratic theory-based interpretations emphasize citizen knowledge, informed decision making, and effective self-government. Within discussions of the marketplace of ideas metaphor, economic theory-based interpretations typically have been associated with arguments against government regulation of the communications industry, whereas democratic theory-based interpretations typically have been associated with calls for such regulation" (1999, pp. 151–152). Media practitioners are satisfied with this distinction because as numerous researchers (e.g., Lavey, 1993; Simon, Atwater, & Alexander, 1988) have demonstrated, government, especially agencies such as the FCC and the Federal Trade Commission, which regulates advertising, "historically has devoted much greater empirical attention to the economic effects of its policies than to the social and political effects" (Napoli, 1999, p. 165).

Government Regulation of Media—The Federal Radio Commission

During the 1920s and 1930s, a new normative theory of mass communication began to emerge that rejected both radical libertarianism and ideas of technocratic control. One source of this theory was Congressional debates over government regulation of radio. In 1927, these debates led to the establishment of the Federal Radio Commission (FRC), which was the forerunner of the Federal Communications Commission (FCC). As the debates raged, some people—especially Progressive and Populist politicians—argued that the excesses of yellow journalism

Instant Access

Marketplace of Ideas Theory

Strengths	Weaknesses
1 Limits government control	1 Mistakenly equates media content with more tangible consumer products
2 Allows "natural" fluctuations in tastes, ideals, and discourse	2 Puts too much trust in profit-motivated media operators
3 Puts trust in the audience	3 Ignores the fact that content that is intentionally "bought" is often accompanied by other, sometimes unwanted, content
4 Assumes "good" content will ultimately prevail	4 Has over-optimistic view of audience's media consumption skills
	5 Mistakenly assumes audience—not advertiser—is consumer
	6 Definition of "good" is not universal (for example, what is "good" for the majority might be bad for a minority)

proved that self-regulation wasn't enough. Overdramatized and fictitious news was so profitable that publishers couldn't resist producing it. Without some sort of regulation, radio was not likely to serve the public interest as well as it should. Even so, Progressives were cautious about turning control of radio over to government technocrats. A compromise solution was sought.

By the 1920s, government regulation of public utilities had become widely accepted as a means of ending wasteful competition while preserving private enterprise. Before government regulation of power and telephone companies, cities were blanketed with competing networks of wires. Anyone who wanted to telephone people on other networks had to buy phones from all the competing companies. The cost of building entirely independent networks increased the cost of phone service and electricity. The solution to these problems was to allow one company to have a monopoly on supplying these needed services. In return for being granted a monopoly, the company submitted to government regulation of prices and services. In this way, public utilities were created with government commissions to oversee their operation. Could a government commission be used to regulate radio as a public utility?

Proponents of a radio commission pointed out the similarities between the early radio industry and the early telephone and power industries. Although broadcasters didn't have to cover a city with wires to send radio signals, they did have to use a particular frequency for their transmission signal. If another broadcaster used this same frequency, she or he would cut into the original broadcast and disrupt it. Initially, radio manufacturers were the only companies who could afford to build large and powerful radio stations. Stations were built to stimulate public interest in the new medium and create a market for radio receivers. Nevertheless, the big stations soon faced growing competition from a variety of sources, including radio enthusiasts who set up stations in their living rooms and garages. Larger cities were blanketed with competing signals. Those who had invested money in the construction of large stations appealed to government to help protect their investment. They requested government regulation as a means of ending competition from stations they thought to be inferior. The public, too, was growing weary of the constant interference in and unpredictability of radio broadcasts, called a "Tower in Babel" by broadcast historian Erik Barnouw. Secretary of Commerce Herbert Hoover himself was moved to remark that this was one of the few instances in history where the country was unanimous in its desire for more regulation (Barnouw, 1966).

In the debate over the establishment of the Federal Radio Commission, Secretary Hoover championed one especially important philosophy—the airwaves belong to the people. If airwaves are public property like other national resources (national forests, for example), then privately operated stations can never own them. Instead, they must be licensed from the people and used in the public interest. If license holders violate the public trust, their licenses can be revoked. The FRC was created to act on behalf of the public. It was given a mandate to make certain that radio stations provided important services to the public in return for the privilege of using public airwaves. The broadcasters were required to serve the "public interest, convenience, or necessity." Unlike the regulation of public utilities, however, the FRC had no mandate to regulate broadcast industry profits. Stations were free to compete against each other and to earn the largest profits possible as long as they continued to provide certain basic public services such as news bulletins or community service programming. Moreover, the FRC had no ability to directly censor content, but it could punish stations that broadcast prohibited content with fines or loss of their license.

The radio industry was the first media industry to ask for and submit to government regulation. The relative success of the FRC encouraged efforts to regulate other media industries. Government censorship of movies was widely advocated, especially by religious groups. Over the years, the movie industry has adopted various forms of self-censorship in an effort to avoid government regulation. As the threat of propaganda grew, even regulation of newspapers was seriously considered. In 1942, for example, the Hutchins Commission on Freedom of the Press was established to weigh the merits of newspaper regulation (we'll say more about this later).

Professionalization of Journalism

As pressure for government regulation of media mounted, industry leaders responded with efforts to professionalize. As noted in Chapter 3, Joseph Pulitzer and William Randolph Hearst established professional awards. The industry lobbied for and subsidized the establishment of professional schools to train media practitioners. Rather than cede control of media to a government agency, media managers went on record with pledges to serve public needs. In 1923, the American Society of Newspaper Editors adopted a set of professional standards entitled "The Canons of Journalism." (The Canons were replaced in 1975 by the ASNE Statement of Principles.) Since then, virtually every association of media practitioners has adopted similar standards. In doing so, they are emulating professionals in fields like law and medicine. These standards typically commit media practitioners to serving the public as effectively as possible.

FOURTH ESTATE
Media as an independent social institution that ensures that other institutions serve the public

Industry codes of ethics began to formalize another important conception about the role of media—that of a watchdog guarding the welfare of the public. Muckraking journalists first articulated this role about the turn of the century. It assumes that media should continually scan the social world and alert the public to problems. Initially, yellow journalists greeted this view of media with skepticism. However, muckraking investigations of corruption proved so popular that eventually the role became widely accepted. In some ambitious formulations of this role, the media are envisioned as an independent social institution, a **Fourth Estate** of government, charged with making certain that all other institutions— the three branches of government, business, religion, education, and family— serve the public. In the words of social critic and veteran journalist Bill Moyers, a properly functioning media are needed "to keep our leaders honest and to arm the powerless with the information they need to protect themselves against the tyranny of the powerful, whether that tyranny is political or commercial" (2001, p. 13). This perspective assumes that once people are informed about wrongdoing, incompetence, or inefficiency, they will take action against it.

In joining the trend toward professionalization, media practitioners, like doctors and lawyers before them, pledged to uphold standards of professional practice. They promised to weed out irresponsible people and give recognition to those who excel. Those who violated standards were to be censured. In extreme cases, they could be barred from professional practice.

Limitations of Professionalization

As an alternative to direct government regulation, media professionalization worked rather well. Certain limitations, however, lead to recurring problems:

1   **Professionals in every field, including journalism, have been reluctant to identify and censure colleagues who violate professional standards.** To do so is often seen as admitting that embarrassing problems exist. Public trust in all media professionals might be shaken if too many people are barred from practice. Professional societies tend to operate as closed groups in which members are protected against outside threats and criticism. Attacks from outsiders are routinely dismissed as unwarranted even when evidence against a practitioner mounts. Often, action is taken only in extreme cases when it cannot be avoided. Even then, news media either avoid covering the case or provide brief and superficial coverage.

2   **Professional standards can be overly abstract and ambiguous.** They can be difficult to implement and enforce. Mission statements and broad codes of ethics are notoriously vague. The Radio-Television News Directors Association's Code of Ethics and Professional Conduct (2000, online), for example, instructs its members to "pursue truth aggressively and present the news accurately, in context, and completely as possible." But news directors must make choices concerning allocation of resources. Increasingly, the news we see consists of corporate and government public relations **video news releases (VNR)**. In fact, 90 percent of all television news operations make use of these outsider-provided public relations pieces (Zoll, 1999). How do editors decide when to stop airing VNRs and start engaging in independent digging and reporting? There might be no reason to doubt the truth of a VNR unless a reporter takes the time to conduct an independent investigation. But what if an independent journalistic investigation leads a large advertiser to cancel its account with the station? Why risk producing stories that might prove embarrassing to someone or some organization? In the news business, telling the truth can sometimes be difficult and expensive. Professional standards are vague, so nothing forces journalists to endanger relationships with friendly sources or their profit margins. And in fact, it is a poorly kept broadcast industry secret that many stations maintain printed lists of people and issues that are untouchable—they may not be covered—"for fear of alienating an advertiser" (Potter, 2001, p. 68).

VIDEO NEWS RELEASE
Report produced by an outside organization, typically a public relations firm, that is distributed on videocassette free of charge to television stations

3 **In contrast with medicine and law, media professionalization doesn't include standards for professional training and licensing.** Other professions mandate that practitioners receive long and closely monitored professional training. For example, doctors and lawyers undergo from 4 to 10 years of specialized training in addition to completing 4 years of college. But media practitioners are unwilling to set standards for professional training and have strongly resisted efforts to license journalists. They argue that these requirements would inevitably be used by government to control the press. If the press is to remain free from control, then it must be free to hire anyone—no matter how untrained or unqualified. Anyone should be able to claim the title of journalist, start a newspaper, and exercise his or her free press rights. No government agency should be able to step in and shut down a paper just because some of its reporters or editors are unlicensed.

Arguments against specialized training and licensing of media practitioners fail to consider how these standards are enforced in other professions. Licensing has not brought doctors and lawyers directly under government control. Even when government agencies issue licenses, professional associations effectively control the standards used to determine who will get a license.

4 **In contrast with other professions, media practitioners tend to have less independent control over their work.** Media practitioners don't work as autonomous practitioners and therefore have difficulty assuming personal responsibility for their work. They tend to work within big, hierarchically structured bureaucracies. Individual reporters, editors, producers, or directors have only a limited ability to control what they do. Reporters are given assignments by editors, advertising designers work for account executives, and television anchors and camera operators follow the instructions of news directors. Editors, account managers, and directors are all responsible to higher management. In these large bureaucracies, it is difficult to assign responsibility. Those at lower levels can claim that they are only "following orders," whereas people at higher levels can simply disavow any knowledge of what was going on below them.

5 **In the media industries, violation of professional standards rarely has immediate, directly observable consequences.** Thus, it is hard for critics to cite violations or to identify the harm that has been done. When doctors fail, people die. When lawyers fail, people go to jail unnecessarily. The results of unethical media practice are harder to see. Sometimes, unethical conduct might even do some good. The classic case of Janet Cooke is instructive. Cooke, a reporter for the *Washington Post,* wrote a series of news stories about ghetto children that was nominated for a Pulitzer Prize in 1980 (Altschull, 1990, pp. 361–364). Later these stories were found to be based on fabricated interviews. Cooke took personal details and comments from several people and then wove them together to create a fictitious interviewee. The resulting stories had great dramatic impact, educating readers about the reality of drugs in the inner city and spurring official action to clean up particularly troublesome areas. Nevertheless, her reports violated professional standards of truth and accuracy. Cooke was fired and the Pulitzer Prize was returned. The *Post* expressed profound embarrassment and its legendary editor, Ben Bradlee, called it the worst failure of his long career.

Social Responsibility Theory of the Press: A Postwar Compromise

Despite moves toward professionalization and self-regulation, pressure for greater government regulation of media mounted throughout World War II and continued during the anti-communist agitation that followed. In response, Henry Luce, CEO of Time Inc., provided funding for an independent commission to make recommendations concerning the role of the press. The Hutchins Commission on Freedom of the Press was established in 1942 and released a major report of its findings in 1947 (Davis, 1990; McIntyre, 1987). Its members consisted of leaders from many areas of society including academics, politicians, and heads of social groups.

Commission members were sharply divided between those who held strongly libertarian views and those who thought some form of press regulation was necessary. Those who favored regulation were fearful that the "marketplace of ideas" was much too vulnerable to subversion by antidemocratic forces. Several of these proponents of regulation were guided by notions about public communication developed by social researchers at the University of Chicago—the **Chicago School.**

CHICAGO SCHOOL
Social researchers at the University of Chicago in the 1940s who envisioned modern cities as "Great Communities" made up of hundreds of interrelated small groups

The Chicago School envisioned modern cities as "Great Communities" comprising hundreds of small social groups—everything from neighborhood social organizations to citywide associations. For these Great Communities to develop, all the constituent groups had to work together and contribute. These were referred to as **pluralistic groups** in recognition of their cultural and racial diversity (Davis, 1990).

PLURALISTIC GROUPS
In a Great Community, the various segments defined by specific, unifying characteristics

The Chicago School opposed marketplace of ideas notions and argued that unregulated mass media inevitably served the interests and tastes of large or socially dominant groups. Small, weak, pluralistic groups would be either neglected or denigrated. This perspective also held that ruthless elites could use media as a means of gaining personal political power. These demagogues could manipulate media to transmit propaganda to fuel hatred and fear among a majority and unite them against minorities. Hitler's use of media to arouse hatred of the Jews was seen as a prime example.

To prevent this tyranny by the majority and to mandate support for pluralistic groups, some Commission members favored creation of a public agency—a Press Council—that would be made up of people much like themselves and that would have the power to prevent publication of hate propaganda. In the view of these

Hutchins Commission members, this "new and independent agency (would) appraise and report annually upon the performance of the press." It would base that appraisal on its comparison of "the accomplishments of the press with the aspirations which the people have for it" (quoted in Bates, 2001, online). This agency might, for example, have required that newspapers devote a certain portion of their coverage to minority groups. Or it might have required that these groups be given regular columns in which they could publish whatever they wanted.

Commission members recognized that such regulations might impose additional costs on newspapers. If this happened, then they favored government subsidies to cover these expenses. By serving pluralistic groups, media would strengthen them and enable them to contribute to the Great Community. This fostering of pluralism and restraint on propaganda was seen as essential to preventing the spread of totalitarianism in the United States.

Although most Hutchins Commission members had some sympathy for Chicago School ideas, they opposed any direct form of press regulation (Davis 1990; McIntyre 1987). The Commission members faced a serious dilemma. On the one hand, they recognized that the marketplace of ideas was not self-regulating and that the media were doing less than they could to provide services to minority groups. However, Commission members feared that any form of press regulation would open the door to official control of media—the very thing they were trying to prevent.

The situation seemed quite dire at the time. Without some form of regulation, a ruthless and cunning demagogue might be able to use hate propaganda to gain power in the United States. However, establishing a national press council might put too much control in the hands of existing elites and they might abuse it. Ultimately, the majority of Hutchins Commission members decided to place their faith in media practitioners and called on them to redouble their efforts to serve the public. The majority members wrote a lengthy report to provide guidance to media practitioners.

The synthesis of ideas put forward in the Hutchins Commission report has become known as the *Social Responsibility Theory of the Press* (Siebert, Peterson, & Schramm, 1956). It emphasized the need for an independent press that scrutinizes other social institutions and provides objective, accurate news reports. The most innovative feature of social responsibility theory was its call for media to be responsible for fostering productive and creative "Great Communities." It said that media should do this by prioritizing cultural pluralism—by becoming the voice of all the people—not just elite groups or groups that had dominated national, regional, or local culture in the past.

In some respects, social responsibility theory is a radical statement. Instead of demanding that media be free to print or transmit whatever their owners want, social responsibility theory imposes a burden on media practitioners. As the Commission argued, "The press is not free if those who operate it behave as though their position conferred on them the privilege of being deaf to ideas which the processes of free speech have brought to public attention" (quoted in Bates, 2001, online).

Social responsibility theory appealed to the idealism of individual media practitioners and tried to unite them in the service of cultural pluralism—even when this might reduce their profits or antagonize existing social elites. Social responsibility theory challenged media professionals' ingenuity to develop new ways of serving their communities. It encouraged them to see themselves as front-line participants in the battle to preserve democracy in a world drifting inexorably toward totalitarianism. By helping pluralistic groups, media were building a wall to protect democracy from external and internal foes. Denis McQuail (1987) summarized the basic principles of social responsibility theory as the following:

- Media should accept and fulfill certain obligations to society.

- These obligations are mainly to be met by setting high or professional standards of informativeness, truth, accuracy, objectivity, and balance.

- In accepting and applying these obligations, media should be self-regulating within the framework of law and established institutions.

- The media should avoid whatever might lead to crime, violence, or civil disorder or give offense to minority groups.

- The media as a whole should be pluralist and reflect the diversity of their society, giving access to various points of view and to rights of reply.

- Society and the public have a right to expect high standards of performance, and intervention can be justified to secure the, or a, public good.

- Journalists and media professionals should be accountable to society as well as to employers and the market.

The Cold War Tests Social Responsibility Theory

The first major test of social responsibility theory occurred during the 1950s with the rise of anti-communist sentiments during the Cold War. Mainland China fell to the communists in 1949. At the same time, most of Eastern Europe was coming under communist control in a series of staged popular uprisings and coups. Spies who stole important secrets aided Soviet development of nuclear weapons. World War II had stopped one form of totalitarianism but had unleashed another that appeared to be even stronger and more deadly. A generation of American politicians, including Richard Nixon and John F. Kennedy, gained national prominence by aggressively opposing the spread of Soviet communism.

Joseph McCarthy led the vanguard opposing communism, as discussed in Chapter 3. Though McCarthy presented himself as a crusader for democracy, he soon exhibited all the traits of the classic demagogue. He successfully used propaganda techniques to draw national attention to himself and stimulate widespread public hatred and suspicion of people or minorities whom he linked, most often inaccurately, to communism. McCarthy charged that many in both government and the media were communist agents or sympathizers and drew strong support from anti-communist groups across the nation. The House Un-American Activities Committee, or HUAC, launched congressional investigations of media practitioners.

Media executives responded to pressure from anti-communist groups and from Congress by blacklisting many people who were accused, even in the absence of evidence, of communist leanings. Prominent practitioners were barred from working in the media. Ultimately, there was little evidence of any widespread conspiracy to subvert democracy in the United States. Though there were Soviet agents at work in the United States, their numbers and effectiveness were never as great as the anti-communist groups asserted.

This Red Scare episode illustrates how difficult it can be for journalists to adhere to social responsibility theory in crisis situations. Most journalists initially hailed McCarthy as someone taking a heroic stand against the Red Menace. His dramatic pronouncements provided ideal material for big headlines and popular front-page news stories. As long as McCarthy confined his witch-hunt to Reds in federal bureaucracies, many reporters printed his charges without criticism. When he began to look for "Pinkos" and communist sympathizers in the media, more journalists began to have misgivings. By then his popularity was so great that it was risky for them to oppose him, so most cowered. Months of Congressional hearings passed before significant media criticism of McCarthy appeared. Many credit Edward R. Murrow with taking the initiative to produce a television news documentary that finally exposed McCarthy's propaganda tactics to public scrutiny.

How should media have reacted if they took social responsibility theory seriously? Should they have made a greater effort earlier to investigate the truth of McCarthy's frequent and dramatic allegations? They would have risked charges that they were pro-communist or the unwitting dupes of the communists. By waiting, they risked the possibility that McCarthy would seize political power and use it to suppress all forms of dissent including media criticism. Without a journalist of Murrow's stature to confront McCarthy, the United States might have turned toward McCarthy's brand of fascism.

Using Social Responsibility Theory to Guide Professional Practice

The ideals of social responsibility theory have proved quite durable, even if their full implications are rarely understood by working journalists. Actually, many scholars argue, "social responsibility doctrine has always been relegated to the fringes of journalism education and the newsroom. Nearly fifty years after the Hutchins Commission report, news personnel generally remain hostile to its focus on the public good and on broad-based reporting about significant events of the day" (Christians, Ferre, & Fackler, 1993, p. 38). Furthermore, in the competing "ethos of news as business (and) that of news as socially responsible institution" (Lind & Rockler, 2001, p. 119), social responsibility often comes in second. In our current era of large media corporations, "Friends of the 'liberty of the press' must recognize that *communication markets restrict freedom of communication* by generating barriers to entry, monopoly and restrictions upon choice, and by shifting the prevailing definition of information from that of a public good to that of a privately appropriated commodity" (Keane, 1991, pp. 88–89, emphasis in original).

So, if social responsibility theory is to remain a viable normative theory, greater effort might be needed to implement it. Compared with the vast amount of research done on media effects, relatively little research has examined whether existing news production practices actually serve the societal goals that they are intended to serve. For example, one primary goal is communicating accurate information about important events to average people. The findings of research on this goal are quite mixed. Evidence indicates that people don't learn much from news reports and what they do learn is quickly forgotten (Graber, 1987). People become easily confused by stories that are poorly structured or use dramatic but irrelevant pictures. Findings from this research have had little or no impact on the practice of journalism. These findings have been largely ignored or misinterpreted by media practitioners (Davis & Robinson, 1989).

In the 1970s and 1980s, sociologists published a series of studies that raised important questions about the value of routine news production practices (Bennett, 1988; Epstein, 1973; Fishman, 1980; Gans, 1979; Glasgow University Media Group, 1976, 1980; Tuchman, 1978). Most of this research has been ignored or dismissed by journalists as biased, irrelevant, and misguided. It deserves a more careful reading. Gaye Tuchman, for example, presents a well-developed argument concerning the role played by media in the discovery and cultivation of social movements. She conceptualizes news production practices as "strategic rituals" and believes that these practices appear to satisfy the requirements imposed by social responsibility norms but fall far short of achieving their purpose. For example, journalists ritualistically construct "balanced" stories in which opposing views are contrasted. However, these rites might actually undermine rather than advance pluralism. She maintains that "balanced stories" about minority groups frequently contain statements from social or political leaders that subtly or blatantly denigrate groups and their ideas. The emotionally charged opinions of little-known group leaders are contrasted with reasoned pronouncements from well-known, credible officials. Little effort is made to create a context for new groups' broader goals or culture. Instead, news reports tend to focus on dramatic events staged by isolated group members.

Tuchman cites early news coverage of the women's movement in the 1960s and early 1970s to illustrate her criticisms. The movement first achieved national prominence with a rally in which bras were purportedly burned (in supposed imitation of the burning of draft cards by antiwar protesters). She maintains that bras might have been brandished but were never burned. The news reports unfairly labeled the women's movement as an extremist group in the same category with the people burning draft cards. Instead of assisting the movement and enabling it to contribute to the larger society, these stories and those that followed hindered it. Pluralism was frustrated rather than advanced.

Is There Still a Role for Social Responsibility Theory?

Although U.S. media have developed many professional practices in an effort to conform to the ideals of social responsibility theory, the long-term objective—the creation of "Great Communities"—has never seemed more elusive. Our cities have undergone decades of urban renewal, yet slums remain, and in some cities, they continue to spread. There have been national "wars" to combat poverty, crime, pollution, disease (from polio to cancer to AIDS), and drugs, but the quality of life for many city dwellers has not improved. Ethnic and racial subcultures are still widely misunderstood. Minority group members continue to be discriminated against and harassed. There is evidence that hate groups are increasing in size and that their propaganda is effectively reaching larger audiences.

Does this mean that social responsibility theory is wrong? Has it been poorly implemented? What responsibility can or should media practitioners assume on behalf of the Great Communities that they serve? More important, how should this responsibility be exercised? With helicopters circling over riots scenes? With inflammatory coverage of hate groups? With boring coverage of the routine work of neighborhood associations? With endless listing of bad news about crime and disease? Was there merit in the Chicago School arguments concerning coverage of pluralistic groups? If so, what forms might that coverage take? Should group members be allowed some direct control of what is printed about them in newspapers or broadcast on television?

LOCAL ORIGINATION (OR MANDATORY ACCESS) RULE *Rule requiring local cable television companies to carry community-based access channels*

Our society's experience with local access channels on cable television suggests that it is not easy to use media to support pluralistic groups. In 1972, the Federal Communications Commission for the first time required local cable companies to provide local access channels in an effort to serve pluralistic groups, and although these **local origination** or **mandatory access rules** have been altered, suspended, and otherwise tinkered with during the last forty years, they have generally failed to serve their intended purpose. Very few people watch the access channels and few groups use them.

Instant Access

Libertarianism

Strengths	Weaknesses
1 Values media freedom	**1** Is overly optimistic about media's willingness to meet responsibilities
2 Is consistent with U.S. media traditions	**2** Is overly optimistic about individuals' ethics and rationality
3 Values individuals	**3** Ignores need for reasonable control of media
4 Precludes government control of media	**4** Ignores dilemmas posed by conflicting freedoms (for example, free press versus personal privacy)

Many observers believe that social responsibility theory will be given new strength by emerging technologies that allow communities greater power to disseminate information. Cable television, though never approaching the re-empowering-the-public revolution predicted for it in the 1960s, has at least made literally hundreds of channels available, many of which are dedicated to ethnic and specific interest communities. Now, with the rapid diffusion of the Internet and World Wide Web, size-of-audience and ability to make a profit have become unimportant concerns for literally thousands of "voices." The Web site for a tribe of Native Americans, for example, sits electronically side-by-side with those of the most powerful media organizations. What many theorists fear, however, is that this wealth of voices—each speaking to its own community—will **Balkanize** the larger U.S. culture. That is, rather than all Americans reading and viewing conscientiously produced content about all the Great Communities that make the United States as wonderfully diverse and pluralistic as it is, communities will talk only to people residing within their borders. The values, wants, needs, and ideas of others will be ignored.

BALKANIZE *Dividing a country, culture, or society into antagonistic subgroups*

The passing of the mass market, national magazine in the face of television's 1950s assault on its ad revenues and audiences is seen as the first step. Where the entire nation once read the *Saturday Evening Post,* individual taste publics now read *Ski, Wired, Mondo 2000, Model Airplane Builder, Ebony,* and *Organic Farmer.* When cable provided scores of alternatives to the big three commercial

Instant Access

Social Responsibility Theory

Strengths

1 Values media responsibility

2 Values audience responsibility

3 Limits government intrusion in media operation

4 Allows reasonable government control of media

5 Values diversity and pluralism

6 Aids the "powerless"

7 Appeals to the best instincts of media practitioners and audiences

8 Is consistent with U.S. legal tradition

Weaknesses

1 Is overly optimistic about media's willingness to meet responsibility

2 Is overly optimistic about individual responsibility

3 Underestimates power of profit motivation and competition

4 Legitimizes status quo

television networks, the same fears were expressed. In the early 1970s, ABC, NBC, and CBS commanded more than 90 percent of the viewing audience. Today, they draw 60 percent. The Internet has exacerbated this trend, leading William Gibson, author of *Neuromancer* and guru to the cyber-generation, to predict that the world will eventually be composed of communities built around brands—Planet Nike and the World of Pepsi—rather than around common values and aspirations (Trench, 1990).

Since the report of the Hutchins Commission on Press Freedom in 1947, and despite these profound changes in the nature of the American media system, there has been relatively little effort to develop a more contemporary normative theory of media in the United States. Social responsibility theory emerged at a time of world crisis and when democracy itself was clearly threatened. Will the end of the Cold War and the establishment of a "New World Order" bring forth a new normative theory? How must this theory be rethought and restructured to reflect the new media environment? It is useful to examine some alternative normative theories that are being practiced in other parts of the world. We will do this after a discussion of a contemporary media movement designed to breathe new life into social responsibility theory.

Civic Journalism

CIVIC JOURNALISM
The journalistic practice of actively engaging audience members in reporting important civic issues (sometimes **public journalism**)

Many media outlets, especially newspapers because of their strong ties to the communities in which they publish, have begun practicing **civic journalism**, actively engaging the members of their areas in reporting important civic issues. This is a direct response to social responsibility theory's call for meeting the needs of the various and disparate groups that make up a Great Community. It is a form of interactive journalism, where the newspaper actively enlists and engages people from all walks of life in the creation of the stories and reports it develops. Shelton Gunaratne (1998, p. 279) presented several definitions, drawn from several sources, for **civic**, or what is sometimes called **public journalism**:

- An effort by print and broadcast journalists to reach out to the public more aggressively in the reporting process, to listen to how citizens frame their problems and what citizens see as solutions to those problems—and then to use that information to enrich their newspaper or broadcast report.

- A movement to create a more active and engaged public by self-consciously giving voice to the people's agenda.

- A movement to steer journalism toward reinvigorating public life, which many see as excluding ordinary citizens and devaluing the need to inform them.

As these definitions suggest, civic journalism can happen in a variety of ways. Often, a paper will devote significant resources to detailed and long-running coverage of important or controversial community issues, employing citizens as part of the coverage and inviting response and debate through devices such as hotlines and open forums. A number of newspapers have developed lengthy series on vexing issues like race relations and the state of public schools, running multiple stories on several days over a number of weeks. In these reports, local people and groups, local problems, and local solutions are highlighted, rather than, for example, national data on minority unemployment or how schools in another state meet challenges.

Another form of civic journalism is the assembly of citizen panels, composed of diverse people and interests, that meet at regular intervals throughout the life of an ongoing news event, for example legislative budget hearings or a political campaign. The reactions of the citizens to developments are reported as news. Several California papers, for example, convened such panels as that state debated and then voted on the abolition of affirmative action. Similarly, many papers develop citizen roundtables, inviting people from antagonistic constituencies to hash out their differences and attempt to find some common ground. These interactions are then reported as news.

Proponents of civic journalism see it as the embodiment of social responsibility theory and a solid form of community service. But there are critics. It's a gimmick, the detractors contend, designed to build circulation by stressing a paper's "localness" in the face of competition for ad revenues from other, more national news media like television and the Web. Others argue that too much professional journalistic judgment is abdicated in favor of the concerns and interests of citizens with personal or narrow agendas. Still others fault civic journalism for its heavy emphasis on very specific issues, and as such, its distortion of the public agenda (Dalton, 1997; Effron, 1997). Nevertheless, as it stands, the civic journalism "experiment" continues the U.S. media's commitment to social responsibility theory.

Other Normative Theories

DEVELOPMENTAL MEDIA THEORY
A normative theory calling for government and media to work in partnership to ensure that media assist in the planned, beneficial development of the country

DEMOCRATIC-PARTICIPANT THEORY
A normative theory advocating media support for cultural pluralism at a grass-roots level

McQuail (1987) cites several normative theories of media that have been developed in other parts of the world. These include development media theory and democratic-participant media theory. Each assigns a particular social role to media. **Developmental media theory** advocates media support for an existing political regime and its efforts to bring about national economic development. Several developing South American countries—Honduras and Brazil, for example—exemplify developmental media theory. By supporting government development efforts, media aid society at large. This theory argues that until a nation is well-established and its economic development well underway, media must be supportive rather than critical of government. Journalists must not pick apart government efforts to promote development but, rather, assist government in implementing such policies. U.S. journalists have been critical of this view. They believe that it is an updated version of authoritarian theory and that media should never surrender the power to criticize government policies even if it risks causing the policies to fail.

Democratic-participant theory advocates media support for cultural pluralism at a grass-roots level. Media are to be used to stimulate and empower pluralistic groups. Unlike social responsibility theory, which assumes that mass media can perform this function, democratic-participant theory calls for development of innovative, "small" media that can be directly controlled by group members. If

WESTERN CONCEPT *A normative theory combining aspects of libertarianism and social responsibility theory*

DEVELOPMENT CONCEPT *A normative theory describing systems in which government and media work in concert to ensure that the media aid the planned, beneficial development of a given nation*

REVOLUTIONARY CONCEPT *A normative theory describing a system where media are used in the service of revolution*

AUTHORITARIAN CONCEPT *A normative theory advocating the complete domination of media by a government for the purpose of forcing those media to serve the government*

COMMUNISM CONCEPT *A normative theory advocating the complete domination of media by a Communist government for the purpose of forcing those media to serve the Party*

they cannot afford such media, then government subsidies should be provided to them. Existing small media should be identified and funded. Training programs should be established to teach group members how to operate small media. Most Scandinavian countries practice some form of democratic-participant theory.

William Hachten (1992) provided a different perspective on normative theories used by various countries and political systems. He identified five "concepts": Western, development, revolutionary, authoritarianism, and communism. The **Western concept**, exemplified by the United States, Great Britain, and most other well-developed industrial nations, combines aspects of libertarianism and social responsibility theory. It recognizes that there are no completely free media systems and that even in the most profit-oriented media systems, there exists not only a public expectation of service and responsibility, but an official expectation as well, one backed by "significant communication related activities of government"—in other words, regulation (Stevenson, 1994, p. 109). The **development concept** describes systems in which government and media work in concert to ensure that media aid the planned, beneficial development of a given nation. This concept is exemplified by the media systems of most developing nations in Africa, Asia, the former Eastern bloc of Europe, and in Latin and South America. Media and government officials work together to produce content that meets specific cultural and societal needs—for example, disease eradication and the dissemination of new farming techniques. There is more government involvement in the operation of the media than there is in the Western concept, but little overt official censorship and control.

The **revolutionary concept** describes a system where media are used in the service of revolution. No country officially embraces this concept, but that does not mean that the people and media practitioners cannot use a nation's communication technologies to upset the government. The goals of media in the revolutionary concept are to end government monopoly over information, building an opposition to the existing government, destroying the legitimacy of an existing government, and bringing down that government (Stevenson, 1994). The revolutionary concept was in clear evidence in the Polish democracy movement Solidarity's adroit manipulation of that country's media system in its 1989 overthrow of its Communist regime and again, more recently, in the banding together of most of the big media outlets in Yugoslavia in opposition to its undemocratic leader Slobodan Milosevic.

Because there are now only three remaining communist countries (North Korea, China, and Cuba), the **authoritarian** and **communism concepts** are typically discussed as one. Both advocate the complete domination of media by the government for the purpose of forcing those media to serve, in the case of the authoritarian system, the government's desires, and in the case of the communism concept, the Communist Party's.

Summary

During the 1940s, social responsibility theory emerged as the predominant normative theory of media practice in the United States. Social responsibility theory represented a compromise between radical libertarian views and technocratic control notions. Control of media content was placed in the hands of media practitioners who were expected to act in the public interest. No means existed, however, to compel practitioners to serve the public. These practitioners were free to decide what services were needed and to monitor the effectiveness of those services.

Since its articulation by the Hutchins Commission, most media practitioners have at least been introduced to the basic ideals of social responsibility theory. As such, when they are questioned about their work, most provide explanations that are based on social responsibility notions. In addition, many different news production practices have been developed in an effort to implement these ideas. Still, there seems to be little enthusiasm among many media professionals for its focus on the public good and on broad-based reporting about significant events. In addition, as the conflict between social responsibility and profitability continues to grow in our increasingly commercialized media, responsibility becomes less central to the mission of many media organizations.

Recently, media critics such as Tuchman (1978) and W. Lance Bennett (1988) have charged that media services to minority groups and social movements have actually impeded or subverted group activities. They argue that ritualistic balancing of news combined with overdramatized coverage has popularized false impressions of groups or reinforced negative stereotypes. Groups get little real assistance from media. Most media services are aimed at demographic segments favored by advertisers—not at those groups in greatest need of help. Media have chronicled the decay of cities but have done little to create "Great Communities." Their target audiences are generally in the affluent suburbs, not the inner city ghettos. The harshest critics of social responsibility theory argue that this ideology simply legitimizes and rationalizes the status quo (Altschull, 1990). We will consider these criticisms in Chapter 10.

Despite little revamping or reexamination, social responsibility theory remains the normative theory that guides most media operation in the United States today. Its enduring appeal can be seen in the practice of civic journalism, where media, especially newspapers, endeavor to connect with diverse groups in the cities they serve.

Recent changes in media technology and world politics make it reasonable to reassess social responsibility theory's usefulness as currently applied. Small media can be provided to ethnic or racial groups at low cost, and the Internet has made it possible for even the smallest groups to air their views. The rise of thousands of small groups is sometimes seen as a Balkanization of the larger U.S. culture. Before the validity of this claim can be decided, however, the normative theory on which our media system is grounded must be reformulated, especially given technological and economic changes that are reshaping the media. This will require a critical re-examination of social responsibility theory and careful consideration of alternatives.

Alternative normative theories, however, already exist, although they may not be a good fit for our political and social system. Developmental media theory advocates media support for an existing political regime in its efforts to foster national economic development. Democratic-participant theory advocates media support for grass-roots cultural pluralism. Hachten offered five concepts, Western, combining libertarian and social responsibility ideals; development, something akin to developmental media theory; revolutionary, when the people and media professionals use mass media to challenge an existing regime; and authoritarian and communism, where media serve the dictates of those in power.

Exploring Mass Communication Theory

1   Following are the home pages for the Web sites of various media industry professional organizations. Examine them to see what you can learn about these self-regulatory bodies. Then link to the codes of ethics or standards of practice for each group. Examine them and determine (a) which set of media professionals does the best job of meeting its own standards, (b) which does the poorest job of doing so, and (c) which has set the highest standards for itself.

Society of Professional Journalists
http://spj.org/

American Society of Newspaper Editors
http://www.asne.org/index.htm

Radio-Television News Directors Association
http://www.rtnda.org

American Advertising Federation
http://www.aaf.org/

Public Relations Society of America
http://www.prsa.org

2   Following are the URLs for a number of Web sites monitoring the performance of those media professionals represented by the organizations just identified. Visit these sites to read their evaluations of our self-regulated mass media industries. Do you think they are too critical of American media performance, or not critical enough?

> http://www.mediawhoresonline.com
> http://www.bartcop.com
> http://www.buzzflash.com
> http://www.americanpolitics.com
> http://www.onlinejournal.com
> http://www.mediatransparency.org
> http://www.fair.org
> http://www.cjr.org

3   Three organizations that pay particular attention, sometimes critical, to civic journalism are listed here. Access these sites and follow the links to their discussions and evaluations of civic journalism. Can you find criticisms or supporting commentary not mentioned in your text? Are you persuaded by any of these groups' advocacy or denial of civic journalism's worth? Does any one of these sites link civic journalism directly to notions of social responsibility? If so, how?

> *Pew Center for Civic Journalism*
> http://www.pewcenter.org
>
> *USC Annenberg Online Journalism Review*
> http://www.orj.org
>
> *The Poynter Institute for Media Studies*
> http://www.poynter.org

4   Use **InfoTrac College Edition** to find articles discussing the operation of the media systems of countries other than the United States. Likely sources might be *Africa Report, Africa Today, African Affairs, the Journal of European Studies,* and the *Journal of Latin American Studies* among others. Search for issues such as *public service* and *media responsibilities.* What can you determine about the operation of the media systems that are detailed? Place those systems into the appropriate normative theory and defend your judgment.

5   Use **InfoTrac College Edition** to find articles dealing with the operation of U.S. media. *American Journalism Review, Broadcasting & Cable, Columbia Journalism Review,* and *Editor & Publisher* are good starting points. Try searching for *advertising ethics* or *journalism ethics.* Can you find differences in perspective between the review journals (*American Journalism Review* and *Columbia Journalism Review*) and the industry journals (*Broadcasting & Cable* and *Editor & Publisher*)?

Critical Thinking Questions

1 What are the most important services that media provide for you? How would you react if one or more of these services were stopped? For example, it might soon be possible for media entrepreneurs to make more money selling National Football League games using a pay-per-view system than they already do using regular network and cable television. How would you react to that?

2 Should minority groups be protected from hate propaganda? Imagine that you are the manager of a local cable television access channel and the Ku Klux Klan approaches you. The group wants you to run its 30-minute video "proving" the inferiority of people of color. It contains no profanity. Do you deny this group its time? Why? Then the Rainbow Coalition approaches you. It wants its video on pluralism aired. Will you air it? If you denied the KKK and allowed the Rainbow Coalition, how would you justify your decisions? Isn't this just a case of you favoring groups you like?

3 How well do you think major media outlets serve minority groups? Do you agree or disagree with the media critics who charge that most news coverage harms rather than helps minority groups or social movements?

4 Develop a new normative theory of media. State at least three important services that media should offer even though little or no profit can be earned by providing them. The theory should justify providing these services. Do you think there should be government subsidies so that the media can afford to provide these services? How would you monitor and compel media outlets to provide mandated services?

5 If you were to develop standards that would qualify someone to be a journalist, what elements would they include? Defend your standards.

Significant People and Their Writing

Altschull, J. Herbert (1990). *From Milton to McLuhan: The Ideas Behind American Journalism.* New York: Longman.

Barnouw, Erik (1966). *A History of Broadcasting in the United States: A Tower in Babel, Vol. I.* New York: Oxford University Press.

Bennett, W. Lance (1988). *News: The Politics of Illusion,* 2nd edition. New York: Longman.

Gunaratne, Shelton A. (1998). "Old Wine in a New Bottle: Public Journalism, Developmental Journalism, and Social Responsibility." In M.E. Roloff, ed., *Communication Yearbook 21.* Thousand Oaks, CA: Sage.

Hachten, William A. (1992). *The World News Prism.* Ames: Iowa State University Press.

McIntyre, Jeryln S. (1987). "Repositioning a Landmark: The Hutchins Commission and Freedom of the Press." *Critical Studies in Mass Communication,* 4: 95–135.

Tuchman, Gaye (1978). *Making News: A Study in the Construction of Reality.* New York: Free Press.

Section 3

The Rise and Fall
of Limited Effects

1951 *Innis's* The Bias of Communication
      Murrow's See It Now *premieres*
      UNIVAC becomes the first successful commercial computer

1953 *Hovland, Janis, and Kelley's* Communication and Persuasion

1954 *Murrow challenges McCarthy on television*

1957 *Mills's* Power Elite
      Soviet Union launches Sputnik, earth's first human constructed satellite

1958 *TV quiz show scandal erupts*

1959 *Mills's* The Sociological Imagination

1960 *Kennedy and Nixon meet in Great Debates*
      TV in 90 percent of all U.S. homes
      Klapper's Effects of Mass Communication

1961 *Key's* Public Opinion and American Democracy
      Kennedy makes nation's first live TV presidential press conference
      Berelson's "Great Debate on Cultural Democracy"
      Schramm team's Television in the Lives of Our Children *published*

1962 *Festinger's cognitive dissonance article appears*
      Kraus's Great Debates
      Air Force commissions Paul Baran to develop a national computer network

Chapter 6

Limited Effects Theory Emerges

Two wars—one imaginary, one real—helped move mass communication theory away from its belief in powerful and malignant mass media to a more moderate view.

What was to become the discipline's long adherence to limited effects theory began on a peaceful evening in late October 1938. On that night, many Americans were listening to a ballroom dance music program on the CBS radio network when the show was interrupted by a series of news bulletins. Early announcements told of strange astronomical observations and sightings of lights in the sky. The reports grew steadily more ominous. An alien spaceship had landed and was attacking the military forces that surrounded it. Transmissions from the scene ended suddenly and were followed by an appeal from the Secretary of the Interior for calm in the face of the alien threat. In cities across the nation, Americans reacted with alarm.

In that year, the medium of radio was still new, but it had become enormously popular. Expansive national networks had been established only a few years earlier. Listeners were starting to rely on the new medium for news, which was free and easily accessible and provided compelling, on-the-spot reports of fast-breaking situations. In a very troubled era, with many unusual and threatening events, such as impending war in Europe, people listened to radio for the latest reports of bad news. Orson Welles, a young radio program producer, conceived a radio theater program in which simulated news bulletins would be used to play a Halloween joke on the entire nation. Borrowing freely from a novel by H. G. Wells entitled *War of the Worlds*, Welles and scriptwriter Howard Koch created a radio drama in which listeners heard a series of compelling eyewitness reports of the alien invasion. Afraid that the program might be too dull, Koch embellished the script with allusions and authentic detail (Lowery & DeFleur, 1995).

The last half of the program recounted the aftermath of the invasion. News bulletins gave way to a monologue from the sole human survivor, telling of the aliens' ultimate defeat by bacteria. Because this portion of the program was clearly fantasy, Welles saw no need to provide announcements of the program's fiction. For many listeners, it was too late anyway. As soon as they heard the early bulletins, they fled their homes and aroused their neighbors.

Many observers saw the invasion from Mars panic as definitive proof of mass society theory. If a single radio program could induce such widespread panic, obviously concerted propaganda campaigns could do much worse. The American masses were clearly at the mercy of any demagogue who could gain control of the airwaves. Eventually, some bully would seize the opportunity and take power, as Adolf Hitler had done in Germany. Propaganda would be used to win a close election. Once sufficient control was gained, opposing political parties would be crushed.

At Princeton University, a group of social researchers set out to determine why the Welles broadcast had been so influential (Cantril, Gaudet, & Herzog, 1940). Their research found that many people acted too hastily after hearing only the first fragmentary reports of the invasion. The simulated news bulletins were trusted without question, especially the eyewitness reports and interviews with phony experts. The people who were most upset by the program didn't stay glued to their radios waiting for updates. In that era, before portable and car radios had become commonplace, these people lost touch with the program once they left their homes. Word of mouth spread news of the ersatz invasion through entire neighborhoods. Often, people who heard about the invasion from others didn't think to turn on their radios to check out the news for themselves. They trusted their neighbors and acted. Even though the researchers found considerable evidence of panic, they also found that most people were not taken in by Welles's practical joke. Most people possessed critical ability that led them to check the validity of the broadcast, so they had little trouble disconfirming news of the invasion. Only listeners who tuned in late and for just a few minutes were likely to be upset. The researchers concluded that these people had one or more psychological traits that made them especially susceptible to media influence: emotional insecurity, phobic personality, lack of self-confidence, and fatalism.

Overview

The *War of the Worlds* researchers, led by Hadley Cantril, were part of a vanguard of social scientists that slowly transformed our view of how media influence society. Within twenty years of that famous broadcast, the way researchers looked at mass media was radically altered. Media were no longer feared as instruments of political oppression and manipulation but, instead, viewed as a relatively benign force with much potential for social good. The media's power over the public was seen as limited—so limited, that no government regulations were deemed necessary to prevent manipulation. The public itself was viewed as very resistant to persuasion and extremist manipulation. The belief was that most people were influenced by others rather than by the media; opinion leaders in every community and at every level of society were responsible for guiding and stabilizing politics. It was argued that only a very small minority of people had psychological traits that made them vulnerable to direct manipulation by media. Media were conceptualized as relatively powerless in shaping public opinion in the face of more potent intervening variables like people's individual differences and group memberships. This new view of media arose and persisted even though television would transform and dominate the media landscape.

How and why did such a radical transformation in media theory take place in such a short time? In this chapter, we trace the rise of what became the dominant **paradigm** in U.S. media research for several decades. We describe the work of researchers who were led by Paul Lazarsfeld, a colleague of Cantril at Princeton University. Lazarsfeld later moved to Columbia University and pioneered the use of sophisticated surveys to measure media influence on how people thought and acted. These surveys provided definitive evidence that media rarely had powerful, direct influence on individuals. The effects were quite limited in scope— affecting only a few people or influencing rather trivial thoughts or actions. These findings eventually led to a perspective on media that was referred to as the **limited effects perspective.**

We also review experimental studies of the persuasive power of media, focusing on the work of Carl Hovland. Like Lazarsfeld, Hovland was a methodological innovator who introduced new standards for evaluating media influence. He too found that media lacked the power to instantly convert average people away from strongly held beliefs. Even in laboratory situations where the potential for media influence was exaggerated, only modest effects were discovered. Many factors were actually found to limit media influence.

Finally, we consider how proponents of limited effects were able to establish this perspective as the dominant way of looking at media. Data from an impressive array of elaborate empirical studies were assembled into an important series of classic reports (for example, Bauer & Bauer, 1960; Campbell, Converse, Miller, & Stokes, 1960; DeFleur & Larsen, 1958; Katz & Lazarsfeld, 1955; Klapper, 1960).

As we trace the rise of the limited effects perspective, it is important to note the parallels to our own times (as well as the important differences). Like the theorists in the 1930s and 1940s, there is seemingly obvious evidence all around us of the power of media to alter our experience of the social world. Most of us have personally experienced the power of media to convey the threat of terrorist attacks. How can this be explained if media are not capable of having powerful ef-

PARADIGM *An organizing theoretical perspective*

LIMITED EFFECTS PERSPECTIVE *The guiding idea that media have minimal or limited effects*

fects? In times of war and national crisis, we turn to media as a means of making sense of what is going on and trying to anticipate what might happen in the future. The more we depend on media to do this, the more we effectively place our faith in media to guide us and the more likely it is that media will influence our lives. To what extent should media be held responsible for altering our views of the social world? To what extent should we be held responsible if we choose to trust the media to provide useful information? It is important to recognize that this apparent power of the media is not inherent in the technology itself or even in the specific media content being transmitted. The power lies in ourselves—in the way we choose to allow media to affect our lives. This is the essential insight that comes out of the limited effects perspective—an insight that continues to have relevance as we seek to assess the role of media today.

Paradigm Shifts

PARADIGM SHIFT
A transformation from one organizing theoretical perspective to another

One way of interpreting what happened to media theory during the two decades from 1940 to 1960 is to view it as a **paradigm shift.** Thomas Kuhn (1970), a science historian, has argued that the way science progresses is through these radical breaks in theory. For a period, a single theoretical perspective or paradigm dominates most research. These paradigms can encompass many closely related theories. Each theory shares certain common assumptions. A paradigm summarizes and is consistent with all known facts. It provides a useful guide for research as long as its basic assumptions are accepted. Most researchers find it easy to work within such a framework. Many are unaware of alternatives or find other ideas or contradictory findings easy to dismiss. As popular scientist writer Stephen Jay Gould eloquently explained, paradigm shifts

> are deep, difficult, and complex. They require a rejection of one view of reality (never an easy task, either conceptually or psychologically), in favor of a radically new order, teeming with consequences for everything held precious. One doesn't discard the comfort and foundation of a lifetime so lightly or suddenly. Moreover, even if one thinker experiences an emotional and transforming eureka, he must still work out an elaborate argument, and gather extensive empirical support, to persuade a community of colleagues often stubbornly committed to opposite views. Science, after all, operates both as a social enterprise and an intellectual adventure. (2000, p. 188)

Though paradigms exercise great influence over the course of scientific research, shifts inevitably occur because no paradigm can provide an adequate explanation for all observations. Sometimes, *small opposition research communities emerge to develop and investigate alternate theories.* Their work is usually ignored or severely criticized, but sometimes they are able to conclusively demonstrate the validity of their perspective. Sometimes *researchers committed to a dominant paradigm uncover important findings that are inconsistent with it.* As they explore these findings, more and more contradictory data are obtained. Eventually, researchers make an effort to account for these inconsistencies and develop a new body of theory. Sometimes *an important role is played by scientific iconoclasts*—people who rebel against key assumptions in the dominant paradigm or who are convinced that new research methods should be used. Iconoclasts often work in isolation as they develop alternate perspectives; the value of their ideas and findings might not be recognized until decades after the original research was done.

The Paradigm Shift in Mass Communication Theory

The people who led the paradigm shift in mass communication theory during the 1940s and 1950s were primarily methodologists—not theorists. Lazarsfeld and Hovland were convinced that we could best assess the influence of media by employing objective, empirical methods to measure it. They argued that new research methods such as experiments and surveys made it possible to observe the effects of media. These observations would permit definitive conclusions to be reached and would guide the construction of more useful theory.

Both Lazarsfeld and Hovland were trained in the empirical research methods that had been developed in psychology. In addition, Lazarsfeld spent time as a social statistician in Austria. Working independently, they demonstrated how their research techniques could be adapted to the study of media effects. Both were successful in convincing others of the validity of their approach. Lazarsfeld secured funding that enabled him to conduct expensive, large-scale studies of media influence at Columbia University. After conducting propaganda experiments during World War II—the real war mentioned at the start of this chapter—Hovland established a large research center at Yale where hundreds of persuasion experiments were conducted. Both Columbia and Yale became very influential research centers that attracted some of the best social researchers of the time.

Neither Lazarsfeld nor Hovland set out to revolutionize mass communication theory. They had broader objectives. During the war years, they were drawn into media studies as part of the larger effort to understand the power of propaganda and the threat it posed. Unlike many colleagues who willingly assumed that media were quite powerful, Lazarsfeld and Hovland were determined to conduct empirical research that could assess that assumption. They hoped that if media's power could be better understood, it might be controlled and used toward good ends.

Lazarsfeld and Hovland argued that scientific methods provided the essential means to control media's power. They were impressed by the tremendous accomplishments being made in the physical sciences. In fields like physics and chemistry, the ability of science to understand and control the physical world was being vividly demonstrated. Some of the most striking examples could be found in new military technology—amazing aircraft, highly destructive bombs, and unstoppable tanks. These weapons could be used for either good or evil, to defend democracy or bolster totalitarianism. Along with Harold Lasswell (Chapter 4), Hovland and Lazarsfeld believed that if democracy were to survive, it would have to produce the best scientists, and these people would have to do a better job of harnessing technology to advance that political ideology.

As both men conducted their research, they found that media were not as powerful as mass society theory indicated. Often, media influence over public opinion or attitudes was hard to locate. Media influence was typically less important than that of factors such as social status or education. Those media effects that were found seemed to be isolated and were sometimes contradictory. Despite the weak findings, funding for additional research proved easy to secure. Study after study provided growing insight into the limited power of media.

During the 1950s, the new paradigm began to take shape. Across the United States, new research centers modeled after those at Yale and Columbia opened. By 1960, many of the "classic studies" were published and became required reading for a generation of communication researchers. This new paradigm dominated during the 1960s, remained quite strong through the 1970s, and its influence echoes even today.

As we discuss the early research, we will illustrate the factors that combined to make development of the paradigm possible. We list these factors here and we will refer to them in later sections.

1 **The refinement and broad acceptance of empirical social research methods was an essential factor in the emergence of the new paradigm.** Throughout this period, empirical research methods were effectively promoted as an ideal means of measuring social phenomena. They were declared to be the only "scientific" way of dealing with social phenomena. Other approaches were dismissed as overly speculative, unsystematic, or too subjective. Because so few people at the time understood the limitations of empirical research methods, findings and the conclusions derived from them were often accepted uncritically. When these outcomes conflicted with past theories, the older theories were questioned.

2 **Empirical social researchers successfully branded people who advocated mass society theories as "unscientific."** Mass society theory advocates were accused of being fuzzy-minded humanists, doomsayers, political ideologues, or biased against media. Also, mass society notions lost some of their broad appeal as the threat of propaganda gradually faded in the late 1950s and 1960s.

3 **Social researchers exploited the commercial potential of the new research methods and gained the support of private industry.** One of the first articles Lazarsfeld wrote after arriving in the United States was about the use of survey research methods as a tool for advertisers (Kornhauser & Lazarsfeld, 1935). Surveys and experiments were promoted as a means of probing media audiences and interpreting consumer attitudes and behaviors. Most of Hovland's persuasion studies had more or less direct application to advertising and marketing. Lazarsfeld coined the term **administrative research** to refer to these applications. He persuasively argued for the use of empirical research to guide administrative decision-making.

ADMINISTRATIVE RESEARCH *Research that examines audiences to interpret consumer attitudes and behaviors; the use of empirical research to guide practical, administrative decisions*

4 **The development of empirical social research was strongly backed by various private and government foundations, most notably the Rockefeller Foundation and the National Science Foundation.** This support was crucial, particularly in the early stages, because large-scale empirical social research required much more funding than previous forms of social research had required. Without support from the Rockefeller Foundation, Lazarsfeld might never have come to the United States or been able to develop and demonstrate the validity of his approach.

5 **After empirical research began to show that media were not as threatening and all-powerful as implied by mass society theory, media companies were encouraged to finance more empirical research.** In time, both CBS and NBC formed their own social research departments and employed many outside researchers as consultants. Two of the most influential early media researchers were Frank Stanton and Joseph Klapper—the former collaborated with Lazarsfeld on numerous research projects and the latter was Lazarsfeld's student. As media corporations grew larger and earned sizable profits, they could afford to fund empirical research—especially when that research helped to justify the status quo and block moves to regulate their operations. Media funding and support were vital to the development of commercial audience ratings services such as Nielsen and Arbitron. These companies pioneered the use of survey research methods to measure the size of audiences and guide administrative decision-making in areas such as advertising and marketing.

Media support was also crucial to the growth of various national polling services such as Gallup, Harris, and Roper. Media coverage of polls and ratings data helped establish their credibility in the face of widespread commonsense criticism. During the 1940s and 1950s, most people were skeptical about the usefulness of data gathered from small samples. They wondered, for example, how pollsters could survey just three hundred or twelve hundred people and draw conclusions about an entire city or nation. To answer these questions, media reported that opinion polls and ratings were valid because they were based on "scientific" samples. Often, there was little explanation of what the term "scientific" meant in this context.

6 Empirical social researchers successfully established their approach within the various social research disciplines—political science, history, social psychology, sociology, and economics. These disciplines, in turn, shaped the development of communication research. As the various communication disciplines developed, empirical social researchers from the more established social sciences provided leadership. Social science theories and research methods assumed an important, often dominant place within university journalism, speech communication, and broadcasting departments. Empirical research became widely accepted as the most scientific way to study communication even though it proved difficult to find conclusive evidence of media influence.

The Two-Step Flow of Information and Influence

INDUCTIVE *An approach to theory construction that sees research beginning with empirical observation rather than speculation*

Lazarsfeld was not a theorist, yet by promoting empirical research, he did more than any of his peers to transform social theory. Lazarsfeld believed theory must be strongly grounded in empirical facts. He was concerned that macroscopic social theories, including the various mass society theories, were too speculative. He preferred a highly **inductive** approach to theory construction—that is, research should begin with empirical observation, not with armchair speculation. After the facts are gathered, they are sifted and the most important pieces of information are selected. This information is used to construct empirical generalizations—assertions about the relationships between variables. Then, researchers can gather more data to see if these generalizations are valid.

This research approach is cautious and inherently conservative. It avoids sweeping generalizations that go beyond empirical observations and demands that theory construction be "disciplined" by data collection and analysis. Theory should never be too far removed from data. The research process proceeds slowly—building step-by-step on one data collection effort after another. Eventually a large number of empirical generalizations will be found and tested.

MIDDLE-RANGE THEORY *A theory composed of empirical generalizations based on empirical fact*

Theory is gradually created by combining generalizations to build what Robert Merton (1967) referred to as **middle-range theory** (see Chapter 7 for a fuller discussion). Unlike earlier forms of grand social theory—mass society theory, for example—middle-range theory comprises empirical generalizations that are solidly based on empirical facts. In this era, most social researchers thought that this was how theories were developed in the physical sciences. They hoped that they would be just as successful in controlling phenomena by emulating physical scientists. If so, the scientific methods that produced nuclear bombs might also eliminate poverty, war, and racism.

During the presidential election campaign of 1940, pitting incumbent Franklin Delano Roosevelt against Republican Wendell Willkie, Lazarsfeld had his first major opportunity to test the validity of his approach. He designed and carried out what was, at the time, the most elaborate field experiment ever conducted. Lazarsfeld assembled a large research team in May 1940 and sent it to Erie County, Ohio—a relatively remote region centered around the town of Sandusky along the shores of Lake Erie, west of Cleveland. The total population of the county was 43,000, and it was chosen because it was considered to be an average American locality. Though Sandusky residents tended to vote Democrat, the surrounding rural area was strongly Republican. By the time the research team left in November, more than 3,000 people had been personally interviewed in their homes. Six hundred were selected to be in a panel that was interviewed seven times—once every month from May until November. Assuming an average household size of five people, one out of every three households in the county was visited by an interviewer (Lazarsfeld, Berelson, & Gaudet, 1944).

In his data analysis, Lazarsfeld focused attention on changes in voting decisions. As people were interviewed each month, their choice of candidates was compared with the previous month's choice. During the six months, several types of changes were possible. Lazarsfeld created labels for each: *Early Deciders* chose a candidate in May and never changed during the entire campaign. *Waverers* chose one candidate, then were undecided or switched to another candidate, but in the end they voted for their first choice. *Converts* chose one candidate but then voted for his opponent. *Crystallizers* had not chosen a candidate in May but made a choice by November.

Lazarsfeld used a very long and detailed questionnaire that dealt extensively with exposure to specific mass media content such as candidate speeches. This focus was not surprising given Lazarsfeld's considerable background and interest in radio research. If propaganda was as powerful as mass society theory predicted, his research should have allowed him to pinpoint media influence. If mass society theory was valid, he should have found that most voters were either Converts or Waverers. He should have observed people switching back and forth between candidates. Those who showed the most change should have been the heaviest users of media.

But Lazarsfeld's results directly contradicted mass society theory. Fifty-three percent of the voters were early deciders. They chose one candidate in May and never changed. Twenty-eight percent were crystallizers—they eventually made a very predictable choice and stayed with it. Fifteen percent were waverers, and only eight percent were converts. He could find little evidence that media played an important role in influencing the crystallizers, the waverers, or the converts. Media use by those in the latter two categories was lower than average and very few of them reported being specifically influenced by media messages. Instead, these voters were much more likely to say that they had been influenced by other people. Many were politically apathetic. They failed to make clear-cut voting de-

cisions because they had such low interest. Often, they de
people closest to them voted—not as radio speeches or new
them to vote.

Lazarsfeld argued that the most important influence of ..
inforce a vote choice that had already been made. Media simply gave peopʌ
reasons for choosing a candidate whom they already favored. For some voters—
the crystallizers, for example—media helped activate existing party loyalties. Republicans who had never heard of Willkie were able to learn his name at least.
Nevertheless, Lazarsfeld found very little evidence that media converted people.
Instead, the converts were often people with divided loyalties—as Lazarsfeld said,
they were "cross-pressured." They had group ties that pulled them in opposing
directions. Willkie was Catholic, so religion pulled some people toward him and
pushed others away. Most Republican voters were rural Protestants—to vote for
Willkie, they had to ignore his religion. The same was true of urban Catholic
Democrats—they had to ignore religion to vote for Roosevelt.

But if media weren't directly influencing voting decisions, what was their role?
As Lazarsfeld worked with his data he began to formulate an empirical generalization that ultimately had enormous importance. He noticed that some of the hard-
core early deciders were also the heaviest users of media. They even made a point
of seeking out and listening to opposition speeches. On the other hand, the people
who made the least use of media were most likely to report that they relied on
others for help in making a voting decision. Lazarsfeld reasoned that the heavy
user/early deciders might be the same people whose advice was being sought by
other, more apathetic voters. The heavy user/early deciders might be sophisticated
media users who held well-developed political views and used media wisely and
critically. They might be capable of listening to and evaluating opposition
speeches. Rather than be converted themselves, they might actually gain information that would help them advise others so that they would be more resistant to
conversion. Thus, these heavy users might act as **gate-keepers**—screening information and only passing on items that would help others share their views. Lazarsfeld chose the term **opinion leader** to refer to these individuals. He labeled those
who turned to opinion leaders for advice as **opinion followers.**

Lazarsfeld designed his subsequent research to directly investigate the empirical generalizations that emerged from the 1940 research. He didn't want to speculate about the attributes of opinion leaders or their role—he wanted empirical
facts. In 1943, Lazarsfeld sent a research team to Decatur, Illinois, to interview
more than 700 housewives about their consumer decisions. Decatur, a city in the
heartland of America, was widely viewed as representative of most small to
medium-sized cities. A "snowball" sampling technique was used. An initial sample of women was contacted. During their interview, these women were asked the
names of people who influenced their thinking on marketing, movies, fashions,

GATE-KEEPERS
*In two-step flow,
people who screen
media messages
and pass on those
messages that help
others share their
views*

OPINION LEADERS
*In two-step flow,
those who pass on
information to
opinion followers*

OPINION FOLLOWERS
*In two-step flow,
those who receive
information from
opinion leaders*

and politics. Subsequently, these influential people were interviewed. In this way, Lazarsfeld hoped to identify and study those who had been named by others as opinion leaders. Their nomination by others was taken as factual evidence of their opinion leader status.

More than ten years passed before the Decatur research was published. With the assistance of a co-author, Elihu Katz, *Personal Influence* was finally published in 1955. This book was very influential in conceptualizing how people use media and formally advanced **two-step flow theory.** Katz and Lazarsfeld reported that opinion leaders existed at all levels of society and that the flow of their influence tended to be horizontal rather than vertical. Opinion leaders influenced people like themselves rather than those above or below them in the social order. Opinion leaders differed from followers in many of their personal attributes—they were more gregarious, used media more, were more socially active—but they often shared the same social status.

TWO-STEP FLOW THEORY *The idea that messages pass from the media, through opinion leaders, to opinion followers*

Limitations in the Lazarsfeld Model

The Lazarsfeld research approach has several important deficiencies that its defenders have been slow to recognize. Although these deficiencies don't invalidate specific findings, they do force us to be very careful in their interpretation. We must recognize what is and is not being measured by such survey research:

1 **Surveys can't measure how people actually use media on a day-to-day basis.** Surveys can only record how people *report* their use of media. As our experience with surveys has grown, we have identified some common biases in reports of media use. For example, more educated people tend to underestimate media influence on their decisions whereas less educated people might overestimate it. Estimates of influence tend to be strongly linked to people's perceptions of various media. For example, because television is widely viewed by educated people as a less socially acceptable medium (that is, the boob tube), they are less willing to admit being influenced by it.

2 **Surveys are a very expensive and cumbersome way to study people's use of specific media content such as their reading of certain news stories or their viewing of specific television programs.** Since Lazarsfeld's early work, most research has dealt with overall patterns of media use rather than use of specific content. Critics have charged that this means that media content is being ignored. The impact of powerful individual messages isn't routinely assessed; only the amount of use being routinely made of a given medium. We can learn a great deal from studying patterns of media use. There are important research questions, however, that can only be addressed if use of specific content is studied.

Instant Access

Two-Step Flow Theory

Strengths	Weaknesses
1 Focuses attention on the environment in which effects can and can't occur	**1** Is limited to its time (1940s) and media environment (no television)
2 Stresses importance of opinion leaders in formation of public opinion	**2** Uses reported behavior (voting) as only test of media effects
3 Is based on inductive rather than deductive reasoning	**3** Downplays reinforcement as an important media effect
4 Effectively challenges simplistic notions of direct effects	**4** Uses survey methods that underestimate media impact
	5 Later research demonstrates a multistep flow of influence

3 The research design and data analysis procedures Lazarsfeld developed are inherently conservative in assessing the media's power. Media influence is gauged by the amount of change media cause in an effect variable (that is, voting decision) after statistically controlling a set of social and demographic variables. Under these conditions, media are rarely found to be strong predictors of effects. Overall patterns of media use tend to be strongly associated with social and demographic variables like age, sex, social status, education, and so forth. When these variables are statistically controlled, there is little impact (variance) left for media-use patterns to explain. Does this mean that media use really isn't very powerful? Or is such a conclusion a methodological artifact?

4 Subsequent research on the two-step flow has produced highly contradictory findings. Most theorists who still find this conceptualization useful talk about multistep flows. These flows have been found to differ greatly according to the type of information being transmitted and the social conditions that exist at a particular point in time (Rogers, 1983). Although information flow from media to audiences has general patterns, these patterns are subject to constant change. Powerful messages could radically alter patterns of flow.

5 Surveys can be useful for studying changes over time, but they are a relatively crude technique. In 1940, Lazarsfeld interviewed people once a month. Considerable change could occur during a 30-day period that isn't measured. Listening or reading that took place days earlier could well be misreported. People tend to selectively remember and report what they think they should be doing rather than what they actually do. If surveys are done more often and at closer intervals, they can become intrusive. But the primary reason these surveys aren't conducted is that they are too expensive.

6   **Surveys omit many potentially important variables by focusing only on what can be easily or reliably measured using existing techniques.** Too often, these variables—for example, how a person was raised—are dismissed as unimportant or unduly speculative. Because they are hard or impossible to measure, their very existence can be questioned. This greatly limits theory construction because entire categories of variables are necessarily eliminated.

7   **The period during which Lazarsfeld conducted his research made it unlikely that he would observe the effects that he tried to measure.** The primary effect that he looked for in his voting research was whether people changed their decisions about whom to vote for in 1940. It's not surprising that very few people altered their voting decision during the summer and fall of 1940 as Nazi troops invaded much of Western Europe. If a national election had been held in November 2001 in the aftermath of the September 11 terrorist attacks in New York and Washington, for example, it's likely that the overwhelmingly high approval ratings for President Bush would have translated into a landslide election victory for him. In such a hypothetical election, would the failure of a Democrat campaign to unseat Bush have been convincing evidence of the weakness of media during all political campaigns? Would the central role of personal influence in this election mean that it would always be so central?

Limited Effects Theory

INDIRECT EFFECTS THEORY *When media do seem to have an effect, that effect is "filtered" through other parts of the society, for example, through friends or social groups*

Two popular labels for the perspective on media that developed out of Lazarsfeld's work are **indirect effects theory** and **limited effects theory**. These labels call attention to key generalizations about the role of media in society. Here are some of the most important that have emerged from the limited effects research work conducted between 1945 and 1960.

1   **Media rarely directly influence individuals.** Most people are sheltered from direct propaganda manipulation by their family, friends, coworkers, and social groups. People don't believe everything they hear or see in the media. They turn to others for advice and critical interpretation. This assumption contradicts mass society notions that viewed people as isolated and highly vulnerable to direct manipulation.

LIMITED EFFECTS
THEORY *The the-*
ory that media
have minimal or
limited effects
because those
effects are miti-
gated by a vari-
ety of mediating
or intervening
variables

2 **There is a two-step flow of media influence.** Media will only be influential if the opinion leaders who guide others are influenced first. Because these opinion leaders are sophisticated, critical media users, they are not easily manipulated by media content. They act as an effective barrier to media influence.

3 **By the time most people become adults, they have developed strongly held group commitments such as political party and religious affiliations that individual media messages are powerless to overcome.** These commitments cause people to reject messages even if other group members are not present to assist them. Media use tends to be consistent with these commitments. For example, voters with Republican affiliations subscribe to Republican magazines and listen mostly to Republican politicians on radio.

4 **When media effects do occur, they will be modest and isolated.** Huge numbers of people across the land will not be converted. Rather, small pockets of individuals might be influenced—usually those who are somehow cut off from the influence of other people or whose long-term group commitments are undermined by social crises.

Attitude Change Theories

Although persuasion and attitude change have been speculated about almost since the beginning of recorded history, systematic study of these phenomena began only in the twentieth century, and World War II provided the "laboratory" for the development of a cohesive body of thought on attitude change and, by obvious extension, media and attitude change. The United States entered that war convinced that it was as much a psychological battle as it was a shooting war. The Nazis had demonstrated the power of the Big Lie. The United States needed to be able to mount an effective counter-offensive. Before the United States could confront the Japanese and the Germans, however, it had to turn its people's attention to the home front. During the 1930s, there were powerful isolationist and pacifist sentiments in the country. These movements were so strong that in the election of 1940, Roosevelt promised to keep the United States out of the war, even though the Nazis were conquering much of Western Europe. Aid to Britain was handled secretly. Until the bombing of Pearl Harbor, peace negotiations were conducted with the Japanese.

Thus, the war provided three important motivations for people interested in attitude research. For one thing, the success of the Nazi propaganda efforts in Europe challenged the democratic and very American notion of the people's wisdom. It seemed that powerful bad ideas might overwhelm inadequately defended good ideas. Strategies were needed to counter Nazi propaganda and defend

American values. Early in the war, for example, Carl J. Friedrich (1943), a consultant to the Office of War Information, outlined the military's ongoing research strategy: detect psychological barriers to persuasion and assess how effectively a given set of messages could overcome those barriers.

A second war-provided research motivation was actually more imperative. Large numbers of men and women from all parts of the country and from all sorts of backgrounds had been rapidly recruited, trained, and tossed together in the armed forces. Remembering that this was before television, universalized higher education, and the country's urbanization, it is easy to see that the military needed to determine what these soldiers were thinking and to find a way to intellectually and emotionally bind them—Yankee and Southerner, Easterner and Westerner, city boy and country girl—to the cause.

The third motivation was simple convenience: Where the military saw soldiers in training, psychologists saw subjects, well-tracked subjects. The availability of many people about whom large amounts of background information already existed proved significant because it helped define the research direction of what we now call attitude change theory. Major General Frederick Osborn, Director of the Army's Information and Education Division, enthused, "Never before had modern methods of social science been employed on so large a scale, by such competent technicians. Its value to the social scientist may be as great as its value to the military for whom the original research was done" (Stouffer, Suchman, De Vinney, Star, & Williams, 1949, p. vii). Equally important to those social scientists was that this groundbreaking research set the tenor for their work for the next two decades.

Carl Hovland and the Experimental Section

The Army's Information and Education Division had a Research Branch. Inside the Research Branch was the Experimental Section, headed by psychologist Hovland. Its primary mission "was to make experimental evaluations of the effectiveness of various programs of the Information and Education Division" (Hovland, Lumsdaine, & Sheffield, 1949, p. v). At first, the Experimental Section focused on documentary films and the War Department's orientation movie series, *Why We Fight,* produced by Hollywood director Frank Capra. But because of the military's increasing use of media, the Experimental Section also studied "other media . . . quite diverse in character" (p. vi). As the researchers themselves wrote (p. vii), "The diversity of topics covered by the research of the Experimental Section made it unfeasible to publish a single cohesive account of all the studies. However, it did appear possible to integrate the group of studies on the effects of motion pictures, film strips, and radio programs into a systematic treatment concerning the effectiveness of mass communication media." They called their account *Experiments on Mass Communication,* and it clearly bore the mark of group leader Hovland.

With his background in behaviorism and learning theory, Hovland's strength was in identifying the essential elements of attitude change and devising straightforward experiments employing **controlled variation**. He took some piece of stimulus material (a film, for example), and systematically isolated and varied its potentially important elements independently and in combination to assess their effects.

CONTROLLED VARIATION *Systematic isolation and manipulation of elements in an experiment*

To meet the military's immediate needs, the Experimental Section began with evaluation research, that is, testing whether or not the *Why We Fight* film series met its indoctrinational goals. Prevailing notions about the power of propaganda implied that the researchers would find dramatic shifts in attitude as a result of viewing the films. According to some versions of mass society theory, every soldier, no matter what his or her background or personality, should have been easily manipulated by the messages in the films. Military training should have induced an ideal form of mass society experience. Individual soldiers were torn from their families, jobs, and social groups. They were isolated individuals, supposedly highly vulnerable to propaganda.

Nevertheless, Hovland's group found that the military's propaganda wasn't as powerful as had been assumed. They discovered that although the movies were successful in increasing knowledge, they were not as effective in influencing attitudes and motivations (their primary function). Even the most effective films primarily strengthened existing attitudes. Conversions were rare. Typically, only the attitudes specifically targeted by the films showed change. More global attitudes such as optimism or pessimism about the war were resistant.

The fact that the films produced little attitude change and that what change did occur was influenced by people's individual differences directly contradicted mass society theory and its assumption that propaganda could radically change even strongly held beliefs and attitudes. If isolated soldiers being hurriedly prepared for battle were resistant to the most sophisticated propaganda available, were average people likely to be more susceptible? As with Lazarsfeld's research, these empirical facts contradicted the prevailing theoretical paradigm and implied that it would be necessary to develop new conceptualizations.

A second outcome of the initial evaluation work was important in determining the direction of future attitude change theory. In examining one of the three films in the series, the 50-minute *The Battle of Britain,* Hovland and his colleagues found that, although initially more effective in imparting factual information than in changing attitudes about the British, as time passed, factual knowledge decreased but attitudes toward the British actually became more positive. Time, the researchers discovered, was a key variable in attitude change.

Possibly propaganda effects were not as instantaneous as mass society theory or behaviorist notions suggested. Hovland's group formulated various explanations for these slow shifts in attitude. But with no precise way to scientifically answer the question of why the passage of time produced increased attitude change in the direction of the original media stimulus, Hovland and his research team developed a new type of research design—controlled variation experiments—"to obtain findings having a greater degree of generalizability. The method used is that of systematically varying certain specified factors while other factors are controlled. This makes it possible to determine the effectiveness of the particular factors varied" (Hovland, Lumsdaine, & Sheffield, 1949, p. 179).

One of the most important variables the researchers examined was the presentation of one or both sides of a persuasive argument. Using two versions of a radio program, they presented a one-sided argument (that the war would be a long one) and a two-sided argument (the war would be long, but the alternative view was addressed). Of course, those who heard either version showed more attitude change than those who had heard no broadcast, but there was no difference between the groups who had listened to the two versions. Hovland had anticipated this. Accordingly, he had assessed the men's initial points of view. What his work demonstrated was that one-sided messages were more effective with people already in favor of the message; two-sided presentations were more effective with those holding divergent perspectives. In addition, Hovland looked at educational level and discovered that the two-sided presentation was more effective with those people who had more schooling.

Thus, this group of psychologists determined that attitude change was a very complex beast and that aspects of the messages themselves can and often did interact with aspects of the people receiving them. An enormous number of significant research questions suddenly could be posed. What happens, for example, when two-sided presentations are directed toward people who are initially predisposed against a position but have low levels of education? Such questions fueled several decades of persuasion research and challenged two generations of researchers.

The Communication Research Program

The concept of attitude change was so complex that Hovland proposed and conducted a systematic program of research that occupied him and his colleagues in the post-war years. Funded by the Rockefeller Foundation, Hovland established the Communication Research Program at Yale University. Its work centered on several of the variables Hovland considered central to attitude change: the communicator, the content of the communication, and the audience.

This research produced scores of scientific articles and a number of significant books on attitude and attitude change, but the most important was the 1953 *Communication and Persuasion*. Although a close reading of the original work is the best way to grasp the full extent of its findings, a general overview of this seminal research offers some indication of the complexity of persuasion and attitude change.

Examining the communicator, Hovland and his group studied the power of source credibility, which they divided into trustworthiness and expertness. As you might expect, they found that high-credibility communicators produced increased amounts of attitude change; low-credibility communicators produced less attitude change.

Looking at the content of the communication, Hovland and his group examined two general aspects of content: the nature of the appeal itself and the organization of that appeal.

Focusing specifically on fear-arousing appeals, the Yale group tested the logical assumption that stronger fear-arousing presentations will lead to greater attitude change. This relationship was found to be true to some extent, but variables such as the vividness of the threat's description and the audience's state of alarm, evaluation of the communicator, and already-held knowledge about the subject either mitigated or heightened attitude change.

The Hovland group's look at the organization of the arguments was a bit more straightforward. Should a communicator explicitly state an argument's conclusions or leave them implicit? In general, the explicit statement of the argument's conclusion is more effective, but not invariably. The trustworthiness of the communicator, the intelligence level of the audience, the nature of the issue at hand and its importance to the audience, and the initial level of agreement between audience and communicator all altered the persuasive power of a message.

Regardless of how well a persuasive message is crafted, not all people are influenced by it to the same degree, so the Yale Group examined the audience for its predispositions. Inquiry centered on the personal importance of the audience's group memberships and individual personality differences among people that might influence their susceptibility to persuasion.

Testing the power of what they called "counternorm communications," Hovland and his cohorts demonstrated that the more highly people value their membership in a group, the more closely their attitudes will conform to those of the group and, therefore, the more resistant they will be to change. If you attend a Big Ten university and closely follow your school's sports teams, it isn't very likely that anyone will be able to persuade you that the Atlantic Coast Conference fields superior athletes. If you attend that same Big Ten college but care little about its sports programs, you might be a more likely target for opinion change, particularly if your team loses to an ACC team in dramatic fashion.

The question of individual differences in susceptibility to persuasion is not about a person's willingness to be persuaded on a given issue. In persuasion research, individual differences refers to those personality factors that render someone generally susceptible to influence. Intelligence is a good example. It is easy to assume that more intelligent people would be less susceptible to persuasive arguments, but this isn't the case. More intelligent people are more likely to be persuaded if the message they receive is based on solid, logical arguments. Self-esteem, aggressiveness, and social withdrawal were several of the other individual characteristics the Yale Group tested. But, as with intelligence, each failed to produce the straightforward, unambiguous relationship that might have seemed warranted. Why? None of a person's personality characteristics operates apart from his or her evaluation of the communicator, his or her judgments of the message, or his or her understanding of the social reward or punishment that might accompany acceptance or rejection of a given attitude. As we'll see, this colored our understanding of media effects for decades.

Emergence of the Media Effects Focus

From the 1950s to the 1990s, persuasion research influenced the study of media. Following the models provided by the early persuasion studies as well as those of Lazarsfeld's group, empirical media research focused heavily on the study of media effects. Melvin DeFleur wrote (1970, p. 118), "The all-consuming question that has dominated research and the development of contemporary theory in the study of the mass media can be summed up in simple terms—namely, 'what has been their effect?' That is, how have the media influenced us as individuals in terms of persuading us."

Although the individual findings of effects research were enormously varied and even contradictory, two interrelated empirical generalizations emerged. These generalizations are consistent with the limited effects perspective outlined earlier and thus served to buttress it. These generalizations assert that the influence of mass media is rarely direct because it is almost always mediated by (a) *individual differences* and (b) *group membership or relationships*. These two factors normally serve as effective barriers to media influence. Study after study confirmed their existence and expanded our understanding of how they operate. DeFleur (1970) summarized this body of research when he offered "specific formulations that summarize contemporary thinking about the effects of mass communication."

Two of these formulations clearly owe their existence to persuasion and attitude change theory:

INDIVIDUAL DIF-
FERENCES *Individ-
uals' different
psychological
make-ups that
cause media influ-
ence to vary from
person to person*

SOCIAL CATEGORIES
*The idea that mem-
bers of given
groups or aggre-
gates will respond
to media stimuli in
more or less uni-
form ways*

1 **Individual differences** theory argued that, because people vary greatly in their psychological make-up and because they have different perceptions of things, media influence differs from person to person. More specifically, "media messages contain particular stimulus attributes that have differential interaction with personality characteristics of members of the audience" (DeFleur, 1970, p. 122).

2 **Social categories** theory "assumes that there are broad collectives, aggregates, or social categories in urban-industrial societies whose behavior in the face of a given set of stimuli is more or less uniform" (DeFleur, 1970, p. 122–123). In addition, people with similar backgrounds (for example, age, gender, income level, religious affiliation) will have similar patterns of media exposure and similar reactions to that exposure. This set of generalizations derives partly from Lazarsfeld's work, but both surveys and the attitude change researchers' experiments have demonstrated the validity of social categories theory.

The Selective Processes

COGNITIVE CONSIS-
TENCY *The idea
that people con-
sciously and uncon-
sciously work to
preserve their
existing views*

COGNITIVE DISSO-
NANCE *Information
that is inconsistent
with a person's
already-held atti-
tudes creates psy-
chological discom-
fort or dissonance*

One central tenet of attitude change theory that was adopted (in one way or another or under one name or another) by influential mass communication theorists from Lazarsfeld to Klapper to DeFleur, is the idea of **cognitive consistency**. We noted earlier that Lazarsfeld found that people seemed to seek out media messages consistent with the values and beliefs of those around them. This finding implied that people tried to preserve their existing views by avoiding messages that challenged them. As persuasion research proceeded, researchers sought more direct evidence. Cognitive consistency was defined as "a tendency (on the part of individuals) to maintain, or to return to, a state of cognitive balance, and . . . this tendency toward equilibrium determines . . . the kind of persuasive communication to which the individual may be receptive" (Rosnow & Robinson, 1967, p. 299). These same authors wrote, "Although the consistency hypothesis is fundamental in numerous theoretical formulations . . . of all the consistency-type formulations, it is Leon Festinger's theory of **cognitive dissonance** which has been the object of greatest interest and controversy" (1967, p. 299–300).

Festinger explained that the bedrock premise of dissonance theory is that information that is not consistent with a person's already-held values and beliefs will create a psychological discomfort (dissonance) that must be relieved; people generally work to keep their knowledge of themselves and their knowledge of the world somewhat consistent. More specifically, Festinger said, "If a person knows various things that are not psychologically consistent with one another, he will, in a variety of ways, try to make them more consistent" (1962, p. 93).

SELECTIVE
PROCESSES *Expo-
sure (attention),
retention, and
perception; psycho-
logical processes
designed to reduce
dissonance*

Collectively, these "ways" have become known as the **selective processes.** Some psychologists consider these to be defense mechanisms that we routinely use to protect ourselves (and our egos) from information that would threaten us. Others argue that they are merely routinized procedures for coping with the enormous quantity of sensory information constantly bombarding us. Either way, the selective processes function as complex and highly sophisticated filtering mechanisms that screen out useless sensory data while quickly identifying and highlighting the most useful patterns in this data.

In arguing that "the (mass) communication itself appears to be no sufficient cause of the effect," Klapper (1960, pp. 18–19) offered his conclusion that "reinforcement is or may be abetted by predispositions and the related processes of selective exposure, selective perception and selective retention." His explanation of how these selective processes protect media content consumers from media's impact neatly echoes Festinger's own presentation. Klapper (1960, p. 19) wrote, "By and large, people tend to expose themselves to those mass communications that are in accord with their existing attitudes and interests. Consciously or unconsciously, they avoid communications of opposite hue. In the event of their being nevertheless exposed to unsympathetic material, they often seem not to perceive it, or to recast and interpret it to fit their existing views, or to forget it more readily than they forget sympathetic material."

Attitude change researchers studied three forms of selectivity: exposure, retention, and perception. Keep in mind that these notions have since been widely criticized and should be interpreted very carefully. We will point out some of the major limitations as we discuss each.

SELECTIVE EXPOSURE
*People tend to
expose themselves
to messages that
are consistent with
their preexisting
attitudes and belief*

Selective exposure is people's tendency to expose themselves to or attend to media messages that they feel are in accord with their already-held attitudes and interests and the parallel tendency to avoid that which might be dissonance-creating. Democrats will watch their party's national convention on television, but go bowling when the GOP gala is aired. Lazarsfeld, Berelson, and Gaudet (1944, p. 89), in their Erie County voter study, discovered that "about two-thirds of the constant partisans (Republicans and Democrats) managed to see and hear more of their own side's propaganda than the opposition's . . . But—and this is important—the more strongly partisan the person, the more likely he is to insulate himself from contrary points of view."

In retrospect, we now realize that during the 1940s people commonly had media use patterns that were strongly linked to their social status and group affiliation. Newspapers still had strong party connections. Most were Republican. Thus, Republicans read newspapers with a strongly Republican bias, and Democrats either read Democratic newspapers or learned how to systematically screen out pro-Republican content. Radio stations tried to avoid most forms of political content but occasionally carried major political speeches. These weren't hard to avoid if you knew you didn't like the politics of the speaker. As media have changed during the intervening six decades, newspapers have become much less partisan and the demographics of their audiences have changed. Today, main-stream broadcast and print media create political news stories that avoid or carefully balance presentation of politically biased content. It has become harder for people to screen out partisan ideas. Candidates increasingly target their campaigns at independent voters by playing down their partisan ties and emphasizing their ability to rise above partisan politics and serve everyone. Not surprisingly, research has documented a steady decline in selective exposure to political information. The obvious content cues that once enabled consumers to avoid or screen out messages are gone.

SELECTIVE RETEN-
TION *People tend to remember best and longest those messages that are most meaningful to them*

Selective retention is the process by which people tend to remember best and longest information that is consistent with their preexisting attitudes and interests. Name all the classes in which you've earned the grade of "A." Name all the classes in which you've earned a "C." The A's have it, no doubt. But often you remember disturbing or threatening information. Name the last class you almost failed. Have you managed to forget it and the instructor or are they etched among the things you wish you could forget? If selective retention always operated to protect us from what we don't want to remember, we would never have any difficulty forgetting our problems. Although some people seem able to do this with ease, others tend to dwell on disturbing information. Contemporary thinking on selective retention ties that retention to the level of importance the recalled phenomenon holds for individuals.

SELECTIVE PERCEP-
TION *People will alter the meaning of messages so they become consistent with preexisting attitudes and beliefs*

Keeping in mind that these processes are not discrete (you cannot retain that to which you have not been exposed), **selective perception** is the mental or psychological recasting of a message so that its meaning is in line with a person's beliefs and attitudes. Klapper offers the famous Allport and Postman (1945) study of rumors as one example of how selective perception works. These two psychologists showed a picture of a fight aboard a train to some people. The combatants were a Caucasian male grasping a razor and an unarmed African American male. Those who saw the scene were then asked to describe it to another person who, in turn, passed it on. In 1945 America, the knife inevitably passed into the hands of the black man. Allport and Postman (1945, p. 81) concluded, "What was outer becomes inner; what was objective becomes subjective."

The attitude researchers who documented the operation of selective processes were good scientists. But their findings were based on people's use of a very different set of media and very different forms of media content than we know today. In the 1940s and 1950s, movies were primarily an entertainment medium; radio disseminated significant amounts of news, but typically as brief, highly descriptive reports that expressed no partisan opinion; newspapers were the dominant news medium; and television did not exist. Television moved all the

Instant Access

Attitude Change Theory

Strengths

1 Pays deep attention to process in which messages can and can't have effects

2 Provides insight into influence of individual differences and group affiliations in shaping media influence

3 Attention to selective processes helps clarify how individuals process information

Weaknesses

1 Experimental manipulation of variables overestimates their power and underestimates media's

2 Focuses on information in media messages, not on more contemporary symbolic media

3 Uses attitude change as only measure of effects, ignoring reinforcement and more subtle forms of media influence

media away from dissemination of information toward the presentation of images and symbols. Many contemporary movies sacrifice storyline and character development for exciting and interesting visuals; your favorite radio station (plus your second and third choices) probably present minimal news, if any; newspaper stories are getting shorter and shorter, the graphics more colorful and interesting, and more than a few papers across the country regularly present pictures snapped from a television screen in their pages. It's not surprising that we process information very differently today than our grandparents did in the 1940s.

Let's transport the valuable Allport and Postman experiment to our times to explain why the selective processes categorized by the attitude theorists and quickly appropriated by mass communication theorists might be less useful now in understanding media influence than they were in Allport and Postman's time.

If a speaker were to appear on television and present the argument, complete with charts and "facts," that a particular ethnic group or race of people was inherently dangerous, prone to violent crime, and otherwise inferior to most other folks, the selective processes should theoretically kick in. Sure, some racists would tune in and love the show. But most people would not watch. Those who might happen to catch it would no doubt selectively perceive the speaker as stupid, sick, beneath contempt. Three weeks later, this individual would be a vague, if not nonexistent memory.

But what if television news—because it is easier to cover violent crime rather than white-collar crime and because violent crime, especially that committed downtown near the studio, provides better pictures than a scandal in the banking industry—were to present inner-city violence to the exclusion of most other crime? What if entertainment programmers, because of time, format, and other pressures (Gerbner, 1990), continually portrayed their villains as, say, dark, mysterious, different? Do the selective processes still kick in? When the ubiquitous mass media that we routinely rely on repeatedly provide homogeneous and biased messages, where will we get the dissonant information that activates our psychological life preservers?

Today, more than fifty years after the Allport and Postman study, would the knife still find its way from the white man's hand into the black man's? Why was our country (police and government officials, the media, we) so willing to accept Charles Stuart's account of a black man shooting his pregnant wife as the expectant parents left their birthing lesson in Boston and that of Susan Smith, who in 1994 convinced a large portion of the country that an African American car-jacker had drowned her two young sons (see Box 6a)? Later chapters that deal with theories that view mass communication as more symbolically, rather than informationally, powerful will address these questions.

The Hovland-Lazarsfeld Legacy

The wealth of empirically based knowledge generated by persuasion research and, more important, the often conflicting, inconclusive, and situationally specific research questions it inspired, have occupied many communication researchers for decades. Together with the survey research findings produced by Lazarsfeld, these data challenged and ultimately undermined mass society notions. In the next chapter, we will discuss how a new and quite powerful paradigm emerged that claimed to be based on all this data. Miller and Burgoon (1978, p. 29) acknowledged the powerful initial influence of the new paradigm when they commented regarding the Hovland work, "The classic volumes of the 'Yale Group' . . . were accorded a seminal status comparable to that conferred on the Book of Genesis by devoted followers of the Judeo-Christian religious faith."

This body of work deserves recognition but not reverence. It was thorough, sophisticated, and groundbreaking—but it was not Truth. Along with Lazarsfeld's research, Hovland's work spawned literally thousands of research efforts on and dozens of intellectual refinements of the process of communication. But now, more than half a century later, we have only begun to put this work into perspective and understand its limitations as well as its considerable merits. Though the new paradigm shed important light on the process of communication, it failed to illuminate all aspects of the process. The beam it cast was narrow, obscuring some important features of the process while highlighting some trivial properties. Thus, its contribution to our overall understanding of the role of mass media in the society at large was at best misleading, and at worst erroneous.

Box 6a Charles Stuart and Susan Smith: Allport and Postman Revisited

Two shameful occurrences in American race relations exemplify the operation of selective perception at the macro, or cultural level. On the night of October 23, 1990, expectant father Charles Stuart phoned Boston's 911 emergency service from his car. "My wife's been shot. I've been shot," he gasped, "It hurts. And my wife has stopped gurgling. She's stopped breathing." The tape of his frantic, desperate call was played on local and national radio and television. A news crew, who happened to be traveling with the emergency team that responded to the plea, caught the gruesome scene in pictures: the 30-year-old pregnant woman, dead, her head smashed by the assailant's bullet, blood flooding the young couple's automobile.

But fortunately Stuart was able to describe the beast who had committed this atrocity. He was a raspy-voiced black man, dressed in a jogging suit, brandishing a snubbed-nose .38. The shootings occurred in a dark street in Boston's racially mixed Mission Hill District. The city's mayor, Raymond Flynn, ordered all available detectives onto the case. Police and prominent government officials attended Carol Stuart's funeral and visited severely wounded Charles in the hospital. Flynn called him a hero.

Soon, police were randomly stopping 200 men a day for questioning and frisking. What made them appear suspicious? They were young and black.

Boston NAACP president, Louis Elisa, likened the atmosphere in the city to that of a "lynch-mob." Prominent African American community leader, Reverend Charles Smith, accused the media of "overkill" in their reports showing "the worst of what black people are supposed to be." Eventually, police arrested William Bennett, an unemployed black man with a long criminal record. Justice was done.

Not quite. Three months later, about to be exposed by the police, Charles Stuart committed suicide by plunging into the frozen Mystic River and drowning. He had killed his wife and shot himself to collect insurance money and set up a new life with his mistress.

How did this happen? Even though federal crime statistics show that one-third of all the women murdered in the United States are killed by their husbands, how was this diabolical man able to fool the police, the media, and the public so dramatically and for so long? How was one man able to move police to terrorize innocent people? Allport and Postman had the answer in 1945.

Limitations of the Experimental Persuasion Research

Like the research approach developed by Lazarsfeld, the Yale approach had important limitations. Here they are listed and compared with those described for the Lazarsfeld research.

1   Experiments were conducted in laboratories or other artificial settings to control extraneous variables and manipulate independent variables. But it was often difficult to relate these results to real-life situations. Many serious errors were made in trying to generalize from laboratory results. Also, most experiments

Box 6a   Charles Stuart and Susan Smith: Allport and Postman Revisited (*continued*)

Time magazine (Carlson, p. 10) had it in 1990: By identifying the killer as a black man, Stuart "raised the curtain on a drama in which the press and police, prosecutors, politicians and the public played out their parts as though they were following the script for the television movie that CBS will make about the case. Instead of suspicion, Stuart was showered with sympathy. The media apotheosized the couple as starry-eyed lovers out of Camelot cut down by an urban savage."

At least the country learned its lesson. Again, not quite. Like Stuart's, the saga of Susan Smith also began with a 911 phone call. "There's a lady who came to our door. Some guy jumped into her car with her two kids in it, and he took off," the caller told the Union, South Carolina, police dispatcher on October 25, 1994 (Gibbs, 1994, p. 44). At least the distraught mother of two boys, one 3 years and the other 14 months old, was able to describe the kidnapper: black, in his twenties, wearing jeans, a plaid shirt, and a knit hat. Soon, thousands of police, FBI, state troopers, and volunteers began the search. A tearful Susan appeared on the *Today* show, begging the kidnapper to return her babies. As the young mother showed videotapes of her precious sons, the nation cried with her. But two weeks after the abduction,

Smith confessed to strapping those very children into their car seats and driving her 1990 Mazda into a lake, drowning them. Again, as with Stuart, Smith wanted to start a new life with her lover—and she thought the kids would just get in the way.

Skeptical police had broken the case. Knowing that a kidnapped child is 100 times more likely to be taken by a family member than by a stranger, they never removed Smith from their list of suspects and pressured her constantly about the details of the crime. But what about the rest of us? What about the searchers? The producers at NBC's *Today*? How could Smith have succeeded in fooling so many people for so long? Again, Allport and Postman offered an answer in 1945. Richard Lacayo, writing in *Time*, offered his in 1994: "Susan Smith knew what a kidnapper should look like. He should be a remorseless stranger with a gun. But the essential part of the picture—the touch she must have counted on to arouse the primal sympathies of her neighbors and to cut short any doubts—was his race. The suspect had to be a black man. Better still, a black man in a knit cap, a bit of hip-hop wardrobe that can be as menacing in some minds as a buccaneer's eye patch. Wasn't that everybody's most familiar image of the murderous criminal?" (p. 46).

take place over relatively short time periods. Effects that don't take place immediately were not found. Hovland found long-term effects only because the military trainees he was studying were readily accessible for a longer period. Most researchers don't have this luxury. Some are forced to study "captive" but atypical populations like students or prisoners.

2 **Experiments have the opposite problems from surveys when researchers study the immediate effects of specific media messages.** As noted earlier in this chapter, it is cumbersome if not impossible to study effects of specific messages using surveys. By contrast, experiments are ideally suited to studying the immediate

effects of specific media content on small or homogeneous groups of people. Experiments aren't, however, suited to studying the cumulative influence of patterns of overall media use within large, heterogeneous populations.

This limitation of experimental research has produced serious biases in the findings that have accumulated. Because the study and comparison of an individual medium's influence was difficult, research often failed to distinguish results based on messages delivered through a mass medium (like film) from those generated in research dependent on messages presented by speakers (for example, an adult speaking about the value of woodcrafts to a group of Boy Scouts) or by printed expressions of opinion. As a result, the persuasion research directed attention away from the power of the media themselves and focused attention on message content. As late as 1972, for example, Alan Elms wrote, "The medium itself may indeed be the principal message in certain artistic productions or entertainments; it is seldom so in communication designed (with any sort of competence) to be persuasive" (p. 184). But if serious lectures extolling young American soldiers to trust the Brits could have done the job, why did the Army commission the movie *Battle of Britain?* If you heard about the terrorist attack on the World Trade Center from another person, were you immediately and completely convinced by this story or did you turn to news media for information? If you were like most Americans, you turned to television for confirmation and programmers cooperated by turning their operations into 24-hour news channels with no commercial interruptions. Clearly, the medium can largely be the message when we are considering persuasion. Not until much later was this proposition seriously considered.

3 **Like the Lazarsfeld approach, the Hovland work is also inherently cautious in assessing media influence, but for very different reasons.** Lazarsfeld insisted on comparing the power of media with that of other social and demographic variables. These other variables were usually stronger. In an experiment, other variables aren't statistically controlled as is done in analyzing survey data; control is exercised by excluding variables from the laboratory and by randomly assigning research subjects to treatment and control groups. In controlling for extraneous variables, however, the researchers often eliminated factors that we now know to be crucial in reinforcing or magnifying media influence. For example, we now know that conversations with other people during or immediately after viewing television programs are likely to strengthen a broad range of media effects. If a researcher eliminates conversation from the laboratory, she or he will systematically underestimate the power of media in situations where personal conversations are otherwise likely.

4 **Like surveys, experiments are a very crude technique for examining the influence of media over time.** Conceivably, a researcher could set up an experimental group and bring it back to a laboratory after weeks or months. This ongoing experimentation could easily affect or bias the results. Imagine yourself as a partici-

pant, required to come into a laboratory every few days over a period of several months so that you can watch films in which women are violently attacked, raped, or murdered. What do you suppose your long-term reaction to these movies would be? Would it be the same as if you were a fan of such movies and regularly sought them out? Research like this has found that male subjects become desensitized to violence against women. They show a greater likelihood to blame rape victims rather than the rapists for causing this crime. What does this research prove? That a persistent researcher can turn an average male into an insensitive animal if he or she can just get him to sit through enough scenes of torture and mayhem? Or does it demonstrate that college students attending biweekly violence filmfests will eventually get bored and stop being aroused by every violent episode? Would you as a male participant be more likely to blame real life rape victims or are you simply more likely to blame the victims that you see on videotapes in the laboratory? Long-term effects of generic forms of media content have been quite hard to establish and have fueled legitimate debates among some of the most skilled researchers.

5 **As with surveys, there are many variables that experiments cannot explore.** For example, some real-life conditions are far too complex to be simulated in laboratories. In other cases, it would be unethical or even illegal to manipulate certain independent variables.

Summary

The 1938 *War of the Worlds* broadcast ushered in the limited effects paradigm. This paradigm shift was led by Paul Lazarsfeld and Carl Hovland and benefited from the refinement of empirical research methods, the failure of the mass society theorists to find evidence for their views, the commercial nature of the new research methods and their support by both government and business, and the spread of these methods to a wide variety of academic disciplines.

Lazarsfeld championed the inductive approach to theory construction and employed it in his 1940 voter studies and other research to develop the idea of a two-step flow of media influence. Along with other research of the time, this helped develop the outlines of the limited effects paradigm: Media rarely have direct effects; media influence travels from media, through opinion leaders, to opinion followers; group commitments protect people from media influence; and, when effects do occur, they are modest and isolated.

Hovland and other psychologists showed support for this limited effects view. Using controlled variation, these scientists demonstrated that numerous individual differences and group affiliations limited media's power to change attitudes.

This led logically to the development of dissonance theory, the idea that people work consciously and unconsciously to limit the influence of messages that run counter to their preexisting attitudes and beliefs. This dissonance reduction operated through selectivity in exposure (attention), retention, and perception.

Exploring Mass Communication Theory

 1   Orson Welles' *War of the Worlds* was important to the early limited effects researchers, as was Frank Capra's documentary film series *Why We Fight*. You can learn more on the Web about these creative geniuses and the works that helped change mass communication theory. Go to these sites to start your search and then follow the links they provide.

> *Orson Welles*
> http://www.fansites.com/orson_welles.html
>
> *Frank Capra*
> http://www.imsa.edu/~mitch/directors/capra.html

 2   Use **InfoTrac College Edition** to scan the tables of contents of as many psychology journals as you can find. Can you identify any articles that focus on persuasion and attitude change? If so, read a few that seem interesting to ascertain how much they rely on the early attitude change research of the Yale Group and its contemporaries.

 3   Use **InfoTrac College Edition** to scan the tables of contents of several political science or sociology journals. Can you find references to two-step flow and voting studies? If you can, read a few that seem interesting to ascertain how much they rely on the early voter studies of researchers like Lazarsfeld and Cantril.

Critical Thinking Questions

1   To what extent did you personally depend on opinion leaders to help you sort out the meaning of the attack on the World Trade Center and to what extent did you turn to media for an explanation? If you depended on other people, where do you think they got their information about the causes of the attack?

2   In the aftermath of the terrorist attack, most Americans strongly embraced U.S. symbols like the flag and the national anthem. Approval of the president exceeded 90 percent. Trust in government returned to levels not seen since the early 1960s before the Vietnam War, Watergate, and Monica-gate. Was this a media effect caused by the overwhelming media coverage of the attack? Or, was it a "natural" reaction to an attack by a foreign enemy?

3   Before the September 11, 2001, terrorist attacks on New York and Washington, what did you know about Islam? The Muslim world? The Taliban? U.S. involvement in Saudi Arabia and in the Russian-Afghan war? How much of what you did know came from the mass media? Which media outlets in particular provided you with the knowledge you did have? What were your attitudes about these things? From where did they come? If not from the media, then where? If you had little knowledge and no opinions or attitudes about these things that would eventually loom so large in American life and history, whose fault was that—the media's or yours?

4   How are you trying to envision your personal future in uncertain times? To what extent are you relying on media to help you assess job prospects in various careers? Are media helping you decide what lifestyle is appropriate or how to form relationships with other people?

5   Is there anything wrong with a political system in which many people rely on others to help them decide how to vote? Should everyone assume the responsibility of becoming well informed about every candidate in every election or is it acceptable if they depend on others and on political parties to decide how to vote. Is democracy in danger if most people are politically apathetic?

6   When it comes to media effects, do you think that you personally are more or less likely to be influenced by media? Were you more influenced by news about the terrorist attacks than your friends? Why or why not? How about advertising? Can you think of a recent advertising campaign that convinced you to buy a product? What was so persuasive about the ad?

Significant People and Their Writing

Allport, Gordon W. (1967). "Attitudes." In M. Fishbein, ed., *Readings in Attitude Theory and Measurement*. New York: Wiley.

Cantril, Hadley, Helen Gaudet, and Herta Herzog (1940). *Invasion from Mars*. Princeton, NJ: Princeton University Press.

Hovland, Carl I., Irving L. Janis, and Harold H. Kelley (1953). *Communication and Persuasion*. New Haven, CT: Yale University Press.

Katz, Elihu, and Paul F. Lazarsfeld (1955). *Personal Influence: The Part Played by People in the Flow of Communications*. New York: Free Press.

Kuhn, Thomas (1970). *The Structure of Scientific Revolutions*, 2nd edition. Chicago: University of Chicago Press.

Lazarsfeld, Paul F., Bernard Berelson, and Helen Gaudet (1944). *The People's Choice: How the Voter Makes Up His Mind in a Presidential Campaign*. New York: Duell, Sloan & Pearce.

Chapter 7

Middle-Range Theory and the Consolidation of the Limited Effects Paradigm

In the United States, the Golden Age of television began in the 1950s and continued throughout the 1960s. New television stations went on the air daily. Sales of television sets soared, and rooftop antennas became a status symbol. The highly successful introduction of color television during the 1960s confirmed the popularity of the new medium. People were willing to pay high prices and cope with sets that delivered unstable, inferior pictures.

In the space of two decades, the everyday life of the nation was radically altered. Visits with friends and extended family members declined sharply as more and more Americans, especially children, stayed at home to watch television. During popular programs, neighborhood streets and playgrounds were deserted.

How was the new medium affecting the nation? Were there negative effects, slowly undermining our mental ability or moral fiber? Among some social elites, mass society arguments resurfaced in new forms. Book after book catalogued speculation about the insidious influences of the mass culture being disseminated by television. Some warned that television was distracting attention from important things in life and turning us into passive couch potatoes. The civilizing influence of high culture was being undermined by mindless entertainment on television. How could we be good citizens if we relied on television for information? Some experts argued that within a few years, people's ability to read and write might disappear entirely—television would make literacy obsolete. Would a nation of illiterates be capable of self-government? How could such a country continue to produce scientists, doctors, or teachers?

Special attention was directed at television's influence on children. Would television so radically alter their experience that enormous social problems might be created in the space of one generation? According to Lawrence Freedman, "Psychiatrists have raised grave questions concerning the pathological implications of prolonged watching of television with its associated surrender of personal, physical, and intellectual ability. They see passivity merging into autism, and predisposing to dependent, schizoid, and withdrawn personalities" (1961, p. 190). Others worried that television violence would lead to widespread juvenile delinquency.

Not surprisingly, these fears spawned numerous research projects. Wilbur Schramm, Jack Lyle, and Edwin Parker (1961) directed one of the most ambitious. In the late 1950s, Schramm was a rising star among empirical media researchers. He had founded one of the first research centers for the scientific study of communication at the University of Illinois and had been hired to establish a similar center at Stanford University. With a large grant from the National Educational Television and Radio Center, he and his Stanford colleagues set out to demonstrate that social science research techniques could provide needed insight into the role of television in the lives of American children.

From 1958 to 1960, the Stanford team conducted 11 studies in 10 different cities. Interviews were conducted with 6,000 children and 2,000 parents. Schramm and his team published their findings in 1961 in a format designed to be read by parents as well as other researchers (all research design and data analyses were placed in methodological appendices). Their book provides a classic example of both the strengths and the limitations of the limited effects paradigm, which had been under development for almost two decades by the time Schramm and his colleagues undertook their work. They used newly refined empirical research methods, primarily survey interviews, to address a full range of questions about the influence of television on children. Computerized data analysis permitted the researchers to examine literally thousands of relationships between variables and to isolate those that were statistically significant.

Yet, the Stanford team conducted its research without using a single, well-articulated theoretical framework. Instead, in keeping with the limited effects paradigm, it relied on a welter of empirical generalizations that had emerged from earlier studies, including notions about selectivity and individual differences. These were combined with others from diverse sources including Freudian psychology and behaviorism. Although Schramm and his team were guided by these ideas, like most limited effects researchers they preferred not to be "biased" by any well-developed theoretical framework. Rather, their ultimate goal was to construct a theory based on systematic empirical observation. To this end, they worked inductively, identifying consistencies in their data and then summarizing and interpreting them. Their conclusions? They wrote,

> No informed person can say simply that television is bad or good for children . . . For *some* children, under *some* conditions, *some* television is harmful. For *other* children under the same conditions, or for the same children under *other*

conditions, it will be beneficial. For *most* children under *most* conditions, *most* television is probably neither particularly harmful nor particularly beneficial. (Schramm, Lyle, & Parker, 1961, p. 1)

The team recognized that some readers wouldn't consider this a particularly satisfactory answer to their concerns. Parents didn't want to know what television did to most children—they wanted to know what it might do to their child. The Stanford approach couldn't explain media's influence on individual children, but it did rule out simplistic, mass society conceptions of media subversion. According to the researchers, the effect of television could most usefully be viewed as "an interaction between characteristics of television and characteristics of viewers."

Unfortunately, in 1960 we knew very little about the nature of this interaction. Therefore, the obvious solution was to do more research that investigated interrelationships between these variables. The researchers were optimistic about the potential of their work. They hoped that modern data analysis techniques would permit causal connections to be efficiently explored so that definitive conclusions about television uses and effects could be reached. Researchers believed that a useful theory of television effects based on hard, empirical facts could be constructed. In the meantime, we could reassure ourselves that whatever television was doing to us, it wasn't doing too much to most of us under most conditions.

In their analysis of the Schramm, Lyle, and Parker study, Shearon Lowery and Melvin DeFleur (1995) point out that throughout their book, Schramm and his team offered an implicit theory that allayed the fears of troubled parents and included comforting, traditional child-rearing truisms. In case after case, specific empirical findings were interpreted as proving the wisdom of these homilies. All was quite simple: "Good" parents had only to do what their family and friends told them to be the right thing and they would have nothing to fear from the new medium. In this view, childhood was seen as an unstable period when children were plagued by wild emotions and drawn toward strange fantasies, so it was not surprising that they were attracted by television that played on these emotions and fantasies. Children hadn't yet learned self-discipline and conformity; they didn't know what was good for them. Parents must provide the discipline and guidance necessary to get children through these crises so that they can mature into rational, responsible adults. Thus, Schramm and his colleagues asserted that the arrival of television hadn't radically altered child rearing. It had merely eliminated some old problems (reading comic books, for example) and substituted new ones. The researchers advised that although television might aggravate some child-rearing problems, these could be handled if parents provided a little extra care and understanding. In the words of Lowery and DeFleur,

> In short, some children could be "damned" by exposure to television. . . . Those who could be "saved" were those who enjoyed the WASP world of love, security, and middle class values. These were the simple solutions to the potential problems of television. (1995, p. 263)

These solutions were offered despite the fact that the data collected and analyzed by the researchers provided only indirect and superficial evidence in support of them. As Lowery and DeFleur (1995) noted, all the studies were cross-sectional (conducted at one particular point in time), but the Schramm team tried to draw firm conclusions about developmental changes in children that take place over time. To do so, they were forced to compare children at different ages and in different cities who had grown up while the medium of television itself was undergoing many changes. On the basis of this circumstantial evidence, the researchers evaluated middle-class child-rearing practices and concluded that they would effectively counteract any potential threat posed by television—a comforting message for troubled parents, but hardly good social science. The television industry and the U.S. government also found this message both plausible and self-serving because it absolved both from taking actions that would have threatened profits or proved politically controversial.

An interesting note of historic irony is that the most persuasive (and potentially damning) early research on children's ability to learn aggression from the media was being conducted at this very same time on Schramm's very same Stanford University campus by psychologist Albert Bandura (for example, Bandura, Ross, & Ross, 1963; see Chapter 8). This should offer some hint about the power of the dominant limited effects paradigm to structure mass communication scientists' interpretation of results.

Overview

During the 1960s and into the 1970s, the limited effects paradigm dominated American mass communication research. The increasing hegemony of a new theoretical paradigm normally goes unheralded, even by its major adherents. Unlike political ideologies, social theories normally aren't debated in public forums. Unlike new cars or brands of toothpaste, they aren't unveiled in front of television cameras before nationwide audiences. As the preceding chapter illustrated, new paradigms are created by loosely knit research communities with inspiration from key individuals like Paul Lazarsfeld and Carl Hovland. Communities form at a handful of universities and their influence gradually spreads outward. Their members share a common perspective that is acquired through collaboration on research and through graduate education. Fledgling researchers are trained to use specific theories and research methods.

As research communities evolve, the paradigm on which they are based gradually matures. At a certain point, if a particular community grows in size and produces widely accepted research, it publishes landmark studies—like the work of Schramm's team. These studies solidify the paradigm's dominance over rival perspectives.

In this chapter, we will discuss several of the "classic" studies that heralded the growing importance and utility of the limited effects perspective. Like the research by Schramm's Stanford group, these studies demonstrated the power of the paradigm and its ability to produce findings that had immediate, practical value. These findings addressed important, troubling questions concerning the role of media. All too often, however, researchers overgeneralized and made sweeping assertions and recommendations based on very marginal and tangential evidence. The view that media had limited effects was one that foundation, corporate, and government sponsors also found comforting. The most successful researchers were good entrepreneurs who sold their approaches and their findings to these sponsors. We will place these theories—functional analysis, information flow theory, information diffusion theory, phenomenistic theory, mass entertainment theory, and Elite Pluralism—into historical perspective and gauge their continuing impact on communication research.

Building a Paradigm

In discussing the development of scientific paradigms, Thomas Kuhn (1970) argued that although great individuals inspire paradigm shifts, the grunt work necessary to solidify an innovative perspective is done by technicians—people who competently execute individual research projects. Each project forms yet another building block for the paradigm. Master researchers such as Lazarsfeld and Hovland are like architects who draw plans for a skyscraper: Without the work of thousands of individual researchers, their blueprints would be useless.

Like buildings, once paradigms are constructed, they take on a life of their own—they reify the dreams of their builders. Unfortunately, reality rarely conforms to the dreamers' fondest hopes. By 1960, the limited effects paradigm was like a half-constructed skyscraper. Thousands of surveys and experiments had been conducted in accordance with the plans devised by the master architects. A structure, much like a framework of steel girders for a skyscraper, had been built but many details remained to be filled in. The research we've been discussing outlines this structure: Media influence *some* people, under *some* conditions, but not *most* people under *most* conditions. But which media influence which people under which conditions? To answer this question, the paradigm needed to be elaborated, and that required lots of research.

Unlike a physical building, you can't see a paradigm. To be serviceable, the limited effects paradigm had to be *envisioned*—an effort had to be made to look at all the pieces of research and locate consistencies in them. Then, new theories had to be created that accounted for these consistencies. Until the late 1950s, social researchers were plagued by a myriad of competing conceptualizations and findings. Once the limited effects paradigm solidly emerged, it quickly gained popularity among empirical researchers because it summarized the bulk of existing findings. Those that didn't fit were relegated to obscurity.

The paradigm, before dominating, passed through a crucial period of development. A new generation of researchers, led by people like Schramm, reinterpreted the work of their predecessors and built upon it. New research was conducted and new theories were developed that were consistent with the paradigm. Most researchers in this second generation had either been trained by pioneer empirical researchers or were strongly influenced by their writing.

The effort to find meaning in the welter of individual empirical studies could have failed. Even with superior resources, researchers might have lost confidence, misinterpreted findings, or based their theories on misleading findings. Given the cost of conducting empirical research, corporate, foundation, and government sponsorship was especially essential during this stage. In addition to paying for this research, sponsorship by elite funding agencies such as the Rockefeller Foundation, the Columbia Broadcasting System, or the National Science Foundation legitimized the paradigm (Gary, 1996).

In the late 1950s, the utility of the limited effects paradigm was not obvious to all or even most social researchers. Many were troubled by its dependence on induction and its rejection of speculative theory. There were strong reactions against its proponents. Often, these judgments were ill conceived—based on misinterpretations of the new paradigm and prejudices against quantitative research. But occasionally people who were knowledgeable about both the paradigm's strengths and limitations made the criticisms. C. Wright Mills, a Harvard sociologist, offered perhaps the most intelligent and devastating criticism. Mills had been personally tutored by Lazarsfeld and served as field director for the survey of housewives in Decatur in 1943. In the early 1950s, he abandoned empirical social research and eventually labeled it "abstracted empiricism." He argued that it stifled the "sociological imagination" (Mills, 1959) and produced highly misleading insights into the social order. He was especially concerned that the new paradigm tended to produce findings that justified the status quo. Mills believed that radical changes were needed in the American social order, and he viewed the paradigm as overly conservative and inhibiting. The basis for his criticisms and the consequences of his challenge will be discussed later in this chapter.

Robert Merton: Master Paradigm Maker

Most of the disciples of the paradigm's architects followed their mentors but did little to advance development of the limited effects paradigm. They were content to simply conduct empirical research and address the many research questions that kept springing up. Nevertheless, a few ambitious or thoughtful devotees tried to take stock of what had been done. They wanted to know how all the individual research findings might be added up or collated. To do this, new theories were needed. As these theories were created, the outlines of the paradigm became clearer.

Fortunately for these thinkers, a master theorist guided and inspired their work. Robert Merton could truly claim to bridge the world of grand sociological theory in the tradition of Émile Durkheim and Karl Marx and the world of microscopic sociological observation as practiced by Lazarsfeld, Hovland, and Schramm. Merton was convinced that empirical research would succeed only if it eventually led to the construction of a body of abstract theory. In the late 1940s, when most empirical researchers were content to write grants, conduct field studies, run experiments, and report data, Merton began writing about the necessity of constructing a paradigm to support the empirical approach to research (Merton, 1949).

The book that made Merton's reputation as a sociologist was *Social Theory and Social Structure* (1949). His work on the art of paradigm construction continued through the 1950s and 1960s and culminated with the publication of *On Theoretical Sociology* (1967). For more than two decades, Merton tutored a host of thoughtful and reflective empirical researchers. He gave them a perspective from which to interpret their work, and he taught them the necessity of combining induction with deduction. More than any other individual, Merton provided a conceptual foundation for the new paradigm.

Merton was a strong advocate for what he called "theories of the middle range." Unlike grand social theories (that is, mass society theory) that attempted to explain all forms of social action, middle-range theories were designed to explain only limited domains or ranges of action that had been or could be explored using empirical research. According to Merton,

> Some sociologists still write as though they expect, here and now, formulation of *the* general sociological theory broad enough to encompass the vast ranges of precisely observed details of social behavior, organization, and change and fruitful enough to direct the attention of research workers to a flow of problems for empirical research. This I take to be a premature and apocalyptic belief. We are not ready. Not enough preparatory work has been done. (1967, p. 45)

Merton described middle-range theory as follows:

1 Middle-range theories consist of limited sets of assumptions from which specific hypotheses are logically derived and confirmed by empirical investigation.

2 These theories do not remain separate but are consolidated into wider networks of theory.

3   These theories are sufficiently abstract to deal with differing spheres of social behavior and social structure, so that they transcend sheer description or empirical generalization.

4   This type of theory cuts across the distinction between micro-sociological problems.

5   The middle-range orientation involves the specification of ignorance. Rather than pretend to knowledge where it is in fact absent, this orientation expressly recognizes what must still be learned to lay the foundation for still more knowledge (1967, p. 68).

Middle-range theory provided a useful rationale for what most empirical researchers, including media scientists, were already doing (Merton, 1967, p. 56). Many were determined to ignore what they considered unnecessary theoretical baggage and to focus on developing and applying empirical research methods. They believed that the future of social science lay in producing and collating empirical generalizations. Following the examples set by Lazarsfeld and Hovland, researchers conducted endless surveys and experiments, gathering data to support or reject individual generalizations and constantly discovering new research questions requiring yet more empirical research. Merton argued that all this research work would eventually be brought together to first create an array of middle-range theories and then to construct a comprehensive theory that would have the power and scope of theories in the physical sciences. Moreover, when it was finally constructed, this theory would be far superior to earlier forms of social theory that were not empirically grounded.

Thus, middle-range theory provided an ideal rationale for limited effects research. It implied that eventually all the individual effects studies would add up and a broad perspective on the role of media could be constructed. Yet, middle-range theory had important shortcomings that were not immediately apparent. Countless empirical generalizations were studied, but the effort to combine them into broader theories proved more problematic than had been expected. Numerous interesting and useful middle-range theories were created, but broader theories based on middle-range notions had crucial limitations. As we describe some of the more influential middle-range theories developed as part of the limited effects paradigm, we touch on a few of those shortcomings.

The Functional Analysis Approach

In *Social Theory and Social Structure,* Merton proposed what he called a "paradigm for functional analysis" that outlined how an inductive strategy centered around the study of social artifacts (such as the use of mass media) could eventually lead

FUNCTIONAL ANALY-
SIS *The study of
media for their
contribution to a
society that is a
"system in bal-
ance"—typically
value neutral*

to the construction of theories that explained the "functions" of these items. Merton derived his perspective on functional analysis from carefully examining research in anthropology and sociology. **Functional analysis** assumes that a society can be usefully viewed as a "system in balance." That is, the society consists of complex sets of interrelated activities, each of which supports the others. Every form of social activity is assumed to play some part in maintaining the system as a whole.

One feature of functional analysis that appealed to Merton and his followers was its apparent *value neutrality*. Older forms of social theory had characterized various parts of society as either "good" or "evil" in some ultimate sense. For example, mass society theory saw media as disruptive and subversive, a negative force that somehow had to be brought under control. Functionalists rejected such thinking and instead argued that empirical research should investigate both the functions and dysfunctions of media. Then a systematic appraisal could be made of media's overall impact. Functionalists believed that social science had no basis and no need for making value judgments about media. Rather, empirical investigation was necessary to determine whether specific media perform certain functions for the society.

This notion can be further illustrated by a functional analysis of primitive tribal society. According to functionalists, all the tribe's activities and practices can be assumed to be interrelated in such a way that the tribe is able to survive in and adapt to a specific physical environment. All practices that contribute to maintaining the tribe can be said to be *functional* rather than good. Any practices that are disruptive or harmful are by definition *dysfunctional* rather than evil. Some individual practices will be found to be functional in certain respects but dysfunctional in others. Some tribal members will be helped or harmed under some conditions. As long as functional practices dominate and dysfunctional practices are kept to some minimum, the tribe will flourish—it can be said to be "in balance" because the functional practices balance out the dysfunctional ones.

MANIFEST FUNC-
TIONS *Intended
and observed con-
sequences of media
use*

LATENT FUNCTIONS
*Unintended and
less easily observed
consequences of
media use*

Merton also distinguished **manifest functions**—those consequences that are intended and readily observed—and **latent functions**—those that are unintended and less easily observed.

This functional analysis was widely adopted as a rationale for many mass communication studies during the 1950s and 1960s. Researchers tried to determine whether specific media or forms of media content were functional or dysfunctional. Manifest and latent functions of media were investigated. What was learned was that functional analysis could be quite complicated. Various forms of media content can be functional or dysfunctional for society as a whole, for specific individuals, for various subgroups in the society, or for the culture. Thus, news that alerts society to a corrupt politician is functional for the society but dysfunctional for the politician. If the politician is a member of an ethnic group—

Instant Access	*Functional Analysis*	

Strengths	Weaknesses
1 Positions media and their influence in larger social system	1 Is overly accepting of status quo
2 Offers balanced view of media's role in society	2 Dysfunctions are too easily "balanced" by functions
3 Is based on and guides empirical research	3 Negative latent functions are too easily "balanced" by positive manifest functions
	4 Rarely permits definitive conclusions about media's role in society

say Irish or Italian—public hostility might be aroused against the group and the news would be dysfunctional for the group. Thus, the functions for society can be offset by the dysfunctions for individuals or for particular minority groups. Individuals might have to endure things that are dysfunctional for them personally as long as these are functional for the society as a whole.

This example illustrates one key problem with functional analysis: It rarely permits any definitive conclusions to be drawn about the overall functions or dysfunctions of media. In general, functional analysis produces conclusions that largely legitimize or rationalize the status quo. Researchers and theorists can easily avoid drawing controversial conclusions by simply noting that dysfunctions are balanced by functions. For example, existing forms of media content and the industries that produce them can be assumed to be functional. After all, if society isn't literally falling apart, then it must be in balance. If it is in balance, then we can deduce that the overall influence of factors such as media must either be positive or only slightly negative. Effects that are obviously negative can be found to be offset by positive effects. If we eliminate the negative effects, then we might also eliminate the positive effects that balance them. Are we willing to pay that price? Researchers were usually content to point to the existence of such balanced effects and then conclude that there was little that could or should be done about them.

Functional analysis and the limited effects paradigm made a good fit. If media influence was modest, media couldn't be too dysfunctional. As we've already seen, for example, in 1961, Schramm, Lyle, and Parker found that although viewing of certain forms of violent television content encouraged *some* children to be aggressive, this was more than offset by *most* children showing little or no influence.

Some might even learn how to anticipate and cope with aggressive peers. Thus, as far as the social system as a whole is concerned, Schramm, Lyle, and Parker concluded that violent television content doesn't make much difference despite being dysfunctional for a few children (those "damned" by their "bad" parents to be manipulated by television violence). By contrast, at precisely the same time, researchers from psychology, bound by neither functional analysis nor the limited effects paradigm, were making significant and persuasive arguments about the harmful effects of mediated violence (Chapter 8).

Information Flow Theory

During the 1950s, many surveys and field experiments were conducted to assess the flow of information from media to mass audiences. Among the types of information flow research that was conducted were studies of how quickly people found out about individual news stories (Funkhouser & McCombs, 1971). The overall objective of this work was to assess the effectiveness of media in transmitting information to mass audiences. The research was patterned after persuasion research, but investigated whether information was learned instead of measuring shifts in attitudes. Survey research rather than controlled experiments were used to gather data.

Information flow research addressed research questions that were thought to be quite important. If our democracy was to survive the challenges of the Cold War, many researchers believed that it was critical that Americans be well informed about a variety of issues. For example, Americans needed to know what to do in the event of a nuclear attack. They also needed to know what their leaders were doing to deal with threats from abroad. Classic theories of democracy assume that the public must be well informed so that people can make good political decisions. The flow of information from elites to the public was considered essential if the United States was to counter the Communist threat.

Persuasion research had identified numerous barriers to persuasion. News flow research focused on determining whether similar barriers impeded the flow of information from media to typical audience members. Some barriers investigated included level of education, amount of media use for news, interest in news, and talking about news with others. The researchers differentiated between "hard" and "soft" news. Hard news typically included news about politics, science, world events, and community organizations. Soft news included sports coverage, gossip about popular entertainers, and human-interest stories about average people.

The news flow research found that most U.S. citizens learned very little about hard news from news media because they were poorly educated, made little use of media for hard news, had low interest in hard news, and didn't talk to other people about hard news (Davis, 1990). Except for major news events such as President Eisenhower's heart attack or the assassination of President John F. Kennedy, most people didn't know or care much about national news events. Soft news generally was more likely to be learned than hard news, but even the flow of soft news was not what might have been hoped. The most important factor that accelerated or reinforced the flow of news was the degree to which people talked about individual news items with others. News of the Kennedy assassination reached most people very rapidly because people interrupted their daily routine to tell others about it (Greenberg & Parker, 1965). Otherwise, learning about most hard news events rarely reached more than 10 to 20 percent of the population and was forgotten by those people within a few days or weeks.

Studies of the flow of civil defense information identified similar barriers (DeFleur & Larsen, 1958). In most cases, the members of the public were even less interested in mundane civil defense information than they were in politics. In a series of field experiments, hundreds of thousands of leaflets were dropped on small, isolated towns in the state of Washington. The researchers wanted to determine how effective they would be in warning people about incoming Soviet bombers. For example, one set of leaflets announced that a civil defense test was being conducted. Every person who found a leaflet was instructed to tell someone else about it and then drop the leaflet in a mailbox.

The researchers were disappointed that relatively few folks read or returned the leaflets. Children were the most likely to take the leaflets seriously. To get the most useful effect, eight leaflets had to be dropped for every resident of a town. Speculating that people were ignoring the leaflets because they only warned of a hypothetical attack, the researchers designed another field experiment in which people were supposed to tell their neighbors about a slogan for a new brand of coffee. Survey teams visited homes in a small town and told people that they could earn a free pound of coffee by teaching their neighbors the coffee slogan. The survey team promised to return the following week and if they found that neighbors knew the slogan, then both families would receive free coffee. The experiment produced mixed results. On the one hand, almost every neighboring family had heard about the coffee slogan and tried to reproduce it. Unfortunately, many gave the wrong slogan. The researchers reported interesting distortions of the original slogan; many people had shortened it, confused it with similar slogans, or recited garbled phrases containing a few key words. The research confirmed the importance of motivating people to pass on information, but suggested that even a free gift was insufficient to guarantee the accurate flow of information. If word of mouth was crucial to the flow of information, the possibility of distortion and misunderstanding was high. Even if media deliver accurate information, the news that reaches most people might be wrong.

Instant Access	*Information Flow Theory*	
Strengths	**Weaknesses**
1 Examines process of mass communication in real world	**1** Is simplistic, linear, source-dominated
2 Provides theoretical basis for successful public information campaigns	**2** Assumes ignorant, apathetic populace
3 Identifies barriers to information flow	**3** Fails to consider utility or value of information for receivers
4 Helps understanding information flow during crises	**4** Is too accepting of status quo

INFORMATION FLOW THEORY *Theory of how information moves from media to audiences to have specific intended effects (now known as* information diffusion theory*)*

SOURCE-DOMINATED THEORY *Theory that examines the communication process from the point of view of some elite message source*

The most important limitation of **information flow theory** is that it is a simplistic, linear, **source-dominated theory.** Information originates with authoritative or elite sources (the established media or the government, for example) and then flows outward to "ignorant" individuals. Barriers to the information flow are to be identified and overcome, and little effort is typically made to consider whether the information has any value or use for average audience members. Audience reactions to messages are ignored unless they form a barrier to information flow. Then, they must be studied only so that they can be overcome. Like most limited effects theories, information flow theory assumes that the status quo is acceptable. Elites and authorities are justified in trying to disseminate certain forms of information and average people will be better off if they receive and learn it. Barriers are assumed to be bad and, where possible, must be eliminated.

Information Diffusion Theory

In 1962, Everett Rogers combined the information flow research findings with studies about the flow of information and personal influence in several fields including anthropology, sociology, and rural agricultural extension work. He developed what he called diffusion theory, which can be seen as an extension of Lazarsfeld's original idea of the two-step flow. Rogers' effort at integrating information flow research with diffusion theory was so successful that information

INFORMATION DIFFU-
SION THEORY *The-
ory that explains
how innovations
are introduced and
adopted by various
communities*

EARLY ADOPTER *In
information diffu-
sion theory, people
who adopt an inno-
vation early, even
before significant
amounts of infor-
mation are received*

flow theory became known as **information diffusion theory.** Rogers assembled
data from numerous empirical studies to show that when new technological innovations are introduced, they will pass through a series of stages before being
widely adopted. First, most people will become *aware* of them, often through information from mass media. Second, the innovations will be adopted by a very
small group of innovators or **early adopters.** Third, opinion leaders learn from
the early adopters and try the innovation themselves. Fourth, if opinion leaders
find the innovation useful, they encourage their friends—the opinion followers.
Finally, after most people have adopted the innovation, a group of laggards or late
adopters make the change. This process was found to apply to most American
agricultural innovations.

Information diffusion theory is an excellent example of the power and the
limitations of a middle-range theory. It successfully integrates a vast amount of
empirical research. Rogers reviewed thousands of studies. Information diffusion
theory guided this research and facilitated interpretation of it but also had many
implicit assumptions limiting its use. Like information flow theory, information
diffusion theory is a source-dominated theory that sees the communication
process from the point of view of an elite that has decided to diffuse an innovation. This theory "improves" on information flow theory by providing more and
better strategies for overcoming barriers to innovations.

Information diffusion theory assigns a very limited role to mass media. Media
mainly create awareness of new innovations. Only the early adopters are directly
influenced by media content. Others adopt innovations only after being influenced by other people. Rogers recommended that diffusion efforts be led by

CHANGE AGENT
*In information
diffusion theory,
those who directly
influence early
adopters and opin-
ion leaders*

change agents, people who could go out into rural communities and directly influence early adopters and opinion leaders. Media are used to draw attention to
innovations and as a basis for group discussions led by change agents. This strategy was patterned after the success of agricultural extension agents in the American Midwest. Thus, information diffusion theory was consistent with other
versions of limited effects thinking.

Rogers' theory was enormously influential. The United States Agency for International Development (USAID) used the strategy to spread agricultural innovations in the Third World. During the Cold War of the 1950s and 1960s, the
United States competed against the U.S.S.R. for influence in the developing nations. The hope was that by leading a Green Revolution and helping them better
feed themselves, America would gain the favor of these emerging countries. But
to help them do this, the United States needed to convince peasants and rural vil-
lagers to adopt a large number of new agricultural innovations as quickly as possible. Rogers' information diffusion theory became a training manual for that
effort. Change agents from around the world were brought to Michigan State University to learn the theory from Rogers himself. Many of these people became

Instant Access

Information Diffusion Theory

Strengths	Weaknesses
1 Integrates large amount of empirical findings into useful theory	1 Is linear, source-dominated
2 Provides practical guide for information campaigns in United States and abroad	2 Underestimates power of media, especially contemporary media
	3 Stimulates adoption by groups that don't understand or want the innovation

academics in their home countries, and unlike many other U.S. theories, information diffusion theory spread through the universities of the developing nations while agricultural innovations were spreading in their fields. In many parts of the world, Rogers' theory became synonymous with communication theory.

Information diffusion theory represented an important advance over earlier limited effects theories. Like the other classic work of the early 1960s, this theory drew from existing empirical generalizations and synthesized them into a coherent, insightful perspective. Information diffusion theory was consistent with most findings from effects surveys and persuasion experiments, and above all, it was very practical. In addition to guiding Third World development, it laid the foundation for numerous promotional communication and marketing theories and the campaigns they support even today.

But information diffusion theory's limitations were also serious. It had some unique drawbacks stemming from its application. For example, it facilitated the adoption of innovations that were sometimes not well understood or even desired by adopters. For example, a campaign to get Georgia farm wives to can vegetables was initially judged a great success until it was found that very few women were using the vegetables. They mounted the glass jars on the walls of their living rooms as status symbols. Most didn't know any recipes for cooking canned vegetables—and those who tried using canned vegetables found that family members didn't like the taste. This experience was duplicated around the world; corn was grown in Mexico and rice was grown in Southeast Asia that no one wanted to eat; farmers in India destroyed their crops by using too much fertilizer; farmers adopted complex new machinery only to have it break down and stand idle after change agents left. Mere diffusion of innovations didn't guarantee long-term success.

Klapper's Phenomenistic Theory

In 1960, Joseph Klapper finally published a manuscript originally developed in 1949 as he completed requirements for a Ph.D. at Columbia University and worked as a researcher for CBS. *The Effects of Mass Communication* was a compilation and integration of all significant media effects findings produced through the mid-1950s and was intended for both scholars and informed members of the public. Klapper was concerned that average people exaggerated the power of media. Though informed academics (that is, empirical researchers) had rejected mass society theory, too many people still believed that media had tremendous power. He wanted to calm their fears by showing how limited media actually were in their ability to influence people.

PHENOMENISTIC THEORY *Theory that media are rarely the sole cause of effects and are relatively powerless when compared with other social factors*

Klapper introduced what he called **phenomenistic theory**. He argued that media rarely have any direct effects and are relatively powerless when compared with other social and psychological factors such as social status, group membership, strongly held attitudes, education, and so forth. According to Klapper,

1 Mass communication *ordinarily* does not serve as a necessary and sufficient cause of audience effects but, rather, functions among and through a nexus of mediating factors and influences.

2 These mediating factors are such that they typically render mass communication as a contributory agent, but not the sole cause, in the process of reinforcing existing conditions (1960, p. 8).

These arguments were not very original, but Klapper expressed them forcefully and cited hundreds of findings to support them. His book came to be viewed as the definitive statement on media effects—especially by those outside the media research community.

REINFORCEMENT THEORY *More common name for phenomenistic theory; stresses that theory's view of media's most common effect, reinforcement*

Klapper's theory is often referred to now as **reinforcement theory** because a key assertion is that the primary influence of media is to reinforce (not change) existing attitudes and behaviors. Instead of disrupting society and creating unexpected social change, media generally serve as agents of the status quo, giving people more reasons to go on believing and acting as they already do. Klapper argued that there simply are too many barriers to media influence for drastic changes to occur except under very unusual circumstances.

Even today, more than forty years after its introduction, phenomenistic theory is still raised by those unconvinced of media's power, although usually by its less formal name, reinforcement theory. Yet, its drawbacks are easily seen through benefit of hindsight. When published in 1960, Klapper's conclusions relied heavily on studies (from Lazarsfeld, Hovland, and so on) of a media environment that did not include the mass medium of television and the restructured newspaper,

Instant Access

Phenomenistic Theory

Strengths	Weaknesses
1 Combines impressive amount of research into a convincing theory	1 Overstates influence of mediating factors
2 Highlights role of mediating variables in the mass communication process	2 Is too accepting of status quo
3 Persuasively refutes lingering mass society notions	3 Downplays reinforcement as an important media effect
	4 Is too specific to its time (pre-1960s) and media environment (no television)

radio, and film industries that arose in response to television. Certainly, it did not envision a world of Internet and digital media. Much of the research Klapper cited examined the selective processes, but with the coming of television, media were becoming more symbolically rather than informationally oriented, producing potentially erroneous conclusions. In addition, the United States that existed after World War II looked little like the one that existed before. As we'll see in later chapters, Klapper's "nexus of mediating variables," that is, church, family, and school, began to lose their powerful position in people's socialization (and therefore in limiting media effects). Finally, Klapper might have erred in equating *reinforcement* with *no effects*. Even if it were true that the most media can do is reinforce existing attitudes and beliefs, this is hardly the same as saying they have no effect. You'll see in Chapter 9, as you did in the Chapter 4 discussion of contemporary propaganda theory, that many contemporary critical scholars see this as media's most negative influence. Box 7a presents Klapper's own explanation of his theory and asks you to assess it in light of some recent momentous events.

An Apology for Mass Entertainment

Another major compilation of media research findings was published by Harold Mendelsohn in 1966. As a young researcher, Mendelsohn was tutored by Lazarsfeld and served as the field director for the 1940 Erie County study. *Mass Entertainment* was intended as a scholarly examination of the role of television entertainment in American society. Like Klapper, Mendelsohn was concerned that

Box 7a   Joseph Klapper's Phenomenistic Theory

Joseph Klapper's own summary of his reinforcement or phenomenistic theory makes it clear that his ideas are very much at home in the limited effects paradigm. The following is drawn directly from his landmark work, *The Effects of Mass Communication*, published in 1960 (p. 8).

Theoretical Statements

1. Mass communication *ordinarily* does not serve as a necessary and sufficient cause of audience effects but, rather, functions among and through a nexus of mediating factors and influences.

2. These mediating factors are such that they typically render mass communication a contributing agent, but not the sole cause, in a process of reinforcing the existing conditions.

3. On those occasions that mass communication does function to cause change, one of two conditions is likely to exist:

   a. The mediating factors will be found to be inoperative and the effect of the media will be found to be direct.

   b. The mediating factors, which normally favor reinforcement, will be found to be themselves impelling toward change.

4. There are certain residual situations in which mass communication seems to produce direct effects, or directly and of itself to serve certain psychophysical functions.

5. The efficacy of mass communication, either as a contributory agent or as an agent of direct effect, is affected by various aspects of the media and communications themselves or of the communication situation.

Your Turn

Can you find hints in Klapper's overview of his theory's links to the dominant paradigm of its time? Can you identify his subtle explanation of why advertising seems to work, an important point to make for a fine scientist who was also chief researcher for broadcast network CBS? After reading his summary of phenomenistic theory, can you explain why it remains, even today, the clearest and most used articulation of media's limited effects? Can you develop an explanation for the power of media on September 11, 2001, based on point number 3 in Klapper's summary? Were the factors that normally mediate the power of media "inoperative"? Or were these factors "themselves impelling toward change?" List some of the factors that normally mediate the power of media. These would include things like personal relationships with friends and family, relationships with opinion leaders, contacts with teachers and classmates, or contacts with church members or religious leaders. Klapper would likely label the power demonstrated by media on September 11 as an anomaly—a rare exception to the rule that media power is constantly checked by "a nexus of mediating factors and influences." Do you agree? Would you argue that media have somehow become more powerful since Klapper developed his theory in the 1940s? If so, how was this power revealed on September 11th?

the influence of media was widely misunderstood. He blamed elite critics of media (mostly mass society theorists) for continuing to foster misconceptions about mass entertainment. He charged that these critics were protecting their own self-interests and were ignoring empirical research findings. His book reviewed

Instant Access

Mass Entertainment Theory

Strengths	Weaknesses
1 Stresses media's prosocial influence	**1** Is too accepting of the status quo
2 Provides cogent explanation for why people seek entertainment from media	**2** Paints negative picture of average people and their use of media

various mass society criticisms of mass entertainment and rejected them all. He dismissed most criticisms as prejudiced speculation that was inconsistent with empirical data. According to Mendelsohn, mass society critics were too paternalistic and elitist. They were upset because television entertainment attracted people away from the boring forms of education, politics, or religion that they, themselves, wanted to promote. Mendelsohn argued that average people needed the relaxation and harmless escapism that television entertainment offered. If television entertainment weren't available, people would find other releases from the tensions of daily life. Television simply served these needs more easily, powerfully, and efficiently than did other alternatives.

Instead of condemning television, Mendelsohn argued that the critics should acknowledge that it performs its function very well and at extremely low cost. He was concerned that critics had greatly exaggerated the importance and long-term consequences of television entertainment and asserted that it had a very limited and ultimately quite minor social role. Television entertainment did not disrupt or debase high culture, it merely gave average people a more attractive alternative to operas or symphony concerts. It did not distract people from important activities like religion, politics, or family life; rather, it helped them relax so that they could later engage in these activities with renewed interest and energy.

MASS ENTERTAIN-MENT THEORY *Theory asserting that television and other mass media, because they relax or otherwise entertain average people, perform a vital social function*

Mendelsohn cited numerous psychological studies to support his **mass entertainment theory**. He admitted that a small number of people might suffer because they became addicted to television entertainment. These same people, however, would most likely have become addicted to something else if television weren't available. Chronic couch potatoes might otherwise become lounge lizards or romance novel fans. Compared with these alternatives, he viewed addiction to television as rather benign: It didn't hurt other people and might even be slightly educational.

Mendelsohn's book provides an excellent example of how limited effects research and its findings can legitimize the status quo. Harmful effects are balanced by an overwhelming number of positive effects. Who can judge whether the harm being done is great enough to warrant making changes? Congress? The courts? The public? When the evidence is mixed, the best course of action would appear to be inaction.

Elite Pluralism

ELITE PLURALISM
Theory that political information in media serves little purpose except to inform the handful of people who are already well informed about politics and already engaged in political activity; they will represent all others intelligently

All the preceding efforts at paradigm construction were limited in scope compared with the development of **elite pluralism.** This idea was spawned partly as an effort to make sense of the voter research initiated by Lazarsfeld. In their report on the 1948 election campaign (Berelson, Lazarsfeld, & McPhee, 1954), Lazarsfeld and his colleagues noted important inconsistencies between their empirical observation of typical voters and the assumptions that classical democratic theory made about those same people. If the Lazarsfeld data were right, then classical democratic theory must be wrong. If so, what did this mean for the long-term survival of our social and political order? Was our political system a façade for a benign ruling class? Could a democratic political system continue to flourish if most citizens were politically apathetic and ignorant?

In characteristic fashion, the Lazarsfeld group offered a guardedly optimistic assessment. Lazarsfeld and his colleagues asserted that classical democratic theory should be replaced with an up-to-date perspective based on empirical findings. Classical democratic theory assumed that everyone must be well informed and politically active. The new perspective was based on empirical data that showed that average people didn't know or care very much about politics. Voting decisions were more likely to be based on personal influence than on reasoned consideration of the various candidates. People voted as their friends, family, and coworkers told them to vote, not as a political theorist would have liked them to vote.

The Lazarsfeld group argued that voter apathy and ignorance weren't necessarily a problem *for the political system as a whole.* A political system in which most people voted based on long-standing political commitments or alliances would be a stable system even if these commitments were based on prejudice and were held in place by emotional bonds to family and friends. The Lazarsfeld group believed that the important factor was not the quality of voting decisions but rather their stability. We are better off if our political system changes very slowly over time as a result of gradual conversions, they argued. We don't want sudden changes that could occur if everyone made rational, informed decisions using information from media. For example, there would be tragic consequences if many people based their vote decisions on bad or biased information from media. Nor could our political system handle the high levels of political activism that would occur if everyone took a strong interest in politics.

These arguments imply rejection of libertarian theory (see Chapter 5). If voters don't need to be informed or if informing them might actually lead to political disorder, then there is no need for communication media to deliver information. Research findings demonstrated that uncensored and independent media typically failed to diffuse political information to most people. If so, then what political role should media be expected to play? To reinforce the status quo except in times of crisis? Was there really a need for media to serve as a public forum as libertarian theory had assumed? If so, how should this forum operate and what resources would be necessary to make it work effectively? Limited effects research findings implied that such a public forum would serve little purpose except for the handful of people who were already well informed about politics and already engaged in political activity. These conclusions directed researchers away from the study of mass media and the formation of media policy and toward political parties, political socialization, and the institutions of government such as legislatures, political executives such as the President, and the legal system. These topics soon dominated the research agenda in political science.

The political perspective implicit in these arguments became known as elite pluralism. During the 1960s, elite pluralism was widely debated in political science and strongly challenged traditional forms of democratic theory. Elite pluralism claimed to be scientific because, in contrast with classical democratic theory, it was based on empirical data. V. O. Key provided one of its best formulations in *Public Opinion and American Democracy* (1961). Like Lazarsfeld, Key was optimistic in the face of apparently discouraging voter data. His book emphasized the strength and enduring value of the American political system, even if it fell short of being a classical democracy.

In some respects, elite pluralism is as contradictory as the two terms that make up its label. "Elite" implies a political system in which power is ultimately in the hands of a small group of influential persons, a political elite. "Pluralism" refers to cultural, social, and political diversity. It implies a political system in which many diverse groups are given equal status and representation. Can there be a political system that is based on both of these principles—a system in which power is centralized in the hands of the few but in which the rights and status of all minority groups are recognized and advanced? V. O. Key not only argued that it is possible to combine these two principles, but he also cited study after study that he interpreted as demonstrating that our political system already accomplished this.

Like the other examples of limited effects theory, elite pluralism assumes that media have little ability to directly influence people. Thus, media alone can't fundamentally alter politics. Elite pluralism rejects libertarian notions and argues that media, in the name of stability, should reinforce political party loyalties and assist the parties to develop and maintain large voter coalitions. Media shouldn't be expected to lead public opinion but, rather, should reinforce it. If change is to occur, it must come from the pluralistic groups and be negotiated and enacted by the leaders of these groups.

It is important to recognize that in constructing his perspective on American society, Key, like most limited effects researchers, went far beyond the small insight provided by his data. Although the ideas he advanced were consistent with the data available to him, other conclusions were equally reasonable. But when Key wrote his book, this was not well understood. His ideas gained widespread acceptance as a definitive interpretation of the data, and his talents as a writer also lent force to his theory.

C. Wright Mills and The Power Elite

Opposition to elite pluralism came from across the political spectrum. Most classical democratic theorists were offended by and disdainful of elite pluralism. They argued that even if the present political system was not a "true" democracy, efforts should be made to move the system in that direction. Either we should recapture the essence of democracy as envisioned by the Founding Fathers or we should take steps to break the power of existing elites. To opponents, elite pluralism was a rationalization of the status quo that provided no direction for future development. In an era when respect for normative and grand social theories was declining, however, it was hard for classical democratic theorists to defend their views against a "scientific" theory like elite pluralism.

The opposition to elite pluralism from the political left was spearheaded by Mills, whom we introduced earlier as a Harvard sociologist and rebel Lazarsfeld protégé. Mills rejected the argument that elite pluralism was more scientific than were other forms of political theory. Based on his knowledge of survey research, he was deeply skeptical of the data marshaled in its support. He argued that in American society, political power was not decentralized across a broad range of pluralistic groups. Instead, he believed that power was centralized in a small group of military-industrial-complex leaders whom he called *The Power Elite* (1957). This elite was not representative of pluralistic groups. Rather it was isolated from them and typically acted against their interests.

For almost a decade, the followers of Mills and those of Key were arrayed against each other. In this conflict, Key and his allies had many crucial advantages. Their research had larger and more secure funding from government agencies and private foundations. As such, elite pluralists successfully defended their claim of being more scientific in their research. Ultimately, Mills brought his own perspective into question by backing Fidel Castro's revolution in Cuba. Then, in 1962, Mills was killed in a tragic motorcycle accident. Criticism of elite pluralism was then muted as the nation turned its attention to Communist threats in Vietnam.

Instant Access

Elite Pluralism

Strengths	Weaknesses
1 Explains a stable U.S. social and political system	1 Legitimizes an undemocratic view of U.S. politics
2 Is based on wealth of empirical data	2 Goes well beyond empirical evidence for conclusions
3 Is a well developed and cogent theory	3 Is too accepting of the status quo
	4 Paints negative picture of average people and their media use

In *The Power Elite* and other books, Mills raised many disturbing questions about American politics. If elite pluralism was operating so effectively, why were so many minority groups receiving so little help? Why did average people feel so powerless and apathetic? Why did people choose to remain ignorant about politics? Why did the same people serve over and over again as leaders of supposedly independent social institutions? Why were the interests of the few so often pursued at the expense of average people? Why did political parties and other social institutions make no determined efforts to educate people about their interests or to mobilize them to take actions that might serve those interests? Why did mass media tend to merely reinforce the status quo rather than inspire people to take action against race- and social class-based discrimination? Mills proved prophetic because these same issues surfaced a decade later as part of a broad-based challenge to American social science and the American political system, and they form the focus of Chapter 9.

Assumptions of the Limited Effects Paradigm

The several views of media's impact described in this chapter are all part of the limited effects paradigm. This perspective of the media's power and influence is based on several assumptions, and it has numerous limitations that we have already discussed. The assumptions are as follows:

1 **Empirical social research methods can be used to generate theory through an inductive research process.** Exploratory, descriptive research is expected to produce empirical generalizations that can later be combined to form middle-range

theories. Eventually, middle-range notions can be combined to create broad, powerful social theories that are firmly grounded in empirical facts.

2   **The role of mass media in society is limited; media primarily reinforce existing social trends and only rarely initiate social change.** The media will cause change only if the many barriers to their influence are broken down by highly unusual circumstances. The empirical mass communication research discussed in this chapter supports this assumption. In study after study, little evidence of strong media influence was found. Even evidence of reinforcement was often lacking.

3   **Mass media's role in the lives of individuals is limited, but it can be dysfunctional for some types of people.** Media provide a convenient and inexpensive source of entertainment and information. But neither use has much long-term or important impact on the daily life of most people. Almost all information is either ignored or quickly forgotten. Entertainment mainly provides a temporary distraction from work, allowing people to relax and enjoy themselves so that they can go back to work refreshed. People who are adversely affected by media tend to have severe personality or social adjustment problems; they would be deeply troubled even if media weren't available.

4   **The U.S. political and social system is both stable and equitable.** Although not democratic in the classical sense, the U.S. system is nevertheless a viable and humane system that respects and nurtures cultural pluralism while preserving social order. There is no need for radical reform. Media play a limited, but nonetheless useful, functional role within the larger society. Potentially harmful effects can be detected and prevented should any appear.

Drawbacks of the Limited Effects Paradigm

We've discussed many of the limitations of the limited effects perspective in this chapter, but here they are briefly listed, accompanied by some new concerns.

1   **Both survey research and experiments have serious methodological limitations that were not adequately recognized or acknowledged.** Empirical researchers were anxious to popularize their approach and sometimes made exaggerated claims for it. Naive people outside the empirical research community made false assumptions about the power and usefulness of this type of research. When empirical researchers were directly challenged in the late 1960s, they were slow to acknowledge limitations of their work and reacted defensively.

2   **The methodological limitations of early empirical social research led to findings that systematically underestimated the influence of mass media for society and for individuals.** Researchers like Lazarsfeld and Hovland were inherently

SPURIOUS EFFECTS
A finding in a research study of a phenomenon that exists only in that study; a research artifact

cautious. They didn't want to infer the existence of effects that might not be there—**spurious effects.** The researchers developed methods designed to guard against this, but they risked overlooking or dismissing evidence that could have been interpreted as an argument for significant media effects. In their conclusions, they often failed to emphasize that they might be overlooking many types of media effects because they had no way of measuring them.

3 **Early empirical social research centered around whether media had immediate, powerful, direct effects; other types of influence were ignored.** This focus was justified for two reasons. First, the mass society paradigm, which had been dominant, asserted that such effects existed and should be easy to observe. This paradigm needed to be evaluated and the early limited effects research did so. Second, the early research methods were best suited to studying immediate, direct effects—if researchers couldn't "see" an effect, it didn't exist. Only later, as we'll see in subsequent chapters, did researchers develop techniques that permitted other types of influence to be empirically assessed.

Contributions of the Limited Effects Paradigm

1 **The limited effects paradigm effectively supplanted mass society theory as the dominant perspective on media.** Thus, the limited effects paradigm lessened unjustified fears about massive, uncontrollable media effects. This benefited media practitioners. Most important, it helped ease pressures for direct government censorship of media and permitted media practitioners to implement useful forms of self-censorship.

2 **The paradigm prioritized empirical observation and downgraded more speculative forms of theory construction.** It demonstrated the practicality and utility of empirical research and inspired development of a broad range of innovative methods for data collection as well as new techniques for data analysis. These empirical techniques have proved to be powerful and useful for specific purposes. If the paradigm had not become dominant, scientists might not have devoted the time and resources necessary to develop these techniques.

3 **Although the limited effects paradigm ultimately turned many established social scientists away from media study, it provided a useful framework for research done in universities and colleges during the 1950s and 1960s.** In hindsight, we can see that the paradigm was, to some extent at least, a self-fulfilling prophecy. It asserted that media had no socially important effects. This belief was based on research findings provided by crude data collection and analysis methods. These methods can now be interpreted as having grossly under-

estimated the influence of media. Unfortunately, by the time more sophisticated research techniques were developed, most social researchers in the established disciplines of sociology, psychology, and political science had stopped looking for important media effects. During the 1960s and 1970s, the work of mass communication researchers was viewed with considerable skepticism. What was there that we didn't already know about the role of media? Quite a lot, as we shall see.

Summary

As the number of research studies began to grow, a unifying framework was needed to combine them into a useable theory. Merton's middle-range theory met that need by legitimizing the value of combining numerous discrete, unrelated "smaller" theories into a convincing overview paradigm. Mass communication theorists seized on the idea and developed several middle-range theories that combined to solidify the limited effects paradigm.

Functional analysis described media as performing certain functions that allowed the larger social system to operate in balance. Information flow theory studied media's effectiveness in transmitting information to mass audiences, and its extension, information diffusion theory, provided an explanation for and guidebook to the use of communication to spread innovations. Klapper's phenomenistic, or reinforcement, theory provided a powerful argument for media as reinforcers of the status quo, unable to have powerful effects. Mendelsohn's mass entertainment theory made a similar argument, even stating that average people needed the relaxation provided by media to allow them to live their lives productively.

Elite pluralism notions, forcefully argued by Key and equally forcefully challenged by Mills, also offered a benign perspective on media influence: As most people were not interested or intelligent enough to use media to form meaningful political attitudes, this ineffectiveness of media actually served the U.S. social system by giving it its stability. As long as those who were more involved in or better at political discourse could get the information they needed, all Americans would be served.

Together, these middle-range theories came to define the limited effects paradigm and shared these assumptions: Empirical research can be used to generate useful theory, the role of media in society is limited, sometimes media can be dysfunctional for some types of individuals, and the U.S. social and political system is stable and fair.

The limited effects paradigm has its drawbacks: Both surveys and experiments have serious methodological limitations, these limitations consistently produced research findings that underestimated media's influence, and "effects" were defined as only those that were immediate and observable, ignoring other, possibly more important effects.

Exploring Mass Communication Theory

 1   Proponents of elite pluralism put their faith in traditional, established sources of political information and political action. This theory values the stability of the mainstream political parties over more populist forms of political action. Visit the Web sites of these political parties and identify themes that echo either Key's faith in elite pluralism or Mills' critique of it.

> *Democratic National Committee*
> http://www.democrats.org

> *Republican National Committee*
> http://www.rnc.org/

> *Green Party of North America*
> http://www.greens.org/

> *The Reform Party of the United States*
> http://www.reformparty.org/

 2   Information diffusion theory became the basis of much of the United States' foreign aid help to developing nations. In fact, the U.S. Agency for International Development explicitly adopted information diffusion theory. Visit the Web sites of these two aid organizations and try to determine if they continue to rely on this view of media.

> *United Nations Educational, Scientific and Cultural Organization (UNESCO)*
> http://www.unesco.org/

> *U.S. Agency for International Development*
> http://www.info.usaid.gov/

 3   Use **InfoTrac College Edition** to scan the tables of contents of several political science journals. *American Political Science Review* and *Political Science Quarterly* are good places to start. Find those articles that argue different sides of the elite pluralism debate. How would you characterize the dispute's current form?

 4   Use **InfoTrac College Edition** to scan the table of contents of *Campaigns & Elections*. Identify at least one article that discusses a campaign or campaigns that seem to have used either information flow or information diffusion theory. Explain your choice.

Critical Thinking Questions

1 Many of the middle-range theories we've discussed assume that the United States provides a viable and humane system that respects and nurtures cultural pluralism while preserving social order. During the 1980s and 1990s, the only apparent threat to social order was domestic crime. As such, recognition and acceptance of cultural pluralism became an important issue in U.S. political debate. But after September 11th, increasing attention has been given to national security and foreign threats. Has the balance shifted in our national political debate? What role should media play in this debate?

2 Assume for the moment that media's primary power is to reinforce the status quo. Do you believe that this is the same as no effect? Why or why not?

3 C. Wright Mills lost much of his stature in the debate over elite pluralism because of his support of Castro and the Cuban Communists. Do you believe that a scientist's politics should invalidate his or her ideas? Are there some positions that a scientist can take that mark him or her as fundamentally nonobjective? What about religious beliefs? Could a sincere Muslim, for example, be trusted to develop a useful perspective on media and its role in democracy?

4 A powerful challenge to elite pluralism is to ask why, if it operates so effectively, are there so many disaffected groups in the United States, for example some minorities, people on the political fringes, and so on? Is this simply the way it always was and always will be even in the most robust democracies? Another question asked of elite pluralism is "Why do so many people feel so powerless and apathetic?" Again, is this simply a given even in good democracies? In the wake of September 11th, the media are paying less attention to the plight of domestic minorities. Are we placing greater emphasis on the "elite" side of elite pluralism and is this emphasis justified by the threats we face from abroad?

5 The last two chapters offered the arguments, seemingly scientifically supported, of the limited effects paradigm. Are you persuaded? To what extent has September 11th altered your view of the power of media to affect your view of the social world? Do you believe that media have little or limited effects on the important things in your life? What about the advertising that constantly reaches us through the media? Are the brands of clothing you wear or other things you own highly advertised? Examine your feelings about media in your life before you read the next several chapters. They paint a much different picture about media's influence. See if you can anticipate some of the major arguments for powerful mass media.

Significant People and Their Writing

DeFleur, Melvin L., and Otto N. Larsen (1958). *The Flow of Information.* New York: Harper.

Key, V. O. (1961). *Public Opinion and American Democracy.* New York: Knopf.

Klapper, Joseph (1960). *The Effects of Mass Communication.* New York: Free Press.

Mendelsohn, Harold (1966). *Mass Entertainment.* New Haven, CT: College and University Press.

Merton, Robert K. (1949). *Social Theory and Social Structure.* Glencoe, IL: Free Press.

———— (1967). *On Theoretical Sociology.* New York: Free Press.

Mills, C. Wright (1957). *The Power Elite.* New York: Oxford University Press.

———— (1959). *The Sociological Imagination.* New York: Oxford University Press.

Rogers, Everett M. (1983). *Diffusion of Innovation.* New York: Free Press.

Schramm, Wilbur, Jack Lyle, and Edwin Parker (1961). *Television in the Lives of Our Children.* Stanford, CA: Stanford University Press.

Wright, Charles R. (1986). *Mass Communication: A Sociological Perspective,* 3rd edition. New York: Random House (updated version of his 1949 book).

Chapter 8

Challenging the Dominant Paradigm: Children, Systems, and Effects

SYSTEMS THEORY
Theory that examines the mass communication process as composed of interrelated parts that work together to meet some goal

SOCIAL COGNITIVE THEORY *Theory of learning through interaction with the environment that involves reciprocal causation of behavior, personal factors, and environmental events*

In the 1960s, the United States stood as the undisputed technological leader of the world. Despite this, the nation's social fabric began to unravel as the decade unfolded. Together, these factors helped reshape mass communication theory.

American technological know-how had helped win World War II and now provided the public with the most comfortable and efficient life ever known. Perhaps, thought some observers, this systematic technological approach could be applied to the study of communication. The resulting **systems theory** offered hope to those who rejected limited effects notions. They saw a changing world. Media, especially television—which by 1960 had reached into 90 percent of all U.S. homes—seemed to be in the middle of that change. Perhaps media's power could be better understood at the macroscopic level, that is, by its influence on the social system.

At the same time, psychologists, unfettered by mass communication theory's adherence to the dominant limited effects paradigm, thought they could explain some of the social turmoil in microscopic—that is, individual—terms. Psychologists turned their attention to how people, especially children, learned from the mass media, especially television. What would eventually be known as **social cognitive theory** and its early focus on children moved communication theorists even further from their belief in limited or minimal media effects.

Overview

In this chapter, we examine changes in post–World War II American society that forced a reconsideration of prevailing thought on mass communication theory.

185

First, much attention was focused on increases in the amounts of real world violence and the possible contribution of television to that rise. Several different perspectives are discussed, including catharsis, social learning, social cognitive theory, aggressive cues, and priming effects. Whereas the latter four perspectives see media as a possible factor in increasing the likelihood of actual violence, catharsis argues just the opposite. The context of mediated violence—that is, how violence and aggression are presented in the media—is described, as are differing understandings of how children interact with the media, specifically the active theory of television viewing and the developmental perspective.

A second avenue of inquiry into media's role in the society came from systems theorists. As such, we define systems and describe the rise of systems theory. The components of systems models are presented, and we discuss their application to the study of communication and mass communication.

Focus on Children and Violence

On August 6, 1945, the United States dropped an atom bomb on Hiroshima, effectively ending World War II. That four-year global conflict forced cataclysmic changes in America's economic, industrial, demographic, familial, and technological character, the impact of which would be felt most powerfully in the 1960s.

The mass medium that transformed that decade had an inauspicious introduction as a novelty at the 1939 World's Fair in New York. Its tiny picture, poor sound quality, and high cost led some to doubt its future as a popular medium. During the next three years, a small number of experimental television stations began broadcasting a limited number and variety of programs to a minuscule audience. When the United States entered the war, television's already limited diffusion to the public halted, as the technologies and materials needed to improve and produce the medium went to the war effort. Technological research, however, did not stop. Therefore, when the war ended and materials were once again available for the manufacture of consumer goods, a technologically mature medium was immediately available. Anticipating not only this, but also dramatic changes in American society that would benefit the new medium, the national commercial radio networks were ready to move their hit shows and big stars to television.

This technological advance occurred simultaneously with profound alterations in U.S. society. The war changed the country from a primarily rural society that boasted an agriculturally based economy into a highly urban nation dependent on an industrially based economy. After the war, more people worked regularly scheduled jobs (rather than the sunrise-to-sunset workday of farmers), and they had more leisure. More people had regular incomes (rather than the seasonal, put-the-money-back-into-the-land farmer's existence), and they had more money to spend on that leisure. Because the manufacturing capabilities developed for the war were still in existence, the economy had the ability to mass produce items on which that money could be spent. Because more consumer goods were competing in the marketplace, there was a greater need to advertise, which provided the economic base for the new television medium. Because non-Caucasian Americans had been enlisted to fight the war and to work in the country's factories, they began to demand their rightful share of the American dream. Because women entered the work force while the men were off to battle, it was more common and acceptable to have both parents working outside the home. Because people had moved away from their small towns and family roots, the traditional community anchors—church and school—began to lose their dominance in the social development of children who were present in the 1960s—in their teenage years—in inordinately large numbers because of the Baby Boom that occurred soon after war's end.

This new social landscape took shape at precisely the same time that the new mass medium arrived. As in all periods of change, there were serious social problems. The rapid expansion in the number of teenagers brought sharp increases in delinquency and crime. The schools were blamed for not doing their job of educating children to be responsible citizens. Crime waves swept one city after another. Successive social movements captured the attention of the nation, especially the Civil Rights and the Anti-Vietnam War Movements. Political instability reached new heights with the assassinations of President John F. Kennedy, Dr. Martin Luther King, Jr., and Robert Kennedy. Young people were behaving strangely. Many were listening more to new, unfamiliar music and less to their increasingly "old fashioned, irrelevant" parents. Sociologists discovered the existence of a "generation gap" between conservative, middle-class parents and their increasingly liberal, even radical children.

Media's role in all these changes was hotly debated. Although social researchers and media practitioners typically argued from the limited effects perspective, a new generation of critics charged that media were harming children and disrupting their lives. Evidence mounted that families, schools, and churches had become less important to children. As Urie Bronfenbrenner (1970) said, the back yards were growing smaller and the school yards growing bigger. In other words, young people were being socialized more and more away from home and classroom. His own research demonstrated that, whereas parents and church had been the primary socializing agents for pre-war American adolescents, by the mid 1960s, media and peers shared top billing in the performance of that crucial function.

It is no surprise, then, that the media, particularly television, became the target of increasing criticism and the object of increasing scientific inquiry, especially where harmful effects were presumed. But these renewed efforts to probe the negative influence of mass media occurred when the limited effects paradigm was cementing its dominance. An intense and continuing debate erupted between those social researchers who had confidence in that perspective and those who were skeptical of its conclusions despite the consistency of its empirical findings (see Chapter 7). Strong advocates of limited effects notions were accused of being paid lackeys of the media industries, and overzealous critics of television were accused of oversimplifying complex problems and ignoring alternative causes.

The argument about the media's role in fomenting social instability and instigating violence reached a peak in the late 1960s. After disruptive riots in the Los Angeles suburb of Watts and in the cities of Cleveland, Newark, and Detroit, President Lyndon Johnson established a National Commission on the Causes and Prevention of Violence in 1968. The Commission offered some serious criticisms of media and recommended a variety of changes in both news reporting and entertainment content. Writing in the preface to the Commission's Staff Report, *Violence and the Media,* editor Paul Briand asked, "If, as the media claim, no objective correlation exists between media portrayals of violence and violent behavior—if, in other words, the one has no impact upon the other—then how can the media claim an impact in product selection and consumption, as they obviously affect the viewers' commercial attitudes and behavior? Can they do one and not the other?" (Baker & Ball, 1969, preface). This question reflected growing public and elite skepticism concerning limited effects assertions.

The federal government itself tried to locate new answers to this problem by establishing the Surgeon General's Scientific Advisory Committee on Television and Social Behavior in 1969. Its purpose was to commission a broad range of research on television effects that might determine whether television could be an important influence on children's behavior.

What did this collection of scientists conclude after two years and a million dollars of study? The Surgeon General, Jesse L. Steinfield, reported to a U.S. Senate subcommittee, "While the . . . report is carefully phrased and qualified in language acceptable to social scientists, it is clear to me that the causal relationship between televised violence and antisocial behavior is sufficient to warrant appropriate and immediate remedial action. The data on social phenomena such as television and violence and/or aggressive behavior will never be clear enough for all social scientists to agree on the formulation of a succinct statement of causality. But there comes a time when the data are sufficient to justify action. That time has come" (Ninety-Second Congress, 1972, p. 26). Dr. Steinfield's adamance was echoed by at least one influential senator, as you can see in Box 8a.

Nevertheless, this report did little to end the controversy over television's effects. Industry officials and lobbyists worked hard to block development and implementation of new Federal Communications Commission regulations for children's programming. They cited inconclusive research and restated limited ef-

---

Box 8a U.S. Senate Hearings on the Surgeon General's Report on Television and Social Behavior

So much controversy was generated by the release and media interpretation of the Surgeon General's Report in 1972 (for example, a *New York Times* article on January 11 was headlined "TV Violence Held Unharmful to Youth," Gould, 1972) that John O. Pastore of Rhode Island convened the U.S. Senate's Communications Subcommittee. He intended to clear the air about the true findings of Dr. Steinfield's Scientific Advisory Committee. The Surgeon General was certain in his understanding of the results, as we see on page 000. But Pastore wanted a more definitive statement before the public. This exchange between the Senator and CBS's Joseph Klapper occurred on March 21, 1972, in Washington, DC.

Dr. Klapper: I have in mind programs which promote admiration for skills and abilities that do not involve the display of anti-social aggression, or of violence, including among such skills and abilities, the solution of interpersonal problems without resort to violence. This would all be undertaken in my hope, in an intensified effort, as I said, to maximize the pro-social potential of television.

Senator Pastore: May I interrupt you, Doctor? You talk about the responsibility of the parents, and I agree with you. You talk about the maximization of pro-social programs, I agree with you. But, why don't we talk about the minimizing of excessive violence? Why isn't that a part of the question? I mean, that is the thing that we are investigating here. I realize that there is a lot of good we can do through television, and television should do it, and that is their responsibility . . . But what we are bothered with here is excessive violence. Now, I realize that a family can do a great deal with a child and should do a great deal with a child, but we have to accept life the way it is. You are a scientist with the broadcasting industry, CBS . . . Don't you think there has been much violence on television that is unnecessary.

Dr. Klapper: Yes.

Senator Pastore: Now, why don't we cut that out? That is what I am talking about. That is what we should do, where we should start. And then all of the other studies you mention, of course, we ought to do them . . . But the question at hand is, does televised violence have to do with the aggressiveness of a child, in spite of everything else? And the question here is, is it something that can be helped, and that is a question we have to decide. If it can be helped, I say for goodness gracious, let's do it.

How would you have answered Senator Pastore had you been the head of social research for CBS? If you were a Senator, what questions would you have asked representatives of the television industry?

---

fects arguments. The primary opposition to the industry was Action for Children's Television (ACT)—a Boston-based group that grew rapidly during the 1970s in response to increasing public fears about television effects. Eventually the industry agreed to a self-imposed family viewing hour in which violent content was ostensibly minimized and, at the time, all three networks tightened their programming standards and worked closely with program producers to limit gratuitous violence.

Television Violence Theories

The most important outcome of the violence research was the gradual development of a set of middle-range theories that summarized findings and offered increasingly useful insight into the media's role in the lives of children. Taken together, they offer strong support for the viewing-aggression link. As Aletha Huston and her colleagues wrote after reviewing decades of scientific research on the question, "The accumulated research clearly demonstrates a correlation between viewing violence and aggressive behavior—that is, heavy viewers behave more aggressively than light viewers . . . Both experimental and longitudinal studies support the hypothesis that viewing violence is causally associated with aggression . . . Field (naturalistic) experiments with preschool children and adolescents found heightened aggression among viewers assigned to watch violent television or film under some conditions" (1992, pp. 54–55). Still, debate and disagreement persist.

Catharsis

The findings from the Surgeon General's Report on one aspect of the television violence debate, catharsis, were quite clear and did generate significant agreement. Testified CBS's Joseph Klapper (Ninety-Second Congress, 1972, p. 60), "I myself am unaware of any, shall we say, hard evidence that seeing violence on television or any other medium acts in a cathartic or sublimated manner. There have been some studies to that effect; they are grossly, greatly outweighed by studies as to the opposite effect."

CATHARSIS *Also called sublimation; the idea that viewing mediated aggression sates, or reduces, people's natural aggressive drives*

Yet **catharsis** (sometimes called **sublimation**)—the idea that viewing violence is sufficient to purge or at least satisfy a person's aggressive drive and, therefore, reduce the likelihood of aggressive behavior—has lived a long, if not thoroughly respectable life in mass communication theory.

Common sense and your own media consumption offer some evidence of the weakness of the catharsis hypothesis. When you watch couples engaged in physical affection on the screen, does it reduce your sexual drive? Do media presentations of families devouring devilish chocolate cakes purge you of your hunger drive? If viewing mediated sexual behavior does not reduce the sex drive and viewing media presentations of people dining does not reduce our hunger, why should we assume that seeing mediated violence can satisfy an aggressive drive? Moreover, think back to when you attended movies like *Black Hawk Down, Collateral Damage, The Fast and the Furious,* or any of the numerous *Die Hard* and *Terminator* films. Do you walk out of the theater a tranquil, placid person? Probably not.

Yet, it isn't difficult to see why the proposition seemed so attractive. For one thing, the philosopher, Aristotle, originally articulated catharsis to explain audience reaction to Greek tragedy. So it has developed a sort of intellectual validity based on tradition rather than observation. For another, catharsis suggested that television violence had social utility, providing young people with a harmless outlet for their pent-up aggression and hostility. In television's early days, many people were anxious to rationalize their use of this attractive, new medium.

There was even early scientific evidence suggesting that catharsis was, indeed, at work. Seymour Feshbach (1961) demonstrated what he said was catharsis by insulting college-aged men with "a number of unwarranted and extremely critical remarks" in an experimental setting and then having them watch either filmed aggression (a brutal prize fight) or a neutral film (on the spread of rumors). The men were then asked to evaluate the experiment and the insulting experimenter. The insultees who had seen the prize fight were less aggressive in their attitudes than those who had seen the other film.

But, as F. Scott Andison wrote in 1977 after reviewing twenty years' worth of scientific evidence, "We can conclude on the basis of the present data cumulation that television, as it is shown today, probably does stimulate a higher amount of aggression in individuals within society. Therefore, it seems reasonable to tentatively accept the 'TV violence as a stimulant to aggression' theory and to reject the . . . 'cathartic' theories" (Andison, 1977 p. 323). Or, as James D. Halloran (1964/65), then-director of Britain's Center for Mass Communication Research at the University of Leicester, more directly put it, catharsis is a "phony argument."

But Feshbach apparently *did* demonstrate a reduction in aggression after viewing in 1961 and he obtained similar results in a 1971 study (Feshbach & Singer) conducted with funding from NBC. The research was undertaken in a group home for preadolescent boys. For six weeks, half of the boys were restricted to watching television programs with little or no violence while the other half were allowed to watch violent content. A variety of behavioral measures indicated that the boys viewing the violent programs were less aggressive. These findings may not have been caused by catharsis, however. The boys who were placed in the nonviolent programming group may have been frustrated because they were not allowed to watch some of their favorite shows. Heightened frustration might account for their increased aggressiveness.

What social scientists would eventually learn, however, is that certain presentations of mediated violence and aggression *can reduce* the likelihood of subsequent viewer aggression. But catharsis is not the reason. Rather, viewers *learn* that violence might not be appropriate in a given situation. Think about the first Feshbach study we mentioned. Maybe those who had seen the brutal boxing match, who had seen unnecessary pain inflicted on another human, simply said to themselves, "Aggression is not a good thing." Their aggressive drive might not have been purged, but they might have simply learned that such treatment of another human is inappropriate. In other words, their inclination toward aggression (remember, they had been insulted) was inhibited by the information in the media presentation. This leads us to the theory that is generally accepted as most useful in understanding the influence of media violence on individuals—social cognitive theory.

Social Learning

IMITATION *The direct reproduction of observed behavior*

Humans learn from observation. There has been some question, however, about how much and what kinds of behaviors people learn from the media. This debate has been fueled, in part, by a definitional problem. No one questions whether people can imitate what they see in the media. **Imitation** is the direct, mechanical reproduction of behavior. A television viewer sees a movie called *Fuzz* in which a gang of teenagers beats and sets a hobo afire. The next day that viewer beats a homeless man sleeping on a beach and sets him on fire. Or two teenagers set fire to a New York subway tollbooth, killing its attendant, after seeing the movie *Money Train*. Both are true stories. Both demonstrate imitation. The problem for mass communication theorists, however, is that these obvious examples of media influence, as dramatic as they are, are relatively rare. Moreover, such gross examples of media influence lend substance to the argument that negative effects occur only in those "predisposed" to aggression—in other words, those crazy to begin with.

IDENTIFICATION *A special form of imitation that springs from wanting to be and trying to be like an observed model relative to some broader characteristics or qualities*

Identification, on the other hand, is "a particular form of imitation in which copying a model, generalized beyond specific acts, springs from wanting to be and trying to be like the model with respect to some broader quality" (White, 1972, p. 252). Although only one or a very few people might have imitated the behaviors seen in the films mentioned above, how many others identified with the movies' characters? How many others might choose a different form of violence against someone they might encounter? How many others identified with the killers' mode of problem solving, although they might never express it exactly as did our cinematic killers? Imitation from media is clearly more dramatic and observable than is identification. But identification with media models might be the more lasting and significant of the media's effects (for a detailed discussion of this distinction and its importance to media theory, see Baran & Meyer, 1974).

The first serious look at learning through observation was offered by psychologists Neal Miller and John Dollard (1941). They argued that imitative learning occurred when observers were motivated to learn, when the cues or elements of the behaviors to be learned were present, when observers performed the given behaviors, and when observers were positively reinforced for imitating those behaviors. In other words, people could imitate behaviors that they saw; those behaviors would be reinforced and therefore learned.

Instead of presenting a means of understanding how people learn from models (including media models), however, Miller and Dollard were simply describing an efficient form of traditional stimulus-response learning. They assumed that individuals behaved in certain ways and then shaped their behavior according to the reinforcement they actually received. The researchers saw imitation as replacing random trial-and-error behaviors. Imitation simply made it easier for an individual to choose a behavior to be reinforced. That actual reinforcement, they argued, ensured learning. But this insistence on the operation of reinforcement limited their theory's application for understanding how people learn from the mass media. The theory's inability to account for people's apparent skill at learning new responses through observation rather than actually receiving reinforcement limited its applicability to media impact.

Two decades later, Miller and Dollard's ideas about what they called **social learning** and imitation were sufficiently developed, however, to become valuable tools in understanding media effects. Where Miller and Dollard saw social learning as an efficient form of stimulus-response learning (the model provided information that helped the observer make the correct response to be reinforced), contemporary **social cognitive theory** (as social learning theory is now known) argues that observers can acquire symbolic representations of the behavior, and these "pictures" provide them with information on which to base their own subsequent behavior. Media characters (models) can influence behavior simply by being depicted on the screen. The audience member need not be reinforced or rewarded for exhibiting the modeled behavior.

SOCIAL LEARNING *Encompasses both imitation and identification to explain how people learn through observation of others in their environments*

SOCIAL COGNITIVE THEORY *Theory that argues that observers can acquire symbolic representations of behaviors, and these "pictures" provide information on which to base subsequent behavior*

Social Cognition from Mass Media

OPERANT LEARNING THEORY *Theory that learning occurs only through the making and subsequent reinforcement of behavior*

BEHAVIORAL REPERTOIRE *The learned responses available to an individual in a given situation*

Traditional or **operant learning theory** as developed by the early behaviorists (see Chapter 4) asserts that people learn new behaviors when they are presented with stimuli (something in their environment), make a response to those stimuli, and have those responses reinforced either positively (rewarded) or negatively (punished). In this way, new behaviors are learned, or added to people's **behavioral repertoire**—the individual's available behaviors in a given circumstance.

Two things are clear, however. First, this is an inefficient form of learning. We all know, for example, how to deal with fire. If each of us had to learn our fire-related behavior individually, we would have overcrowded hospitals. According to operant learning theory, each of us, when presented with that stimulus (fire), would render a chance response (put our hand in it), and be burned. To ensure that we would not be scorched in the future, we would add avoidance to fire to our behavioral repertoire. Because that initial burnt hand "increases the

NEGATIVE RE-
INFORCER *The removing, reducing, or preventing of a particular stimulus that increases the probability of a given behavior over time*

probability of a given behavior over time (in our case, avoiding flames), the stimulus (the burnt hand) is a **negative reinforcer** (Zimbardo & Weber, 1997, p. 215). This process is very inefficient. Instead, we observe, in a variety of settings (mass mediated and otherwise), the operation of that stimulus, response, and reinforcement chain, and we, in turn, add avoidance to the store of behaviors that we can use when confronted in everyday life by the stimulus. In essence, then, we have substituted a representation of an experience for an actual (and, in this case, painful) experience.

A second obvious point is that we do not learn in only this operant manner. We have all experienced learning through observation, even when we have not seen the stimulus/response/reinforcement chain; that is, when there has been no reinforcement, either to us or to the person in the representation. Observation of a behavior is sufficient for people to learn that behavior. Even people who have never shot an arrow from a bow, for example, know how it's done.

MODELING *The acquisition of behaviors through observation*

Modeling from the mass media, then, is an efficient way to learn a wide range of behaviors and solutions to problems that we would otherwise learn slowly or not at all, or pay too high a price to learn in the actual environment.

This learning from observation of the environment, or social cognition, is the basis of social cognitive theory. According to Albert Bandura, "Social cognitive theory explains psychosocial functioning in terms of triadic reciprocal causation. In this model of reciprocal determinism, behavior; cognitive, biological, and other personal factors; and environmental events all operate as interacting determinants that influence each other bidirectionally" (1994, p. 61). In other words, things they experience in their environments (for example, mass media) can affect people's behaviors and that affect is influenced by various personal factors specific to those people.

This social cognition through the use of media representations operates in one or all of three ways (see Bandura, 1971 and 1994, for excellent extended discussions):

OBSERVATIONAL LEARNING *When the observation of a behavior is sufficient to learn that behavior*

1 **Observational Learning.** Consumers of representations can acquire new patterns of behavior by simply watching these representations. We all know how to shoot a gun, although many of us have never actually performed or been reinforced for that act. Many of us probably even think that we can rob a convenience store. We have seen it done.

INHIBITORY EF-
FECTS *Seeing a model punished for a behavior is sufficient to reduce the likelihood that the observer will make that behavior*

2 **Inhibitory Effects.** Seeing a model in a representation punished for exhibiting a certain behavior decreases the likelihood that the observers will make that response. It is as if the viewers themselves are actually punished. We see the villain brought low for evil deeds. We see Helga hated by the kids on *Hey Arnold!* because of her duplicity and selfishness. Our likelihood of responding to various real-world stimuli in similar ways is reduced. Experimental studies using film and

video of people being punished for various behaviors have shown that these representations can inhibit in observers such things as aggression, exploratory behavior, and antisocial interaction with peers.

DISINHIBITORY **3**
EFFECTS *Seeing a model rewarded for a prohibited or threatening behavior increases the likelihood that the observer will make that behavior*

Disinhibitory Effects. A media representation that depicts reward for a threatening or prohibited behavior is often sufficient to increase the likelihood that the consumer of the representation will make that response. A young man sees a contestant on NBC's *Fear Factor* emerge from brief captivity in a pit of snakes or suffer no ill effects from eating beetles or drinking a martini of blended earthworms. His likelihood of responding to various real-world stimuli in similar ways is increased. Experimental studies using film and television representations of various threatening and prohibited encounters have successfully reduced fear of dentists, dogs, and snakes and increased aggression by reducing viewers' inhibitions toward such action.

VICARIOUS
REINFORCEMENT
Reinforcement that is observed rather than directly experienced

REINFORCEMENT
CONTINGENCIES
The value, positive or negative, associated with a given reinforcer

Vicarious reinforcement is central to social cognition through the mass media. Although observational learning can occur in the absence of any reinforcement, vicarious or real, whether observers *actually make* that learned behavior is a function of the **reinforcement contingencies** (positive or negative) they associate with it.

For, example, when we see a television character rewarded or punished for some action, it is as if we ourselves have been actually rewarded or punished. This vicarious reinforcement tells us where to place the observationally learned behavior in our behavioral hierarchy—the likelihood that we will choose a given behavior. When presented with certain stimuli in our environment, we will be likely to choose a highly placed behavior for demonstration. One that promises punishment will be given a lower place in that hierarchy. We do not actually have to experience those rewards and sanctions; we have done it vicariously through the use of media representations.

Clearly, there might be times when we ignore the negative vicarious reinforcement and perform a behavior that we have seen represented as associated with punishment, such as running into a burning house. In these cases, sufficient incentive is present in the actual environment (saving a child from the flames, for example) to move that behavior up the hierarchy to a point where we can choose it from among a number of alternatives.

Bandura (1965) conducted what is now considered a classic experiment in modeling aggressive behavior from television, one that has direct bearing on several aspects of the media effects debate. He showed nursery school children a television program in which a character, Rocky, was either rewarded for aggression (given candy and a soft drink and called a "strong champion") or punished for those same behaviors (reprimanded, called a "bully," and spanked with a rolled-up magazine). Those who saw aggression rewarded showed more aggressive activity in a "free play" period (disinhibition) and those who saw it punished displayed less (inhibition). You can almost hear those people who believe that media have no effects on viewer aggression crowing, "See, the bad guy is punished, so media portrayals of violence actually reduce subsequent aggression." But Bandura went one step further. He then offered those in the inhibited group "sticker-pictures" for each of Rocky's aggressive acts they could demonstrate. Boys and girls alike could produce the "forbidden" behaviors. The environment offered them sufficient reward to demonstrate those observationally learned, but previously inhibited behaviors. The response to the "TV violence apologists," then, is simple: The bad guy is usually "out-aggressed" by the good guy who is rewarded for his or her more proficient display of aggression, and besides, that might not matter because the behaviors are observationally learned and can appear later when the conditions in the viewer's world call them (or similar ones) forward.

Aggressive Cues

AGGRESSIVE CUES
Information contained in media portrayals of violence that suggests (or cues) the appropriateness of aggression against specific victims

One direct outgrowth of social cognitive theory focuses on the **aggressive cues** inherent in media portrayals of violence. People who see mediated violence are believed to show higher levels of subsequent aggression. The question is when and against whom do they aggress. The answer is that media portrayals of violence are almost always in some dramatic context, and that context provides information, or *cues,* that tell viewers when and against whom violence is acceptable.

Leonard Berkowitz (1965) produced a representative piece of research, in which male college students were shown a film of a brutal boxing scene (the closing sequence of the movie, *The Champion*). To some it was presented in the context of a story that said the loser deserved his beating, that is, the violence against him was justified. In a second version of the tale, the defeated boxer was victimized, that is, the violence against him was unjustified.

The students were then given an opportunity to "grade" another student's design of "an original and imaginative floor plan for a house." Unbeknownst to them, all the participants were given the same floor plan from that other student (who was actually Berkowitz's accomplice). In half the cases, that accomplice introduced himself as a "college boxer" and in the other as a "speech major." A "new form of grading" was to be used, grading by electrical shock: one shock was very good, ten was very bad. Of course, the accomplice was not actually zapped; the shocks administered by the participants were read by a metering device and the accomplice feigned a response. Any differences in shocking the other student would be the result of differences in what they had seen on the screen. To confuse matters even more, half the participants were insulted (angered) by the experimenter before they began. What happened? The "college boxer" was shocked more than the speech major; the angered subjects gave more shocks regardless of whom they were shocking; and those who had seen the justified version of the film also gave more shocks. Berkowitz's conclusions? First, viewers' *psychological state* can lead them to respond to cues in programs that meet the needs of that state. Second, viewers who see justified violence not only learn the behavior, but also learn that it can be a good or useful problem-solving device (disinhibition). Third, cues associated with a victim, in this case a boxer, can disinhibit viewers toward aggression against similar people in the real world. Berkowitz said, "The findings show that the film context can affect the observer's inhibitions against aggression and that the people encountered soon afterwards vary in the extent to which they can evoke aggressive responses from the observer" (Berkowitz, 1965, p. 368). In a later study (Berkowitz & Geen, 1966), Berkowitz produced similar results simply by having the real-world target of the viewers' aggression share the same first name (Kirk) as the victim in the film.

PRIMING EFFECTS
The idea that presentations in the media heighten the likelihood that people will develop similar thoughts about those things in the real world

This idea of aggressive cues is supported by contemporary thinking on **priming effects**, which "maintains that the presentation of a certain stimulus having a particular meaning 'primes' other semantically related concepts, thus heightening the likelihood that thoughts with much the same meaning as the presentation stimulus will come to mind" (Jo & Berkowitz, 1994, p. 46). Aggressive cues and priming form the core of some of the most interesting and controversial media violence research now being conducted. With the media violence-viewer aggression link generally accepted, attention turned to the issue of violence against a specific target—women. In terms of aggressive cues, media portrayals cue viewers to consider women as likely or appropriate targets of violence. In terms of priming effects, media presentations of women as victims of violence heighten the likelihood that viewers, when confronted by real-life women, will have similar thoughts about them.

Richard Frost and John Stauffer (1987, p. 29) wrote, "But even though members of an audience for a violent film or television program may not be moved to actual behavioral imitation, do they not experience different levels of emotional arousal? . . . Could arousal also be influenced by the type of violence being portrayed, such as violence against women as opposed to men . . . ?" Peterson and Pfost (1989) and Johnson, Jackson, and Gatto (1995) demonstrated that rock music and rap videos featuring aggression against women could, indeed, lead—in the Peterson and Pfost work—to negative evaluations of women and—in the Johnson, Jackson, and Gatto work—to greater acceptance of violence toward women and heightened intention to use violence to resolve conflicts with females.

The Context of Mediated Violence

Writing in 1994, Bandura summed the accumulated knowledge of social cognitive theory to conclude that television viewers "acquire lasting attitudes, emotional reactions, and behavioral proclivities towards persons, places, or things that have been associated with modeled emotional experiences" (p. 75). What is it about specific presentations of media violence that encourage this acquisition through modeling? W. James Potter (1997) identified seven important **contextual variables:**

CONTEXTUAL VARIABLES *The information (or context) surrounding the presentation of mediated violence*

1 **Reward/punishment**—Rewarded aggression is more frequently modeled; punished aggression is less frequently modeled. We know this to be disinhibitory and inhibitory effects, respectively.

2 **Consequences**—Mediated violence that is accompanied by portrayals of negative or harmful consequences produces less modeling. Again, this shows inhibitory effects at work.

3 **Motive**—Motivated media aggression produces greater levels of modeling, and unjustified media violence results in less viewer aggression. Viewers are "cued" to the appropriateness (or inappropriateness) of using aggression.

4 **Realism**—Especially with boys, realistic media violence tends to produce more real-world aggression. As Potter explained (1997, p. 234), "realistic (media) perpetrators are more likely to reduce inhibitions because their behaviors are more applicable to real life situations than are unrealistic perpetrators such as cartoon or fantasy characters."

5 **Humor**—Because it reduces the seriousness of the behavior, humorously presented media violence leads to the greater probability that viewers will behave aggressively in real life.

6 **Identification with media characters**—The more a viewer identifies with media characters (for example, with those they consider like themselves or attractive), the more likely it is that he or she will model the behaviors demonstrated by those characters.

7 **Arousal**—Potter explained, "Emotional appeals can serve to increase the dramatic nature of the narrative, and this can increase attention . . . positive dispositions toward the characters using violence . . . and higher levels of arousal which is more likely to result in aggressive behavior" (1997, p. 235).

Active Theory of Television Viewing

The operation of these contextual variables underscores the idea that media consumers do indeed bring something to the viewing situation. That is, they make judgments about what it is they are seeing as they consume; for example, is this violence justified? What are the consequences of making that behavior? Presenting "a theory of visual attention to television which has as its central premise the cognitively active nature of television viewing," Daniel Anderson and Elizabeth Lorch (1983, pp. 27–28), as well as several others (for example, Bryant & Anderson, 1983, and Singer & Singer, 1983) challenged the idea that "television viewing is fundamentally reactive and passive." This **active theory** of television viewing sees viewers in general—and in the violence debate, particularly children—as actively and consciously working to understand television content. The researchers argue that by the age of two and a half, children have sufficiently developed **viewing schema** that allow them to comprehend specific television content conventions. "Beyond two and a half years," they wrote, "visual attention to television increases throughout the preschool years . . . and may level off during the school-age years . . . We suggest this increase reflects cognitive development, increased world knowledge, and an understanding of the cinematic codes and format structures of television" (Anderson & Lorch, 1983, p. 13).

ACTIVE THEORY *View of television consumption that assumes viewer comprehension causes attention and, therefore, effects or no effects*

VIEWING SCHEMA *Interpretational skills that aid people in under-standing media content conventions*

Those who argue for this active theory of viewing claim that social cognitive theorists generally subscribe "to the proposition that the child is an active, cognitive, and social being (but) television is seen as providing such an exceptionally powerful influence that the child becomes reactive in its presence" (Anderson & Lorch, 1983, p. 5). This pessimistic view of children's viewing and cognitive abilities, they claim, inevitably leads social cognition advocates to overestimate the power of the medium and underestimate the influence that individual viewers have in determining effects. Put another way, "reactive theory" assumes that attention causes comprehension and therefore, effects. The active theory of television viewing assumes that comprehension causes attention and, therefore, effects (or no effects).

The Developmental Perspective

DEVELOPMENTAL PERSPECTIVE *The view of learning from media that specifies different intellectual and communication stages in a child's life that influence the nature of media interaction and impact*

But obviously not all viewers, especially children, are active viewers, and not all are equally active. This has led to support for the **developmental perspective**, one that assumes that children undergo "extensive and varied cognitive growth between birth and adulthood . . . that is extremely rich, complex, and multifaceted" (Flavell, 1992, p. 998). As such, it also assumes that an important aspect of people's power to deal with television is their ability to comprehend it at different stages in their intellectual development. Logically, older children will "read" television differently than will younger children. As Ellen Wartella wrote, this developmental perspective "seeks to describe and explain the nature of the communicative differences between four year olds, six year olds, 10 year olds, etc., and adults" (1979, p. 7). This notion of developmental stages in children's communicative abilities was drawn from developmental psychology, especially the work of Jean Piaget, who argued that children, as they move from infancy through adolescence, undergo qualitative changes in the level of cognitive and intellectual abilities available to them. Although it might be easy to assume that older children's processing of television's messages is more developed and, therefore, somehow better at insulating them from television effects, this was neither the conclusion of developmental research, nor was it the goal. Wartella said, "While questions of children's modeling of televised behavior have been the major focus of experimental and survey research" the developmental perspective asks "new questions and (deals with) different sorts of communication issues regarding children's learning from television and use of television" (1979, p. 8–9). Much of this research actually focused on differences in attention and comprehension at different stages of development to better tailor educational programming to specific groups of children.

Media and Children's Socialization

The focus on children extends beyond social cognition. The issue of media's contribution to children's socialization has attracted significant attention, especially in the areas of the loss of (or changing the meaning of) childhood, understandings of gender or sex roles, and advertising.

EARLY WINDOW
The idea that television allows children to see the world before they have the skill to successfully act in it

Television is an **early window**. That is, it allows children to see the world well before they are capable of competently interacting with it. Or, as Joshua Meyrowitz explained, television "escorts children across the globe even before they have permission to cross the street" (1985, p. 238). What happens to children's social development when television treats them as "little adults?" Children's books, for example, are the only types of books that children are capable of reading and their themes are geared to children's interests and experiences. Yet, as Meyrowitz argues, because all television is "educational television," there's no such thing as "children's television." Television

allows the very young child to be "present" at adult interactions. Television removes barriers that once divided people of different ages and reading abilities into different social situations. The widespread use of television is equivalent to a broad social decision to allow young children to be present at wars and funerals, courtships and seductions, criminal plots and cocktail parties. Young children may not fully understand the issues of sex, death, crime, and money that are presented to them on television. Or, put differently, they may understand these issues only in childlike ways. Yet television nevertheless exposes them to many topics and behaviors that adults have spent several centuries trying to keep hidden from children. Television thrusts children into a complex adult world, and it provides the impetus for children to ask the meanings of actions and words they would not yet have heard or read about without television. (1985, p. 242)

Instant Access

Social Cognitive Theory

Strengths	Weaknesses
1 Causal link between media and behavior is demonstrated	1 Laboratory demonstration raises question of generalizability
2 Applies across several viewer and viewing situations	2 Experimental demonstration might overestimate media power
3 Has strong explanatory power (for example, catharsis, cues)	3 Has difficulty explaining long-term effects of media consumption
	4 Underestimates people's active use of media messages
	5 Focuses too narrowly on individual rather than on cultural effects

One thing that children do learn about from the early window is gender or sex roles. George Comstock (1991) reviewed decades of research on children's sex role socialization and concluded that a "modest but positive association" exists between television exposure and the holding of traditional notions of gender and sex roles (p. 175). He also acknowledged that those who consume nontraditional portrayals of gender can and do develop similarly nontraditional perceptions of sex roles. Moreover, not only can media portrayals socialize children by encouraging certain expectations of themselves, these portrayals can encourage expectations of others. Comstock wrote, "Portrayals in television and other media of highly attractive persons may encourage dissatisfaction or lowered evaluations of the attractiveness of those of the pertinent sex in real life" (1991, p. 176).

Advertising's impact on children's socialization has been studied from several different angles. Research indicates that although even children as young as seven can tell the difference between commercials and other televised content, they might not understand the commercials' selling intent and that much advertising, especially premium advertising (ads that promise a gift or toy with purchase), can cause conflict between parents and children. In addition, the failure of many products to live up to the expectations created for them by children's advertising can lead to frustration and even cynicism (Liebert & Sprafkin, 1988).

The question remains, however, as to the contribution of social cognition and socialization from media, especially television, on children's behavior, especially aggression. Despite continued resistance from those Bernard Berelson would call Practicus (Chapter 3), the most accepted contemporary view is that "children have many influences operating on them, but the media stand out as the best resource for surveying and understanding the larger social environment, its threats, and its opportunities" (Ball-Rokeach, 2001, p. 16). And, according to Dr. Brandon Centerwall in the *Journal of the American Medical Association,* "Manifestly, every violent act is the result of an array of forces coming together—poverty, crime, alcohol and drug abuse, stress—of which childhood exposure to television is just one. Nevertheless, the epidemiological evidence indicates that if, hypothetically, television technology had never been developed, there would today be 10,000 fewer homicides each year in the United States, 70,000 fewer rapes, and 700,000 fewer injurious assaults" (quoted in Vander Neut, 1999, p. 40).

Systems Theories of Communication Processes

Although psychologists led communication researchers to the possibility of individual (micro level) media effects, engineers alerted these researchers to the possibility of developing holistic explanations for societal or systemwide (macro level) effects.

SYSTEM *Any set of interrelated parts that can influence and control one another through communication and feedback loops*

A **system** *consists of a set of parts that are interlinked so that changes in one part induce changes in other parts.* System parts can be directly linked through mechanical connections or they can be indirectly linked by communication technology. Because all parts are linked, the entire system can change as a result of alterations in only one element. Systems can be *goal directed* if they are designed to accomplish a long-term objective. Some systems are capable of *monitoring the environment and altering their operations in response to environmental changes.*

Interest in systems began with electronics engineers who developed systems that could be programmed to pursue goals, monitor the environment, and adjust actions so that the goals were achieved. These engineers were concerned with designing systems in which communication links functioned efficiently and transmitted information accurately. Communication was a means to an end. If a communication link didn't work properly, then the solution was obvious: Communication technology had to be improved so that desired levels of effectiveness and accuracy were achieved. Thus, in designing and engineering systems of this type, communication problems were solved by technological change. As a result, during the 1950s and 1960s, there was optimism that important, societal-level communication problems might also be solved by improving the accuracy of message transmissions.

The Rise of Systems Theories

After World War II, social theorists became intrigued by systems notions as a way of conceptualizing both macroscopic and microscopic phenomena. Some decided that the idea of systems offered a heuristic means of constructing useful models of various social processes, including communication. Rather than merely adding more variables, these models fundamentally altered how relationships between variables were understood. In developing these models, theorists drew on a variety of sources. Walter Buckley (1967) traced systems notions to seventeenth-century mechanical models, nineteenth-century organic models, and early twentieth-century process models. But most 1960s social systems theorists acknowledged that the greatest and most recent impetus toward the development of systems theories came from an engineering subfield known as **cybernetics**, the study of regulation and control in complex machines. Cybernetics investigates how communication links between the various parts of a machine enable it to perform very complex tasks and adjust to changes taking place in its external environment.

CYBERNETICS *The study of regulation and control in complex systems*

Cybernetics emerged as an important new field during World War II, partly because of its use for designing sophisticated weapons (Wiener, 1954, 1961). Cybernetics proved especially useful for communications engineering—the design of powerful new communication systems for military applications, such as radar. Communications engineers had abandoned simple, linear models of the communication process by the 1940s. A circular but evolving communication process was conceptualized in which messages come back from receivers to influence sources that in turn alter their messages. These circular processes were referred to as **feedback loops.** In these systems, ongoing mutual adjustment is possible that ultimately leads to achieving a long-term objective or function.

FEEDBACK LOOPS *Ongoing mutual adjustments in systems*

Complex machines rely on feedback loops as a means of making ongoing adjustments to changes caused by the environment. Feedback loops enable sources to monitor the influence of their messages on receivers. But just as important, receivers can in turn influence sources. If the effects are not what is expected or desired, a source can keep altering a message until the desired feedback is obtained. As World War II progressed, machines were built that used ever more powerful forms of communication technology, such as radar and television cameras, to monitor the environment. These provided sophisticated means of detecting subtle changes so that a weapons system could achieve its objective. We refer to these as **communication systems** if their function is primarily to facilitate communication. By this definition, a guided missile is not a communication system: It is a weapons system that contains a communication subsystem.

COMMUNICATION SYSTEMS *Systems that function primarily to facilitate communication*

Mathematical Theory of Communication

SIGNAL *The flow of communication from one part of a system to another*

INFORMATION BIT *Individual elements of a signal*

NOISE *The difference between the signal sent and the signal received*

REDUNDANT *When a signal contains many bits carrying the same information*

CHANNEL *The carrier of a signal*

CHANNEL CAPACITY *The ability of a channel to transmit an accurate signal*

Communications engineers also made another important breakthrough, one central to the current revolution in communications technology (Shannon & Weaver, 1949). Accuracy in message transmission is essential if systems are to operate effectively and achieve long-term goals. Even minor errors can compound over time and lead to serious problems. To address this situation, communications engineers developed a very sophisticated way of conceptualizing the flow of communication from one part to another within a system. The flow was referred to as a **signal** and each element in it was labeled an **information bit**. The ultimate information bit is a digital bit—one that is either present or absent. Methods of monitoring the accuracy of transmissions of bits were developed. The signal transmitted by one part was compared with the signal received by another. Any differences between the signal sent and the signal received were viewed as errors or **noise.** Because a signal can be composed of thousands or even millions of bits, some level of noise can usually be tolerated before it creates a problem. High levels of noise can be tolerated if a message is **redundant,** that is, if it contains many bits that carry the same information. All redundant bits must be lost or distorted before noise becomes a problem. Every communication link can be seen as a **channel,** and every channel can be seen as having a certain capacity to transmit an accurate signal. This **channel capacity** can be quite high, permitting a very complex signal to be carried with few errors or it can be low, permitting only a very simple signal to be accurately transmitted. Obviously, it is better to have channels that can accurately transmit complex signals. When accuracy is a problem, redundancy can be increased, but this reduces efficiency because the same information is being sent more than once.

For example, when you listen to an AM radio, you hear static. The static is actually thousands of erroneous bits of information that have somehow entered the signal as it moves from the radio transmitter to your receiver. The importance of minimizing these errors in signal transmission depends on the purpose or function of the communication link. FM signals aren't as subject to the introduction of errors as the signal moves from transmitter to receiver, so you receive a more accurate transmission of the original signal—that is, higher fidelity. This is why all-talk and sports stations tend to be on AM radio, and music—where static would be more troublesome—tends toward FM.

This example illustrates a common trend in communication engineering. As technology develops, ways are found to reduce or even eliminate noise, improve efficiency, and increase channel capacity. The dominant strategy for doing this currently involves digital technology. A signal is first broken into or encoded into digital bits, the digitized signal is transmitted and received, and then the original signal is reconstructed or decoded from the digital information. The channel capacity of existing communication links can be increased tremendously using digital technology. There is less need for transmission of redundant information so the links are more efficient. This is the basis for contemporary work on digital high-definition television (HDTV). Rather than transmit 30 frames a second as does traditional television, HDTV transmits only digital information about the changes that occur between those frames. Imagine two newscasters reading the news. The background set does not change, nor do their clothes, hairstyle and color, or even their faces. Only their mouths and facial expressions change. After the initial transmission of the information necessary to re-create the scene on home sets, all that is subsequently transmitted and received in a digital HDTV system is information about changes in that original scene. Noise is reduced, efficiency is improved, and channel capacity is increased as only *necessary* information enters the system (Fisher & Fisher, 1996, pp. 343–345).

Notions about signals, noise, bits, efficiency, redundancy, and channel capacity have found their way into mass communication theory through a variety of sources. One of the first and most important books was the *Mathematical Theory of Communication* written by Claude Shannon and Warren Weaver in 1949. Shannon was a research mathematician at Bell Telephone Laboratories, and Weaver was a consultant on scientific projects at the Sloan Foundation. They believed that these new concepts would transform how all forms of communication were understood. They were optimistic that it might even be possible to remedy macroscopic, societal-level communication problems using these very microscopic notions. Their ideas came to be referred to as **information theory.**

INFORMATION THEORY *The application of mechanical notions of information flow to the understanding of all forms of communication*

The highest ambitions for Shannon and Weaver's information theory have yet to be realized. In communications technology and the design of communications systems, the theory has been enormously successful. Technology based on this theory is providing the building blocks for constructing the Information Superhighway. Designers of this super-communications system promised that it would provide us with vast quantities of information at low cost in convenient, user-friendly formats, and that promise seems to have been fulfilled.

But efficient, accurate transmission of information isn't enough. Entry into the information age has been accompanied by a troubling escalation in social problems. Ideally, systems notions could also provide a powerful way of conceptualizing complex, social systems and analyzing the role played by communication in them. Important social problems might be solved.

Modeling Systems

The term *system* is used in communication engineering and cybernetics to refer to any set of interrelated parts that can influence and control one another through

MODEL *Any representation of a system, whether in words or diagrams*

INTERDEPENDENCE *Each element of a system has a specialized function, but changes in one element affect all others*

SELF-REGULATION *System characteristic that allows the overall system to operate properly and regulate itself so that goals are achieved*

communication and feedback loops. Any representation of a system, whether in words or diagrams, is a **model.** In systems, a change in one part affects all the others because all are interconnected through channels. **Interdependence** and **self-regulation** are key attributes of systems. Each part can have a specialized role or function, but all must interrelate in an organized manner for the overall system to operate properly and regulate itself so that goals are achieved. Systems can be relatively simple or quite complex. They can display a high or low level of internal organization. They can operate in a static fashion, or they can evolve and undergo profound change over time. They can operate in isolation or be interconnected with a series of other machines to form an even larger system.

Another key attribute of systems is that they are **goal-oriented.** That is, they constantly seek to serve a certain overall or long-term purpose. We usually associate goals with thinking and planning. But, of course, machines can't think. Their goal orientation is built-in, hardwired, or otherwise programmed. Once a machine is started, it will seek its goal even if the goal is mistaken or can't be achieved. Like the robots in a bad science fiction movie, machines carry out their mission even if it makes no sense.

A Simple Systems Model

GOAL ORIENTED *The effort to serve a specific overall or long-term purpose*

Although complex systems can be hard to describe and understand, the basic principles of a self-regulating system can be illustrated by looking at the way the furnace or air conditioner in your home operates. Both of these are parts of a self-regulating system that uses a simple feedback loop to adjust to the external environment. Both the furnace and the air conditioner communicate with a thermostat that monitors the environment and signals them when they need to turn on or off. As long as the temperature in your home remains within a desired range, the furnace or air conditioner remains inactive. When the thermostat detects a temperature that is below the desired range, it sends an electronic message to the furnace and it turns on. The furnace communicates with the thermostat by heating the air in your home. The thermostat monitors the air temperature and when that reaches the desired level, the thermostat sends another message telling the furnace to turn off. In this simple system, the furnace and the thermostat work together to keep the temperature in balance. Communication in the form of a simple feedback loop linking the furnace and the thermostat enables the system to operate effectively.

Applying Systems Models to Human Communication

Even simple systems models can be used to represent some forms of human communication. You and a friend can be seen as forming a system in which your friend plays the role of "thermostat." By maintaining communication with him or her, you find out whether your actions are appropriate or inappropriate. Are these the right clothes to wear now? Should you go to a dance or join friends for a movie? When you talk to this friend, you might not be trying to affect her but rather want her to guide you. You want her feedback so you can adjust your actions.

This example also illustrates key limitations of systems models when they are used to represent human communication—the easiest models to create tend to be too simple and too static. Unless you and your friend have a very unusual relationship, you will play many other kinds of roles and communicate with each other across a very broad range of topics. If the only function your friend serves for you is that of a thermostat, you probably need to reexamine your relationship. Assuming that you do have a more complex relationship with your friend, you could probably spend weeks trying to map out a systems model to represent the intricacies of your interrelationship. By the time you finished, you would discover that significant changes have occurred and the model is no longer accurate. Unlike mechanical parts linked by simple forms of communication, both you and your friend can easily alter your roles, your communication links, and the content of your messages. In other words, you regularly and routinely transform the system that links you to others. New feedback loops spring up while old ones vanish. Only recently have systems theorists begun to recognize and try to develop more complex models that allow ongoing transformation of systems.

Adoption of Systems Models by Mass Communication Theorists

TRANSMISSIONAL MODEL *The view of mass media as mere senders or transmitters of information*

Along with other social scientists, mass communication researchers were drawn to systems models. Moderately complex systems models came to be seen as an ideal means of representing communication processes—a big advance over simplistic, linear communication process models that were common before 1960. Gradually, systems models replaced the **transmissional model** that was implicit in most of the early effects research. Harold Lasswell (1949) provided a cogent, succinct version of this model when he described the communication process as *Who says What to Whom through what Medium with what Effect*. The transmissional model assumes that a message source dominates the communication process and that the primary outcome of the process is some sort of effect on receivers—usually one intended by the source. Influence moves or flows in a straight line from source to receivers. The possibility that the message receivers might also influence the source is ignored. Attention is focused on whether a source brings about intended effects or whether unintended negative effects occur. Mutual or reciprocal influence is not considered.

Communication theorists proposed new models of communication processes with feedback loops in which receivers could influence sources and

Box 8b   The Westley-MacLean Model of the Communication Process

The Westley-MacLean Model offers a clear picture of communication as a system.

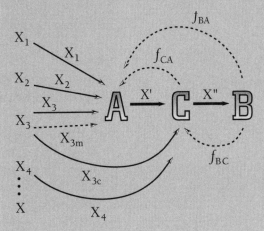

Source: Reproduced from *Journalism Quarterly,* Vol. 34, No. 1, Winter, 1957, pp. 31–38 with permission of the Association for Education in Journalism and Mass Communication.

The messages C transmits to B (X″) represent his selections from both messages to him from A's (X′) and C's selections and abstractions from Xs in his own sensory field (X_{3c}, X_4), which may or may not be Xs in A's field. Feedback not only moves from B to A (f_{BA}) and from B to C (f_{BC}), but also from C to A (f_{CA}). Clearly, in the mass communication situation, a large number of Cs receive from a very large number of As and transmit to a vastly larger number of Bs, who simultaneously receive from other Cs.

mutual influence was possible. The potential for modeling mutual influence was especially attractive for theorists who wanted to understand interpersonal communication. Bruce Westley and Malcolm MacLean (1957) provided a good example of this type of model, as you can see in Box 8b. Most conversations involve mutual influence. Participants send out messages, obtain feedback, and then adjust their actions. In everyday life, people are constantly adjusting to one another. The overall social environment can be understood as something that is created by ongoing negotiation between actors.

The usefulness of systems models for representing mass communication processes was less obvious. With most traditional forms of mass media, there are few if any *direct* communication links from receivers to sources. Message sources can be unaware of the impact of their messages or find out only after days or weeks have elapsed. During the 1960s, however, refinement of media-ratings systems and improved, more scientific public opinion polls allowed indirect communication links to be established between message sources and receivers. Ratings and opinion poll results provided message producers with feedback about audience reaction to their messages. This feedback was quite crude for ratings—either people watch a television show or they don't. If they don't, you change the message without much understanding of what people want. If ratings are high, then you provide more of the same—until people get so tired of the same programming that they finally tune to something else. With opinion polls, the feedback can provide a bit more information to message sources, but not much. Politicians, for example, are constantly experimenting with messages in an effort to alter voter opinions and produce favorable evaluations of themselves.

Closed versus Open Systems

HOMEOSTATIC
A closed system; performs the same task endlessly

DYNAMICALLY BALANCED *Open systems in which the parts interrelate so the system can monitor and adjust to its environment*

Two fundamentally different types of systems can be differentiated and used to model different forms of communication. Systems can be *closed* and **homeostatic** or they can be *open* and **dynamically balanced.** Closed systems are like simple machines that perform a task endlessly. There is limited monitoring of the external environment. The machine works well as long as all the parts interrelate in the same, unchanging manner. If a part becomes so worn that it stops working or a wire that is part of a communication link frays, the system will fail. It has no capacity to adjust to problems. The system can't maintain itself when parts wear out or communication links break down. The role played by communication in these closed systems tends to be highly structured and predictable. The parts of a simple machine don't have much to say to each other. They often communicate in very simple digital messages—turn on and turn off.

Open systems are very different. An open system consists of parts that interrelate in such a way that the overall system can monitor its environment and adjust to both internal and external changes. The parts of open systems can alter their functions so that if one part fails, others can adjust and take over its function. These systems can be capable of growth and change over time. Often, their relationship to the environment can change as well. These systems are said to be dynamically balanced—that is they are able to maintain their integrity and a high level of organization while undergoing significant changes. They are able to combine stability with change.

A classic example of an open system is a biological organism. In your body, the various organs communicate in a variety of ways—using electrical and chemical messages transmitted by the nervous and circulatory systems. As you grow, the relationship between organs changes. Some enlarge and take on more important functions, and others decline. The body can adapt in very complex ways to the failure of some of its parts and to changes in the external environment. Complex adjustments occur—yet the body as a whole maintains its physical integrity—it can grow and change and yet remain highly organized.

Systems theory had its greatest practical impact on mass communication theory several decades after the burst of initial interest in the 1960s. We will examine media-oriented system theory in the discussion of information processing theory in Chapter 10. But for now, it is important to remember that the two bodies of thought that we have studied in this chapter—social cognitive theory and system theory, both of which came to mass communication theory from outside the discipline itself—signaled an important shift in thinking about mass communication.

The Utility of Systems Models

Critics of systems models fall into two major categories—humanistic scholars who reject the mechanistic analogies inherent in systems models and social scientists who argue that research must stay focused on development of causal explanations and predictions. These critics have very different concerns.

Humanists who are fundamentally opposed to the use of systems models perceive them to be dehumanizing and overly simplistic. They argue that systems models are often nothing more than elaborate metaphors—sets of descriptive analogies. Humanists are dissatisfied with the ability of systems models to adequately represent complex human or societal interrelationships. After all, people aren't parts of machines. The relationships in a family aren't like the mechanism in an old-fashioned pocket watch. Even complex mechanical systems are simple when compared with the human relationships that are found within a family. Humanists are fearful that in applying mechanistic analogies we demean or trivialize human existence.

Systems theorists admit to using mechanical models as a starting point but argue that systems models can be refined to represent quite complicated phenomena. New types of models have been created that are based on biological rather than mechanical systems. Computers now permit the development and application of a new, promising type of model. **Simulation models** of complex social systems can be created in which complicated interrelationships between agents are represented. The operation of the system can be simulated over time in a computer (Simon, 1981).

SIMULATION MODEL
Model that represents the operation of complex social systems

After a simulation model is run for some time in a computer, its results can be compared with real-world outcomes. If major differences are found, the model can be refined until results are obtained that closely mimic or parallel the operation of actual systems. Can or should these models be used to predict the future? Should they be used as a basis for making changes in systems? Simulation models have already proved useful for controlling and managing complex machines. Could they work for social systems?

Systems theorists tend to be optimistic about their ability to create ever more useful models. These theorists are careful to temper the claims they make, however, and to specify the limitations of these models. Often, theorists only model parts of larger systems or model complex systems over brief periods. Models of large systems can be useful in predicting the long-term operation of the system as a whole but useless in explaining the operation of specific parts.

Estimating Causality

In the heating and cooling system model, which is the causal agent and which agent is being affected? Does the furnace cause the thermostat to act? Yes. Does the thermostat cause the furnace to act? Yes. So, which is dominant in this relationship? Which controls the other? In these models, neither agent is clearly dominant. Each causes the other to change. Thus, in even a very simple process involving feedback, causality can be hard to assess. If you measure the furnace and the thermostat at only one point in time, you are likely to get a completely mistaken impression of their relationship. When these processes become more complicated with more agents and more feedback loops, you need a schematic diagram to sort out the flow of influence. The effort to assign causality soon becomes a meaningless exercise. For example, given the complexity of the systems we create when we interact with other people, it becomes literally impossible to sort out causality—except for the most simple and narrowly defined systems or parts of systems.

Explanation of causality and identification of powerful causal agents are at the core of the limited effects paradigm, and they are what many social researchers still consider to be the essence of the scientific method. It is not surprising, therefore, that some social researchers, our second set of critics, find systems models troublesome because they don't permit development of definitive causal explanations. Systems models permit complex patterns of interrelationships to be traced, but the more complex these patterns are, the harder it is to make precise estimates of the causal influence of various agents on one another.

Should we be concerned about the difficulty of assigning causality in systems models? Is assignment of causality necessary to have a truly scientific theory? Or should we be satisfied if our theories are useful for certain other, more limited purposes? If we could simulate a set of interrelationships that provides insight into people playing certain roles in a particular situation over a limited time span, is that enough? Do we need to be able to say that the person playing role X has .23 causal dominance over the person playing role Y, whereas the person in role Y has .35 dominance over person X? Just how precise must our understanding of these interrelationships be for the simulation to be of value? Just how precise can we afford to make our simulations given the time and research effort necessary?

Researchers who assert the importance of assigning causality are concerned that if we lower our concern for causality we will create and use systems models that are based on little more than informed speculation. Although sophisticated systems models might allow us to construct fascinating computer simulations, will they serve any practical purpose? How can the utility of these models be evaluated if we don't use explanation of causal variance as our standard? It might appear that a model fits a particular set of relationships and gives insight into interconnections between parts. How can we be sure? How can we choose between two competing models that seem to represent a particular set of relationships equally well? These critics are deeply skeptical of the value of constructing models that contain complex interconnections between agents. Critics view systems models as **unparsimonious**—containing too many unnecessary variables and overly complex interrelationships.

UNPARSIMONIOUS
Containing too much unnecessary information (opposite of parsimonious)

A Focus on Structure and Function

Systems models have a third limitation that some critics find troublesome. A status quo bias in systems models can tend to concentrate our attention on observable structures (that is, the parts of a machine) and lead us to assume that the primary function or role of these structures is to maintain and serve the overall system. We are led to ask research questions like, "Is a particular part doing what it should, is it communicating properly, is it maintaining a proper relationship to other parts, is it enabling the system to operate properly?" The value of each part is assessed by its contribution to the whole. When we view systems in this way, we might be concerned about communication, but only in a limited way. We tend to view communication as something that merely interconnects parts in much the same way that our nervous and circulatory systems interconnect the organs in our bodies. Communication is something that primarily serves as a means of command and control. In our body, one organ tells another organ what to do. In this biological system, we judge the success of communication by looking at its overall operation. If the system is doing what we think it should, then we conclude that communication must be appropriate. If we think the system is failing, then we look for communication problems. But sometimes systems should fail. Sometimes systems go through necessary transformations in which existing structures break down and give way to new structures. In such cases, communication will necessarily play a very different role.

Given their concern for command and control, systems theories with a status quo bias tend to give only superficial attention to the substance of individual messages. If messages are examined, they tend to be quickly categorized according to their function in the overall system—the interconnection that they help maintain or the adaptation that they help manage. Accuracy and clarity of messages are viewed as important because inaccurate or ambiguous messages could lead the system to degrade and fail. Messages are often seen as having no purpose other than interconnection and system regulation. In such systems theories, there is little potential for communication to have unanticipated or far-reaching consequences. These theories don't recognize that communication can and should sometimes have transformative power that fundamentally alters the structure or long-term goals of the system.

SECOND-ORDER CYBERNETICS *The theory that many systems often or continually undergo fundamental, frequently chaotic, transformation*

A more recent form of systems theory, **second-order cybernetic theory**, seeks to overcome status quo biases. These theorists argue that many important systems often or continually undergo fundamental, frequently chaotic, transformations in their structures. These changes are said to be *nonlinear*, that is they can't be predicted by simply examining past behavior of a system. James Gleick put it in these words:

> In our world, complexity flourishes, and those looking to science for a general understanding of nature's habits will be better served by the laws of chaos . . . Nature forms patterns. Some are orderly in space but disorderly in time, others orderly in time but disorderly in space. (1987, p. 380)

Gleick offers the development of ecological systems theory as an example. Simple models assumed the existence of a "natural balance." "Models supposed that equilibriums would exist and that populations of plants and animals would remain close to them" (1987, p. 315). But these models are giving way to more complex ones. According to Gleick, "the traditional models are betrayed by their linear bias. Nature is more complicated . . . Chaos may undermine ecology's most enduring assumptions" (1987, p. 315).

In mechanical or biological systems undergoing profound change, transformative messages can play a central role. They might be necessary if the system is to move through chaotic developmental stages or overcome the limitations of existing structures. On the surface, these changes appear to be catastrophic. From the point of view of the older system structure, they are devastating. But for the old structure to be overcome, change might have to be quite radical. New linkages need to be formed and new substructures created, so that a transformed system can emerge. For example, this is the thinking behind contemporary ecological notions that some, if not most, forest fires actually serve rather than damage environmental balance. Second-order cybernetic theory focuses on such transformations and seeks to understand rather than fear them or suppress them (Gleick, 1987).

Thus, within simple, dynamically balanced, unchanging systems, the role of communication can be quite limited; we can make many assumptions about this role and our examination of communication can focus on accuracy and clarity. In

Instant Access

Systems Theory

Strengths	Weaknesses
1 Can be conceptualized as either micro- or macro-level theory	1 Has difficulty assessing causal relationships
2 Represents communication as a process	2 Is often too simplistic to represent complex communication patterns
3 Can be used to model a limitless variety of communication processes	3 Is perceived by some as overly mechanistic and dehumanizing
4 Moves mass communication theory beyond simple linear effects notions	4 Focuses attention on observable structures, ignoring the substance of communication
	5 Is unparsimonious

complex systems undergoing continual transformations, messages can have many functions. For example, ambiguous messages might be deliberately transmitted because they can serve many different functions simultaneously. Klaus Krippendorf (1986) pointed out that "noise need not be undesirable as in creative pursuits or in political discourse, in which ambiguity may be intentional" (p. 21). He argued that it is possible to develop useful models of systems in which noise is functional rather than inherently disruptive.

Critics charge that too often systems models have restricted concern to a narrow range of communication. Complex problems are reduced to simple questions involving accuracy and channel capacity. But these criticisms have been addressed by second-order cybernetic theorists who argue that we can have systems models that deal with more sophisticated forms of communication.

Summary

New media are always blamed for societal troubles that happen to occur at the time of their introduction. Yet, most limited effects research that examined media effects on young people concluded that media influence was, if not inconsequential, at least tempered by traditional forces like church, family, and school. In the 1960s, however, the mass diffusion of a new, powerful medium—television—the clear presence of significant social upheaval, and a weakening of those traditional forces' influence over young people gave rise to several penetrating looks at media and viewer aggression.

Catharsis, the idea that viewing violence substitutes for the actual demonstration of aggression by the viewer, was ultimately discredited.

Social cognitive theory proved to be a useful way of understanding how people learn behaviors from television, but it left many questions unanswered, especially as its insights were extrapolated from micro-level analyses (where they were initially formulated) to more macro-level explanations of effects.

Aggressive cues and priming effects research attempted to add some specificity to social cognitive theory, as did the developmental perspective. Another conception of the young audience—the active theory of television viewing—although not dismissing media effects, did suggest that viewers have more influence over their interaction with media than social cognitive theory seemed to imply.

The rise of systems theories in the 1950s and 1960s encouraged theorists to move beyond simplistic, linear models of mass communication. Concepts developed by communications engineers were applied to mass media systems. The study of systems, which consist of sets of parts that are interlinked so that changes in one part induce changes in other parts, evolved from cybernetics, the study of the regulation and control of complex machines. Systems theory allows the creation of models that demonstrate the interdependence, self-regulation, and goal-orientation of systems. Systems theory also permits the visualization of closed (homeostatic) and open (dynamically balanced) systems. The application of systems theories to mass communication, although raising many important questions during this period of reconsideration of the limited effects paradigm, would bear its most valuable fruit decades later, as we'll see in Chapter 10.

Exploring Mass Communication Theory

1 The relationship between media portrayals of violence and subsequent viewer aggression is among the most discussed media effects. There are literally hundreds of good Web sites on the issue. Here are a few particularly interesting ones:

The American Psychological Association
http://www.apa.org/

Center for Research on the Effects of Television
http://www.ithaca.edu/cretv

Centre for the Study of Children, Youth, and Media
http://www.ccsonline.org.uk/mediacentre/main.html

The Office of the Surgeon General of the United States
http://www.surgeongeneral.gov/sgoffice.htm

 2 Systems theory and cybernetics are naturally of interest to people committed to the Internet and the World Wide Web. Among the scores of sites is this one that should be valuable to students with a general understanding of these fields. It links to a host of other fascinating and challenging sites:

The Principia Cybernetics Project (links to general background material on the field of cybernetics and systems theory)
http://pespmc1.vub.ac.be/masthead.html

 3 Use **InfoTrac College Edition** to scan the tables of contents of as many psychology journals as you can find. Look for the names Albert Bandura and Leonard Berkowitz. Bandura is the name most identified with social learning and social cognitive theories, and Berkowitz is among the leaders in applying these theories to the issue of media effects, especially violence. Choose one article from each of these researchers that you find interesting and examine how each tests his theory in the experiments they use.

 4 Use **InfoTrac College Edition** to scan the tables of contents of as many psychology, sociology, political science, economic, and communication journals as you can find. Search for the words *system, systems theory,* and *cybernetics.* Can you find themes that are particular to the individual disciplines? In other words, do economists use systems theory one way, sociologists another way, and communication theorists a third way?

Critical Thinking Questions

1 What was your family's attitude toward television when you were growing up? Were there viewing rules for the children in your home?

2 Think back to when you were in your pre- and early-teen years. Which lessons from those days are still with you? Those from school, church, and family or those from media and friends? What are they?

3 Can you think of an example of social cognition from the media in your own life? Examples of imitation? Of identification?

4 Briefly list and explain the essential elements of a systems model. Now describe your peer group as a system. What are its interrelated elements? What are its goals? How does the system help insure the meeting of those goals?

Significant People and Their Writing

Ball-Rokeach, Sandra J. (2001). "The Politics of Studying Media Violence: Reflections 30 Years After the Violence Commission." *Mass Communication & Society,* 4, 3–18.

Bandura, Albert (1971). *Psychological Modeling: Conflicting Theories.* Chicago: Aldine Atherton.

Bryant, Jennings, and **Daniel R. Anderson** (1983). *Children's Understanding of Television: Research on Attention and Comprehension.* New York: Academic.

Buckley, Walter (1967). *Sociology and Modern Systems Theory.* Englewood Cliffs, NJ: Prentice Hall.

Jordan, Amy B. (1996). *The State of Children's Television: An Examination of Quantity, Quality, and Industry Beliefs.* Philadelphia: Annenberg Public Policy Center.

Krippendorf, Klaus (1986). *Information Theory: Structural Models for Qualitative Data.* Newbury Park, CA: Sage.

Liebert, Robert M., and **Joyce N. Sprafkin.** (1988). *The Early Window: Effects of Television on Children and Youth.* New York: Pergamon.

Potter, W. James (1997). "The Problem of Indexing Risk of Viewing Television Aggression." *Critical Studies in Mass Communication,* 14, 228–248.

Wiener, Norbert (1954). *The Human Use of Human Beings: Cybernetics and Society.* Boston: Houghton Mifflin.

Section 4

Contemporary Mass Communication Theory—
Searching for Consensus and Confronting Challenges

1975 *ASNE's Statement of Principles replaces Canons*
      Bill Gates and Paul Allen develop operating system for personal computers

1977 *Steve Jobs and Stephen Wozniak perfect Apple II*

1978 *Digital audio and video recording adopted as media industry standard*

1981 *IBM introduces the PC*

1983 Journal of Communication *devotes entire issue to "Ferment in the Field"*

1985 *Meyrowitz's* No Sense of Place

1987 *Chaffee and Berger formalize "communication science"*

1990 *Signorielli and Morgan's* Cultivation Analysis

1991 *Gulf War explodes, CNN emerges as important news source*

1992 *ACT disbands, says work is complete*
      World Wide Web released

1993 *Ten years after "Ferment,"* Journal of Communication *tries again with special issue, "The Future of the Field"*

1996 *Telecommunications Act passes, relaxes broadcast ownership rules, deregulates cable television, mandates television content ratings*

1998 Journal of Communication *devotes entire issue to media literacy*

Chapter 9

Emergence of Critical and Cultural Theories of Mass Communication

Moviegoers in the late 1950s and early 1960s could see the same type of Hollywood spectacular with which they had become familiar before World War II. *The Ten Commandments* (1956), *Ben Hur* (1959), *El Cid* (1960), *Spartacus* (1960), and *Cleopatra* (1963) were gigantic productions filled with color and grandeur. But other movies were appearing on theater screens with increasing frequency. In the United States, they were called message movies, and they depicted an America that was not universally fair and democratic, a jarring message for the world's mightiest power. Hadn't the United States and its allies just made the world safe for democracy?

The Men (1950) focused on the difficult lot of returning injured GIs. *Blackboard Jungle* and *Rebel Without a Cause,* both released in 1955, provided stark, pessimistic views of the alienation of youth. *12 Angry Men* (1957), *Imitation of Life* (1959), and *To Kill a Mockingbird* (1962) challenged prejudice and racism in the "Land of the Free." *The Pawnbroker* (1965) examined the clash of class and culture in urban America. In Great Britain, message movies became the basis of a powerful cinematic movement, the British New Wave. *Room at the Top* (1959), *The Entertainer* (1960), *A Taste of Honey* (1961), *The L-Shaped Room* (1962), and *The Loneliness of the Long Distance Runner* (1962), dark, brooding films, "emphasized the poverty of the worker, the squalor of working-class life, the difficulty of keeping a home and keeping one's self-respect at the same time, (and) the social assumptions that sentence a person with no education and a working-class dialect to a lifetime of bare survival . . . In the midst of this gray world, the directors focus on a common man reacting to his surroundings—bitter, brutal, angry, tough" (Mast & Kawin, 1996, p. 412).

Anger might have run deeper in England than in the United States, but these films reflected a disillusionment and frustration common to both countries. Soldiers—especially minorities and working class people—and women who had served their countries well during the war, wanted to know why they were denied the full benefits of their countries' wealth and freedoms. Their curiosity turned to resentment because they were unwilling to return to the way things had been before the war. This social unrest manifested itself in both England and in the United States in many profound ways—for example, the rise of the Civil Rights and feminist movements in the United States and the erosion of Great Britain's rigid class structures. The unrest also shaped mass communication theory.

Overview

Challenge to the limited effects paradigm came from ideas other than social cognitive learning and systems theories. During the 1950s and 1960s, interest in cultural theories of mass communication began to develop and take hold. As we have noted in previous chapters, limited effects theory makes several questionable assumptions and has many serious limitations. Limited effects theory focuses on whether media content can have an immediate and direct effect on specific thoughts and actions of individuals. Researchers typically seek evidence for these effects in experiments or through surveys. But, it is possible to approach the study of mass media in quite another way. Instead of focusing on specific effects on individuals, we can focus instead on changes in culture, on how shared understandings and social norms change. Instead of trying to locate hundreds of small effects and add them all up, we can ask whether the development of mass media has profound implications for the way we create, share, learn, and apply culture.

In this chapter, we will trace the emergence of theories that directly address questions about the way media might produce profound changes in social life. These new perspectives argued that media might have the power to intrude into and alter how we make sense of ourselves and our social world. Political, economic, and educational institutions might be disrupted and transformed as media institutions play an increasingly central role in contemporary societies. These theories are quite diverse and offer very different answers to questions about the role of media in social life. In all these theories, the concept of **culture** is central. Media affect society because they affect how culture is created, shared, learned, and applied. Cultural theories offer a broad range of interesting ideas about how media can affect culture and provide many different views concerning the long-term consequences of the cultural changes affected by media.

CULTURE *The learned behavior of members of a given social group*

Changing Times

Children begin watching television attentively by the age of three. Before most children start school or form close relationships with peers, they have learned the names of countless television characters and are fans of particular programs. By the first day of elementary school, they are already watching nearly three hours a day. By eight years old, they are watching four full hours. By the time they finish high school, average teenagers will have spent more time in front of their television sets than they will have been engaged in any other activity except sleep; this means more time with television than in school. Most children also spend more time with their television sets than they do communicating with their friends or family. If other forms of media like radio, records, movies, video games, magazines, the Internet, and newspapers are considered, the contrast between the time spent with media and with the "actual" world and "real" people becomes even more striking (Arnett, 1999).

Modern mass media dominate everyday communication. From the time children learn to talk, they are mesmerized by the sounds and moving images of *Sesame Street*. During the teen years, media supply vital information on peer group culture and most important—the opposite sex. In middle age, as people rear families, they turn to television for convenient entertainment and to magazines for tips on raising teenagers. In old age, as physical mobility declines, people turn to television for companionship and advice.

Media have become a primary means by which many of us experience or learn about many aspects of the world around us. Even when we don't learn about these things directly from media, we learn about them from other people who get their ideas of the world from media. With the advent of mass media, many forms of folk culture fell into sharp decline. Everyday communication was fundamentally altered. Storytelling and music making ceased to be important within extended families. Instead, nuclear families gathered in front of an enthralling, electronic storyteller. Informal social groups dedicated to cultural enrichment disappeared—along with vaudeville and band concerts. It is no coincidence that our culture's respect for older people and the wisdom they hold has fallen in the age of media. If respected theorists like Joshua Meyrowitz (1985) and George Gerbner (Cultural Environment Movement, 1996) are correct, we're losing touch with locally based cultures and are moving into a media-based, global cultural environment.

Mass society theory (see Chapter 3) viewed these changes with alarm. Mediated culture was assumed to be inferior to elite culture. As mass culture spread, theorists feared it would undermine the social order and bring chaos. People's lives would be ruined. The sudden rise of totalitarian social orders in the 1930s seemed to fulfill these prophecies. In Fascist and Communist nations alike, media were used to propagate new and highly questionable forms of totalitarian culture. But were media ultimately responsible for their creation and promotion? Was the linkage between the new media and their messages so great that the drift into totalitarianism was inevitable? Or could media promote individualism and democracy as easily as collectivism and dictatorship? We have struggled with these questions throughout nearly a century of mass communication theory.

During the 1950s and 1960s, as the overt threat of a totalitarian take-over of the United States and the world declined, so too did interest in mass society theory. As we've seen, most social researchers in the United States adopted the limited effects perspective that media rarely produce significant, long-term changes in people's thoughts and actions. Limited effects researchers no longer assumed that mediated mass culture was inherently anti-democratic. American media had become highly effective promoters of capitalism, individualism, and free enterprise. Some critics now argue that newer media technologies, such as personal computers, the Internet, and camcorders, are actually biased toward individualism and market economies rather than toward collectivism and state control. So the role of media in culture seems to be settled—doesn't it? After all, we've won the Cold War. Shouldn't we conclude that media are benign? Can't we safely ignore the warnings in books like *1984* and *Brave New World?*

Critical theory suggests that it isn't safe to do so quite yet. As Hanno Hardt explained, the paradigm shift away from limited effects and toward theories postulating important media influence was "the result of complex social, political, and cultural developments that enable(d) ideas to rise and take hold of the imagination of individuals in their own struggle against a dominant professional ideology" (1999, p. 181).

The Cultural Turn in Media Research

CULTURAL STUDIES *Focus on use of media to create forms of culture that structure everyday life*

HEGEMONIC CULTURE *Culture imposed from above or outside that serves the interests of those in dominant social positions*

POLITICAL ECONOMY THEORIES *Focus on social elites' use of economic power to exploit media institutions*

It is possible to differentiate the various cultural theories of media in several ways. In this chapter, we will use a dichotomy that is widely used by cultural theorists to differentiate their scholarship (Garnham, 1995). There are *microscopic, interpretive theories* that focus on how individuals and social groups use media to create and foster forms of culture that structure everyday life. These theories are referred to as **cultural studies** theories. And *macroscopic, structural* theories focus on how social elites use their economic power to gain control over and exploit media institutions. These theories argue that elites effectively use media to propagate **hegemonic culture** as a means of maintaining their dominant position in the social order. They are called **political economy theories** because they place priority on understanding how economic power provides a basis for ideological and political power. Some researchers speculate about how alternate forms of culture and innovative media uses are systematically suppressed. These theories directly challenge the status quo by exposing elite manipulation of media and criticizing hegemonic culture.

Macroscopic versus Microscopic Theories

Cultural studies theories are less concerned with the long-term consequences of media for the social order and more concerned with looking at how media affect our individual lives. These theories, as we've seen throughout this book, are said to be micro-level or *microscopic* because they de-emphasize larger issues about the social order in favor of questions involving the everyday life of average people. Political economy theories by contrast are *macroscopic* cultural theories, which are less concerned with developing detailed explanations of how individuals are influenced by media and more concerned with how the social order as a whole is affected. Ideally, these theories ought to be complementary. Individual-level explanations of what media do to people should link to societal-level theories. Yet, until recently, macroscopic and microscopic cultural theories developed in relative isolation. Theorists were separated by differences in geography, politics, and research objectives. But that may be changing, as we'll see in Chapter 12.

Microscopic cultural studies researchers prefer to understand what is going on in the world immediately around them. These researchers believe the social world is an endlessly fascinating place. They are intrigued by the mundane, the seemingly trivial, the routine. They view our experience of everyday life and of reality itself as an artificial construction that we somehow maintain with only occasional, minor breakdowns. They want to know how mass media have been incorporated into the routines of daily life without creating serious disruptions. Perhaps the media do cause problems that are somehow being compensated for or concealed. If so, how is this being done? Will there be a breakdown eventually—are we being systematically desensitized and trained to be aggressive? Or is everyday life being transformed in useful ways—are we somehow becoming kinder and gentler?

Macroscopic researchers are troubled by the narrow focus of microscopic theory. So what if some people experience everyday life in certain ways? Why should we care about things that might affect only a few people? These researchers demand answers to larger questions. How do media affect the way politics is conducted, the way that a national economy operates, or the delivery of vital social services? Macroscopic researchers want to know if media are intruding into or disrupting large-scale social processes. For example, have media disrupted the conduct of national politics and therefore increased the likelihood that inferior politicians will be elected? Macroscopic researchers believe that such large-scale questions can't be answered if you focus on individuals.

Critical Theory

Some cultural studies and political economy theories are also referred to as critical theories because they openly espouse certain values and use these values to

Instant Access

Critical Theory

Strengths	Weaknesses
1 Is politically based, action-oriented	**1** Is too political; call to action is too subjective
2 Uses theory and research to plan change in the real world	**2** Typically lacks scientific verification; based on subjective observation
3 Asks big, important questions about media control and ownership	**3** When subjected to scientific verification, often employs innovative but controversial research methods

CRITICAL THEORIES
Theories openly espousing certain values and using these values to evaluate and criticize the status quo, providing alternate ways of interpreting the social role of mass media

evaluate and criticize the status quo. Those who develop **critical theories** seek to initiate social change that will implement their values. Political economy theories are inherently critical but some cultural studies theories are not. A critical theory raises questions and provides alternate ways of interpreting the social role of mass media. For example, some critical theorists argue that media in general sustain the status quo—even, perhaps especially, when that status quo is under stress or breaking down. Critical theory often provides complex explanations for this tendency of media to consistently do so. For example, some critical theorists identify constraints on media practitioners that limit their ability to challenge established authority. They charge that few incentives exist to encourage media professionals to overcome those constraints and that media practitioners consistently fail to even acknowledge them.

Critical theory often analyzes specific social institutions, probing the extent to which valued objectives are sought and achieved. Mass media and the mass culture they promote have become a focus for critical theory. Mass media and mass culture have been linked to a variety of social problems. Even when mass media are not seen as the source of specific problems, they are criticized for aggravating or preventing problems from being identified or addressed and solved. For example, a theorist might argue that content production practices of media practitioners either cause or perpetuate specific problems. A common theme in critical theories of media is that content production is so constrained that it inevitably reinforces the status quo and undermines useful efforts for constructive social change.

Consider, for example, the last time you read news reports about members of a social movement that strongly challenged the status quo. How were the movement's actions described? How were members and their leaders portrayed? Why were the college students who protested against the Communist Chinese government in Tiananmen Square "heroes of democracy" and those in the Anti-World Trade Organization/International Monetary Fund protests in Seattle, Washington, and Genoa of 2000 and 2001 "anarchists," "radicals," and "extremists"?

Stories about movements imply problems with the status quo. Movements frequently defy the authority of existing elites and make demands for social change. Media professionals are caught in the middle of the confrontation. Movement leaders demand coverage of their complaints, and they stage demonstrations designed to draw public attention to their concerns. Elites seek to minimize coverage or to exercise "spin control" so that coverage favors their positions. How do journalists handle this? How should they handle it? Existing research indicates that this coverage almost always denigrates movements and supports elites (FAIR, 2000; Gitlin, 1980; Tuchman, 1978).

Comparing Cultural Theories with Those Based on Empirical Research

It is useful to keep in mind both the strengths and limitations of the theories we will introduce in this chapter. Many of the theorists whose ideas we will discuss believe in powerful media effects and ask us to accept their view of media influence using logic, argument, and our own powers of observation rather than by presenting us with scientific "proof." They describe compelling examples to illustrate their arguments. Others offer empirical evidence for their belief in powerful media, but they use innovative research methods, and so their work is challenged and questioned by other social scientists. Supporters of the limited effects paradigm are especially troubled by the rise of cultural theories. They have been quick to question the evidence offered by cultural theorists to support their views of powerful media. Limited effects researchers believe that cultural theories are too speculative and the empirical research generated from these theories has been too loosely structured.

QUALITATIVE METH-ODS *Research methods that highlight essential differences (distinctive qualities) in phenomena*

Cultural studies and political economy theorists employ a broad range of research methods and theory generation strategies, including some that are unsystematic and selective. In contrast with the quantitative, empirical research methods described in previous chapters, these techniques are labeled as **qualitative**; that is, they highlight essential differences (distinctive qualities) in phenomena. Evaluation of ideas tends to be accomplished through debate and discussion involving proponents of contrasting or opposing theoretical positions. Theory is advanced through the formation of schools of thought in which there is consensus about the validity of a specific body of theory. Rival schools of theory emerge that work to undermine opposing theories while defending their own. Proof of a theory's power lies in its ability to attract adherents and be defended against attacks from opponents.

Not surprisingly, researchers who adopt a more traditional social science perspective find cultural theories hard to accept. They are skeptical of theories that are evaluated more through debate than through empirical research. Quantitative media researchers place far less stress on theory development or criticism. Their research methods are used for theory testing rather than as a means of making qualitative differentiations. They argue that if empirical research is conducted according to prevailing standards, findings can be readily accepted throughout the research community. If other researchers doubt the validity of specific findings, they can replicate (duplicate) the research and then report conflicting findings. Actually, these conflicting reports are rare and provoke considerable controversy when they are published. Though there is verbal debate between those who espouse conflicting, empirically based theories, these debates rarely appear in print. When they do, both sides present empirical findings to support their positions. Arguments often center around methodological disputes rather than the strength of the theoretical propositions—researchers disagree about whether appropriate methods were used, question the application of specific methods, or argue that the data were improperly analyzed. Much less attention is given to the structure and consistency of theoretical propositions.

Rise of Cultural Theories in Europe

GRAND SOCIAL THE-ORY *Highly ambitious, macroscopic, speculative theory that attempts to understand and predict important trends in culture and society*

MARXIST THEORY *Theory arguing that the hierarchical class system is at the root of all social problems and must be ended by a revolution of the proletariat*

Despite its long life in American social science, the limited effects paradigm never enjoyed great popularity in Europe. European social research has instead been characterized by what U.S. observers regard as **grand social theories**—highly ambitious, macroscopic, and speculative theories that attempt to understand and predict important trends in culture and society. In Chapter 3, we presented an early example of a European-style, grand social theory—mass society theory—that illustrated both the strengths and the limitations of grand theory. In Chapter 6, we explained why American social researchers, especially those trained in the Columbia School of empirical social research, preferred middle-range theories.

In Europe, the development of grand social theory remained a central concern in the social sciences and humanities. Mass society theory gave way to a succession of alternate ideas. Some were limited to specific nations and others spread across many countries. Some of the most widely accepted have been based on the writings of Karl Marx. **Marxist theory** influenced even the theories that were created in reaction against it. Marxist ideas formed a foundation or touchstone for much post–World War II European social theory and research. Cold War politics colored much of the U.S. response to it. Ironically, in the 1970s and 1980s, at the

Instant Access

Cultural Studies Theory

Strengths	Weaknesses
1 Provides focus on how individuals develop their understanding of the social world	1 Has little explanatory power at the macroscopic level
2 Asks big, important questions about the role of media	2 Focuses too narrowly on individual compared with societal effects
3 Respects content consumption abilities of audience members	3 Typically lacks scientific verification; based on subjective observation
	4 When subjected to scientific verification, often employs nontraditional (controversial) research methods

very time that Marxism failed as a practical guide for politics and economics in Eastern Europe, grand social theories based on Marxist thought were gaining increasing acceptance in Western Europe (Grossberg & Nelson, 1988). We will briefly summarize key arguments in the Marxist perspective and pay particular attention to media. Then we will present some more recent theories that are based on these ideas.

Marxist Theory

Karl Marx developed his theory in the latter part of the nineteenth century during one of the most volatile periods of social change in Europe. In some respects, his is yet another version of mass society theory—but with several very important alterations and additions. Marx was familiar with the grand social theories of his era. He drew on them or constructed his ideas in opposition to them. He identified industrialization and urbanization as problems but argued that these changes were not inherently bad. Instead, he blamed ruthless, robber baron capitalists for exacerbating social problems because they maximized personal profits by exploiting workers. Where mass society theorists demanded restoration of the old order, Marx was a utopian, calling for the creation of an entirely new social order in which all social classes would be abolished. The workers would rise against capitalists and demand an end to exploitation. They would band together to create an egalitarian, democratic social order.

Marx argued that the hierarchical class system was at the root of all social problems and must be ended by a revolution of the workers or proletariat. He believed that elites dominated society primarily through their direct control over the means of production (that is, labor, factories, and land), which he referred to as the **base** of society.

BASE *In Marxist theory, the means of production*

SUPERSTRUCTURE *In Marxist theory, a society's culture*

IDEOLOGY *In Marxist theory, ideas present in a culture that mislead average people and encourage them to act against their own interests*

But elites also maintained themselves in power through their control over culture, or the **superstructure** of society. He saw culture as something that elites freely manipulated to mislead average people and encourage them to act against their own interests. He used the term **ideology** to refer to these forms of culture. Marx believed an ideology operated much like a drug. Those who are under its influence fail to see how they are being exploited. In the worst cases, they are so deceived that they actually undermine their own interests and do things that increase the power of elites while making their own lives even worse.

Marx concluded that the only hope for social change was a revolution in which the masses seized control of the base—the means of production. Control over the superstructure—over ideology—would naturally follow. He saw little possibility that reforms in the superstructure could lead to social evolution, or if it could, that that transformation would be very slow in coming. Elites would never willingly surrender power. Power must be taken from them. Little purpose would be served by making minor changes in ideology without first dominating the means of production.

Neomarxism

BRITISH CULTURAL THEORY *A hybrid theory that traces historic domination over culture, criticizes that domination, and demonstrates how it continues*

NEOMARXIST THEORY *Contemporary incarnation of Marxist theory focusing attention on the superstructure*

Most **British cultural studies** theories discussed in this chapter can be labeled **neomarxist**. They deviate from classic Marxist theory in at least one important respect—they focus concern on the superstructure issues of ideology and culture rather than on the base. The importance that neomarxists attach to the superstructure has created a fundamental division within Marxism. Many neomarxists assume that useful change can begin with peaceful, ideological reform rather than violent revolution in which the working class seizes control of the means of production. Some neomarxists have developed critiques of culture that call for radically transforming the superstructure whereas others call for modest reforms. Tensions have arisen among scholars who base their work on Marx's ideas over the value of the work being done by the various neomarxist schools.

Textual Analysis and Literary Criticism

Modern European cultural studies theories have a second, very different source—a tradition of humanist criticism of religious and literary texts that is referred to as hermeneutics (Chapter 2). Humanists have specialized in analyzing written texts since the Renaissance. One common objective was to identify those texts that had greatest cultural value and to interpret them so that their value would be appreciated and understood by others. Texts were seen as a civilizing force in society (Bloom, 1987). Hermeneutics was used to enhance this force. Humanist scholars ranged from religious humanists who focused on the Bible or the writings of great theologians to secular humanists who worked to identify and preserve what came to be known as the "literary canon"—a body of the great literature. The literary canon was part of what was referred to as **high culture**, a set of cultural artifacts including music, art, literature, and poetry that humanists judged to have the highest value. By identifying and explaining these important texts, humanists attempted to make them more accessible to more people. Their long-term goal was to preserve and gradually raise the level of culture—to enable even more people to become humane and civilized.

HIGH CULTURE *Set of cultural artifacts including music, art, literature, and poetry that humanists judged to have the highest value*

Over the years, many different methods for analyzing written texts have emerged from hermeneutics. These methods are now being applied to many other forms of culture, including media content (Littlejohn, 1996, pp. 208–225). They share a common purpose: to criticize old and new cultural practices so that those most deserving of attention can be identified and explicated and the less deserving can be dismissed. This task can be compared with that of movie critics who tell us which films are good or bad and assist us in appreciating or avoiding them. The primary difference is that many movie critics are typically not committed to promoting higher cultural values; they only want to explain which movies we are likely to find entertaining.

As we shall see in Chapter 12, contemporary critical theory includes both neomarxist and hermeneutic approaches. Hybrid theories combine both. Before examining these, we will look at some of the historically important schools of critical theory that have produced work that is still influential.

The Frankfurt School

FRANKFURT SCHOOL *Group of neomarxist scholars who worked together in the 1930s at the University of Frankfurt*

One early prominent school of neomarxist theory developed during the 1930s at the University of Frankfurt and became known as the **Frankfurt School.** Two of the most prominent individuals associated with the school were Max Horkheimer, its long-time head, and Theodor Adorno, a prolific and cogent theorist. In contrast with some later forms of neomarxism, the Frankfurt School combined Marxist critical theory with hermeneutics. Its writings identified and promoted various forms of high culture such as symphony music, great literature, and art. Like most secular humanists, members of the Frankfurt School viewed high culture as something that had its own integrity, had inherent value, and could not be used by elites to enhance their personal power.

Though high culture was extolled by the Frankfurt School, mass culture was denigrated (Arato & Gebhardt, 1978). Horkheimer and Adorno were openly skeptical that high culture could or should be communicated through mass media. Adorno argued that radio broadcasts or records couldn't begin to adequately reproduce the sound of a live symphony orchestra. He ridiculed the reproduction of great art in magazines or the reprinting of great novels in condensed, serialized form. He claimed that mass media reproductions of high culture were inferior and diverted people from seeking out (and paying for) the "real thing." If bad substitutes for high culture were readily available, he believed, too many people would settle for them and fail to support better forms of culture.

The Frankfurt School has been criticized along with other forms of traditional humanism for being too elitist and paternalistic. By rejecting the possibility of using media to disseminate high culture, most of the population was effectively denied access to it. Many of the school's criticisms of media paralleled those of mass society theory and had the same limitations that we listed in Chapter 3.

The Frankfurt School eventually had a direct impact on American social research because the rise of the Nazis forced its Jewish members into exile. Horkheimer, for one, took up residency at the New School for Social Research in New York City. During this period of exile, however, Frankfurt School theorists remained productive. They devoted considerable effort, for example, to the critical analysis of Nazi culture and the way it undermined and perverted high culture. In their view, Nazism was grounded on a phony, artificially constructed folk culture that had been cynically created and manipulated by Hitler and his propagandists. This hodgepodge of folk culture integrated many bits and pieces of culture borrowed from various Germanic peoples. But Nazism did appeal to a people humiliated by war and deeply troubled by a devastating economic depression. Nazism helped them envision the Germany they longed to see—a unified, proud nation with a long history of achievement and a glorious future. As they rose to power, the Nazis replaced high culture with their pseudo-folk culture and discredited important forms of high culture, especially those created by Jews.

Development of Neomarxist Theory in Britain

During the 1960s and 1970s two important schools of neomarxist theory emerged in Great Britain: British cultural studies and political economy theory. British cultural studies combines neomarxist theory with ideas and research methods derived from diverse sources including literary criticism, linguistics, anthropology, and history (Hall, 1980a). This theory has attempted to trace historic elite domination over culture, to criticize the social consequences of this domination, and to demonstrate how it continues to be exercised over specific minority groups or subcultures. British cultural studies criticizes and contrasts elite notions of culture, including high culture, with popular, everyday forms practiced by minorities. The superiority of all forms of elite culture including high culture is challenged and compared with useful, valuable forms of popular culture. Hermeneutic attention is shifted from the study of elite cultural artifacts to the study of minority group "lived culture."

Graham Murdock (1989b) traced the rise of British cultural studies during the 1950s and 1960s. Most of the important theorists came from the lower social classes that were the focus of the movies discussed at the beginning of this chapter. The British cultural studies critique of high culture and ideology was an explicit rejection of what its proponents saw as alien forms of culture imposed on minorities. They defended indigenous forms of popular culture as legitimate expressions of minority groups. A dominant early theorist was Raymond Williams, a literary scholar who achieved notoriety with his reappraisals of cultural development in England. Williams pieced together a highly original perspective of how culture develops based on ideas taken from many sources, including literary theories, linguistics, and neomarxist writing. He questioned the importance of high culture and seriously considered the role of folk culture. Not surprisingly, Williams' ideas were viewed with suspicion and skepticism by many of his colleagues at Cambridge University. Throughout most of his career, he labored in relative obscurity.

Toward the end of the 1960s and into the 1970s, Williams (1967, 1974) turned his attention to mass media. Although media weren't the focus of his work, he developed an innovative, pessimistic perspective of mass media's role in modern society. His ideas inspired a generation of young British media scholars, first at the Centre for Contemporary Cultural Studies at the University of Birmingham and then at other universities across England and Europe. Williams was more broadly concerned with issues of cultural change and development as well as elite domination of culture. Committed to certain basic, humanistic values including cultural pluralism and egalitarianism, he argued that mass media posed a threat to worthwhile cultural development. In contrast with most humanists of his time, Williams rejected the literary canon as a standard, and with it traditional notions of high culture. But he was equally reluctant to embrace and celebrate folk culture—especially when it was repackaged as popular, mass media content. If there were to be genuine progress, he felt, it would have to come through significant reform of social institutions.

The first important school of cultural studies theorists was formed at the University of Birmingham during the 1960s and was led by Stuart Hall. Hall (1982) was especially influential in directing several analyses of mass media that directly challenge limited effects notions and in introducing innovative alternatives. Building on ideas developed by Jürgen Habermas (1971, 1989) and Williams, Hall understood ideology to be "those images, concepts, and premises which provide frameworks through which we represent, interpret, understand, and make sense of some aspect of social existence" (1981b, p. 31). As such, he argued that mass media in liberal democracies can best be understood as a **pluralistic public forum** in which various forces struggle to shape popular notions about social existence. In this forum, new concepts of social reality are negotiated and new boundary lines between various social worlds are drawn. Unlike traditional Marxists, however, Hall did not argue that elites can maintain complete control over this forum. In his view, elites don't need that power to advance their interests. The culture expressed in this forum is not a mere superficial reflection of the superstructure but is instead a dynamic creation of opposing groups. To Hall, popular culture "is the ground on which the transformations are worked" (1981a, p. 228). Elites, however, *do* retain many advantages in the struggle to define social reality. Counter-elite groups must work hard to overcome them. Hall acknowledged that heavy-handed efforts by elites to promote their ideology can fail and well-planned efforts to promote alternative perspectives can succeed even against great odds. Nevertheless, the advantages enjoyed by elites enable them to retain a long-term hold on power.

A key strength *and* limitation of some British cultural studies theorists is their direct involvement in various radical social movements. In keeping with their commitment to critical theory, these theorists not only study movements, they enlist in them and even lead them. Some cultural studies advocates (O'Connor, 1989) argue that a person cannot be a good social theorist unless he or she is personally committed to bringing about change. Cultural studies theorists have been active in a broad range of British social movements including feminism, youth movements, racial and ethnic minority movements, and British Labour party factions. But active involvement can make objective analysis of movements and movement culture difficult. These cultural studies theorists usually don't worry about this because they reject the possibility of objectivity anyway and doubt its utility for social research. Their aim is to do research that aids the goals of movements rather than conduct work that serves the traditional aims of scholarship or science.

British cultural studies has produced a variety of research on popular media content and the use that specific social groups make of that content. Many questions have been addressed. Does this content exploit and mislead individuals or does it enable them to construct meaningful identities and experiences? Can people take ambiguous content and interpret it in new ways that fundamentally alters its purpose for them? Can useful social change be achieved through cultural reform rather than through social revolution?

In the United States, British cultural studies is influencing research by scholars in many fields, particularly the work of feminists (Long, 1989) and those who

PLURALISTIC PUBLIC FORUM *In critical theory, the idea that media may provide a place where the power of dominant elites can be challenged*

Instant Access

British Cultural Studies

Strengths	Weaknesses
1 Asserts value of popular culture	1 Is too political; call to action is too subjective
2 Empowers "common" man	2 Typically lacks scientific verification; is based on subjective observation
3 Empowers minorities and values their culture	3 When subjected to scientific verification, often employs innovative but controversial research methods
4 Stresses cultural pluralism and egalitarianism	

study popular culture (Grossberg, 1989). We will examine some of the most important recent work in Chapters 10 and 11. Cultural studies is seen as providing an innovative way of studying media audiences that has many advantages over approaches grounded in limited effects theory.

Political Economy Theory

Political economy theorists study elite control of economic institutions such as banks and stock markets and then try to show how this control affects many other social institutions, including the mass media (Murdock, 1989a). In certain respects, political economists accept the classic Marxist assumption that the base dominates the superstructure. They investigate the means of production by looking at economic institutions, then expect to find that these institutions will shape media to suit their interests and purposes. For example, Herb Schiller, "one of the most widely recognized and influential political economists of communication" (Gerbner, 2001, p. 187), wrote for decades that "corporate influence pervades nearly every aspect of society. From simple things, like our daily diet and the clothes we wear, to matters of larger scale, like the way we communicate with each other" (Schiller, 2000, p. 101). Political economists have examined how economic constraints limit or bias the forms of mass culture that are produced and distributed through the media. These economists are less concerned with investigating how mass culture influences specific groups or subcultures and are more concerned with understanding how the processes of content production and dis-

Instant Access

Political Economy Theory

Strengths	Weaknesses
1 Provides focus on how media are structured and controlled	1 Has little explanatory power at microscopic level
2 Offers empirical investigation of media finances	2 Is not concerned with scientific verification; is based on subjective analysis of finances
3 Seeks link between media content production and media finances	

tribution are constrained. Why do some forms of culture dominate prime-time television schedules whereas other forms are absent? Does audience taste alone explain those differences or can other, less obvious reasons be linked to the interests of economic institutions?

During the past four decades, political economy theorists have worked in relative obscurity compared with cultural studies theorists. Although political economy theories gained respect in Europe and Canada, they were largely ignored in the United States. Even though American communication theorists were intrigued by cultural studies theory, few found the views of political economists interesting or persuasive until quite recently, as we'll see in Chapter 11.

Although the two schools of neomarxist theory—British cultural studies and political economy theory—appear to be complementary, there has been considerable rivalry between them (Murdock, 1989b). Some genuine theoretical differences separate the two, but they also differ in their research methods and the academic disciplines in which they are based. With their macroscopic focus on economic institutions and their assumption that economic dominance leads to or perpetuates cultural dominance, political economists were slow to acknowledge that cultural changes can affect economic institutions. Nor do political economists recognize the diversity of popular culture or the variety of ways in which people make sense of cultural content. Murdock suggested that the two schools should cooperate rather than compete. For this to happen, however, researchers on both sides will have to give up some of their assumptions and recognize that the superstructure and the base—culture and the media industries—can influence each other. Both types of research are necessary to produce a complete assessment of the role of media. In Chapters 11 and 12, we examine some recent proposals for creating integrated perspectives. One of the most interesting and powerful of these proposals conceptualizes media as culture industries and argues that the production and distribution of cultural commodities have profoundly disrupted modern social orders (Cultural Environment Movement, 1996; Enzensberger, 1974; Hay, 1989; Jhally, 1987).

The Debate Between Cultural Studies and Political Economy Theorists

Despite their shared concerns and assumptions, key differences have led to serious debates between these two major schools of cultural theory. Cultural studies theorists tend to ignore the larger social and political context in which media operate. These theorists focus instead on how popular culture content is consumed by individuals and groups. Their research has led them to become increasingly skeptical about the power of elites to promote hegemonic forms of culture. Instead, they have found that average people often resist interpreting media content in ways that would serve elite interests (see the discussion of oppositional decoding in Chapter 10). Cultural studies theorists have been less interested in making or influencing social policy, and their research often doesn't provide a clear basis for criticizing the status quo. Political economy theorists often accuse cultural studies theorists of abandoning the historical mission of critical theory and instead adopting the value-free stance toward research that dominates social science in the United States. Political economy adherents argue that it is important for theorists to actively work for social change.

Political economy theorists have remained centrally concerned with the larger social order and elites' ownership of media. These theorists have criticized the growing privatization of media in Europe and the increasing centralization of media ownership around the world. They take pride in remaining true to the mission of critical theory by being politically active and by seeking to shape social policy. They have formed social movements and serve as leaders within other movements. Above all, political economy theorists are critical—they have an explicit set of values that provides a basis for their evaluation of the status quo.

Cultural Studies: Transmissional versus Ritual Perspectives

James Carey has been a leading American proponent of cultural studies during the past three decades. Drawing on the work of British and Canadian scholars, he contrasted cultural studies with the limited effects paradigm in a series of seminal essays (1989). One essential difference that he found is that limited effects theories focus on the transmission of accurate information from a dominant source to passive receivers whereas cultural studies are concerned with the every-

TRANSMISSIONAL
PERSPECTIVE *View
of mass communi-
cation as merely
the process of
transmitting mes-
sages from a dis-
tance for the pur-
pose of control*

day rituals that we rely on to structure and interpret our experiences. Carey argued that the limited effects view is tied to the **transmissional perspective**—the
view that mass communication is a "process of transmitting messages at a distance for the purpose of control. The archetypal case . . . then is persuasion, attitude change, behavior modification, socialization through the transmission of
information, influence, or conditioning" (Newcomb & Hirsch, 1983, p. 46). In
the transmissional perspective, car commercials attempt to persuade us to buy a
certain make of automobile, and political campaign messages are simply that,
campaign messages designed to cause us to vote one way or another. They might
or might not be effective in causing us to act as they intend.

RITUAL PERSPECTIVE
*View of mass com-
munication as the
representation of
shared belief where
reality is produced,
maintained, re-
paired, and
transformed*

The **ritual perspective**, on the other hand, views mass communication as "not
directed toward the extension of messages in space but the maintenance of society
in time; not the act of imparting information but the representation of shared beliefs" (Newcomb & Hirsch, 1983, p. 46). Carey (1975a, p. 177) believed, in other
words, that "communication is a symbolic process whereby reality is produced,
maintained, repaired, and transformed." According to Carey, a car commercial sells
more than transportation. It is, depending on its actual content, possibly reaffirm-
ing the American sense of independence ("It's a Chevy, it's your freedom"), reinforcing cultural notions of male and female attractiveness (we don't see many
homely actors in these ads), or extolling the personal value of consumption, regardless of the product itself ("Be the first on your block to have one"). Similarly,
political campaign messages often say much more about our political system and
us as a people than they say about the candidates featured in them.

Carey traced the origin of the ritual view to hermeneutic literary criticism.
Scholars who study great literary works have long argued that these texts have far-
reaching, long-lasting, and powerful effects on society. A classic example is the
impact that Shakespeare has had on Western culture. By reshaping or transforming culture, these works indirectly influence even those who have never read
them or even heard of them. Literary scholars argue that contemporary cultures
are analyzed and defined through their arts, including those arts that depend on
media technology. These scholars have not been interested in finding evidence of
direct media effects on individuals. They are more concerned with macroscopic
questions of cultural evolution—the culture defining itself for itself. Thus, ritual
perspective theorists presume a grand-scale interaction between the culture, the
media used to convey that culture, and the individual media content consumers
of that culture.

During the 1970s and 1980s, some communication theorists began to move
away from more transmissionally oriented questions like "What effects do media
have on society or on individuals?" and "How do people use the media?" toward
broader examinations of how cultures organize themselves, how people negotiate
common meaning and are bound by it, and how media systems interact with the

culture to affect the latter's definition of itself. This, as we'll see, allowed cultural theories to become home for a variety of people who presumed the operation of powerful mass media, for example advertising and market researchers, neomarxist media critics, and even sophisticated social researchers. The primary issue was no longer whether media have certain effects on individuals, but what kind of people we are, we have become, or we are becoming in our mass mediated world.

Symbolic Interaction

SYMBOLIC INTER-
ACTION *Theory that people give meaning to symbols and those meanings come to control those people*

SOCIAL BEHAVIORISM *View of learning that focuses on the mental processes and the social environment in which learning takes place*

Symbolic interaction was one of the first social science theories to address questions of how we use culture to learn. Symbolic interaction theory developed during the 1920s and 1930s as a reaction to and criticism of behaviorism (see Chapter 3), and it had a variety of labels until Herbert Blumer gave it its current name in 1969. One early name was **social behaviorism**. Unlike traditional behaviorists, social behaviorists rejected simplistic conceptualizations of stimulus-response conditioning. They were convinced that attention must be given to the mental processes that mediate learning. Social behaviorists believed that the social environment in which learning takes place must be considered. Traditional behaviorists tended to conduct laboratory experiments in which animals were exposed to certain stimuli and conditioned to behave in specific ways. Social behaviorists believed these experiments were absurd. They believed that human existence was far too complex to be understood through conditioning of animal behavior.

George Herbert Mead (1934), a University of Chicago philosopher and social activist, provided a way of understanding social life that differed profoundly from behaviorist notions. Rather than observe rats running through mazes, he proposed that a better way to understand how people learn is to look at how people learn to play baseball (or any team sport). How do we learn to play these games? Surely not by reading textbooks on *The Theory of Playing Second Base*. Not through stimulus-response conditioning. Mead argued that what occurs on a playing field is a sophisticated form of *mutual conditioning*—the players teach each other how to play the game while they are playing it. Players must learn to structure their actions in very complex ways to cover their positions effectively. But each position must be played differently, so teammates can't simply mimic one another. According to Mead, each player learns a social role—the pitcher role, the catcher role, or the left fielder role. Each is learned by observing and modeling good players and by interacting with other team members. As they play, team members receive encouragement and friendly criticism from teammates and fans. If they play well, they have the satisfaction of being accepted by others as a productive member of a social unit.

Mead believed a baseball team could be regarded as a microcosm of society. Each of us learns many different social roles through interaction with others. Our actions are being subtly "conditioned" by others while we are affecting their actions. The goal is not to manipulate or dominate each other but rather to create and sustain a productive social unit—a group that provides its members with certain rewards in return for their willingness to take on specific roles. We learn social roles through interaction, through experiences in daily life situations. Over time, we internalize the rules inherent in the situations and structure our actions accordingly. Only in rare cases do we consciously reflect on and analyze our actions. If asked to explain what we are doing and why we are doing it, we are puzzled—the question seems strange. Why don't you call your mother by her first name? Why do you wear clothes to school? We are doing something because it is common sense, it's the way everybody does it, it's the normal, the logical, the right way to do things. Once internalized, these roles provide us with a powerful means of controlling our actions. In time, our identity becomes bound up with them—we feel good about ourselves because we play certain roles that are respected by others. And sometimes, like athletes whose physical skills inevitably fail, we experience identity crises because we can't play a role as we or others expect us to play it.

Mead's analogy is insightful and powerful, but it has some important limitations common to microscopic theories. Mead assumes that baseball teams operate as a sort of miniature democracy. But where do the teams come from? How do they get established? Who defines the rules of baseball games? Who sells the tickets, pays expenses, and profits from the game? The team members mutually influence each other, but often a few older or more experienced players will dominate the others. And what about teams as a whole? They have managers and owners who hire and fire team members.

The baseball team analogy also isn't very helpful for understanding how mass media might affect socialization. Players interact directly with one another. What happens when communication occurs through media? Perhaps a more up-to-date analogy would be a group of people who use computers to engage in an interactive, role-playing game like *Ultima On-Line*. Unlike baseball players who confront each other physically on the field, these role players meet each other as characters in a complex fantasy-drama. They each sit at their personal computers, linked to a remote server via modems and phone lines. The game can go on endlessly with the computer taking over roles as players drop in and out. Players choose a role as they enter the game and use it to structure their interaction with others. To take on a role and enjoy the game, players must acquire considerable knowledge about the fantasy world. They could get this knowledge only from playing the game, but this would be inefficient and frustrating—they would figuratively die a thousand deaths. A more efficient way of learning the game is through media—comic books, books, magazines, and television programs. Once you have found or constructed a role you think you might enjoy playing, you are ready to log on and try it. In this example, there is mutual conditioning, but it occurs after use of media and reinforces knowledge gained through media.

Mead offered another important insight into the socialization process. Unlike animals that are conditioned to respond to stimuli in predetermined ways, human socialization permits more or less conscious interpretation of stimuli and planned responses. What is the secret that enables us to do what animals cannot? *Symbols.* **Symbols** are arbitrary, often quite abstract representations of unseen phenomena. Think of the words you use—all are arbitrary vocalizations that are essentially meaningless except to others who know how to decode them. When we write we cover pages with complicated markings. To read them, someone must be literate in our language. According to Mead, the use of symbols transforms the socialization process—freeing it from the bonds of both space and time. Using symbols, we can create vivid representations of the past and we can anticipate the future. We can be transported anywhere on the globe or even into the far reaches of space.

In *Mind, Self, and Society,* Mead (1934) argues that we use symbols to create our experience of consciousness (Mind), our understanding of ourselves (Self), and our knowledge of the larger social order (Society). In other words, symbols mediate and structure all our experience because they structure our ability to perceive and interpret what goes on around us. This argument is similar to the one made by information processing theorists (see Chapter 10). In information processing theory, sets of symbols called **schemas** enable us to routinely make sense of the sensory information we take in. Mead believed that mind, self, and society are internalized as complex sets of symbols. They serve as filtering mechanisms for our experiences. For information processing theorists, schemas perform a similar function.

This might seem to be an extreme argument. Most of us take for granted our ability to look at the world around us and see the things that are obviously there. You might assume that you were born with this ability. But think about it. Why do you notice certain things and not others? Unless you are unusually fastidious, for example, you will not notice small amounts of dust and dirt when you enter a room. According to Mead, human perceptual processes are extremely malleable and can be shaped by the sets of symbols we learn so that we will see only what our culture has determined is worth seeing (were you taken in by Charles Stuart and Susan Smith as discussed in Chapter 6? How aware of Islam and Afghanistan were you before September 11, 2001?). Mead's arguments anticipated cognitive psychology research that is beginning to empirically demonstrate much of what he hypothesized.

Thus, symbolic interactionism posits that our actions in response to symbols are mediated (or controlled) largely by those same symbols. Therefore, a person's understanding of and relation to his or her physical or objective reality is medi-

SYMBOLS *In general, arbitrary, often abstract representations of unseen phenomena*

SCHEMAS *In information processing, mental categories used in interpretation*

ated by the symbolic environment—the mind, self, and society that we have internalized. Put another way, the meanings we give to symbols define us and the realities that we experience. As we are socialized, culturally agreed-upon meanings assume control over our interactions with our environments.

Consider the meaning that you attach to the sewn red, white, and blue cloth that constitutes an American flag. A flag is, in reality (objectively), little more than a piece of colored cloth. That is, it is little more than a piece of cloth until someone attaches symbolic meaning to it. We have decided that a particular array and formulation of colors and shapes should become our flag. Each of us experiences the flag differently, yet there is shared meaning as well. To Afghan civilians who saw it fly from the rear of tanks and jeeps in the 2001 war on terrorism, the Stars and Stripes signified liberation from Taliban oppression. To Somalis in 1992, it became associated with food and medical care. To people from some other countries—Serbs during the 1999 Kosovo war, for example—it might represent oppression. Regardless of the meaning we attach to our flag, however, we are not free from its power. When a color guard passes before you at a sporting event, how free are you to remain sitting? At a school function, how free are you to continue chatting with your friends during the pledge of allegiance to that tri-colored piece of fabric? Box 9a offers the idea of sensemaking as one way to better understand the close relationship between communication and a culture's definitions of certain symbols.

Although Mead first articulated his ideas in the 1930s, not until the 1970s and 1980s did mass communication researchers give serious attention to symbolic interaction. Given the great emphasis that Mead placed on interpersonal interaction and his disregard for media, it is not surprising that media theorists were slow to see the relevancy of his ideas. Michael Solomon (1983), a consumer researcher, provided a summary of Mead's work that is especially relevant for media research:

- Cultural symbols are learned through interaction and then mediate that interaction.

- The "overlap of shared meaning" by people in a culture means that individuals who learn a culture should be able to predict the behaviors of others in that culture.

- Self-definition is social in nature; the self is defined largely through interaction with the environment.

- The extent to which a person is committed to a social identity will determine the power of that identity to influence his or her behavior.

Among the most notable efforts by communication scholars to apply this symbolic interactionist thinking to our use of mass media was the book, *Communication and Social Behavior: A Symbolic Interaction Perspective*, written by Don F. Faules and Dennis C. Alexander in 1978. Basing their analysis on their definition

Box 9a   Sensemaking: The Intersection of Communication and Culture

by Dennis Jaehne, Professor of Communication, San José State University.

As obvious as the link between culture and communication may seem to researchers and theorists who work in the cultural studies tradition, not all observers are aware of (or convinced of the power of) that relationship. But one easy way to conceptualize this interaction is to think of it in terms of *sensemaking*.

Linking culture with communication may be logical in the large sense, but such a generalization doesn't make clear how this process works to produce an effect. To understand the communication-culture relationship, we need to distinguish culture as an abstract body of knowledge from culture as a process or performance by real actors (like you) in real time (your life). The performance/process that links culture and communication is the process of sensemaking that each of us goes through to make the world meaningful.

To grasp the significance of this idea, imagine yourself in a world before meaning. This is difficult, if not impossible to do, so we'll need a metaphor to help us. Suppose I plunk you down in a strange place in total darkness. Now suppose I give you a flashlight. Your first reaction is to shine the light on something so you can see it, so you can begin to make sense of where you are. Gradually, as you shine your beam of light

in more and more places, you render your situation more and more meaningful. Places where you don't shine your light remain in darkness and have no meaning for you yet. Now imagine that words and their concepts work just like your flashlight. When you have a word/concept for something it becomes real to you, and meaningful. You can see it in your mind's eye or in the world around you. You can talk about it to yourself (that is, you can think about it) or to others.

Once you open your eyes in the morning and become conscious, your sensemaking apparatus is switched on and it operates for as long as you are awake. In fact, it is useful to think of consciousness as the ongoing process of sensemaking.

Obviously, communication requires a sender and a message, but also a receiver. You will always alternate between both sender and receiver roles. But both roles require you to interpret the world so that it is meaningful (so that it makes sense) to both you and your fellow communicators. As creatures, we have evolved so far into the "second nature" of communication that we take for granted the actual sensemaking process we go through.

Consider something as simple as a smile. If you look it up in the dictionary, it will probably tell you what you already know: to show plea-

of communication as "symbolic behavior that results in various degrees of shared meaning and values between participants," they offered three fundamental propositions on symbolic interaction and communication:

1   People's interpretation and perception of the environment depend on communication. In other words, what we know of our world is largely a function of our prior communication experiences in that world. This conforms to Solomon's idea

Box 9a   Sensemaking: The Intersection of Communication and Culture (*continued*)

sure by an upward curving of the mouth. The very act of defining a concept is to involve a set of distinctions that sets the smile apart from what it is not. For example, it shows pleasure, not pain; the curve is upwards, not downwards or sideward; it is a curving, not a rounding or straightening. But when does a smile actually begin? And how do you distinguish the brave smile that masks deep pain from the smile of innocent joy you get while interacting with a newborn child, or the smile that says I just betrayed you, I one-upped you, or I'm smarter than you?

When you smile one of these smiles, you enact a distinction between types of smiles that you have learned as part of your cultural repertoire. Indeed, you probably just pictured in your mind what each of these various smiles might look like, perhaps recalling specific instances of your experience of such smiles. Furthermore, you expect that the receivers of your communication also share the repertoire of smile distinctions and that they will know which smile you "mean." They will correctly interpret your smile as meaning pain, joy, betrayal, and so on.

Chances are, however, that until you just now processed our example, you didn't consciously realize that you had a menu of smile distinctions. The point is, you did (you DO)—and so

do all the rest of the competent members of your cultural group. Thus, what culture comes to mean for us is an indication of a whole range of distinctions for making sense of the world that a group of people share. And of course, the range of distinctions is quite broad and complex—distinctions among frowns, for example, and all our other facial expressions, among all our words, our tones of voice, our body postures, our hand gestures. As we grow up in a culture, we continually build up our personal repertoire of distinctions we can make in this culture. We are becoming enculturated. When we communicate with others, we enact (or embody or make present) some specific sets of distinctions for that communicative situation. Those others invoke the same set of distinctions in order to interpret the communication and make it meaningful. Thus, culture provides us with the total set of categories and distinctions while communication selects certain specific categories and distinctions to use from moment to moment as we attempt to create and share a jointly meaningful world with others.

Can you find a rearticulation of the ritual perspective of communication in Dr. Jaehne's essay? Can you find support for symbolic interaction and social construction of reality?

of interaction with cultural symbols. As Faules and Alexander wrote, "Communication allows for the reduction of uncertainty without direct sensory experience. The media are a prime source of indirect experience and for that reason have impact on the construction of social reality" (1978, p. 23).

2   Communication is guided by and guides the concepts of self, role, and situations, and these concepts generate expectations in and of the environment. Put

SIGN *In symbolic interaction, any element in the environment used to represent another element in the environment*

NATURAL SIGNS *In symbolic interaction, things occurring in nature that represent something else in nature*

ARTIFICIAL SIGNS *In symbolic interaction, elements that have been constructed to represent something else in the social world*

SIGNALS *In symbolic interaction, artificial signs that produce highly predictable responses*

SYMBOLS *In symbolic interaction, artificial signs for which there is less certainty of response*

differently, our use of communication in different settings is related to our understanding of ourselves and others in those situations. This is analogous to Solomon's point about learning a culture and predicting the behavior of others.

3 Communication consists of complex interactions "involving action, interdependence, mutual influence, meaning, relationship, and situational factors" (1978, p. 23). Here we can see not only a communication-oriented restatement of Solomon's precepts three and four, but also a rearticulation of the ritual perspective. Faules and Alexander are clearly reminding us that our understanding of our world and our place in it are created by us in interaction and involvement with media symbols.

Before we get any further into symbolic interaction, however, we must mention some definitional differences between this perspective and its close relative, social construction of reality, discussed in the next section of this chapter. In symbolic interaction theory, a **sign** is any element in the environment used to represent another element in the environment. Signs can be classified in two ways. One is **natural signs**, those things in nature—like the changing color of leaves—that represent something else in nature—the coming of autumn. The second is **artificial signs**, elements that have been constructed—like a handshake—to represent something else in the social world—like a friendly greeting. These artificial signs only work if the people using them agree on their meaning, that is, if they are "interactive"; two or more people must agree on their meaning and must further agree to respond to that sign in a relatively consistent fashion. Social construction of reality uses the concept of signs somewhat differently, as you'll soon see.

Another difference is symbolic interaction's distinction between signals and symbols. **Signals** are artificial signs that produce highly predictable responses, like traffic signals. **Symbols**, on the other hand, are artificial signs for which there is less certainty of response, like the flag. As Faules and Alexander explained (1978, p. 36), "Signals are used to regulate normative behavior in a society, and symbols are used to facilitate communicative behavior in a society."

Social Construction of Reality

What all theories that are classified as cultural studies theories have in common is the underlying assumption that our experience of reality is an ongoing, social construction, not something that is only sent, delivered, or otherwise transmitted to a docile public by some authority or elite. This assumption contrasts sharply with both mass society theory and the limited effects perspective. Mass society theory envisioned vast populations living in nightmare realities dominated by demagogues. Limited effects research focused on the effective transmission of

SOCIAL CONSTRUC-
TION OF REALITY
*Theory that as-
sumes an ongoing
correspondence of
meaning because
people share a
common sense
about its reality*

ideas and information from dominant sources to passive receivers. When **social construction of reality** is applied to mass communication, it implies an *active* audience. Audience members don't just passively take in and store bits of information in mental filing cabinets, they actively process this information, reshape it, and store only what serves culturally defined needs.

Active audience members use the media's symbols to define their environments and the things in it, but those definitions have little value unless others share them. A Porsche, for example, can be as expensive an automobile as a Rolls Royce and both are functionally the same thing—automobiles that transport people from here to there. Yet, the "realities" that surround both cars (and the people who drive them) are quite different. Moreover, how these different drivers are treated by other people may also vary, not because of any true difference in them as humans, but because the "reality" that is attached to the car of each is used to define them (see, for example, Baran & Blasko, 1984). We'll discuss this more later.

Alfred Schutz (1967, 1970), a banker whose avocation was sociology, provided some early systematic discussions of social construction of reality ideas. He was fascinated by what he regarded as the mysteries of everyday existence. Just how do we make sense of the world around us so that we can structure and coordinate our daily actions? How can we do this with such ease that we don't even realize that we are doing it? To answer these questions Schutz used a body of social theory that had been developed in Europe, **phenomenology**. Relying on phenomenological notions, he asked his students at the New School for Social Research in New York to *bracket* or set aside their commonsense, taken-for-granted explanations for what they were doing and recognize that everyday life was actually much more complicated than they assumed. Schutz argued that we can conduct our lives with little effort or thought because we have developed *stocks of social knowledge* that we use to quickly make sense of what goes on around us and then structure our actions. One of the most important forms of knowledge that we possess is **typifications**. Typifications enable us to quickly classify objects and actions that we observe and then structure our own actions in response. But typifications operate to some extent like stereotypes—though they make it easy to interpret our experiences, they also distort and bias these experiences.

PHENOMENOLOGY
*Theory developed
by European
philosophers focus-
ing on individual
experience of the
physical and social
world*

TYPIFICATIONS
*"Mental images"
that enable people
to quickly classify
objects and actions
and then structure
their own actions
in response*

The concept of typifications is similar to Mead's conception of symbols and the notion of schemas in information processing theory. It differs from these by reminding us of the negative consequences of typifications. When we rely on typifications to routinely structure our experience, we risk making serious mistakes.

Schutz's ideas were elaborated in *The Social Construction of Reality,* written by sociologists Peter Berger and Thomas Luckmann. Published in 1966, the book made virtually no mention of mass communication, but with the explosion of interest in the media that accompanied the dramatic social and cultural changes of that turbulent decade, mass communication theorists (not to mention scholars from numerous other disciplines) quickly found Berger and Luckmann's work and identified its value for developing media theory.

In explaining how reality is socially constructed, the two sociologists assumed first that "there is an ongoing correspondence between *my* meanings and *their* meanings in the world (and) that we share a common sense about its reality" (1966, p. 23). Let's use a common household article as our example. Here are three symbols for that object:

1 KNIFE

2

3

SYMBOLS *In social construction of reality, an object that represents some other object*

In social construction of reality, a **symbol** is an object (in these instances, a collection of letters or drawings on paper) that represents some other object— what we commonly refer to as a knife. Here are three other symbols for that same object:

1 MESSER

2 CUCHILLO

3

But unless you speak German or Spanish, respectively, or unless you understand what truly horrible artists we are, these symbols have no meaning for you, there is no correspondence between our meaning and yours, we share no common sense about the reality of the object being symbolized.

But who says that KNIFE means what we all know it to mean? And what's wrong with those people in Germany and Mexico? Don't they know that it's KNIFE, not MESSER or CUCHILLO? In English-speaking countries, the culture has *agreed* that KNIFE means that sharp thing we use to cut our food, among other things. Just as the folks in German- and Spanish-speaking lands have agreed on something else. There is no inherent truth, value, or meaning in the ordered collection of letters K-N-I-F-E that gives it the reality that we all know it has. We have given it meaning, and because we share that meaning, we can function as a people (at least where the issue is household implements).

SIGNS *In social construction of reality, objects explicitly designed to serve as an index of subjective meaning*

But Berger and Luckmann recognized that there is another kind of meaning that we attach to the things in our environments, one that is *subjective* rather than *objective*. They call these **signs**, objects explicitly designed "to serve as an index of subjective meaning" (1966, p. 35); this is analogous to symbolic interaction's concept of symbols. If you were to wake up tomorrow morning, with your head on your pillow, to find a knife stuck into the headboard inches above your nose, you'd be fairly certain that this was some sort of sign. In other words, people can produce representations of objects that have very specific, very subjective agreed upon meanings. What does the knife in the headboard signify? Says who? What does a Porsche signify? Says who? What do several pieces of cloth—some red, some white, some blue—sewn together in a rectangle in such a way to produce thirteen alternating red and white stripes and a number of stars against a blue field in the upper left hand corner signify? Freedom? Democracy? Food and medicine? The largest car dealer on the strip? Says who?

Remember that symbolic interaction defines signs and symbols in precisely the opposite way that social construction of reality does. This small problem aside, how do people use these signs and symbols to construct a reality that allows a culture to function? Berger and Luckmann developed Schutz's notion of typifications into what they refer to as **typification schemes,** collections of meanings we have assigned to some phenomenon, that come from our social stock of knowledge to pattern our interaction with our environments and the things and people in it. A bit more simply, we, as a people, through interaction with our environment, construct a "natural backdrop" for the development of "typification schemes required for the major routines of everyday life, not only the typification of others . . . but typifications of all sorts of events and experiences, both social and natural" (1966, p. 43).

Of course, what media theorists and practitioners, especially advertisers and marketing professionals, now understand is that whoever has the greatest influence over a culture's definitions of its symbols and signs also controls the construction of the typification schemes that individuals use to pattern their interactions with their various social worlds. Why, for example, is one beer more "sophisticated" than another? Are you less likely to serve generic beer to your houseguests than you are to serve Michelob or Heineken? Why?

TYPIFICATION SCHEMES *In social construction of reality, collections of meanings assigned to some phenomenon that come from a social stock of knowledge to pattern interaction with the environment and things and people in it.*

Research on Popular Culture in the United States

During the 1960s and 1970s, some American literary scholars began to focus their research on popular culture. By 1967, this group had grown large enough to have its own division (Popular Literature Section) within the Modern Language Association of America and to establish its own academic journal, *The Journal of Popular Culture.* They were influenced by British cultural studies and by the Canadian media scholar, Marshall McLuhan (see Chapter 11). The members of this group have adapted a variety of theories and research methods to study various forms of popular culture including hermeneutics and historical methods. Unlike British critical theorists, most have no links to social movements. Much of their attention is focused on television and, now, the Internet as the premier media of the electronic era. Many share McLuhan's optimism about the future and the positive role of electronic media rather than the pessimistic vision of Williams.

Some of the best examples of popular culture research have been provided by Horace Newcomb in *TV, The Most Popular Art* (1974) and in a much-respected anthology, *Television: The Critical View*, that has had several updated editions (2000). These books summarize useful insights produced by popular culture researchers, emphasizing that popular media content generally, and television programming specifically, are much more complex than they appear on the surface. Multiple levels of meaning are often present, and the content itself is frequently ambiguous. Sophisticated content producers recognize that if they put many different or ambiguous meanings into their content, they will have a better chance of appealing to different audiences. If these audiences are large and loyal, the programs will have high ratings. Though Newcomb wrote long before the advent of *Twin Peaks, The Simpsons, Ally McBeal*, and cable television series such as *The Sopranos* and *Queer as Folk*, these programs illustrate his argument. They make an art of layering one level of meaning on top of another so that fans can watch the same episode over and over to probe its meaning.

A second insight well articulated by Newcomb is that audience interpretations of content are likely to be quite diverse. Some people make interpretations at one level of meaning whereas others make their interpretations at other levels. Some interpretations will be highly idiosyncratic, and some will be very conventional. Sometimes groups of fans will develop a common interpretation, and sometimes individuals are content to find their own meaning without sharing it.

One person whose work has combined the popular culture approach with neomarxist theory is Larry Grossberg (1983, 1989). His take on popular culture "signals (the) belief in an emerging change in the discursive formations of contemporary intellectual life, a change that cuts across the humanities and the social sciences. It suggests that the proper horizon for interpretive activity, whatever its object and whatever its disciplinary base, is the entire field of cultural practices, all of which give meaning, texture, and structure to human life" (Grossberg & Nelson, 1988, p. 1). Although his synthesis has proved controversial (O'Connor, 1989), it gained wide attention. Part of this popularity stems from Grossberg's application of contemporary European theories to the study of popular culture. Recently, he has moved more toward neomarxist theory and has coedited two large anthologies of research, *Marxism and the Interpretation of Culture* (Nelson & Grossberg, 1988) and *Cultural Studies* (Grossberg, Nelson, & Treichler, 1992).

The serious study of popular culture poses a direct challenge to mass society theory, the limited effects paradigm, and notions of high culture for several reasons. In asserting the power of audiences to make meaning, researchers of popular culture grant a respect to *average* people that is absent from mass society and limited effects thinking. In treating popular culture as culturally important and worthy of study, theorists challenge high culture's bedrock assumption of the inherent quality of high culture artifacts like symphonies and opera. In suggesting that individual audience members use media content to create personally relevant meaning, theorists open the possibility of media effects, albeit content consumer-generated or allowed. In short, in arguing the crucial cultural role played by the interaction of people and media texts, researchers studying popular culture lend support to all the cultural theories.

Summary

During the past four decades, cultural studies and political economy theory have emerged as important, alternative perspectives on the role of media in society. These approaches have their intellectual roots in Marxist theory but have been influenced by and incorporate other perspectives, including literary criticism. Theorists argue that mass media often support the status quo and interfere with the efforts of social movements to bring about useful social change. But they also argue that ordinary people can resist media influence and that media might provide a pluralistic public forum in which the power of dominant elites can be effectively challenged.

Most forms of theory and research examined in this book are based in the social sciences. Much cultural theory, however, is critical theory. It is more or less explicitly based on a set of specific social values. These values are used to critique existing social institutions and social practices. Institutions and practices that undermine or marginalize important values are criticized. Alternatives to these institutions or practices are offered. Theory is developed to guide useful social change.

Unlike earlier schools of Marxist theory, some neomarxist cultural theorists reject the view that mass media are totally under the control of well-organized, dominant elites who cynically manipulate media content in their own interest. Instead, media are viewed as a public forum in which many people and groups can participate. However, elites are seen as enjoying many advantages. Most media content is found implicitly or explicitly to support the status quo. Also, critical theorists reject simplistic notions of audience effects like those found in mass society theory. Even when media content explicitly supports the status quo, audiences can misunderstand or reject this content.

The ritual perspective of mass communication as articulated by James Carey sees the media as central to the representation of shared beliefs rather than as mere imparters of information. This contrasts with the transmissional perspective that views the media as mere transmitters of information, usually for the purpose of control. As dissatisfaction with the limited effects paradigm grew in the 1970s and 1980s, more and more communication theorists, even those with a social science orientation, began to move toward this former perspective.

One such theory is symbolic interaction, which assumes that our experience of reality is a social construction—that when we learn to assign meaning to symbols, we give them power over our experience. Social construction of reality also assumes that people have a correspondence of meaning when they use symbols (an object that represents some other object) and signs (objects explicitly designed to serve as indices of subjective meaning). These signs and symbols combine into collections of meanings, or typification schemes, that form the social stock of knowledge that patterns people's interactions with their environments.

Current research on media has begun to converge on a common set of themes and issues. These are shared by many qualitative and quantitative researchers (see Chapter 12). Cultural studies and political economy theory have played an important role in identifying these themes and prioritizing these issues. Despite the serious questions that have been raised about the value of these approaches, they have proven heuristic. Cultural theorists make bold assertions and explicitly incorporate values into their work. They provide a useful challenge to mainstream media theory, as do popular culture researchers who grant much power to audiences and cultural value to such popular culture texts as television series and popular music.

Exploring Mass Communication Theory

1   You can test Mead's arguments about symbolic interaction yourself by going on the Internet to study and play *Ultima On-Line*. Select some of the links that are provided before you play the game. In this way, you can shape your environment as it shapes you when you do actually engage others.

    Ultima On-Line
    http://www.owo.com/

2   Get the videos of any of the movies that were mentioned at the beginning of this chapter. If possible, get one of the American films and one of the British New Wave movies. After viewing them, see if you can identify a worldview in them that resonates with cultural and critical cultural theory. Then see if you can identify differences in ideology between your U.S. and British movies.

3   Use **InfoTrac College Edition** to scan the tables of contents of as many marketing and advertising research journals as you can. *Consumers' Research Magazine, Journal of Advertising,* and *Journal of Advertising Research* are good places to start. Can you find symbolic interaction and social construction of reality among the articles you uncover? How are these theories used? Don't assume

that these theories' names will appear in the titles of the research that uses them; keep an eye out for those titles that suggest using advertising or products for sensemaking or meaning making.

4   Use **InfoTrac College Edition** to scan the tables of contents of popular culture journals like *Differences: A Journal of Feminist Cultural Studies, Film Comment,* and *Film Quarterly.* Can you identify writing that, although text-based, borrows ideas from any of the theories we've discussed in this chapter? For example, can you find hints of Marxism, neomarxism, or British cultural studies in the analysis of some piece of media content?

Critical Thinking Questions

1   What examples of failure to share meaning of signs and symbols can you recall from your own experience? What was the outcome of those experiences? Why do you think errors occurred (try to frame your answer in terms of the intersection of communication and culture)?

2   Do you ever make judgments about people based solely on how they look? What kinds of evaluations do you make? Why do you do this? What are the advantages and disadvantages of this very human ability?

3   To what extent do you think media content fosters support for the status quo? Do you agree or disagree with critical cultural studies arguments that this tendency limits the growth of richer, more pluralistic cultures?

4   Many U.S. journalists found themselves in difficult positions in the aftermath of the September 11, 2001, terrorist attacks on New York and Washington, D.C. Were they Americans or journalists first? Many opted for nation over profession. For example, CBS anchor Dan Rather told an interviewer, "George Bush is President, he makes the decisions and, you know, as just one American, he wants me to line up, just tell me where." The issue is not whether you supported America's action in Afghanistan. The issue is that there was a variety of opinion on the best, most effective, most just, most humane response to the attacks, and media should have provided the forum for its debate. They did in mainstream media around the world, even that of our closest allies. Did U.S. media fail the American people by so obviously supporting the official government position, the status quo? Might you answer differently if reporters' pro-establishment biases, on any topic, were in opposition to your own?

5   Discuss Frankfurt School assertions about mass culture and high culture. Can or should mass media be used to promote high culture? What about the notion of high culture itself? Is this concept inherently elitist? Why, for example, should a city fund symphonies, opera, and ballet companies and not jazz, rock 'n roll, and rap music?

6 Popular culture researchers assert the value of popular culture texts like television shows, movies, and popular music. Their argument seems valid when we talk about examples such as television series *The Sopranos* and *The X-Files*, movies like *Dogma* and *Pulp Fiction*, and the music of a rocker like Sting and a rapper like Queen Latifah. What about other texts, things like television's *The Beverly Hillbillies, Everyone Loves Raymond,* and *Sabrina the Teenage Witch,* or movies like the *Die Hard* series or *The Nutty Professor,* or Barry Manilow music? Can you still make the popular culture argument using these texts?

Significant People and Their Writing

Adorno, Theodor, and Max Horkheimer (1972). *Dialectic of Enlightenment.* New York: Herder & Herder.

Arato, Andrew, and Eike Gebhardt, eds. (1978). *The Essential Frankfurt School Reader.* New York: Urizen.

Berger, Paul L., and Thomas Luckmann (1966). *The Social Construction of Reality: A Treatise in the Sociology of Knowledge.* Garden City, NY: Doubleday.

Carey, James (1975). "Culture and Communications." *Communication Research,* 2: 173–191.

Faules, Don F., and Dennis C. Alexander (1978). *Communication and Social Behavior: A Symbolic Interaction Perspective.* Reading, MA: Addison-Wesley.

Hall, Stuart, Dorothy Hobson, Andrew Lowe, and Paul Willis, eds., (1982). *Culture, Media, Language.* London: Hutchinson.

Nelson, Cary, and Lawrence Grossberg, eds. (1988). *Marxism and the Interpretation of Culture.* Urbana: University of Illinois Press.

Newcomb, Horace M. (1974). *TV, The Most Popular Art.* Garden City, NY: Anchor.

———. (2000). *Television: The Critical View.* New York: Oxford University Press.

Schiller, Herb I. (2000). *Living in the Number One Country: Reflections from a Critic of American Empire.* New York: Seven Stories Press.

Williams, Raymond (1967). *Communications.* New York: Barnes and Noble.

———. (1974). *Television: Technology and Cultural Form.* London: Fontana.

Chapter 10

Media and Audiences: Theories About the Role of Media in Everyday Life

Consider the ways that you use media during a typical day in your life. For most of us, the use of media is a very routine activity that takes up a considerable amount of our free time and not much planning. With the development of new media and new technology applied to old media, we can surround ourselves with powerful forms of media wherever we go. In the past, we could carry print media with us, but now we can enjoy rich audiovisual media wherever and whenever we choose. If there are empty spaces in our daily routines, we can easily fill them with media content. But why do you use media the way you do? What are you seeking from media, and are you getting what you seek? Do media easily satisfy you or do you constantly change your uses of media in a search for something more? Has the increasing availability of new media enabled you to make some changes so that media serve you better?

When the Internet music service Napster was at the height of its popularity, college students across the country traded hundreds of thousands of MP3 music files over the Internet every day. Completely new media use activities gained widespread popularity as students ripped music files off their CDs, uploaded and downloaded music files, and burned CDs. Sales of CD burners and blank CD-R disks rose exponentially. What was going on? Why were so many people becoming so active in their use of media that they were willing to buy expensive new forms of technology and learn somewhat complicated media use skills? If you were one of the students who used Napster, why did you do it and how satisfied were you with your use of it? Did you enjoy experimenting with the technology? Did you compete with friends to download more files? Did Napster give you easy access to unusual, highly specialized music that you couldn't get from a local music store? Did you appreciate being able to create highly personalized collections of music? Did you feel a sense of loss when the music industry forced Napster to block distribution of copyrighted music? Did you transfer your music copying activity to another file sharing Web site, such as BearShare, KaZaa, or Morpheus?

The Napster phenomenon provides a dramatic example of how availability of a new media service can bring about widespread changes in what people do with media. In turn, these changes can have a powerful impact on the media industries, technology manufacturers, and on ourselves and on the people around us. Even if we don't change our uses of media, we can be affected if others change their uses. It's important to remember that our personal uses of media are never unique to ourselves—thousands and often millions of other people engage in the same activities—often at the same time. As we have seen in previous chapters, this widespread, simultaneous use of media has long been of interest to media researchers. Media audience research dates from the beginning of the 20th century. Early researchers focused mostly on describing audiences, however, and determining whether media had direct effects on people. By the 1960s, this research had ceased to produce new insights. During the last thirty years, however, researchers have turned their attention to new research questions and developed new theories of media that have produced a new understanding of why people use specific media and the meaning that media use has for them.

This simple idea—that people put specific media and specific media content to specific use in the hopes of having some specific need or set of needs gratified—forms the basis of the theories we will review in this chapter. Unlike many of the perspectives we've examined already, these that we call **active-audience theories** do not attempt to understand what the *media do to people* but, rather, focus on assessing what *people do with media*. For this reason, these theories are referred to as *audience-centered* rather than *source-dominated* theories. Logically, they are micro-level rather than macro-level perspectives.

Much of the empirical research that we reviewed in preceding chapters was "effects research," which assumed that media do things to people, often without their consent or desire. This research typically focused on negative effects—the bad things that happen to people because they use media. Effects were caused by a variety of content, from political propaganda to dramatized presentations of sex and violence.

In this chapter, we will consider a very different type of media effect—those we consciously or routinely seek every time we turn to media for some particular purpose. Study of these effects was slow to develop. Mass society theory and the response to it focused researchers' attention on the unintended, negative consequences of media. Audience members were seen as passively responding to whatever content media companies made available to them. There were some early critics of this viewpoint. For example, John Dewey (1927) argued that educated

ACTIVE-AUDIENCE THEORIES *Theories that focus on assessing what people do with media; audience-centered theories*

people could make good use of media. He saw the problem of propaganda as one that should be solved through public education rather than through censorship: If people could be taught to make better use of media content, they wouldn't need to be sheltered from it (see Chapter 4). Despite such arguments, empirical research remained focused on locating evidence of how average people could be manipulated by media.

Eventually, effects research found that people weren't as vulnerable to propaganda as had been predicted by mass society theory. People were protected from manipulation by opinion leaders and well-formed, intensely held attitudes. But even this seemingly optimistic conclusion was associated with a pessimistic view of the average person. If the barriers protecting them were broken down, individuals could be easily manipulated. Researchers were slow to develop the perspective that average people can be responsible media consumers who use media for their own worthwhile purposes—an active audience.

Overview

During the 1970s and 1980s, empirical and cultural media researchers became increasingly focused on media audiences. Their goal was to gain a more useful understanding of what people were doing with media in their daily lives. Television use increased exponentially during the 1960s, but very little research was done to examine what people were doing when they viewed television. Were viewers primarily passive consumers of entertainment or was television viewing serving more important purposes? As this research developed, new and less pessimistic conceptualizations of audiences began to develop. Empirical researchers reexamined limited effects assumptions about audiences and argued that people were not as passive as these effects theories assumed. At the same time, cultural studies researchers were conducting their own audience research and finding that the power of elites to manipulate audiences was not as great as had been assumed by critical theorists (Chapter 9).

Of course, the possibility of responsible audience activity was never totally ignored in early media research, but much of it gave audiences insufficient credit for selection, interpretation, and use of media content. We will see that the early development of the audience-centered theories was hampered by confusion about the ideas of "functions" and "functionalism" and by methodological and theoretical disputes. We will discuss what it means to be an active audience member and examine in detail several audience-centered approaches.

The theories introduced in this chapter are important because they were among the first to make a priority of studying audience activity and to view that activity in a more or less positive way. As we shall see, this doesn't mean that they ignored the possibility of long-term negative consequences. Active audiences can still be misled by poorly constructed or inaccurate media presentations. We will explain how the development of audience-centered theories challenged the limited effects paradigm. In doing so, we revisit functional analysis and discuss how it formed the basis of much audience-centered theory. We describe the uses and gratifications approach, both as initially conceived and as it matured and developed. We explore some of its central notions, for example, what is meant by an active audience, how is activity measured, and the use of the approach to understand effects.

We also study other audience-centered theories. Reception studies and framing, two theories that focus on how people make meaning, are described, as is information processing theory, a very micro-level perspective that focuses on the conscious and unconscious processes used by individuals to extract meaning from media messages.

Audience Theories: From Source-Dominated to Active Audience Perspectives

As early as the 1940s, the work of people like Herta Herzog, Paul Lazarsfeld, and Frank Stanton reflected at least the implicit concern for studying an active, gratifications-seeking audience.

Lazarsfeld and Stanton (1942) produced a series of books and studies throughout the 1940s that paid significant attention to how audiences used media to organize their lives and experiences. For example, the researchers studied the value of early morning radio reports to farmers. As part of the Lazarsfeld and Stanton series, Bernard Berelson (1949) published a classic media use study of the disruption experienced by newspaper readers during a strike. He reported convincing evidence that newspapers formed an important part of many people's daily routine.

USES AND GRATIFICA-
TIONS *Approach to media study focusing on the uses to which people put media and the gratifications they seek from that use*

Herta Herzog, a colleague of Lazarsfeld, is often credited as the originator of the **uses and gratifications** approach, although she most likely did not give it its label. Her 1944 article, entitled "Motivations and Gratifications of Daily Serial Listeners," was the first published research to provide an in-depth examination of media gratifications. She interviewed 100 radio soap-opera fans and identified "three major types of gratification." They were (including her editorial comments) first, "merely a means of emotional release," "a second and commonly recognized form of enjoyment concerns the opportunities for wishful thinking," and the "third and commonly unsuspected form of gratification concerns the advice obtained from listening to daytime serials." Herzog wanted to understand why so many housewives were attracted to radio soap operas. In contrast with the typical effects research being done in Lazarsfeld's shop, Herzog didn't try to measure the influence that soap opera listening had on women. She was satisfied with assessing their reasons and experiences—their uses and gratifications.

One of the first college mass communication textbooks, *The Process and Effects of Mass Communication,* offered an early active-audience conceptualization. Author Wilbur Schramm (1954, p. 19) asked the question, "What determines which offerings of mass communication will be selected by a given individual?" The answer he offered is called the **fraction of selection,** and it looks like this:

FRACTION OF SELECTION *Schramm's graphic description of how individuals make media and content choices based on expectation of reward and effort required*

$$\frac{\text{Expectation of Reward}}{\text{Effort Required}}$$

His point was that people weigh the level of reward (gratification) they expect from a given medium or message against how much effort they must make to secure that reward. Review your own news consumption, for example. Of course, it's easier to watch the network television news or flip on CNN than it is to get your news online. Television news is presented attractively and dramatically. The images are usually arresting, and the narration and anchorperson's report are typically crisp and to the point. You never have to leave your chair to watch, once you settle on a specific news broadcast you don't have to touch the remote again, and when the show you're watching ends, you're already in place for *Wheel of Fortune.* This concerns only the denominator, effort required, and there is little effort required to consume a televised news program. But you might choose to get your news from the Internet instead of from television because the reward you expect from your online news (more detail, greater depth, more variety of approach, more sophisticated reports, alternative perspectives) makes the additional effort (logging on, waiting for the server to connect you to your search engine, identifying the sites you're interested in, selecting specific reports, reading them, searching for alternative accountings, accessing related links) worthwhile. You can develop your own fractions for your own media use of all kinds, but the essence of Schramm's argument remains—we all make decisions about which content we choose based on our expectations of having some need met, even if that decision is to not make a choice—say between two early evening situation comedies, for example, because we can't find the remote control and it's too much trouble to get up and change the channel—because all we really want is some background noise while we sit and daydream.

Limitations of Early Audience-Centered Research

If this is all so seemingly logical and straightforward, why didn't the early theories that saw audiences as active and important in the mass communication process quickly emerge as strong alternatives to limited effects theories? There are many possible answers to this question. We have seen how mass society theory exaggerated the influence of media and centered widespread public concern on negative media effects. Since the 1930s, government agencies, private foundations, and the media industry all have been willing to provide funding to study a broad range of positive and negative effects, but little money was available for the study of active audiences. Also, researchers thought that it was possible to study effects more objectively than media uses could be studied. For example, behavioral or attitudinal effects might be observed in a laboratory following exposure to media content. On the other hand, studying uses meant asking people to report on their subjective experience of content. During the 1940s and 1950s, social science researchers were determined to avoid approaches that didn't meet what they regarded as scientific standards. They chose to focus their efforts on developing what they thought would be definitive, powerful *explanations for the consequences* of media use. They didn't see as much purpose or value in *describing and cataloguing people's subjective reasons* for using media.

For example, in the area of media and attitude change, early researchers hoped to find the magic keys to persuasion (see Chapter 6). The discovery of these keys would enable media to be used by benevolent communicators to eliminate all sorts of bad attitudes (that is, racism and fascism) and replace them with good attitudes (that is, middle-class values). This would provide many benefits to society—and to the researchers. The Cold War could be ended. Ethnic conflict could be avoided. A new era of peace could be initiated. Of course, there would be problems if these keys fell into the wrong hands (such as people like Adolf Hitler or Joseph McCarthy), but that was another matter.

Thus, for these researchers, studying people's reasons for using media was difficult using available scientific methods, hard to fund, and unlikely to be productive. Most attitude researchers had strong behaviorist biases that led them to be suspicious of taking people's thoughts and experiences at face value. Researchers regarded people's reasons for doing things as rationalizations for actions. The real reasons people acted as they did could only be determined by studying the stimuli people were exposed to and the responses that they learned for them.

Early active-audience research was also widely criticized by social scientists as being too descriptive—it did little more than group people's reasons for using media into sets of arbitrarily chosen categories. Why one set of categories rather than another? Moreover, the categorization process itself was dismissed as too arbitrary and subjective. For example, Herzog placed her listeners' reasons into three categories—why not five? Where did her categories come from and how could we be certain she wasn't arbitrarily putting reasons into these categories? In contrast, experimental attitude change research used what most researchers regarded as a scientifically sound set of procedures. This type of research produced causal explanations rather than simple descriptions of subjective perceptions. As long as this effects research (even that based on the limited effects model) offered the hope of producing significant new insight into the causal power of media, researchers had little motivation to test alternate approaches.

Confusion of Media Functions and Media Uses

In Chapter 7, we described functional analysis and its use by early media researchers. By the 1960s, notions of an active and gratification-seeking audience had been absorbed by and confused with functional analysis. Failure to adequately differentiate media uses from media functions impeded the design and interpretation of audience-centered research. Charles Wright explicitly linked the active audience to functionalism in his 1959 textbook. Explained Wright (1959, p. 16), "Harold Lasswell, a political scientist who has done pioneering research in mass communications, once noted three activities of communication specialists: (1) surveillance of the environment, (2) correlation of the parts of society in responding to the environment, and (3) transmission of the social heritage from one generation to the next." To these, Wright added a fourth, entertainment.

CLASSIC FOUR FUNCTIONS OF THE MEDIA *Surveillance, correlation, transmission of the social heritage, and entertainment*

These have become known as the **classic four functions of the media**, and we'll discuss them later, but what's more important immediately is how this linkage to functions influenced the development of active-audience theories.

Although Wright cautioned his readers to distinguish "between the consequences (functions) of a social activity and the aims or purposes behind the activity" (p. 16), *functions* were assumed by most communication theorists to be equivalent to (synonymous with) the aims or goals of the media industries themselves. As explained in Chapter 7, functionalism became equated with legitimization of the status quo. To the extent that active-audience notions were linked to functionalism, they were seen by critics as merely another way to rationalize the way things are.

Let's use the classic four functions as an example. *Surveillance of the environment* refers to the media's collection and distribution of information. We know who was elected governor of Illinois because it was in the newspaper, and we know whether to wear a sweater to school because the radio weatherperson said that it would be chilly today. *Correlation of parts of society* refers to the media's interpretive or analytical activities. We know that the failure of the highway bond proposition means that gasoline taxes will rise to cover necessary road repair because of the editorial in the Sunday paper. *Transmission of the social heritage* relates to the media's ability to communicate values, norms, and styles across time and between groups. What were typical attitudes toward women in the 1930s? What did a normal American home look like in the 1950s? Any of two hundred old movies can answer the former question, and *Leave It To Beaver* and *Father*

Knows Best answer the latter. What's happening in French fashion today? Pick up a recent copy of *Paris Match*. Finally, *entertainment* means media's ability to entertain or amuse.

These seem like perfectly reasonable aims of the media, but there is a problem. These might be *aims* of given media organizations, but they might not necessarily be the functions they serve for the people who consume those media, and these functions can be different from the intended uses of audience members. For example, you might intentionally watch an old black and white gangster movie to be entertained, and you might even learn (unintentionally) a bit about how people at the time viewed lawlessness. But you might also, in the course of watching, inadvertently learn how to use a pistol. The filmmaker's aim was to entertain, but the use (the purpose) to which you ultimately put the content was much different. Transmission of the cultural heritage occurred (although that was not the filmmaker's aim), as did some learning of potentially dangerous behavior (although that, too, was no one's aim). In other words, the aim is not always the ultimate function. If we confine our research to an investigation of functions intended by media practitioners (their aims), we are likely to ignore many negative effects. Because much early functional analysis was restricted to *intended* functions (again, aims), critics have charged that it is too apologetic to the media industries.

Wright, realizing how his functions were misinterpreted, later wrote,

> Our working quartet of communications—surveillance, correlation, cultural transmission, and entertainment—was intended to refer to common kinds of activities that might or might not be carried out as mass communications or as private, personal communications. These activities were not synonymous for functions, which . . . refer to the consequences of routinely carrying out such communication activities through the institutionalized processes of mass communications. (1974, p. 205)

To clarify even further, he added that in understanding how functionalism relates to mass communication, it is necessary to draw a distinction between functions (the consequences of routinely carrying out communication activities) and the effects of those activities.

The surveillance activity, its functions in our society, and the effects of those functions offer a good example of how Wright intended functionalism to be applied to media studies (and uses and gratifications). Newspapers and television news devote significant energy and effort to covering political campaigns and delivering the product of that effort to their audiences. If readers and viewers ignore (that is, fail to use) the reports, no communication happens and the intended functions fail to occur. But if readers and viewers do consume the reports, then the intended function we've been calling surveillance of the environment should take place. Thus, media cannot serve their intended function unless people make certain uses of their content. For surveillance to occur, routine transmission of news information about key events must be accompanied by active audience use that results in widespread learning about those events. Thus, news media can achieve this societal level function only if enough audience members are willing and able to make certain uses of content.

As was implied in our earlier discussion of libertarianism (Chapter 5), one historically important and widely intended function of public communication is the creation and maintenance of an enlightened and knowledgeable electorate, one capable of governing itself. But many of us might argue that most current day news media transmit "infotainment" that actually serves a negative function (a dysfunction) in that it produces ill-educated citizens or citizens who actually become *less* involved in the political process because they substitute pseudo-involvement in overdramatized media depictions of campaign spectacles for actual involvement in real campaign activities (Edelman, 1988).

What we've done here, though, is confused intended functions with unintended effects, just as Wright warned us against. The intended function of the reporting of those events and our intended use of the reports might be consistent with a normative theory (libertarianism) that underlies our political and media system. The effects of that activity, however, might well be something completely different. As political campaigns cater more and more to the time, economic, and aesthetic demands of the broadcast media (less complexity, more staging of campaign spectacles, less talk about complex and controversial issues, more reliance on negative ads, and so on), voters can become repelled by politics, which might create disrespect for government and increase the influence of well-organized special interest groups. Voters' use of media can gradually change so that instead of seeking information that isn't there, they turn to media for the mesmerizing spectacles that are available. In this example, the intended function of media hasn't changed, but its practical consequences have. Such gaps between intended functions and observed effects have impressed media critics and have led them to be suspicious both of functional analysis and of theories that presume an active audience, those that can be categorized under what is now called the uses and gratification approach.

Revival of the Uses and Gratifications Approach

Interest in studying the audience's uses of the media and the gratifications it receives from them had two revivals. The first occured during the 1970s partly as a response to the inconsequential and overqualified findings of run-of-the-mill effects research. As we have discussed earlier, by 1970 most of the important tenets of the limited effects paradigm had been worked out and demonstrated in study after study. In all this research, media's role was found to be marginal in comparison with other social factors. But how could this be true when media audiences were so vast and so many people spent so much time consuming media? Why were advertisers spending billions to purchase advertising time if their messages had no effect? Why were network television audiences continuing to grow? Didn't any of this media use have important consequences for the people who were engaging in it? If so, why didn't effects research document this influence? Was it overlooking something—and if so, what?

The limited effects paradigm had become so dominant that it was hard to ask questions about media that weren't stated in terms of measurable effects. There just didn't seem to be anything else worth studying. But if researchers restricted their research to the study of effects, all they could obtain would be predictable, modest, highly qualified results. Though they were frustrated by this situation, few could see any practical alternative.

This first revival of interest in the uses and gratifications approach can be traced to three developments—one methodological and two theoretical:

1 **New survey research methods and data analysis techniques allowed important new strategies for conducting studies of and interpreting audience uses and gratifications to be developed.** Researchers developed innovative questionnaires that allowed people's reasons for using media to be measured more systematically and objectively. At the same time, new data analysis techniques provided more objective procedures for developing categories and for assigning reasons to them. These developments overcame some of the most serious methodological criticisms of earlier research.

2 **During the 1970s, some media researchers developed increasing awareness that people's active use of media might be an important mediating factor that made effects more or less likely.** These researchers argued that a member of an active audience can decide whether certain media effects are desirable and set out to achieve those effects. For example, you might have decided to read this book to learn about media theories. You intend the book to have this effect on you, and you work to induce the effect. If you lack this intent, use of the book is less likely to result in learning. Does the book cause you to learn? Or do you make it serve this purpose for you? If you hold the latter view, then you share the perspective of uses and gratifications theorists.

3 **Some researchers began expressing growing concern that effects research was focusing too much on unintended, negative effects of media while intended, positive uses of media were being ignored.** By 1975, we knew a lot about the influence of television violence on small segments of the audience but much less about how people were able to make media do things that they wanted.

The second revival of interest in uses and gratifications, as you might have guessed from this chapter's opening, is the product of the relatively recent development and diffusion of the Internet and World Wide Web, most specifically because of the interactivity these digital media allow. Arguing that "uses and gratifications has always provided a cutting-edge theoretical approach in the initial stages of each new mass communications medium," Thomas Ruggiero (2000, p. 3) identified three characteristics of computer-mediated mass communication that "offer a vast continuum of communication behaviors" for uses and gratifications researchers to examine:

- *Interactivity* "significantly strengthens the core U&G notion of active user" (Ruggiero, 2000, p. 15) because interactivity in mass communication has long been considered "the degree to which participants in the communication process have control over, and can change roles in their mutual discourse" (Williams, Rice, & Rogers, 1988, p. 10).

- *Demassification* is "the ability of the media user to select from a wide menu . . . Unlike traditional mass media, new media like the Internet provide selectivity characteristics that allow individuals to tailor messages to their needs" Ruggeriero, 2000 (p. 16).

- *Asynchroneity* means that mediated messages "may be staggered in time. Senders and receivers of electronic messages can read mail at different times and still interact at their convenience. It also means the ability of an individual to send, receive, save, or retrieve messages at her or his convenience. In the case of television, asynchroneity meant the ability to of VCR users to record a program for later viewing. With electronic mail (email) and the Internet, an individual has the potential to store, duplicate, or print graphics and text, or transfer them to an online Web page or the email of another individual. Once messages are digitized, manipulation of media becomes infinite, allowing the individual much more control than traditional means" (p. 16).

Actually, researchers studying new technology have found uses and gratifications to be quite helpful in studying a wide range of new media, especially email. Bonka Boneva, Robert Kraut, and David Frohlich (2001) report that women find email more useful than men in maintaining social relationships. They found increasing use of email by women to keep in touch with family and friends. John Dimmick and his colleagues at Ohio State are conducting an on-going series of studies tracing the uses and gratifications of the telephone, email, and the Internet (Dimmick, Sikand, & Patterson, 1994; Stafford, Kline, & Dimmick, 1999). Uses and gratifications theory may prove to be essential in assessing how and why various computer-based or wireless communication services are used to supplement and in some cases replace older media.

The Active Audience Revisited

Whether they are engaged in new or traditional media use, the question remains, How active are media audiences? And what forms does this activity take? Mark Levy and Sven Windahl attempted to put the issue in perspective by writing,

> As commonly understood by gratifications researchers, the term "audience activity" postulates a voluntaristic and selective orientation by audiences toward the communication process. In brief, it suggests that media use is motivated by needs and goals that are defined by audience members themselves, and that active participation in the communication process may facilitate, limit, or otherwise influence the gratifications and effects associated with exposure. Current thinking also suggests that audience activity is best conceptualized as a variable construct, with audiences exhibiting varying kinds and degrees of activity. (1985, p. 110)

Jay G. Blumler (1979) claimed that one problem in the development of a strong uses and gratifications tradition is the "extraordinary range of meanings" given to the concept of "activity." He identified several meanings for the term, including

- **Utility:** Media have uses for people and people can put media to those uses.
- **Intentionality:** Consumption of media content can be directed by people's prior motivations.
- **Selectivity:** People's use of media might reflect their existing interests and preferences.
- **Imperviousness to influence:** Audience members are obstinate; they might not want to be controlled by anyone or anything, even mass media. Audience members actively avoid certain types of media influence.

Blumler's list summarized the forms of audience activity that the early uses and gratifications researchers studied. These forms related to overall choices of content and media use patterns. These types of audience activity did not, however, consider what people actually did with media content once they had chosen it. Recent research has begun to focus on this type of audience activity—the manner in which people *actively impose meaning* on content and *construct new meaning* that serves their purposes better than any meaning that might have been intended by the message producer or distributor. The classic television program *All in the Family* is a good example. Creator Norman Lear and his writers might have intended their show to be satire, poking fun at narrow-mindedness and bigotry, but a substantial portion of the audience chose not to look at it that way—the meaning that many people made from Archie Bunker's battles with his politically and socially liberal son-in-law was something completely different. They "read" Archie as correct and Mike as a dumb bleeding heart. More recently, in 1997, ABC encountered significant protest over its critically acclaimed series *Nothing Sacred.* Its producers attempted a realistic representation of the life of a modern inner-city priest. Many conservative Catholics "read" the show as an attack on holy doctrine.

Two ways to clarify the issue are to distinguish between "activity" and "activeness" and to see the "active audience" as a relative concept. "Activity" and "activeness" are related, but the former refers more to what the audience does (for example, chooses to read the newspaper rather than to watch television news), and the latter is more what the uses and gratifications people had in mind—that is, the audience's freedom and autonomy in the mass communication situation, as exemplified in the *All in the Family* and *Nothing Sacred* scenarios just described. This activeness, no doubt, is relative. Some audience members are more active, some are more passive. This is obvious; we all know too many couch potatoes, people who live their lives through the movies, or people who bend to every fad and fashion presented in the mass media. But we also know many people who fit none of these descriptions. An inactive user can become active. Our level of activity might vary by time of day and by type of content. We might be active users of the World Wide Web by day and passive consumers of late night movies.

What the uses and gratifications approach really does, then, is provide a framework for understanding when and how different media consumers become more or less active and what the consequences of that increased or decreased involvement might be.

The classic articulation of this framework remains that offered by Elihu Katz, Jay Blumler, and Michael Gurevitch (1974). These theorists described five elements, or basic assumptions, of the uses and gratifications model:

1   **The audience is active and its media use is goal oriented.** We've seen some confusion about exactly what is meant by "active," but clearly, various audience members bring various levels of activity to their consumption (if nothing else, at least in choice of preferred medium in given situations or preferred content within a given medium).

2   **The initiative in linking his or her need gratification to a specific media choice rests with the audience member.** Neither Quentin Tarantino nor Samuel L. Jackson can make you see *Pulp Fiction.* Dan Rather and Tom Brokaw cannot compel you to be a news junkie.

3   **The media compete with other sources for need satisfaction.** This is what Joseph Klapper meant when he said that media function "through a nexus of mediating factors and influences." Simply put, the media and their audiences do not exist in a vacuum. They are part of the larger society, and the relationship between media and audiences is influenced by events in that environment. If all your needs for information and entertainment are being satisfied by conversations with your friends, then you are much less likely to turn on a television set or go online

for news. When students enter college, their media use tends to sharply decline. In this new environment, media don't compete as well.

4   **People are self-aware enough of their own media use, interests, and motives to be able to provide researchers with an accurate picture of that use.** This, as we've seen earlier, is a methodological issue that is debated. As research methods are refined, however, researchers should be able to offer better evidence of people's awareness of media use. Evidence suggests that as media choices grow with the continued diffusion of technologies like VCR, cable, and the Internet, people are being forced to become more conscious of their media use. You can blunder into watching television shows by flipping on a channel and leaving the set tuned to one station all night. But if you pay money to rent a video, you are more likely to make an active choice. You don't pick the first tape on the shelf. You scan over rows of tapes, weigh the merits of one versus another, read the backs of video boxes, and then settle on a tape. Your choice is much more likely to reflect your interests than when you "zone out" viewing one channel.

5   **Value judgments of the audience's linking its needs to specific media or content should be suspended.** For example, the "harmful effects" of consumer product advertising on our culture's values might only be harmful in the researcher's eyes. If audience members want those ads to help them decide what's "cool," that's their decision. This is perhaps the most problematic of Katz and his associates' assertions. Their point is that people can use the same content in very different ways and therefore the same content could have very different consequences. Viewing movies that show violent treatment of minorities could reinforce some people's negative attitudes and yet lead others to be more supportive of minority rights. On September 11, 2001, news coverage of the attack on the World Trade Center repeatedly showed scenes of the second plane hitting the tower and later scenes of the towers collapsing. Many viewers reported being traumatized by this coverage. We each construct our own meaning of such reports and that meaning ultimately influences what we think and do.

This synopsis of the perspective's basic assumptions raises several questions. What factors affect an audience member's level of activeness or her or his awareness of media use? What other things in the environment influence the creation or maintenance of the audience's needs and their judgments of which media use will best meet those needs? Katz, Blumler, and Gurevitch (1974, p. 27) argued that the "social situations" that people find themselves in can be "involved in the generation of media-related needs" in any of the following ways:

1   **Social situations can produce tensions and conflicts, leading to pressure for their easement through media consumption.** You're going dancing with a group of friends next weekend, so you plan a steady diet of MTV so you can pick up on the latest steps, or you rent a video of *Dirty Dancing, Strictly Ballroom,* or *Dance With Me,* or you borrow a friend's magazine with an article on dance fads.

2 **Social situations can create an awareness of problems that demand attention, information about which might be sought in the media.** In our dance example, you notice that the most popular people in your circle of friends are those who are the most socially outgoing; you also see that they get invited to do things that you do not. You increase your consumption of style and fashion magazines to better understand the social scene.

3 **Social situations can impoverish real-life opportunities to satisfy certain needs, and the media can serve as substitutes or supplements.** Your student budget does not allow you to buy the "in" clothes or to pay the cover charge at the dance club, so MTV's *Dance Party* keeps you company on Saturday night. When you move to a new city, you might use media as a substitute until you make new friends.

4 **Social situations often elicit specific values, and their affirmation and reinforcement can be facilitated by the consumption of related media materials.** The fact that you are a single, young adult in college often means that you are part of a group that values dancing. And if you want to be reassured that is true, just check out VH1, MTV, and *Soul Train.* This media content also promotes dancing and will reinforce your attitude toward dancing.

5 **Social situations can provide realms of expectations of familiarity with media, which must be met to sustain membership in specific social groups.** What? You don't watch MTV? You don't know how Courtney Love became famous? You didn't know that Queen Latifah was a rap star before she became a movie star? You haven't seen the latest dating flick?

Of course, if you see media as important sources of effects, you might ask if the mass media themselves might have been instrumental in creating certain social situations (such as the one in our example) *and* for making the satisfaction of those situation's attendant needs so crucial *and* for making themselves, the media, the most convenient and effective means of gratifying those needs. But that is typically not of concern in traditional uses and gratifications thinking because the members of the audience personally and actively determine what gratifications of what needs will and will not occur from their own exposure to media messages.

Uses and Gratifications and Effects

This refusal to consider the possibility of effects, however, has led many researchers to dismiss uses and gratifications as interesting, but ultimately of little

Instant Access

Uses and Gratifications

Strengths	Weaknesses
1 Focuses attention on individuals in the mass communication process	1 Reliance on functional analysis can create a status quo orientation
2 Respects intellect and ability of media consumers	2 Cannot easily address the presence or absence of effects
3 Provides insightful analyses of how people experience media content	3 Measurement of key concepts is criticized
4 Differentiates active use of media from more passive uses	4 Is too micro-level oriented
5 Studies the use of media as a part of everyday social interaction	
6 Provides useful insight into adoption of new media	

value. As a result, some contemporary proponents of the approach have taken on the challenge of linking gratifications and effects.

Windahl (1981) argued that a merger of uses and gratifications and the effects traditions was overdue and proposed what he called a "uses and effects" model that viewed the product of the use of media content as "conseffects." In a similar vein, Phillip Palmgreen, Lawrence Wenner, and Karl Rosengren (1985, p. 31) wrote, "studies have shown that a variety of audience gratifications (again, both sought and obtained) are related to a wide spectrum of media effects, including knowledge, dependency, attitudes, perceptions of social reality, agenda-setting, discussion, and various political effects variables."

Blumler (1979) also presented his ideas on how the uses and gratifications and effects approaches could be harmonized. You'll notice that his perspective still centers responsibility for the control of effects with the consumer rather than the media. He wrote,

How might propositions about media effects be generated from . . . gratifications? First, we may postulate that cognitive motivation will facilitate information gain . . . Second, media consumption for purposes of diversion and escape will favour audience acceptance of perceptions of social situations in

line with portrayals frequently found in entertainment materials . . . Third, involvement in media materials for personal identity reasons is likely to promote
reinforcement effects. (pp. 18–19)

In 1994, Alan Rubin summarized the state of uses and gratifications thinking
by echoing Windahl's (1981) call for a synthesis of the uses and gratifications and
effects perspectives. Rubin wrote, "Media perceptions and expectations guide
people's behavior; besides needs, motivation is derived from interests and externally imposed constraints; there are functional alternatives to media consumption;
and media content plays an important role in media effects" (1994, pp. 431–432).

Development of Reception Studies: Decoding and Sensemaking

At the same time that audience-centered theory was attracting the attention of U.S.
empirical social researchers, British cultural studies researchers were developing a
different but compatible perspective on audience activity. In Chapter 9, we introduced the Birmingham University Centre for Contemporary Cultural Studies and
the work of Stuart Hall, its most prominent scholar. Initially, Hall (1973) produced
a mimeographed report that proved quite central in developing and focusing the
work of his center. It was later published as a book chapter (Hall, 1980a). The report argued that researchers should direct their attention toward: (a) analysis of
the social and political context in which content is produced (encoding); and
(b) the consumption of media content (decoding). Researchers shouldn't make unwarranted assumptions about either encoding or decoding but, rather, should conduct research that permits them to carefully assess the social and political context
in which media content is produced and the everyday life context in which it is
consumed. According to Shaun Moores (1993), Hall developed his approach in
part as a reaction against a tradition of Marxist film criticism that was centered
around the film journal, *Screen*. This tradition viewed mainstream, popular films
as inherently deceptive and supportive of an elite-dominated status quo. *Screen's*
critics favored *avant guarde* films in which there was no pretense about trying to
depict a "real" social world. Hall objected to the cultural elitism that was inherent
in this criticism. He believed that it was wrong to assume that popular films necessarily served to deceive and subvert working class audiences. There might well
be cases where such films actually made moviegoers less supportive of the status
quo. In fact, the message and British New Wave films mentioned at the start of
Chapter 9 offered explicit and strong challenge to a United States and Great Britain
committed to business-as-usual. In addition, Hall did not think that it was reasonable to expect that working class audiences should embrace *avant guarde* films as
providing a better way of understanding the social world.

RECEPTION STUDIES
Audience-centered theory that focuses on how various types of audience members make sense of specific forms of content (sometimes referred to as reception analysis)

PREFERRED READING
In critical theory, the producer-intended meaning of a piece of content; assumed to reinforce the status quo (sometimes referred to as the dominant reading)

NEGOTIATED MEANING
In critical theory, when an audience member creates a personally meaningful interpretation of content that differs from the preferred reading in important ways

OPPOSITIONAL DECODING
In critical theory, when an audience member develops interpretations of content that are in direct opposition to a dominant reading

In laying out his views about decoding, Hall proposed an approach to audience research that has come to be known as **reception studies** or **reception analysis.** A central feature of this approach is its focus on how various types of audience members make sense of specific forms of content. Hall drew on French semiotic theory to argue that any media content can be regarded as a *text* that is made up of signs. These signs are structured; that is, they are related to one another in specific ways. To make sense of a text—to *read* a text—you have to be able to interpret the signs and their structure. For example, when you read a sentence you must not only decode the individual words but you also need to interpret the overall structure of the sentence to make sense of the sentence as a whole.

Hall argued that most texts can be read in several ways but that the producers of a message generally intend a **preferred** or **dominant reading** when they create a message. As a critical theorist, Hall assumed that most popular media content will have a preferred reading that reinforces the status quo. But in addition to this dominant reading, it is possible for audience members to make alternate interpretations. They might disagree with or misinterpret some aspects of a message and come up with an alternative or **negotiated meaning** that differs from the preferred reading in important ways. In some cases, audiences might develop interpretations that are in direct opposition to a dominant reading. In that case, they are said to engage in **oppositional decoding.** As explained by Jesus Martin-Barbero (1993, p. 225), although people are susceptible to domination by communication technologies, "they are able to exploit contradictions that enable them to resist, recycle, and redesign those technologies . . . and people are capable of decoding and appropriating received messages and are not necessarily duped by them."

A student and colleague of Hall, David Morley, published one of the first detailed studies that applied Hall's insights (1980b). Morley's work served as a model for subsequent reception analysis. He brought together 29 groups of people drawn from various levels of British society. The groups ranged from business managers to trade unionists and apprentices. These groups were asked to view an episode from *Nationwide,* a British television news magazine program. The program they watched assessed the economic consequences for three families of the government's annual budget. After the program finished, the groups discussed the program and offered their interpretations of it. *Nationwide* was chosen because an earlier analysis had identified it as a program that routinely offered status quo explanations for social issues (Brunsdon & Morley, 1978). Moreover, it was produced in a way that was designed to appeal to lower and middle class audiences. Thus, the researchers expected that the program would be able to communicate status quo perspectives to middle and lower class audiences.

Morley tape-recorded all the group discussions and then analyzed them by placing them into one of three categories: dominant, negotiated, or oppositional decoding. He found that although an upper class group of business managers dismissed the program as mere entertainment, they had no complaints about the views it offered. Morley labeled their decoding as a dominant reading. At the other extreme, a group of shop stewards liked the format for the program but objected to its message. They saw it as too sympathetic to middle management and as failing to address fundamental economic issues. Morley labeled their decoding as oppositional. In the negotiated decoding category were groups of teacher trainees and liberal arts students. Very few groups articulated only a dominant reading of the program. Aside from managers, only a group of apprentices was found to merely repeat the views offered by the program. Most groups offered a negotiated reading and several provided oppositional readings.

More recently, Judith Mayne, in *Cinema and Spectatorship* (1993), applied a sophisticated and many-layered reception analysis to three case studies—readings of Oscar Wilde's persona in *The Picture of Dorian Gray,* Bette Davis' star image, and white viewers' readings of race in the films *Field of Dreams* and *Ghost.* Her study is driven by the belief that "the relationship between the 'subject,' the position supposedly assigned to the film viewer by the institutions of the cinema, and the 'viewer,' the real person who watches the movies," is a very real and not fully understood dichotomy" (p. 8).

As the reception studies approach has developed in cultural studies, researchers have been careful to differentiate their audience research from that conducted by empirical social researchers. They stress their effort to combine macroscopic encoding research with microscopic decoding studies. They also point to their reliance on qualitative rather than quantitative research methods. Reception studies are often done with focus groups. For example, people who frequently use certain types of content (fans) are sometimes brought together to discuss how they make sense of the content. In other cases, groups of people who belong to certain racial or ethnic groups are chosen so that the researcher can assess how these groups are routinely interpreting media content. In some cases, in-depth interviews are done to probe how individuals engage in "meaning making." In other cases, the researcher tries to assess how a focus group reaches a consensus concerning the meaning of content.

Sociologist Pertti Alasuutari (1999) recently argued that reception research has entered a third stage. The first stage was centered on Hall's encoding and decoding approach. The second stage was dominated by Morley's pioneering audience ethnography work. "The third generation," Alasuutari wrote,

> entails a broadened frame within which one conceives of the media and media use. One does not necessarily abandon ethnographic case studies of audiences or analyses of individual programmmes, but the main focus is not restricted to finding out about the reception or "reading" of a programme by a particular audience. Rather the objective is to get a grasp of our contemporary "media

---

Instant Access

Reception Theory

Strengths	Weaknesses
1 Focuses attention on individuals in the mass communication process	1 Usually based on subjective interpretation of audience reports
2 Respects intellect and ability of media consumers	2 Cannot address presence or absence of effects
3 Acknowledges range of meaning in media texts	3 Qualitative research methods preclude causal explanations
4 Seeks an in-depth understanding of how people interpret media content	4 Has been too micro-level oriented (but is attempting to become more macroscopic)
5 Can provide an insightful analysis of the way media are used in everyday social contexts	

---

culture," particularly as it can be seen in the role of the media in everyday life, both as a topic and as an activity structured by and structuring the discourses within which it is discussed . . . The big picture that one wants to shed light on, or the big question to pursue, is the cultural place of the media in the contemporary world. It may entail questions about the meaning and use of particular programmes to particular groups of people, but it also includes questions about the frames within which we conceive of the media and their contents as reality and as representations–or distortions–of reality . . . The big research programme also includes questioning the role of media research itself. (pp. 6–7)

Thus, this third generation of reception studies attempts to return to some of the more macroscopic concerns that first motivated critical theorists. It represents an effort to integrate these critical theory concerns with reception analysis to establish a challenging research agenda. This trend toward macroscopic concerns in reception studies parallels developments in frame analysis theory that we will discuss in Chapter 12.

Feminist Reception Studies

Janice Radway (1984) was one of the first American cultural studies researchers to exemplify the shift away from an exclusive focus on textual analysis and toward an increased reliance on reception studies. Her work has provided an influential model for American scholars and is frequently cited as one of the best examples of recent feminist cultural studies research. Radway initially analyzed the content of popular romance novels. She found that romance characters and plots are derived from patriarchal myths in which a male-dominated social order is assumed to be both natural and just. Men are routinely presented as strong, aggressive, and heroic whereas women are weak, passive, and dependent. Women must gain their identity through their association with a male character.

After completing her content analysis of romance novels, Radway (1986) went on to interview women who regularly read them. She was surprised to find that many readers used these books as part of a silent rebellion against male domination. They read them as an escape from housework or child rearing. Many of them rejected key assumptions of the patriarchal myths. They expressed strong preferences for male characters who combined traditionally masculine and feminine traits, for example, physical strength combined with gentleness. Similarly, readers preferred strong female characters who controlled their own lives but still retained traditional feminine attributes. Thus, romance reading could be interpreted as a form of passive resistance against male dominated culture. Romance readers rejected the preferred reading and instead engaged in oppositional decoding. British research on soap opera viewers offered similar interpretations of their decoding of program content (Brunsdon & Morley, 1981; Hobson, 1982; Lovell, 1981).

Another feminist cultural studies researcher offers evidence that women routinely engage in oppositional decoding of popular media content. Linda Steiner (1988) examined 10 years of the "No Comment" feature of *Ms.* magazine in which readers submit examples of subtle and not so subtle male domination. She argued that *Ms.* readers routinely engage in oppositional decoding of texts. They form a community that can act together to construct oppositional readings of these texts. Magazine examples can teach women how to identify these texts and help them make an interpretation that serves their own interests rather than those of a patriarchal elite. Angela McRobbie came to a similar conclusion in her study of teenage girls' negotiated readings of the movies *Flashdance* and *Fame.* She concluded that young girls' "passion" for these films "had far more to do with their own desire for physical autonomy than with any simple notion of acculturation to a patriarchal definition of feminine desirability" (1984).

Framing and Frame Analysis

While critical cultural researchers were developing reception analysis during the 1980s, a new approach to audience research was taking shape in the United States. This approach had its roots in theories that we discussed in Chapter 9—symbolic interaction and social construction of reality. Both of these theories argue that the expectations we form about ourselves, other people, and our social world are one of the basic elements in social life. You have probably encountered many terms in this and other textbooks that refer to such expectations—stereotypes, attitudes, typification schemes, and racial or ethnic bias. All these concepts emphasize that our expectations: (a) are based on previous experience of some kind, whether derived from a media message or direct personal experience (that is, we aren't born with them); (b) can be quite resistant to change even when they are contradicted by readily available factual information; (c) are often associated with and can arouse strong emotions such as hate, fear, or love; and (d) may be free of our conscious control over them, especially when strong emotions are aroused that interfere with our ability to make sense of new information available in the situation.

Developing and using expectations is a normal and routine part of everyday life. As human beings, we have cognitive skills that allow us to continually scan our environment, make sense of it, and then act on these interpretations. Our inability to adequately understand these skills in no way prevents them from operating, but it does impede our ability to make sense of our own sensemaking. You inevitably make an interpretation of the world around you. Sometimes you will understand what you are doing but more often you won't—typically it doesn't matter whether you do or not. But if you would like to assume more responsibility for your actions, then you should be concerned.

FRAME ANALYSIS
Goffman's idea about how people use expectations to make sense of everyday life

Sociologist Erving Goffman (1974) introduced a theory of **frame analysis** to provide a systematic account of how we use expectations to make sense of everyday life situations and the people in them (it is graphically represented in Box 10a on page 277). He was fascinated by the mistakes we make as we go through daily life—including the mistakes we never notice, for example, when we mistake courtesy for flirting. Like Alfred Schutz (see Chapter 9), Goffman was convinced that daily life is much more complicated than it appears. Goffman argued that we constantly and often radically change the way we define or typify situations, actions, and other people as we move through time and space. In other words, our experience of the world is constantly shifting, sometimes in major ways, yet we usually don't notice these shifts. We can step from one world to another without noticing that a boundary has been crossed. According to Goffman, we don't operate with a limited or fixed set of expectations about social roles, objects, or situations. Rather, we have enormous flexibility in creating and using expectations.

But if our sensemaking ability is so great and so flexible, how can we structure it so that we can coordinate our actions with others and experience daily existence as having order and meaning? Life, Goffman argued, operates much like a staged dramatic performance. We step from one social world to another in much the same way that actors move between scenes. Scenes shift, and as they shift we are able to radically alter how we make sense of them. But just how do we know

SOCIAL CUES *In frame analysis, information in the environment that signals a shift or change of action*

when such shifts are to be made? How do we know when one scene is ending and another beginning? According to Goffman, we are always monitoring the social environment for **social cues** that signal when we are to make a change. For example, when you view a play in a theater, you rely on many conventional cues to determine when a shift in scenes takes place. One of the oldest and most obvious cues involves using a curtain—it rises when a new scene begins and it falls when a scene ends. Other cues are more subtle—shifts in lights and music tempo often signal changes. As lights dim and music becomes ominous, we know that danger threatens. Goffman believes that we use the same cognitive skills to make sense of daily life as we do to make sense of plays. His theory also implies that social cues learned from using media could also be used to mark the boundaries of social worlds in everyday life.

FRAME *In frame analysis, a specific set of expectations used to make sense of a social situation at a given point in time*

Goffman used the term **frame** to refer to a specific set of expectations that are used to make sense of a social situation at a given point in time. Frames are like the typification schemes described by Peter Berger and Thomas Luckmann (see Chapter 9) but they differ in certain important respects. According to Goffman, individual frames are like notes on a musical scale—they spread along a continuum from those that structure our most serious and socially significant actions to those that structure playful, trivial actions. Like the notes on a musical scale, each is different even though there is underlying structural continuity. For social action, the continuity is such that we can learn how to frame serious actions by first learning frames for playful actions. Using the musical scale analogy, we can first learn to play simple tunes that use a narrow range of the scale in preparation for playing complex musical scores. For example, many of our games and sports provide useful preparation for more serious forms of action. If we can perform well under the pressures of a big game, we may handle the demands of other life situations better. Goffman argued that we are like animal cubs that first play at stalking frogs or butterflies and then are able to transfer these skills to related but more serious situations.

DOWNSHIFT AND UPSHIFT *In frame analysis, to move back and forth between serious and less serious frames*

When we move from one set of frames to another, we **downshift** or **upshift**. We reframe situations so that we experience them as being more or less serious. Remember when you were pretending to fight with a friend but one of you got hurt and the fight turned serious. You both downshifted. Suddenly, you no longer pulled punches but tried to make them inflict as much pain as possible. Many of the fighting skills learned during play were used but with a different frame—you were trying to hurt your friend. Perhaps, as you both got tired, one of you told a joke and cued the other that you wanted to upshift and go back to a more playful frame. According to Goffman, daily life involves countless shifts in frames and these shifts are negotiated by using social cues. Some cues are very conventional and universal, like the curtain on a stage; others are very subtle and used by small groups. For example, couples often develop a very complex set of cues to signal when to upshift or downshift their interaction. During the course of a conversation, many upshifts and downshifts can occur. Upshifting and downshifting add a dimension of complexity to everyday interaction that Goffman argued shouldn't be ignored.

So where do media come into this theory? Goffman made only limited but heuristic explorations of the way that media might influence our development and use of frames. In *Gender Advertisements* (1979), he presented an insightful argument concerning the influence that advertising could have on our perception of members of the opposite sex. He argued that advertising that uses the sex appeal of women to attract the attention of men inadvertently teaches us social cues that could have serious consequences. He showed how women are presented as less serious and more playful than men in numerous advertisements. Women smile, place their bodies in nonserious positions, wear playful clothing, and in various ways signal deference and a willingness to take direction from men. They are not only vulnerable to sexual advances, they signal their desire for them. No wonder these ads attract the attention of men. No wonder these ads are useful in positioning products. But could these representations of women be teaching social cues that have unexpected consequences?

We might be learning more than product definitions from these ads. We could be learning a vast array of social cues, some blatant but others quite subtle. Once learned, these cues could be used in daily life to make sense of members of the opposite sex and to impose frames on them, their actions, and the situations in which we encounter them. One possibility is that this advertising leads men to be overly sensitive to playful cues from women and increases the likelihood that they will upshift. Men learn such a vast repertoire of these cues that it might be hard for women to avoid displaying them. Men could routinely misinterpret inadvertent actions by women. Advertising might make it hard for women to maintain a serious frame for their actions. If they smile, bend their elbows in a particular way, or bow their heads even briefly, men might perceive a cue when none was intended. The more physically attractive the woman, the more likely this problem might arise because most advertising features good-looking women.

Goffman's theory provides an intriguing way of assessing how media can elaborate and reinforce a dominant public culture. Advertisers didn't create sex-role stereotypes, but Goffman argues that they have homogenized how women are publicly depicted. He contrasts the variety of ways that women are represented in private photos with their standardized depiction in advertising. Powerful visual imagery is routinely used to associate products with women who explicitly and implicitly signal their willingness to be playful, sexual partners. There are many subtle and not-so-subtle messages in these ads. Consume the product and get the girl is one dominant message. Another is that physically attractive women are sexually active and fun-loving. Ads both teach and reinforce

Box 10a   The Framing Process

In a different book (Davis & Baran, 1981), we developed this version of Goffman's theory of framing. Can you explain how it allows for up and downshifting? Can you speculate on how errors in framing can occur?

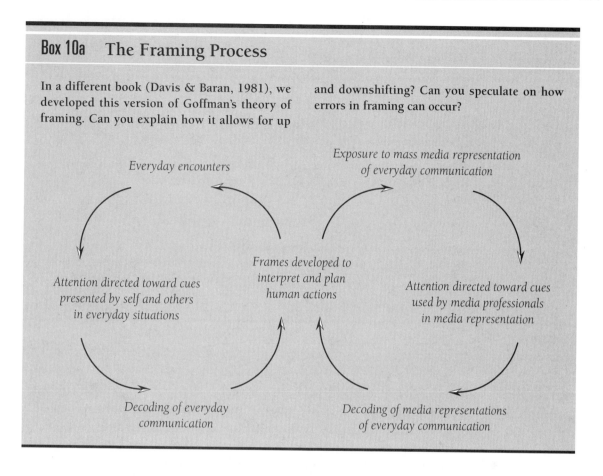

Everyday encounters

Exposure to mass media representation of everyday communication

Frames developed to interpret and plan human actions

Attention directed toward cues presented by self and others in everyday situations

Attention directed toward cues used by media professionals in media representation

Decoding of everyday communication

Decoding of media representations of everyday communication

cues. The specific message that each of us gets from the ads will be very different, but their long-term consequence may be similar—dominant myths about women are retold and reinforced.

By comparison with the other theories we have examined in this chapter, Goffman's is the most open-ended and flexible. He was convinced that social life is a constantly evolving and changing phenomenon. And yet, we experience social life as having great continuity. Though we have the capacity to constantly reframe our experience from moment to moment, most of us can maintain the impression that our experiences are quite consistent and routine. According to Goffman, we do this by firmly committing ourselves to live in what we experience as the **primary** or **dominant reality**—a real world in which people and events obey certain conventional and widely accepted rules. We find this world so compelling and desirable that we are constantly reworking and patching up flaws in our experience, and we don't notice when rule violations occur. He argued that we work so hard to maintain our sense of continuity in our experience that we

PRIMARY REALITY *In frame analysis, the real world in which people and events obey certain conventional and widely accepted rules (sometimes referred to as the dominant reality)*

Instant Access

Frame Analysis

Strengths

1 Focuses attention on individuals in the mass communication process

2 Micro-level theory but is easily applicable to macro-level effects issues

3 Is highly flexible and open-ended

4 Is consistent with recent findings in cognitive psychology

Weaknesses

1 Is highly flexible and open-ended (lacks specificity)

2 Is not able to address presence or absence of effects

3 Precludes causal explanations because of qualitative research methods

4 Assumes individuals make frequent framing errors; devalues individuals' abilities

inevitably make many framing mistakes. We literally see and hear things that aren't there but that should be there according to the rules we have internalized. For example, most college campuses in America today face the problem of date rape. And ultimately, what is the basic issue in most of these occurrences? Goffman might answer upshifting and downshifting problems between men and women as they attempt to frame the situations (dating) they find themselves in.

From Goffman's viewpoint, we are virtual prisoners of primary reality. We permit ourselves only brief and socially acceptable escapes into clearly demarcated alternative realities that we experience as fantasy worlds. But as the date rape example suggests, when we make framing mistakes in our primary realities, the results can be devastating.

Frame analysis theory as developed by Goffman is a microscopic theory that focuses on how individuals learn to routinely make sense of their social world. But this theory can be combined with macroscopic concerns to create a conceptual framework that considers: (a) the social and political context in which framing takes place, and (b) the long-term social and political consequences of the frames learned from media. In the next chapter, we will consider the work of researchers who have done this, drawing on frame analysis ideas, but using its ideas to address macroscopic questions about the role of media in politics. This current trend in frame analysis research is best illustrated by a recently published collection of studies entitled *Framing Public Life: Perspectives on Media and Our Understanding of the Social World* (Reese, Gandy, & Grant, 2001), which we will discuss in Chapter 11.

Information Processing Theory

INFORMATION PRO-
CESSING THEORY
*Theory that uses
mechanistic analo-
gies to describe and
interpret how
people deal with all
the stimuli they
receive*

For more than two decades, cognitive psychologists have been developing an innovative perspective on the way that individuals routinely cope with sensory information: **information processing theory**. The theory is actually a large set of quite diverse and disparate ideas about coping mechanisms and strategies and provides yet another way to study media audience activity. Researchers work to understand how people take in, process, and store various forms of information that are provided by media.

Closely related to systems theory (Chapter 8), information processing theory uses mechanistic analogies to describe and interpret how each of us takes in and makes sense of the flood of information that we receive from our senses every moment of each day. This theory describes individuals as complex computers with certain built-in information handling capacities and strategies. Each day we are exposed to vast quantities of sensory information; we filter this information so that only a small fraction of it ever reaches our conscious mind; then only a tiny fraction of this information is singled out for attention and processing; and then we finally store a tiny fraction of this in long-term memory. According to some cognitive theorists, we are not so much information handlers as information avoiders—we have developed sophisticated mechanisms for screening out irrelevant or useless information. Thus, very little of what goes on around us ever reaches our consciousness, and most of this is soon forgotten.

Some cognitive psychologists argue that many of the processing mechanisms we use to screen in and screen out information must have developed when early human beings were struggling to adapt to and survive in a hostile, physical environment (Wood & McBride, 1997). In that environment, it was critical that potential predators and prey be quickly identified so that swift action could be taken. There was no time for conscious processing of such information and no need for conscious reflection before action. If you sensed a predator nearby, you ran away. If you sensed nearby prey, you attacked. Those that didn't either died at the hands of predators or died of starvation. Humans that did develop the requisite cognitive skills survived. Some psychologists argue that many of these cognitive processing mechanisms are critical to adapting to and surviving in close social relationships with other human beings. Those theorists argue that much of the cognitive processing capacity of the human brain is effectively devoted to taking in and unconsciously interpreting subtle body and facial movements that enable us to sense what others are feeling and anticipate how they are likely to act. These processing mechanisms might have been more important to survival than processing information about prey and predators precisely because human beings are relatively weak and defenseless compared with many predators. Humans quickly die when food supplies fluctuate or temperatures vary. Human children require nurturing for much longer periods than do those of other mammals. As a result, it is essential that humans form communities in which they can band together to survive. But living in communities requires cognitive skills that are far more sophisticated that those needed to sense predators and prey.

How relevant is this theory for understanding how we deal with sensory information? Think about it for a moment. As you sit reading this book, consider your surroundings. Unless you are seated in a white, soundproof room with no other people present, there are many sensory stimuli around you. If you have been sitting for some time, your muscles might be getting stiff and your back might have a slight ache. Those around you might be laughing. A radio might be blaring. All this sensory information is potentially available but if you are good at focusing your attention on reading, then you are routinely screening out most of these external and internal stimuli in favor of the printed words on this page.

Consider what you do when you watch a television program. Unless you have a VCR and can play back scenes in slow motion, you can't pay attention to all the images and sounds. If you do watch them in slow motion, the experience is totally different from viewing them at normal speed. Viewing television is actually a rather complex task that uses very different information processing skills than does reading a textbook. You are exposed to rapidly changing images and sounds. You must sort these out and pay attention to those that will be most useful to you in achieving whatever purpose you have for your viewing. But if this task is so complex, why does television seem to be such an easy medium to use? Because the task of routinely making sense of television appears to be so similar to the task of routinely making sense of everyday experience. And making sense of that experience is easy, isn't it?

Information processing theory offers fresh insight into our routine handling of information. It challenges some basic assumptions about the way we take in and use sensory data. For example, we assume that we would be better off if we could take in more information and remember it better. But more isn't always better in the case of information. Some people actually experience severe problems because they have trouble routinely screening out irrelevant environmental stimuli. Such people are overly sensitive to meaningless cues such as background noise or light shifts. Other people remember too much information. You might envy someone with a photographic memory—especially when it comes to taking an exam covering textbook material. But total recall of this type can pose problems as well. Recall of old information can intrude on one's ability to experience new information. A few cues from the present can trigger vivid recall of past experiences. If you've watched reruns of the same television show several times, *South Park* or *The X-Files* for example, you probably have found that as you watch one episode it triggers recall of bits and pieces of previous episodes. If you were asked to reconstruct a particular episode of either program, you would likely weave together pieces from several different shows. What if everyday life was like that—the past constantly intruding into the present? Forgetting can have its advantages.

Another useful insight from information processing theory is a recognition of the limitations of conscious awareness. Our culture places high value on conscious thought processes, and we tend to be skeptical or suspicious of the utility of mental processes that are only indirectly or not at all subject to conscious control. We associate consciousness with rationality—the ability to make wise decisions based on careful evaluation of all available, relevant information. We associate unconscious mental processes with things like uncontrolled emotions, wild intuition, or even mental illness. We sometimes devalue the achievements of athletes because their greatest acts are typically performed without conscious thought. No wonder we are reluctant to acknowledge our great dependency on unconscious mental processes.

According to information processing theory, we can never be conscious of more than a very small fraction of the information present in our environment. As we absorb large quantities of information, we are consciously aware of only a small fraction of it. Our conscious awareness could be compared with a lone engineer in a nuclear power complex. The engineer's primary task is to remain in a master control room and confine his or her activity to reading the output from the equipment that directly monitors the activity of the plant. The engineer rarely observes any of the automated plant operations directly—to do so would be to risk a breakdown in some other part of the plant. The engineer scans the output from the instruments and then records only the most noteworthy information for long-term recall. As long as the plant operates smoothly, the engineer will have little reason to make direct observations or tinker with the equipment.

The point of this analogy is that the overall task of coping with information is much too complex for conscious control to be either efficient or effective. We have to depend on routinized processing of information and must normally limit conscious efforts to only those instances when intervention is crucial. For example, when there are signs of a breakdown of some kind, when routine processing fails to serve our needs properly, then conscious effort might be required.

One advantage of the information processing perspective is that it provides a more objective perspective on learning. Most of us view learning subjectively. We blame ourselves if we fail to learn something that we think we should have learned or that appears to be easy to learn. We assume that with a little more conscious effort, failure could have been avoided. How often have you chided yourself by saying, "If only I'd paid closer attention," "I should have given it more thought," "I made simple mistakes that could have been easily avoided if only I'd been more careful"? But would a little more attention really have helped all that much? A little more attention to one aspect of information processing might simply have led to a breakdown in some other aspect of processing. Of course, sometimes additional conscious effort can do wonders. But what you might need is

---

Instant Access

Information Processing Theory

Strengths

1 Provides specificity for what is generally considered routine, unimportant behavior

2 Provides objective perspective on learning; mistakes are routine, natural

3 Permits exploration of wide variety of media content

4 Produces consistent results across a wide range of communication situations and settings

Weaknesses

1 Is too micro-level oriented

2 Overemphasizes routine media consumption

3 Focuses too much on cognition, ignoring such factors as emotion

---

some overall revamping of your routine information handling skills and strategies—a transformation of your information processing system. This can take considerable time and effort—not just trying harder in one specific instance.

Thus, information processing theory provides a means of developing a more objective assessment of the mistakes we make when processing information. These mistakes are routine outcomes from a particular cognitive process or set of processes—not personal errors caused by personal failings. For example, the theory implies that blaming autistic people for failing to relate to others is like blaming blind people for failing to see. Thus, this theory doesn't blame audience members for making mistakes when they use media content. Information processing theory links errors to breakdowns in cognitive processes and suggests that solutions should be sought that anticipate these breakdowns and avoid them. For example, research has repeatedly demonstrated that poorly structured news stories will be routinely misinterpreted (Gunter, 1987) even if journalists who write them are well intentioned and news consumers try hard to understand them. Rather than retraining people to cope with badly structured stories, it is more efficient to change stories so that more people can use them without making mistakes.

An Information Processing Model

According to information processing theory, what we need is an ability to routinely scan our environment—taking in, identifying, and routinely structuring the most useful stimuli and screening out irrelevant stimuli. Then we must be able to process the structured stimuli that we take in, hold these structures in memory long enough so that we can sort out the most useful ones, put the useful ones into the right categories, and then store them in long-term memory. Described in this way, the process seems simple, but cognitive psychologists are finding that the process is quite complex with many different information screening skills and various processing stages.

Processing Television News

Information processing theory has been used most extensively in mass communication research to guide and interpret research about how people decode and learn from television news broadcasts. Numerous studies have been conducted, and useful reviews of this literature are now available (Davis, 1990; Davis & Robinson, 1989; Graber, 1987; Gunter, 1987; Robinson & Davis, 1990; Robinson & Levy, 1986). Remarkably similar findings have been gained from very different types of research, including mass audience surveys and small-scale laboratory experiments. A rather clear picture of what people do with television news is emerging.

Though most of us view television as an easy medium to understand and one that can make us eyewitnesses to important events, television is actually a difficult medium to use. Frequently, information is presented on television in ways that inhibit rather than facilitate learning. Part of the problem rests with audience members. Most of us view television primarily as an entertainment medium. We have developed many information processing skills and strategies for watching television that serve us well in making sense of entertainment content but that interfere with effective interpretation and recall of news. We approach the news passively and rely on routine activation of **schemas** (more or less highly structured sets of categories or patterns; sets of interrelated conceptual categories). We rarely engage in deep, reflective processing of news content, so most of it is quickly forgotten. Even when we do make a more conscious effort to learn from news, we often lack the schemas necessary to make in-depth interpretations of content or to store these interpretations in long-term memory.

SCHEMAS *More or less highly structured sets of categories or patterns; sets of interrelated conceptual categories*

But although we have many failings as an audience, news broadcasters also bear part of the blame. The average newscast is often so hard to make sense of that it can be said to be "biased against understanding." The typical broadcast contains too many stories, each of which tries to condense too much information into too little time. Stories are individually packaged segments that are typically composed of complex combinations of visual and verbal content—all too often, the visual information is so powerful that it overwhelms the verbal. Viewers are left with striking mental images but little contextual information. Often pictures are used that are irrelevant to stories—they distract but don't inform.

Findings presented by Dennis Davis and John Robinson (1989) are typical of this body of research. They were part of a research team that interviewed more than four hundred people to assess what viewers learned or failed to learn from three major network news broadcasts. The researchers identified numerous story attributes that enhanced or inhibited learning. Stories with complex structure and terminology or powerful but irrelevant visual images were poorly understood. Human-interest stories with simple but dramatic storylines were well understood.

Information processing theory has great potential to permit exploration of a wide variety of media content. Researchers are beginning to apply it to such diverse topics as advertising (Lang, 1990), televised political content, and children's programming. This research is rapidly revealing how we tailor our innate cognitive skills so that we can make sense of and use media content. Our ability to do this is most strikingly demonstrated by children as they learn to watch television. Within a few years children move from being dazzled by shifting colors and sound on the television screen to making complex differentiations (good/bad, strong/weak, male/female) about program characters and making accurate predictions about the way program storylines will unfold. For example, they come to recognize that Disney stories will have happy endings despite the efforts of evil characters. But underlying these seemingly simple and routine acts of sensemaking are complex cognitive processes that have been adapted to the task of watching television.

Some Final Words to Clear the Mist

Of all the chapters you have or will read in this book, this one may leave you the most unsatisfied. Social cognitive theory was easy: People learn from the mass media through a process called modeling. Attitude change theory is simple: Cognitive dissonance helps people protect themselves from persuasive messages. But the various audience theories that we have reviewed in this chapter often raise as many questions about the role of media in our lives as they answer. These theories suggest that our use of media is actually much more complicated than we might like to assume. When you relax by clicking the remote and watching *Friends* or *The Drew Carey Show*, you might like to assume that you are only being amused by these well-known programs. Theories that argue that you are constantly reinforcing status quo conceptions of the social world, theories that assert that you are actually unconsciously but expertly processing enormous amounts of information, or theories that claim that this seemingly routine choice is the result of your seeking a particular set of gratifications from a quite specific use of media might seem to be making something out of nothing. But they aren't. Our use of media is an infinitely complex process and, because of our belief in a well informed citizenry, an extremely important one. Proponents of media literacy, as we'll see in Chapter 12, not only understand this, but offer ways to help us all become more skilled consumers of media and their content.

A second reason that audience theories leave many observers unsatisfied is the difficulty these theories have in explaining media effects. Several authors we've cited told us that uses and gratifications developed as a "counter" to the effects research that was dominant at the time. Blumler (1979, p. 10) for example, wrote that it developed "at a time of widespread disappointment with the fruits of attempts to measure the short-term (media) effects on people." Palmgreen, Wenner, and Rosengren (1985, p. 12) wrote, "The dominance of the 'effects' focus in pre- and post-World War II communication research tended to overshadow . . . concern with individual differences." In a sense, uses and gratifications thinkers could not allow themselves the luxury of demonstrating or even postulating media-initiated effects because that would have been heresy to the then dominant paradigm.

Critical cultural theorists like Stuart Hall had quite another reason for disregarding media effects. Hall was convinced that effects research was useless because it largely served the status quo. He regarded the American focus on empirical effects research with great suspicion, believing that it largely served the interests of the media industries. When effects were found, as with advertising, these findings were exploited to manipulate audiences. When effects were not found or were found to be quite limited, then these findings were used to argue that media industries should not be regulated because they had no important or serious effects. Hall thought this was nonsense. He believed that the dominant readings embedded in most media content were obviously propping up a status quo in which most people were exploited. But how could he demonstrate this in a way that would be convincing to someone other than a neomarxist? His answer was reception analysis—a qualitative research strategy that permitted in-depth exploration of how groups "read" popular media content from television sitcoms to punk rock videos.

Finally, these audience theories might not seem as "clean" or straightforward as some of the other ideas we've studied because they are best regarded not as highly coherent, systematic conceptual frameworks (true theories) but rather as loosely structured perspectives through which a number of ideas and theories about media choice, consumption, sensemaking, and even impact can be viewed. As Blumler himself said,

> There is no such thing as *a* or *the* uses and gratification theory, although there are plenty of theories about uses and gratification phenomena, which may well differ with each other over many issues. Together, they will share a common field of concern, an elementary set of concepts indispensable for intelligibly carving up that terrain, and an identification of certain wider features of the mass communication process with which such core phenomena are presumed to be connected. (1979, p. 11–12)

Similarly, there is no one theory of reception analysis, framing, or information processing. All these theories are quite open ended and at relatively early stages of development. Although all three began as microscopic theories with a focus on how and why people make sense of and learn from specific media content, all have recently moved to address more macroscopic issues. Important recent publications have demonstrated the usefulness of these theories and increase the likelihood that they will emerge as dominant approaches over the next decade. These theories show the potential to provide quite significant insights into media audiences. These insights don't reveal a mass audience mesmerized by powerful elites, however, nor do they reveal an increasingly informed citizenry that benefits from the flood of information available via mass media and the Internet. Instead, they show a very complex interrelationship between media, media programming, and audiences in which considerable mutual influence is possible and likely. These theories, taken together, offer exciting challenges to the next generation of media researchers.

So where do we go from here? How does someone who believes in the concept of an active audience but who is also working to understand mass communication do so using contemporary audience theories? We will provide our answers to these questions in Chapter 12. But we will leave you now with hints provided by Elihu Katz and Jay Blumler, two of the creators of the original 1974 volume, *The Uses of Mass Communication.* When asked to write the concluding comments for a book to celebrate the tenth anniversary of that work, they, along with the colleague who wrote the original volume's introductory chapter, had this advice. This advice can be applied to any of the audience theories we have reviewed in this chapter:

> Philosophically, lingering traces of "vulgar gratificationism" should be purged from our outlook. This implies the following: (1) *Rejection of audience imperialism.* Our stress on audience activity should not be equated with a serene faith in the full or easy realization of audience autonomy . . . (2) *Social roles constrain audience needs, opportunities, and choices* . . . The individual is part of a social structure, and his or her choices are less free and less random than a vulgar gratificationism would presume. (3) *Texts are also to some extent constraining.* In our zeal to deny a one-to-one relationship between media content and audience motivation, we have sometimes appeared to slip into the less warranted claim that almost any type of content may serve any type of function. (Blumler, Gurevitch, & Katz, 1985, p. 259–260)

Their fourth assertion is that these three "propositions inject into the uses and gratifications paradigm an essential (but sometimes neglected) element of *realism*— without reducing . . . our normative commitment to the would-be active audience member and to the provision of media materials designed to enable him or her to realize his or her purposes" (Blumler, Gurevitch, & Katz, 1985, p. 259–260).

Summary

The audience has never been completely absent from mass communication theory, but the uses and gratifications approach brought it to a more central position in thinking about media. Its assertion that audiences are active proved quite valuable in refining our understanding of the mass communication process.

Audience activity can be defined in several ways—utility, intentionality, selectivity, imperviousness to influence, and meaning construction, for example—but activity should be seen as a relative concept; that is, some people are more active media consumers than others are. Other audience-centered theories accept this fact. Reception studies focuses on people's ability to make sense of specific forms of content, presumably for personally relevant ends. Readers of media texts often apply their own negotiated and oppositional meanings to the preferred readings intended by content producers.

Frame analysis assumes that people use their expectations of situations to make sense of them and to determine their actions in them. Individuals use the cues inherent in these situations to determine how to frame, or understand, the situation and whether they should downshift or upshift, that is, the level of seriousness they should bring to their actions. Media's contribution to this framing is in influencing people's expectations, or readings of those cues.

Information processing theory describes how individuals process and make sense of the overwhelming amounts of information present even in the simplest media message and has been successfully applied to such situations as how people read television news.

The audience perspectives described in this chapter were developed as a counter to both mass society notions and the dominant limited effects paradigm. These perspectives argue that the media do not do things to people; rather, people do things with media. The basic tenet is that audiences are active and make media do things to serve their purpose.

Each of these perspectives has met resistance. Some theorists criticize the uses and gratifications approach, for example, because of questions about the definition of an active audience, its seeming basis in functional theory, and the methods of conducting research within its framework.

Uses and gratifications theory is largely based on research that uses survey methods. But just how should this survey data be interpreted? Is it safe to assume that audience members can adequately articulate the reasons and outcomes of their use of media? If you can make this assumption, then you can do what some uses and gratifications research does and simply add up people's reasons for using media. On the other hand, reception analysis, which employs qualitative interview methods, assumes that some audiences will interpret content according to a dominant reading (a passive interpretation) while other audiences will engage in oppositional decoding. But how do you differentiate between these readings when you are analyzing focus group discussions?

These concerns aside, audience-centered theory placed the audience in a more central role in our understanding of mass communication, but it also had a second beneficial effect. This theory provides the theoretical basis for and has fueled interest in media literacy (see Chapter 12). If audiences are central to the mass communication process, their effectiveness in that process should be significant.

Exploring Mass Communication Theory

1   Feminist reception studies are a good example of the contemporary state of cultural studies' focus on reception and meaning making. Several Web sites are devoted to feminist readings of media content. Among the best are the following:

> *differences: A Journal of Feminist Cultural Studies*
> http://iupjournals.org/differences

> *The Feminist Majority Foundation's Links to Feminist Media*
> http://www.feminist.org/arts/linkfilm.html

2   It began on the Internet and it lives not only on television but also on the Web. Visit a few *South Park*-oriented Web sites. See what others say about the show and its content and stories. In other words, determine how others process information or how they go about the task of sensemaking. If you'd rather, substitute *The X-Files, Queer as Folk*, or your favorite program for *South Park*. Start with these sites:

> *South Park*
> http://www.comedycentral.com/tv_shows/southpark/

> *The X-Files—Official Web Site*
> http://www.thex-files.com/

> *Queer as Folk*
> http://sho.com/queer/

3   Use **InfoTrac College Edition** to scan the tables of contents of as many advertising journals as you can. *The Journal of Advertising* and *The Journal of Advertising Research* are two examples. Identify those articles that focus on image advertising. Read one or two of the articles you find and redefine what they have to say relative to framing and frame analysis.

4   Use **InfoTrac College Edition** to scan the tables of contents of *differences: A Journal of Feminist Cultural Studies, Film Comment,* and *Film Quarterly.* Look for pieces that promise negotiated or oppositional readings of a film with which you

are familiar. Compare your reading with the dominant reading and then to the reading offered by the writer of the piece you've chosen.

Critical Thinking Questions

1   How active a media consumer are you? Are you always thoughtful in your choice of individual television programs, for example? Are you more active with one medium than another? Why?

2   How has your willingness and ability to be intentional in your media choices changed as you've grown older? Do you find yourself being more thoughtful in your choices at different times? If you regularly use the Internet, has that use caused you to become more or less active in your media activity?

3   Just how good are your information processing skills? Try watching a news broadcast as you usually do. When you finish, write down what you can remember. Did you come up with a detailed report with lots of factual information or did you remember fragments of a few stories?

4   When you enter the room where your television is, do you turn it on and then flip around the channels, searching for something to watch or do you first examine some sort of listing to determine what you will watch and then turn the set to that choice? What does this say about audience-centered theory?

5   Have you ever made a serious framing error? That is, have you ever approached a situation with one set of expectations, only to have to downshift or upshift to perform appropriately? Describe the situation. Were you successful in making the necessary adjustment?

6   Do you use the Internet to download, swap, or otherwise acquire copyrighted music? If you do, subject this media use to the fraction of selection. That is, complete the equation for your use of "legitimate" music sites such as pressplay.com (from Sony and Universal Records), emusic.com (Universal and Vivendi), and musicnet.com (AOL/Time Warner). Now complete the equation for your use of "illegitimate" sites such as BearShare and KaZaa. How do the factors you consider in the numerators and denominators of each differ? What were the "final scores" of each type of service? Were they accurate predictors of your preferences? If you do not file share on the net, use the experience of a friend who does to complete this exercise.

Significant People and Their Writing

Blumler, Jay G., and Elihu Katz, eds., (1974). *The Uses of Mass Communication: Current Perspectives on Gratifications Research*. Beverly Hills, CA: Sage.

Goffman, Erving (1979). *Gender Advertisements.* New York: Harper & Row.

_____. (1974). *Frame Analysis: An Essay on the Organization of Experience.* New York: Harper & Row.

Graber, Doris (1987). *Processing the News,* 2nd edition. New York: Longman.

Hall, Stuart (1982). "The Rediscovery of 'Ideology': Return of the Repressed in Media Studies." In M. Gurevitch, T. Bennett, J. Curran, and J. Woollacott, eds., *Culture, Society and the Media.* New York: Methuen.

Rubin, Alan M. (1994). "Media Uses and Effects: A Uses-and-Gratifications Perspective." In J. Bryant and D. Zillman, eds., *Media Effects: Advances in Theory and Research.* Hillsdale, NJ: Lawrence Erlbaum.

Chapter 11

Theories of Media, Culture, and Society

Remember the last news report you saw or read concerning a natural disaster or major accident such as a plane crash. Most likely, it focused on the factual details of the disaster—how much damage was done, what was destroyed, how many people were hurt. Considerable detail may have been used to describe the emotional reactions of the people involved, especially those whose relatives were killed or who "lost everything." But were there things that the report didn't tell you? Were questions not asked or left unanswered? Could or should the disaster have been prevented? Disasters and major accidents represent important disruptions in the social order. Their occurrence prompts us to wonder, "Are we doing something wrong?" "Should changes be made?" "Are the people running things doing their job?"

Media reports rarely raise these questions. Instead, they typically focus on offering us reassurance that the disruption will be resolved. Everyone involved in the disaster is all right. Services are being restored. Your government is working hard to get problems under control. One researcher (Gans, 1979) found that 85 percent of the news reports of social disruptions focused on restoration of order by social elites. But why does news give so much attention to the actions of elites and so little attention to factors that cause problems? Why is there so much coverage of emotional reactions?

Media practitioners have several plausible answers to these questions. First, they have little time to do in-depth, investigative reports. When a disaster happens, all their attention must be focused on getting out accurate, factual reports of what took place. By sticking to the facts about a disaster, journalists are able to remain objective at a time when objectivity is crucial. During a crisis, there is little time or opportunity to raise questions of blame or determine if changes are needed. News media can expect to be sued if coverage incorrectly blames persons who later are discovered to be innocent. Richard Jewell, the security guard who was the focus of the investigation into the Olympic bombing in Atlanta, reportedly reached a settlement of more than $500,000 from NBC when it incorrectly identified him as the bomber. So, most journalists would argue it is not their job to place blame or recommend changes. Highly trained and well-paid experts or officials are expected to do that. By offering reassurance and emphasizing that order is being restored, journalists calm public fears and rumors that might otherwise create even more problems. They say it is socially responsible for news media to calm rather than ignite public fears.

One of the controversies that arose concerning news coverage of the terrorist attacks on September 11th was that coverage had unnecessarily alarmed the public and failed to provide sufficient reassurance. Journalists responded by saying that they were merely reflecting what government officials were telling them. This event illustrates quite well how media coverage can reinforce (many would say justifiably in this case) public fears concerning threats to social order. After a "routine" air disaster, for example, Federal Aviation Administration officials come to the scene within hours and take control of the crash investigation. News coverage focuses on their efforts to find the causes of the crash but the results of this investigation typically aren't released for several months. Clearly, reporters would be irresponsible to blame the pilot in their early reports only to discover a year later that there had been an equipment failure. Why not tell people that air travel is still safe? Why promote what are likely to be groundless fears about air safety?

Soon after the September 11th event, President Bush himself placed blame on Osama bin Laden. Rather than offer reassurance, Bush warned Americans that a real threat still existed and that more attacks were likely. The airline industry was thrown into chaos as thousands of Americans cancelled plans to fly. Instead, people chose to stay at home and focus on immediate family and friends. If the larger social world was "changed forever," we could at least find refuge in our homes. In this case, journalists decided that it was their responsibility to report the warnings that the President and other officials provided. They also provided extensive coverage of the terrorist threat. Some experts later argued that they should have done more to calm fears (more on this in Box 11a on page 295). Just how should journalists be expected to deal with news about crises? How and when should they be expected to criticize the status quo and the elites who maintain the existing social order? What should they do if they feel that government officials or other elites are covering up real dangers? Remember when the anthrax threat first appeared after the September 11 terrorist attacks? Public officials responded by minimizing the threat. Post office officials, along with public health experts, staged a news conference in a Washington, D.C., mail sorting facility. But after two post office workers fell ill with anthrax, officials quickly admitted that the threat was greater than they had first believed. Clearly, some important constraints will always limit what media practitioners can be expected to do. They are human beings working for fallible social organizations. But not every constraint is as powerful as media practitioners assert. Some constraints could be overcome without great expense or effort. Still others might be countered if industry groups or professional associations chose to address them. Taken as a whole, the U.S. news media are a major industry that commands enormous resources, but these resources are rarely marshaled in any systematic way to address even the most serious social issues. Instead, they are fragmented across hundreds of competing agencies that work against artificially imposed time deadlines.

Overview

The media theorists that we consider in this chapter argue that the failings of news and other media raise important questions about the motives of media practitioners and their professional norms. Are they really doing everything they can and should to provide us with useful services? Or are they part of the problem? To what extent do their professional norms actually lead them to be socially irresponsible? These questions about the ideal social role of media are much like those raised in Chapter 5 in our discussion of normative theories of mass media. Moreover, these questions imply that the dominant normative theory, social responsibility theory, should be radically changed or replaced.

The earliest mass communication theories arose out of a concern for the creation and preservation of social order. Ever since the appearance of modern mass media in the middle of the nineteenth century, social theorists have speculated about the power of media to create community on the one hand or disrupt important social institutions on the other. Technology was embraced as a panacea or feared as a corrupting force. In Chapters 3 and 4, we traced the rise of mass society theory along with that of the mass media industries. At its height, mass society theory painted a dire picture of a totalitarian future in which media were manipulated by a cynical elite bent on creating and maintaining absolute power.

In this chapter, we will consider theories that address many of the same questions and issues that sparked the development of mass society theory. We live today in an era that is being transformed by powerful new media—by communications satellites that span the globe while computer-based media invade our homes. These media give rise to unrealistic hopes and inspire inordinate fears. Like our ancestors at the end of the nineteenth century, we harbor doubts about our political system. Though we aren't threatened by totalitarian propaganda, we are regularly deluged by negative political advertising that feeds our cynicism about politics. Finally, concerns about the media barons of the nineteenth century are echoed by concerns about contemporary media power brokers best exemplified by Rupert Murdoch and his News Corporation.

The contemporary media theories we consider in this chapter might seem familiar to you based on your reading of previous chapters. Most of these ideas draw on older theories to offer cogent and insightful analyses of the role of media in both culture and society. Some of the theories discussed in this chapter are grounded in empirical social research whereas others are based on qualitative research such as text analysis, reception analysis, historiography, or participant observation. Although this research is quite diverse, the theories it supports have many similarities. As you will see, the assessment these theories provide of contemporary media and their social role is, with two exceptions (the ideas of Marshall McLuhan and social marketing theory), uniformly negative. Some of the theories we cover view media industries as primarily commercial enterprises with little commitment to public service (knowledge gap and cultivation analysis). Other theories argue that media routinely disrupt important social institutions such as politics or education (spiral of silence, media systems dependency theory, news production research).

It is important to keep in mind that despite their negative tone, none of these contemporary media theories should be confused with mass society theory. None argues that media will inevitably destroy high culture, bring an end to democracy, and plunge us into a dark age of totalitarianism. The conceptions of culture found in these theories are far more sophisticated than the elitist notions of high culture central to mass society theory. Their view of individuals is generally positive, based on active audience assumptions similar to those described in Chapter 10. Media don't manipulate passive individuals. Instead, media's power lies in their ability to provide communication services that are routinely used by individuals and are central to the maintenance of our social order.

Contemporary theories of media, culture, and society also have a darker side. Modern theorists are quite concerned about the forms of culture that are most easily and widely cultivated by mass media. According to some theorists, mass media have turned culture into a commodity (commodification of culture) and political institutions are being eroded (media intrusion theory). Powerful elites are playing an increasingly central role in determining how new media systems will be created and the purposes they will serve. These theories argue that the structure and content of our media system both reflect and create our overall social structure and our culture.

Marshall McLuhan: The Medium Is the Message and Massage

During the 1960s, a Canadian literary scholar, Marshall McLuhan, gained worldwide prominence as someone who had a profound understanding of electronic

Box 11a   Media Response to Terrorism

In the wake of the September 11th terrorist attacks, a group of prominent academics and media practitioners examined media's performance in the aftermath of that horrible day. Led by communication researcher Kathleen Hall Jamieson and psychologist Martin E. P. Seligman (2002), this group released a report that offered advice to both government officials and journalists concerning news coverage of future attacks. Their recommendations reflect insights based on the best current theory in both mass communication and psychology.

Six Rules for Government and Press on Terrorism: Undercutting Fear Itself

The main weapon the terrorists have is not bombs or anthrax, but fear itself. The U.S. government and press can either play into the hands of the terrorists by magnifying anxiety and fear or help thwart their efforts by instilling courage and calm.

Although the dictionaries of quotations have abbreviated it to "the only thing we have to fear is fear itself," Franklin Roosevelt made a more complex point in his first inaugural when he said, "So, first of all, let me assert my firm belief that the only thing we have to fear is fear itself—nameless, unreasoning, unjustified terror which paralyzes needed efforts to convert retreat into advance." Scientific psychology provides guidance for public officials attempting to blunt nameless, unreasoning, unjustified terror.

Fear is an important and sensible human response to events such as those that transpired on September 11 and to bioterrorism. Fear and anxiety increase adaptive vigilance, ready us to fight or flee, and prompt searches for means of coping. High fear-provoking messages can be a powerful means of changing attitudes and inducing action if they convince audiences that: the problem is real, they are vulnerable to it, the

solution will eliminate the problem, and they are able to carry out the solution.

Fear and anxiety very easily become maladaptive. When people feel helpless to do anything about the objects of their fears, they become paralyzed, depressed, and demoralized. When people cannot distinguish safe from dangerous situations, they become chronically anxious, and avoid many innocent activities, like flying and shopping. When people cannot see a clear upper limit to the danger, fear can easily turn to panic. Here are six principles that can be incorporated into the reporting of terrorism and into government announcements about terrorism to undercut these dysfunctional states.

Principles

- **Reduce Helplessness.** A danger that is uncontrollable evokes much more fear than the identical danger when it is controllable. When individuals believe that they can take action that might influence the danger, even slightly, fear is much reduced. Government and press announcements should include recommendations for actions that citizens can take. Truisms such as "be vigilant" are unhelpful unless they specify how, where, and why. If there are conceivable actions that citizens can take to avoid, minimize, or influence the danger, these should be spelled out. These actions need not result in capture of terrorists for the fear-reducing value to take hold.

- **Blunt Availability.** Heuristics are cognitive shortcuts that drive generalizations. Because evocative images are more available in memory, we tend to over-estimate how likely they are to occur. When news brings vivid photos of a plane crash, people overestimate the likelihood that planes crash. Dramatic, vivid,

(continues)

Box 11a   Media Response to Terrorism (*continued*)

repeated visually evocative materials can be tools of terror or vehicles that reassure. By repeatedly showing the hijacked planes hitting the towers, news increased our sense that such crashes were likely to happen. By repeatedly showing the towers collapsing, news magnified our fear that we could be trapped in a tall building as it collapsed. By repeatedly airing stories about anthrax, news increased the likelihood that we would be fearful as we open our mail. News, of course, should be reported. However, narratives of reassurance and base-rate information should be included to blunt the overgeneralizing effect produced by the availability heuristic.

- **Reframe.** Our perception of risk is a function of framing. Frame a choice in terms of loss and people become risk averse. Frame it in terms of gain and people are more likely to accept the risk. Although the risk expressed in each is mathematically the same, there will likely be two different responses to the following scenarios: (1) Of the 18 people exposed to anthrax in the past weeks, 14 were treated with appropriate antibiotics and survived. (2) Of the 18 exposed to anthrax in the past weeks, 4 have died. By focusing on those who have died not those who have survived, news magnifies our sense of risk. Similarly, by focusing on the 4,000–4,500 people

killed on September 11 and not the 20,000 or more survivors of the World Trade Center, the news magnifies our perception that terrorists will kill us and minimizes our sense that we will survive a terrorist attack. By focusing on the handful of letters thought to contain anthrax, we lose track of the over 600 million other pieces of mail that are unaffected each day. By focusing on the four planes that were downed on September 11 and not on the 39,996 scheduled to fly that day that were unaffected, we increase the fear of flying.

- **Tell Stories of Survival and Triumph.** The stories we tell matter. In a contest between data and dramatic narrative, the narrative is likely to be believed. The press has focused too much attention on stories of the country's lack of preparedness to cope with bioterrorism and too little on the capacity of the country to respond to challenges. Officials have invited stories about unpreparedness by offering the public misinformation and sometimes conflicting claims. What is missing in much of the commentary from appointed officials and also from the news media are the stories that recall past crises that were surmounted by diligence and scientific commitment. For example, many remember the fear of polio in the early fifties.

---

media and their impact on both culture and society. McLuhan was highly trained in literary criticism but also read widely in communication theory and history. Although his writings contain few citations to Marx (McLuhan actually castigated Marx for ignoring communication), he based much of his understanding of media's historical role on the work of Harold Innis, a Canadian political economist. Still, in his theory, McLuhan synthesized many other diverse ideas. We place him at the start of this chapter for two reasons. McLuhan is important to the de-

Box 11a Media Response to Terrorism (*continued*)

Parents kept children away from swimming pools, public drinking fountains, and movie theaters. Every child and adult who lived through those times remembers children in leg braces and children in iron lungs. Fear was pervasive. Uncertainty was high. Then Jonas Salk and his colleagues created the polio vaccine. We no longer feared polio. Remember AIDS? Diagnosis was once a death sentence. Who would have imagined that a combination of pills taken faithfully could control the virus? Smallpox? We have already proven that we can beat it. Anthrax? The drugs to save lives exist. Our challenge is detection. Here are the warning signs. Just as we met these challenges, we will likely meet any posed by bioterror.

- **Model Courage; It is Contagious.** Just as fear is contagious so too is courage. Those who model courage and heroism inspire it in others. Some of the high government officials making announcements convey courage; others do not. Some of the press conveys courage, but others do the opposite. The courage-enhancing techniques of Winston Churchill and Edward R. Murrow are trainable, and we suggest such "media training" for those making these announcements. Reporters and anchors who show anxiety or sound frightened should stay off the air.

- **Use Safety Signals.** During the London Blitz, there were warning sirens and all-clear sirens. People were anxious during the warning signals, but could relax and go about their lives after the all-clear signal. Our situation is more ambiguous, but we emphasize the well-documented principle that in the absence of safety signals, people are anxious all the time. The public has been receiving warning signals, but no safety signals. The "indefinite extension" of the late October warning is an egregious example. Continuous states of high alert create the cry wolf effect and produce chronic anxiety, depression, and helplessness. If there are times, or places, or actions during which there is reduced danger, these should be spelled out.

What do you think of these recommendations? If the media and government officials had followed them post–September 11, do you think you might have been less fearful, less anxious? But isn't some fear and anxiety in time of disaster of this magnitude a good thing? If it had been one of your family members killed by anthrax, would you have wanted more calm or more warning? If you were a journalist, how would you strike the proper balance between your professional obligation to inform people and the natural desire to reduce people's fears?

velopment of cultural theory because his work did much to inspire and legitimize macroscopic theories of media, culture, and society in North America. He wrote at a time when the limited effects paradigm had reached the peak of its popularity among academics, a time when most American communication researchers regarded macroscopic theory with suspicion, if not outright hostility. In the humanities, it was a time when the high culture canon consisted largely of "classic" work (novels, symphonies, serious theatre) produced by dead Anglo-Saxon males. McLuhan's focus on the cultural role of popular media quickly posed a challenge both to limited effects notions and to the canon.

The second reason for our attention to McLuhan is that he and his ideas are again in vogue. It is no small irony that McLuhan, hailed (or denigrated) in the 1960s as the "High Priest of Popcult," the "Metaphysician of Media," and the "Oracle of the Electronic Age" has been declared the patron saint of *Wired* magazine, the "Bible of Cyberspace." McLuhan, featured on the March 3, 1967, cover of *Newsweek,* graces the cover of the January 1996 *Wired* 29 years later.

McLuhan's "theory" is actually a collection of lots of intriguing ideas bound together by some common assumptions. The most central of these assumptions is that *changes in communication technology inevitably produce profound changes in both culture and social order.* Even though McLuhan drew on critical cultural theories such as political economy theory to develop his perspective, his work was rejected by political economists because it failed to provide a basis on which to produce positive social change. McLuhan had no links to any political or social movements. He seemed ready to accept whatever changes were dictated by and inherent in communications technology. Because he argued that technology inevitably causes specific changes in how people think, in how society is structured, and in the forms of culture that are created, McLuhan is said to be a **technological determinist.**

TECHNOLOGICAL DETERMINIST *A person who believes that all social, political, economic, and cultural change is inevitably based on the development and diffusion of technology*

Harold Innis: The Bias of Communication

Innis was one of the first scholars to systematically speculate at length about the possible linkages between communication media and the various forms of social structure found at certain points in history. In *Empire and Communication* (1950) and *The Bias of Communication* (1951), he argued that the early empires of Egypt, Greece, and Rome were based on elite control of the written word. He contrasted these empires with earlier social orders dependent on the spoken word. Innis maintained that before elite discovery of the written word, dialogue was the dominant mode of public discourse and political authority was much more diffuse. Gradually, the written word became the dominant mode of elite communication, and its power was magnified enormously by the invention of new writing materials (that is, paper) that made writing portable yet enduring. With paper and pen, small, centrally located elites were able to gain control over and govern vast regions. Thus, new communication media made it possible to create empires.

Innis argued that written word-based empires expanded to the limits imposed by communication technology. Thus, expansion did not depend as much on the skills of military generals as it did on the communication media used to disseminate orders from the capital city. Similarly, the structure of later social orders also depended on the media technology available at a certain point in time. For example, the telephone and telegraph permitted even more effective control over larger geographic areas. Thus, the development of media technology has gradually given centralized elites increased power over space and time.

Innis traced the way Canadian elites used various technologies, including the railroad and telegraph, to extend their control across the continent. As a political economist, he harbored a deep suspicion of centralized power and believed that newer forms of communication technology would make even greater centralization inevitable. He referred to this as the inherent **bias of communication**. Because of this bias, the people and the resources of outlying regions that he called *the periphery* are inevitably exploited to serve the interests of elites at *the center.*

BIAS OF COMMUNICA-
TION *Innis' idea
that communication
technology makes
centralization of
power inevitable*

McLuhan: Understanding Media

Although he borrowed freely from Innis, McLuhan didn't dwell on issues of exploitation or centralized control. He was fascinated instead by the implications of Innis' arguments concerning the transformative power of media technology. If media could create empires, what else could they do? Was it possible that media could transform our sensory experiences as well as our social order? After all, the acts of reading a book and viewing a movie or television program employ different sensory organs. During the 1960s, we were clearly moving from an era grounded in print technology to one based on electronic media. McLuhan asked if communication technology plays such a critical role in the emergence of new social orders and new forms of culture, what were the implications of abandoning print media in favor of electronic media?

THE MEDIUM IS THE
MESSAGE
*McLuhan's idea
that new forms of
media transform
our experience of
ourselves and our
society, and this
influence is ulti-
mately more impor-
tant than the
content of specific
messages*

In a series of books so densely written as to be almost unreadable (the ironically titled *Understanding Media* [1964] is a good example), McLuhan outlined his vision of the changes that were taking place as a result of the spread of radio and television. He proclaimed that **the medium is the message** (*and the massage*). In other words, new forms of media transform (massage) our experience of ourselves and our society, and this influence is ultimately more important than the content that is transmitted in its specific messages.

GLOBAL VILLAGE
*McLuhan's concep-
tion of a new form
of social organiza-
tion emerging as
instantaneous,
electronic media tie
the entire world
into one great so-
cial, political, and
cultural system*

McLuhan coined several phrases and terms that have become part of the common vocabulary we use to talk about media and society. He suggested the term **global village** to refer to the new form of social organization that would inevitably emerge as instantaneous, electronic media tied the entire world into one great social, political, and cultural system. Unlike Innis, McLuhan didn't bother to concern himself with questions about control over this village or whether village members would be exploited. To McLuhan, these questions didn't matter. He was more concerned with microscopic issues, with the impact of media on our senses.

THE EXTENSIONS OF MAN *McLuhan's idea that media literally extend sight, hearing, and touch through time and space*

McLuhan proclaimed media to be **the extensions of man** [sic] and argued that media quite literally extend sight, hearing, and touch through time and space. Electronic media would open up new vistas for average people and enable us to be everywhere, instantaneously. But was this an egalitarian and democratic vision? What would ordinary people do when their senses were extended in this way? Would they succumb to information overload? Would they be stimulated to greater participation in politics? Would they flee into the virtual worlds that were opened up to them by their extended senses? In a series of books, McLuhan tossed out cryptic and frequently contradictory ideas that addressed such questions. Occasionally, his ideas were profound and prophetic. More often, they were arcane, mundane, or just confusing.

McLuhan's observations concerning the global village and the role of electronic media in it continue to be prophetic. At a time when satellite communication was just being developed, he seemed to foretell the rise of the Cable News Network with its ability to seemingly make us eyewitnesses to history as it's made on the battlefield or at the barricade. At a time when mainframe computers filled entire floors of office buildings, he seemed to envision a time when personal computers would be everywhere and the Internet would give everyone instant access to immense stores of information. But as one media critic (Meyrowitz, 1985) noted, to be everywhere is to be nowhere—to have no sense of place. To have access to information is not the same thing as being able to select and use information effectively. The global village isn't situated in space or time. Is it possible to adjust to living in such an amorphous, ambiguous social structure? Or will the global village merely be a façade used by cynical elites to exploit people? These questions go far beyond the paeans to electronic media that can be found throughout *Understanding Media*.

McLuhan's ideas achieved enormous public popularity. He became one of the first pop culture gurus of the 1960s. His pronouncements on Nixon and Kennedy propelled him to national prominence. His ideas received serious attention but then fell into disfavor. Why the rise and sudden fall?

Initially, McLuhan's work fit the spirit of the early 1960s—the age of Camelot. In sharp contrast with Innis, he was unabashedly optimistic about the profound but ultimately positive changes in our personal experience, social structure, and culture that new media technology would make possible. McLuhan was the darling of the media industries—their prophet with honor. For a brief period, he commanded huge fees as a consultant and seminar leader for large companies. His ideas were used to rationalize rapid expansion of electronic media with little concern for their negative consequences. His mantra became broadcast industry gospel: So what if children spend most of their free time in front of television sets and become functionally illiterate? Reading is doomed anyway, why prolong its demise? Eventually, we will all live in a global village where literacy is as unnecessary as it was in preliterate tribal villages. Why worry about the negative consequences of television when it is obviously so much better than the hot, old media it is replacing? Just think of the limitations that print media impose. Linear, logical thinking is far too restrictive. If the triumph of electronic media is inevitable, why not get on with it? No need for government regulation of media. The ideal form of media can be expected to evolve naturally, no matter what we try to do. No need to worry about media conglomerates. No need to complain about television violence. No need to resist racist or sexist media content. Adopt McLuhan's long-term, global perspective. Think big. Think nonlinearly. Just wait for the future to happen.

But even as his work became more accepted within the media industries, it aroused increasing criticism within academia. Perhaps the most devastating criticism was offered by other literary critics who found his ideas too diverse and inconsistent. They were astounded by his notion that literacy was obsolete and found his praise of nonlinear thinking nonsensical or even dangerous. These critics thought nonlinear thinking was just another label for logically inconsistent, random thoughts. McLuhan's books were said to be brainstorms masquerading as scholarship. McLuhan answered by charging that these critics were too pedantic, too concerned with logic and linear thinking. The critics were too dependent on literacy and print media to be objective about them. They were the elitist defenders of the high culture canon. Their jobs depended on the survival of literacy. He recommended that they work hard to free their minds from arbitrary limitations. Not surprisingly, few were willing to do so.

Empirical media researchers were also uniformly critical of McLuhan, but for different reasons. Although a few tried to design research to study some of his notions, most found his assumptions about the power of media to be absurd. Most were indoctrinated in the limited effects perspective and were skeptical about the possibility that media could transform people's experience. Even if this was possible, how could research be designed to systematically study something as amorphous as "people's experience"? When early, small-scale empirical studies failed to support McLuhan's assertions, these suspicions were confirmed. McLuhan was just another grand theorist whose ideas were overly speculative and empirically unverifiable.

McLuhan fared even less well with most critical cultural theorists. Although many of them respected Innis, these theorists found McLuhan's theory to be a perversion of Innis' basic ideas. Rather than attempt reform of the superstructure or lead a revolution to take control of the base, McLuhan was content to wait for technology to lead us forward into the global village. Our fate is in the hands of media technology, and we are constrained to go wherever it leads, he seemed to say. Political economists saw this as a self-fulfilling prophecy, encouraging and sanctioning the development of potentially dangerous new forms of electronic media. These might well lead us to a painful future—a nightmare global village in which we are constantly watched and coerced by remote elites. As long as existing elites remain in power, political economists saw little hope

Instant Access

McLuhanism

Strengths	Weaknesses
1 Is comprehensive	1 Is empirically unverifiable
2 Is macro-level	2 Is overly optimistic about technology's influence
3 Resonates with general public	3 Ignores too many important effects issues
4 Elevates cultural value of popular media content	4 Calls for nonlinear thinking are criticized
5 Enjoys longevity as a result of introduction of new electronic media	5 Is overly apologetic of electronic media

for positive change. They condemned McLuhan for diverting attention from more important work and for perverting the radical notions found in Innis' writing. Some political economists even saw McLuhan's ideas as a form of disinformation, deliberately designed to confuse the public so that neomarxist work would be ignored or misinterpreted.

Despite these criticisms of McLuhan's work, much in it merits attention. Everett Rogers (2000) recently argued that McLuhan's perspective deserves more attention by mass communication scholars, especially those interested in studying new media. Some young scholars find it an exciting starting point for their own thinking (Wolf, 1996). This is possible because McLuhan's work is so eclectic and open-ended. If you start with McLuhan and are excited by ideas he introduces, you can trace them back to the theorists who developed them. Lewis Mumford (1975), for example, claimed that he introduced the global village notion 30 years before McLuhan. Although it is advisable to go back and read the original works, McLuhan does introduce some important thinking—just don't expect that ideas will be presented logically. At his best, he seized the central ideas in other works and expressed them in interesting, cogent ways.

Social Marketing Theory

During the early 1970s, a new macroscopic theory of media and society began to take shape that is quite unlike any of the other theories we will consider in this

SOCIAL MARKETING
THEORY *Collection
of middle-range
theories concerned
with promoting
socially valuable
information*

chapter. The theory is known as **social marketing theory.** This theory is not a unified body of thought but, rather, a collection of middle-range theories dealing with the promotion of information deemed by elite sources to be socially valuable. Rather than describing each one, we will provide an overarching theoretical framework for them and then discuss some of the important features. Readers interested in a more extended discussion of these theories should consult other sources (Goldberg, Fishbein, & Middlestadt, 1997; Rice & Atkin, 1989; Rogers, 1983).

Social marketing theory differs from other contemporary macroscopic theories in that it is a working theory (Chapter 2), and it is essentially source-dominated. It assumes the existence of a benign information provider who is seeking to bring about useful, beneficial social change. The theory gives such providers a framework for designing, carrying out, and evaluating information campaigns. In its most recent forms, this theory gives increasing attention to audience activity and the need to reach active audiences with information they are seeking. Target audiences are identified according to their information needs. Recommendations are made for stimulating audiences to seek information and for packaging and distributing information so that audiences will find it easy to get and use.

Social marketing theory can be regarded as a logical extension of the persuasion theories outlined in Chapter 6 and of diffusion theory discussed in Chapter 7. It represents an effort to increase the effectiveness of mass media–based information campaigns through greater understanding and manipulation of aspects of societal and psychological factors. Social marketing theory does this by identifying a variety of social system-level barriers and psychological barriers to the flow of information and influence through the mass media. The theory anticipates these barriers and includes strategies for overcoming them. Some strategies are ingenious; others involve the brute force of saturation advertising. Social marketing theory has several key features:

1 Methods for *inducing audience awareness* of campaign topics or candidates. A key first step in promoting ideas or candidates is to make people aware of their existence. The easiest but most costly way to do this is with a saturation television advertising campaign. As social marketing theories have gained sophistication, other methods have been developed that are almost as effective but much less costly. These include using news coverage and new media channels to induce awareness. During the last three presidential campaigns, the candidates successfully experimented with many new channels for reaching voters, including radio and television talk shows like *Larry King Live,* the MTV cable channel, late night variety shows like *Late Night with David Letterman,* and the Internet. These efforts permitted the candidates to reach voter segments that are difficult to reach effectively through mainstream media. Most young people, for example, no longer read newspapers and have learned to selectively screen out political news stories

on television. Thus, new media channels—especially the Internet and the World Wide Web—offer a means of overcoming barriers to the flow of information that arise over time. Republican hopeful Steve Forbes went so far as to launch his presidential bid for 2000 not with the usual press conference but on the Web. His intention was to signal "a new way of talking to the people."

2 **Methods for *targeting messages* at specific audience segments that are most receptive or susceptible to those messages.** Limited effects research demonstrated how to identify audience segments that are most vulnerable to specific types of messages. Once these segments are identified, messages can be targeted at them. **Targeting** is one of several concepts borrowed from product marketing research and converted to the marketing of ideas or political candidates. By identifying the most vulnerable segments and then reaching them with the most efficient channel available, targeting strategies reduce promotional costs while increasing efficiency.

TARGETING *Identifying specific audience segments and reaching them through the most efficient available channel*

3 **Methods for *reinforcing messages* within targeted segments and for encouraging these people to influence others through face-to-face communication.** Even vulnerable audience members are likely to forget or fail to act on messages unless they are reinforced by similar messages coming from several channels. Various strategies have been developed to make certain that multiple messages are received from several channels. These strategies include visits by change agents, group discussions, messages placed simultaneously in several media, and door-to-door canvassing.

4 **Methods for *cultivating images and impressions* of people, products, or services.** These methods are most often used when it is difficult to arouse audience interest. If people aren't interested in a topic, it is unlikely that they will seek and learn information about it. Lack of interest forms a barrier against the flow of information. But it is still possible to transmit images. The most prominent method used to cultivate images is image advertising in which easily recognizable, visually compelling images are presented. Relationships are implied between these and the objects being promoted. For example, a soft drink will be shown being consumed by very attractive people in an interesting setting. To what extent are your impressions of the U.S. Army or Pepsi shaped by ads that invited you to "Be an Army of One" or a member of the "Pepsi Generation"?

5 **Methods for *stimulating interest and inducing information seeking* by audience members.** Information seeking occurs when a sufficient level of interest in ideas or candidates can be generated. Numerous techniques have been developed that stimulate interest and induce information seeking. During political campaigns, candidates stage dramatic events designed to call attention to and stimulate interest in their positions on issues (or the positions of their opponents). Politicians have replaced cutting the ribbon at new supermarket openings with standing in

the food line at a homeless shelter to demonstrate their concern for the poor, or hiking to a pristine mountain lake to represent their commitment to the environment. Once information seeking is induced, various methods have been developed to provide easy access to those forms of information that serve the interest of the campaign planners.

6 Methods for inducing *desired decision-making or positioning.* Once people are aware and informed, or at least have formed strong images or impressions, they can be moved either toward a conscious decision or unconscious prioritization or positioning. Media messages can be transmitted through a variety of channels and used to highlight the value of choosing a specific option or of prioritizing one product, service, or candidate relative to others. Change agents and opinion leaders can also be used, though these are more expensive. This is a critical stage in any communication campaign because it prepares people to take an action desired by campaign planners.

7 Methods for *activating audience segments,* **especially those that have been targeted by the campaign.** Ideally, these audiences will include people who are properly positioned and have decided to act but have not yet found an opportunity. In other cases, people will have prioritized a product, service, or candidate but need to be confronted with a situation in which they are compelled to make a choice. Many communication campaigns fail because they don't have a mechanism for stimulating action by audience members. People seem to be influenced by campaigns but that influence isn't effectively translated into action. A variety of techniques can be used to activate people, including change agents, free merchandise, free and convenient transportation, free services, moderate fear appeals, and broadcast or telephone appeals from high-status sources.

HIERARCHY OF EF-FECTS MODEL *Practical theory calling for the differentiation of persuasion effects relative to the time and effort necessary for their accomplishment*

One of the simplest, yet most comprehensive social marketing theories is the **hierarchy of effects model** (Rice & Atkin, 1989), which states that it is important to differentiate a large number of persuasion effects—some that are easily induced and others that take more time and effort. This model permits development of a step-by-step persuasion strategy in which the effort begins with easily induced effects, such as awareness, and monitors these effects using survey research. Feedback from that research is used to decide when to transmit messages designed to produce more difficult effects such as decision-making or activation. Thus, the effort begins by creating audience awareness, then cultivates images or induces interest and information seeking, reinforces learning of information or images, aids people in making the "right" decisions, and then activates those people. At each step, the effectiveness of the campaign to that point is monitored, and the messages are changed when the proper results aren't obtained.

The hierarchy of effects model was first developed by product marketers but has now been widely applied to social marketing. Critics argue that the assumption that it makes about certain effects necessarily preceding others in time is unwarranted. Some people, for example, can be moved to act without ever being informed or even making a decision about an issue or a candidate. Social marketers argue that although they can't hope to induce all the desired effects in every targeted person, they have evidence that a well-structured, step-by-step campaign that uses survey data to provide feedback is much more successful than persuasion efforts based on simple linear effects models.

Critics of social marketing point to limitations that are very similar to those that we summarized in Chapter 7 in our discussion of information flow and diffusion theories. This is not surprising because social marketing theory is an extension of the two. Though social marketing theory can squeeze some usefulness out of the older source-dominated, linear effects models, it also has many of their limitations. In social marketing models, sources use feedback from target audiences to adjust their campaigns. This use is generally limited to changes in their messages; however, their long-term persuasion or information goals don't change. If audiences seem resistant, new messages are tried in an effort to break down the resistance. Little thought is given to whether the audience might be justified or correct in resisting information or influence. If the effort to get out information fails, the audience is blamed for being too apathetic or ignorant—people simply don't know what's good for them.

Thus, the social marketing model is tailored to situations where elite sources are able to dominate elements of the larger social system. These powerful sources can prevent counter-elites from distributing information or marshaling organized opposition. The theory doesn't allow for social conflict and thus can't be applied to situations where conflict has escalated to even moderate levels. It applies best to trivial forms of information and works best when politics is reduced to marketing of competing candidate images or the transmission of innocuous public health messages.

Brenda Dervin (1989) tried to develop an audience-centered, social marketing theory that could serve some of the same purposes while overcoming obvious limitations. She argued that campaign planners must conceive of communication as a dialogue between elite sources and various audience segments. There must be a genuine commitment to the flow of information and ideas upward from audiences even at early stages of campaigns. The purpose of campaigns should not be understood as inducing audiences to do things that elite sources want them to do, but rather to help people learn to responsibly reconstruct their lives in ways that will be useful to them. For example, public health campaigns shouldn't scare people into adopting better diets but should encourage people to fundamentally reorient their lives so that better eating habits are formed as one aspect of a larger lifestyle change.

Instant Access

Social Marketing Theory

Strengths	Weaknesses
1 Provides practical advice for media campaigns	1 Is source-dominated
2 Can be applied to serve good ends	2 Doesn't consider ends of campaigns
3 Builds on attitude change and diffusion theories	3 Underestimates intellect of average people
4 Is gaining acceptance among media campaign planners and researchers	4 Ignores constraints to reciprocal flow of information
	5 Can be costly to implement
	6 Has difficulty addressing cultural barriers to influence

Dervin's model includes many of the systems theory notions we introduced in Chapter 8. She assumes that mutual interaction between sources and audiences is more effective than a source-dominated communication process. Sources will become better informed about the everyday situations faced by audiences, and audiences will gradually learn useful information for restructuring their lives. She argued that elite sources should learn to respect their audiences. Then these audiences will be more likely to see the wisdom of some of the things that those sources want them to do.

Unfortunately, Dervin's model will work only if the many constraints that inhibit or prevent this mutual interaction between elite sources and various audiences—especially lower status or minority group audiences—can be overcome. This will not be easy. Current mass media–based communication systems permit only indirect, usually delayed, often very crude forms of feedback from audiences. This feedback is suitable for redesigning promotional messages but not for gaining deep insight into the life situation and information needs of audience members.

The greater the gap between the life situation of elite sources and that of lower status audiences, the more unlikely it is that useful feedback will be obtained and used. Typically, message sources must be able to pay for sophisticated audience research and then be willing and able to act on it. Dervin believes that new communication technologies might significantly reduce the cost of maintaining mutual interaction between sources and audiences. Those who advocate

Dervin's more egalitarian social marketing theory see the Internet as so unlike more traditional media technologies that it might allow this greater interaction and exchange. So they oppose the overregulation and overcommercialization of the net, fearing that these will render the Internet no different than television and other elite-dominated media.

The Knowledge Gap

During the past three decades, a team of researchers at the University of Minnesota (Donohue, Tichenor, & Olien 1986; Tichenor, Donohue, & Olien 1970, 1980) developed a theory of society in which mass media and the use of media messages play a central role. This model focuses on the role played by news media in cities and towns of various sizes. These areas are conceptualized as subsystems within larger state and regional social systems. The team began by empirically establishing that news media systematically inform some segments of the population, specifically persons in higher socioeconomic groups, better than the media inform others. Over time, the differences between the better informed and the less informed segments tend to grow—the **knowledge gap** between them gets larger and larger. This research team conducted numerous surveys for twenty-five years to develop and support its theory.

KNOWLEDGE GAP
Systematic differences in knowledge between better informed and less informed segments of a population

But just how should these knowledge gaps be interpreted? Do they pose long-term problems for subsystems or for the overall system? Could knowledge gaps actually be functional in some way? If we rely on classical democratic Libertarian theory (see Chapter 5) to answer these questions, knowledge gaps are troubling. We can be concerned that the people who are less well informed will not be able to act as responsible citizens. If they act at all, they will do so based on ignorance. On the other hand, if we use elite pluralism theory (Chapter 7) to speculate about the consequences of knowledge gaps, we are less concerned. After all, there is a strong correlation between political ignorance and political apathy. If the less informed don't vote, then they can't upset the system. As long as there is an active, informed minority of societal leaders, the overall system should function smoothly—problems should be resolved by this elite based on their superior knowledge.

Phillip Tichenor, George Donohue, and Clarice Olien (1980) recognized that documenting the existence of knowledge gaps was only the first step in assessing media's role in social systems at various levels. In the next phase of their research, the team explored the long-term implications of knowledge gaps for the operation of local communities by studying the role played by news media when communities confront social conflicts. Would news media enable communities to effectively resolve these conflicts or would the conflicts be exacerbated? What would happen to knowledge gaps?

The researchers studied conflicts in nineteen different cities that were debating environmental pollution, wilderness logging, and the construction of high-voltage power lines. These conflicts could have been resolved in several ways. If the elite pluralism perspective was accurate, news media would only inform a politically active minority and this group would take control of the conflict and resolve it. If classical democratic libertarian theory was accurate, news media would inform everyone and the conflict would be resolved through negotiation and public debate. In fact, neither of these older theories was very useful in predicting what happened. A more complicated, systems theory–based perspective (see Chapter 8) proved useful in interpreting the empirical findings.

In nearly every case, external agents initiated conflicts. Local leaders, including newspaper publishers, were often co-opted by powerful regional businesses such as electrical power companies or big manufacturers. The research team found that as conflicts escalated, more and more groups were activated from all segments of a community. Even normally apolitical or apathetic people were eventually drawn into an escalating conflict. News coverage of conflict-related issues increased. But within small communities, most of the information came from outside media. Local media either avoided reporting about conflicts or severely limited their reports. Little useful information was provided. As time passed, ordinarily uninformed individuals made better use of outside news media and gradually became better informed about the specific issues that were directly related to the conflict. Thus, the knowledge gap tended to narrow between those population segments that were initially well informed about these issues and those that were ignorant.

The knowledge gap findings are somewhat reassuring. They imply that all segments of a community will become informed when (a) the relevancy of that knowledge has been increased by an escalating social conflict and (b) increased news coverage from either local or outside sources provides better access to information. Closing the knowledge gap should increase the likelihood that a solution will be negotiated based on the best information available. The findings also indicate that news media can help close these gaps. As systems, communities appear to be capable of adapting the roles played by parts (population segments) so that the system as a whole changes its ability to adapt to the environment.

But these optimistic conclusions were tempered by other findings. The researchers also found evidence that within the larger social system, the smaller, rural communities were dominated by large urban centers. Most conflicts were not resolved through local negotiations. Rather, solutions were imposed by outside elites who found ways to control local negotiations and direct them toward conclusions favored by urban elites. And in their more recent research (Donohue, Tichenor, & Olien, 1986), the team found that outside media, most notably the major urban newspapers, have "pulled back" from their long-standing mission of

Instant Access

Knowledge Gap

Strengths	Weaknesses
1 Identifies potentially troublesome gaps between groups	1 Assumes gaps are dysfunctional; not all agree
2 Provides ideas for overcoming gaps	2 Limits focus to gaps involving news and social conflicts
3 Presumes reciprocity and audience activity in communication	3 Can't address fundamental reasons for gaps (for example, poor schools or limited access to information sources)
4 Is grounded in systems theory	

serving a regional or statewide audience. This might be making it harder for less knowledgeable people in small communities to get access to the information they need to effectively address conflicts in their communities.

The knowledge gap research demonstrates the potential for using systems theory to guide and interpret empirical research. It also addresses questions of information supply in a way that is not source-dominated like social marketing theory is. Knowledge gap researchers have demonstrated the utility of conceptualizing information access, use, and gaps within a macroscopic social system. In this system, local communities are only small parts. Resolution of knowledge gaps proved to be less important than might have been hoped. The researchers demonstrated that knowledge gaps decreased when conflicts escalated. This should have facilitated informed, democratic, decision-making at local levels. But this didn't happen because elites from the larger social system intervened. These findings imply that social conflict might be "functional" within smaller social systems because it can improve the flow and use of information. But the escalation of conflict also motivates elites from the larger social system to intervene, and they ultimately control the conflict by imposing a solution.

Knowledge gap research also demonstrates that social systems are constantly evolving. Social institutions that manage conflict can and do change. Moreover, the role of media in these systems also undergoes profound alterations over time. Metropolitan newspapers might stop making their content accessible to local communities. If broadcast media fail to effectively fill in and provide such access, conflicts will have to be managed within informed public debate. The Internet, with its presumed "democracy" might alter the system even further.

Agenda-Setting

What were the crucial issues in the 2000 presidential election? The United States was faced with its first budget surplus in decades and the money could have been turned back to citizens in the form of tax breaks or it could be used to shore up Social Security. Proponents from different sides of the culture debate seemed as divided as ever—attacks on organizations and doctors that provided legal abortions continued; harassment of gay people was common. American educational standards were diminishing. Billions were being spent on weapons systems despite the end of the Cold War. An overwhelming number of Americans were disgusted by the influence of money in politics and favored significant campaign-finance reform. What do you remember from the mass media as the important issues and images of that campaign? The debate over noncandidate President Clinton's character? George Bush's "youthful drinking" and National Guard service during the Vietnam War? Al Gore's stiffness? The lock-box? Bush's fractured syntax? Gore inventing the Internet and serving as the model for *Love Story*. Of all the issues that should or could have been aired and examined, only a few became dominant. This is **agenda-setting**.

AGENDA-SETTING
The idea that media don't tell people what to think, but what to think about

With or without the label, the idea of agenda-setting has been with us since the days of the penny press. Walter Lippmann, in *Public Opinion,* argued that the people do not deal directly with their environments as much as they respond to "pictures" in their heads. He wrote (1922, p. 16), "For the real environment is altogether too big, too complex, and too fleeting for direct acquaintance. We are not equipped to deal with so much subtlety, so much variety, so many permutations and combinations. And although we have to act in that environment, we have to reconstruct it on a simpler model before we can manage with it." If you remember our discussion of Lippmann in Chapters 4 and 5, then you know that he concluded that average people just can't be trusted to make important political decisions based on these simplified pictures. Average people have to be protected, and the important decisions have to be made by technocrats who use better models to guide their actions. Thus, modern agenda-setting notions derive more or less directly from a mass society perspective. Critics have noted this connection.

Although he did not specifically use the term itself, Bernard Cohen is generally credited with refining Lippmann's ideas into the theory of agenda-setting. He wrote (1963, p. 13), "The press is significantly more than a purveyor of information and opinion. It may not be successful much of the time in telling people what to think, but it is stunningly successful in telling its readers what to think *about*. And it follows from this that the world looks different to different people, depending not only on their personal interests, but also on the map that is drawn for them by the writers, editors, and publishers of the papers they read." Parenthetically, it's hard to ignore the limited effects bias in Cohen's thinking. He first argued that the press is rarely successful in telling people what to think, but then said that the world looks different to different people depending on what the press offers them. Another way of interpreting this is that Cohen took a mass society perspective and revised it to make it compatible with the limited effects paradigm.

Cohen's writing became the basis for what we now call the agenda-setting function of the mass media. This perspective might have lingered in obscurity had it not been empirically confirmed by research conducted by Maxwell E. McCombs and Donald Shaw. They articulated their interpretation of agenda-setting (1972, p. 176): "In choosing and displaying news, editors, newsroom staff, and broadcasters play an important part in shaping political reality. Readers learn not only about a given issue, but how much importance to attach to that issue from the amount of information in a news story and its position . . . The mass media may well determine the important issues—that is, the media may set the 'agenda' of the campaign."

During September and October of the 1968 presidential election, these researchers interviewed one hundred registered voters who had not yet committed to either candidate (presumably these people would be more open to media messages). By asking each respondent "to outline the key issues as he [sic] saw them, regardless of what the candidates might be saying at the moment," these researchers were able to identify and rank by importance just what these people thought were the crucial issues facing them. Then, these results were compared with a ranking of the time and space accorded to various issues produced by a content analysis of the television news, newspapers, newsmagazines, and editorial pages available to voters in the area where the study was conducted. The results? "The media appear to have exerted a considerable impact on voters' judgments of what they considered the major issues of the campaign . . . The correlation between the major item emphasis on the main campaign issues carried by the media and voters' independent judgments of what were the important issues was +.967," they wrote, continuing, "In short, the data suggest a very strong relationship between the emphasis placed on different campaign issues by the media . . . and the judgments of voters as to the salience and importance of various campaign topics" (McCombs & Shaw, 1972, p. 180–181).

This important and straightforward study highlights both the strengths and limitations of agenda-setting as a theory of media effects. It clearly establishes that there is an important relationship between media reports and the people's ranking of public issues. On the negative side, we can see that the logic of agenda-setting seems well suited for the question of news and campaigns, but what of other kinds of content and other kinds of effects? More important, though, is the question of the actual nature of the relationship between news and its audience. Maybe the public sets the media's agenda and then the media reinforce it. The McCombs and Shaw analysis, like most early agenda-setting research, implies a direction of influence from media to audience—that is, it implies causality. But the argument that the media are simply responding to their audiences can be easily made. Few newspeople have not uttered at least once in their careers, "We only give the people what they want." McCombs (1981) himself acknowledged these limitations.

It is important not to judge the utility of the agenda-setting approach based on the earliest studies. Although these had many limitations, they have inspired other research that is providing intriguing if still controversial results. For example, Shanto Iyengar and Donald Kinder attempted to overcome some of the problems of earlier work in a series of experiments published in 1987. Because of the unanswered questions about causality, they lamented, "agenda-setting may be an apt metaphor, but it is no theory. The lack of a theory of media effects has significantly impeded our understanding of how democracy works" (1987, p. 3). To develop such a theory they offered a *testable* "agenda-setting hypothesis: Those problems that receive prominent attention on the national news become the problems the viewing public regards as the nation's most important" (1987, p. 16). Their series of experiments examined agenda-setting, the vividness of news reports, the positioning of stories, and what they called **priming**.

PRIMING *In agenda-setting, the idea that media draw attention to some aspects of political life at the expense of others*

- *Agenda-setting:* Iyengar and Kinder demonstrated causality. They wrote, "Americans' view of their society and nation are powerfully shaped by the stories that appear on the evening news. We found that people who were shown network broadcasts edited to draw attention to a particular problem assigned greater importance to that problem—greater importance than they themselves did before the experiment began, and greater importance than did people assigned to control conditions that emphasized different problems. Our subjects regarded the target problem as more important for the country, cared more about it, believed that government should do more about it, reported stronger feelings about it, and were much more likely to identify it as one of the country's most important problems" (Iyengar & Kinder, 1987, p. 112).

- *Vividness of presentation:* Iyengar and Kinder found that dramatic news accounts undermined rather than increased television's agenda-setting power. Powerfully presented, personal accounts (a staple of contemporary television news) might focus too much attention on the specific situation or individual rather than on the issue at hand.

- *Position of a story:* Lead stories had a greater agenda-setting effect. Two possible reasons were offered. First, people paid more attention to the stories at the beginning of the news and these were less likely to fall victim to the inevitable interruptions experienced when viewing at home. Second, people accepted the news program's implicit designation of a lead story as most newsworthy.

- *Priming:* This is the idea that even the most motivated citizens cannot consider all that they know when evaluating complex political issues. Instead, people consider the things that come easily to mind, or as the researchers said, "those bits and pieces of political memory that are accessible." Iyengar and Kinder's research strongly demonstrated that "through priming (drawing attention to some aspects of political life at the expense of others) television news (helps) to set the terms by which political judgments are reached and political choices made" (1987, p. 114). Writing in a later study, Iyengar (1991, p. 133) offered this distinction, "While agenda-setting reflects the impact of news coverage on the perceived importance of national issues, priming refers to the impact of news coverage on the weight assigned to specific issues in making political judgments."

AGENDA-BUILDING *A collective process in which media, government, and the citizenry reciprocally influence one another in areas of public policy*

Agenda-setting, primarily a micro-level effects perspective, has another interesting contemporary articulation as a more macro level theory—**agenda-building**, "the often complicated process by which some issues become important in policy making arenas" (Protess et al., 1991, p. 6). Kurt Lang and Gladys Lang defined "-agenda-building—a more apt term than agenda-setting—(as) a collective process in which media, government, and the citizenry reciprocally influence one another" (1983, pp. 58–59). The Langs provided a useful case study of agenda-building during the Watergate crisis.

Agenda-building presumes cognitive effects (increases in knowledge), an active audience (as seen in the Lang and Lang definition), and societal level effects (as seen in both of the previous definitions). Its basic premise—that media can profoundly affect how a society (or nation or culture) determines what are its important concerns and therefore can mobilize its various institutions toward meeting them—has allowed this line of inquiry, in the words of David Protess and his colleagues (1991), to "flourish."

Recently McCombs has begun an effort to expand and develop agenda-setting theory by linking it to a broad range of other media theories, for example framing theory (McCombs & Ghanem, 2001). Alan Rubin and Paul Haridakis (2001) offer a similar view. McCombs argues that agenda-setting operates at two levels—the object level and the attribute level. Conventional agenda-setting research has focused at the object level and assessed how media coverage could influence the priority assigned to objects (e.g., issues, candidates, events, and problems). In doing this, media told us "what to think about." But media can also tell us "how to think about" some objects. Media do this by influencing "attribute agendas." They tell us which object attributes are important and which ones are not. McCombs argues that the two theories share common concerns for attribute agendas (frames), the dynamics of the agenda-setting process (framing process), and agenda-setting influence (framing effects). McCombs believes that the integration of agenda-setting theory with framing theory will help clarify some of the concepts in framing theory. He advocates "explication of a more general theoretical structure describing the frames and attributes that are important to the com-

Instant Access

Agenda-Setting

Strengths	Weaknesses
1 Focuses attention on audience interaction with media	1 Has roots in mass society theory
2 Empirically demonstrates links between media exposure, audience motivation to seek orientation, and audience perception of public issues	2 Is too situationally specific to news and political campaigns
3 Integrates a number of similar ideas including priming, story positioning, and story vividness	3 Direction of agenda-setting effect is questioned by some

munication process" (p. 79). But Dietram Scheufele provides an overview of agenda-setting, priming, and framing theories in which he argues that agenda-setting and priming are compatible theories, but that framing is quite different because it involves activation of entire interpretive schemas–not merely prioritization of individual objects or attributes. He wrote,

> agenda-setting and priming rely on the notion of attitude accessibility. Mass media have the power to increase levels of importance assigned to issues by audience members. They increase the salience of issues or the ease with which these considerations can be retrieved from memory . . . Framing, in contrast, is based on the concept of prospect theory; that is, on the assumption that subtle changes in the wording of the description of a situation might affect how audience members interpret this situation. In other words, that influences how audiences think about issues, not by making aspects of the issue more salient, but by invoking interpretive schemas that influence the interpretation of incoming information. (2000, p. 309)

The Spiral of Silence

A somewhat more controversial theory of media and public opinion is the concept of the **spiral of silence**. This can be regarded as a form of agenda-setting but one that is focused on macro-level rather than micro-level consequences. In the words of its originator, Elisabeth Noelle-Neumann (1984, p. 5), "Observations

SPIRAL OF SILENCE
Idea that people holding views contrary to those dominant in the media are moved to keep them to themselves for fear of rejection

made in one context (the mass media) spread to another and encouraged people either to proclaim their views or to swallow them and keep quiet until, in a spiraling process, the one view dominated the public scene and the other disappeared from public awareness as its adherents became mute. This is the process that can be called a 'spiral of silence.'" In other words, because of people's fear of isolation or separation from those around them, they tend to keep their attitudes to themselves when they think they are in the minority. The media, because of a variety of factors, tend to present one (or at most two) sides of an issue to the exclusion of others, which further encourages those people to keep quiet and makes it even tougher for the media to uncover and register that opposing viewpoint.

Noelle-Neumann's focus is not on micro-level conceptualizations of how average people come to perceive the public agenda; rather, she is concerned with the macro-level, long-term consequences of such perceptions. If various viewpoints about agenda items are ignored, marginalized, or trivialized by media reports, then people will be reluctant to talk about them. As time passes, those viewpoints will cease to be heard in public and therefore cannot affect political decision-making. Her arguments are especially noteworthy because she has a reputation as being one of the foremost public-opinion pollsters in Germany. In a series of empirical studies, she has demonstrated links between media reports of viewpoints on issues and trends in what people are willing to say about those issues.

Noelle-Neumann (1973) argued that her perspective involves a "return to the concept of powerful mass media." She believes that the limited effects perspective erred in its assertion that selective perception limits media to reinforcement effects—that people interpret media messages based on preexisting attitudes and beliefs and, therefore, reinforcement of those attitudes and beliefs is the result. Incorrect, she wrote, because "as regards the connection between selective perception and the effect of the mass media, one can put forward the hypothesis that the more restricted the selection the less the reinforcement principle applies, in other words the greater the possibility of mass media changing attitudes" (1973, p. 78).

The way news is collected and disseminated, she continued, effectively restricts the breadth and depth of selection available to citizens. She identified three characteristics of the news media that produce this scarcity of perspective:

- **Ubiquity:** The media are virtually everywhere as sources of information.

- **Cumulation:** The various news media tend to repeat stories and perspectives across their different individual programs or editions, across the different media themselves, and across time.

- **Consonance:** The congruence or similarity of values held by newspeople influences the content they produce.

She identified six parts of working journalists' everyday lives as factors that produce this consonance:

1 The concurring assumptions and experiences held by all journalists at all levels and in all fields about the public's criteria for acceptance of both the style and content of journalists' work.

2 Journalists' common tendency to confirm their own opinions, to demonstrate that theirs is the proper interpretation, and to confirm that their predictions have indeed been correct.

3 Their dependence on common sources, such as the relatively few wire and news video services.

4 Their "reciprocal influence in building up frames of reference"; newspaper people watch what's on the television news, television news programs monitor one another, and broadcast newspeople scour the newspapers for consensus and information.

5 Their striving for acceptance from colleagues and superiors.

6 Journalists' relative uniformity of views as a result of demographic and attitudinal attributes shared by the news profession's practitioners.

This view of media effects suggests that two different social processes, one macro-level and one micro-level, are operating simultaneously to produce effects. Audience members, because of their desire to be accepted, choose to remain silent when confronted with what they perceive to be prevailing counter opinion. Newspeople, because of the dynamics of their news-gathering function and their need to be accepted, present a restricted selection of news, further forcing into silence those in the audience who wish to avoid isolation. This led Klaus Merten (1984) at first to praise spiral of silence as comprising features that are "significant for any advanced social theory . . . The theory is a *dynamic* theory; that is, it possesses features of a process theory . . . (and) the theory relies heavily on an important structural feature of communication processes, *reflexivity in the social dimension*" (p. 33), but later to call it "a highly pretentious theory" (p. 42).

Elihu Katz (1983), in an essay critical of spiral of silence theory, summarized Noelle-Neumann's thinking this way:

(1) Individuals have opinions; (2) Fearing isolation, individuals will not express their opinions if they perceive themselves unsupported by others; (3) A "quasi-statistical sense" is employed by individuals to scan the environment for signs of support; (4) Mass media constitute the major source of reference for information about the distribution of opinion and thus the climate of support/nonsupport; (5) So do other reference groups . . . ; (6) The media tend to speak in one voice, almost monopolistically; (7) The media tend to distort the

distribution of opinion in society, biased as they are by the . . . views of journalists; (8) Perceiving themselves unsupported, groups of individuals—who may, at times, even constitute a majority—will lose confidence and withdraw from public debate, thus speeding the demise of their position through the self-fulfilling spiral of silence. They may not change their own minds, but they stop recruitment of others and abandon the fight; (9) Society is manipulated and impoverished thereby. (p. 89)

This understanding led Katz to conclude that these "more subtle, more sociological (macro-level) definitions of effect" (p. 96) would have us "consider the dark side of mass communication. Even in the democracies, media—like interpersonal communication—can impose acquiescence and silence in defiance of the free flow of information" (Katz, 1983, p. 91). This commentary is especially noteworthy because it is offered by someone who helped pioneer uses and gratifications research and who co-authored a classic limited effects study based on the data collected in Decatur (Katz & Lazarsfeld, 1955). Katz clearly was reluctant to accept Noelle-Neumann's assertions and discredited them by arguing that they are an updated version of mass society theory.

Spiral of silence has encountered other criticisms as well. Charles Salmon and F. Gerald Kline (1985) wrote that the effects explained by spiral of silence could just as easily be understood as the product of the bandwagon effect (everybody wants to join a winner) or of projection (people's natural tendency to use their own opinions to form perceptions of the general climate of opinion around them). In addition, these critics argued that individual factors, such as a person's degree of ego-involvement in an issue, should be considered (regardless of the climate of opinion surrounding you, if you feel very strongly about the issue, you might not want to remain silent, even if isolation is a threat). Salmon and Kline call, too, for further examination of individual demographic differences that Noelle-Neumann suggested would combine to produce people who are more likely to speak out—males, younger people, and members of the middle and upper classes, for example.

Drawing on the notion that pluralistic groups can mediate media effects, Carroll Glynn and Jack McLeod (1985) faulted the spiral of silence for underestimating the power of people's communities, organizations, and reference groups in mitigating media influence on the larger society. Regardless of the consonant view of racial equality presented in the news, they might say, a Ku Klux Klan member would probably feel no great threat of alienation for expressing his views to his team mates between innings of a Klan softball game. Glynn and McLeod also questioned the generalizability of Noelle-Neumann's research (conducted almost exclusively in what was then West Germany) to the American situation, and they raised the possibility of situations in which media can actually move people to speak up rather than remain silent.

Instant Access	*Spiral of Silence*

Strengths

1 Has macro- and micro-level explanatory power

2 Is dynamic

3 Accounts for shifts in public opinion, especially during campaigns

4 Raises important questions concerning the role and responsibility of news media

Weaknesses

1 Has overly pessimistic view of media influence and average people

2 Ignores other, simpler explanations of silencing

3 Ignores possible demographic and cultural differences in the silencing effect

4 Discounts power of community to counteract the silencing effect

Noelle-Neumann (1985) responded simply that the media, especially television, adopt a prevailing attitude in any controversy as a matter of course, and as a result, they present a "dominant tendency." Holders of the minority viewpoint are willing to speak out if they feel that they are supported by the media dominant tendency (as during the Civil Rights movement). Moreover, she offered an alternative perspective of the media's ability to increase speaking out in the face of rejection when she wrote, "It appears that the intensive articulation of a certain viewpoint in the media gives the followers of this viewpoint the advantage of being better equipped to express their point of view . . . The resulting willingness to talk has nothing to do with fear of isolation, it only makes talking easier. By using words and arguments taken from the media to discuss a topic, people cause the point of view to be heard in public and give it visibility, thus creating a situation in which the danger of isolation is reduced" (Noelle-Neumann, 1985, p. 80).

As with any theoretical proposition that challenges the prevailing view of the time—specifically, the limited effects paradigm—spiral of silence and agenda-setting both suffered intense criticism and their adherents had to overcome a fear of isolation and rejection from others in the discipline, just as Noelle-Neumann might have predicted. Nonetheless, these articulations of powerful mass media helped move mass communication theory toward its more contemporary stance, as can be seen in a number of interesting, potentially useful formulations of public opinion formation. For example, Moy, Domke, and Stamm (2001) offer a useful integration of spiral of silence theory with reference group theory. They argue that these two theories offer compatible rather than

competing explanations for an individual's willingness to speak out on a controversial public issue. Fear of isolation is assumed to be the overarching reason
why people will choose to be silent. Spiral of silence theory predicts that when
media reports imply that one viewpoint on an issue is gaining influence, most
people will stop verbally supporting alternative viewpoints to avoid isolating
themselves. Reference group theory predicts that the most important source of
support is from immediate family and friends, so if these people support alternate viewpoints then an individual will go on speaking out with no fear of isolation. Thus, spiral of silence theory can make useful predictions except in those
cases where reference group theory applies.

Media System Dependency Theory

MEDIA SYSTEM DE-
PENDENCY THEORY
*Idea that the more
a person depends
on having needs
gratified by media
use, the more im-
portant the media's
role will be in the
person's life and,
therefore, the more
influence those
media will have*

In its simplest terms, **media system dependency theory** assumes that the more a
person depends on having his or her needs gratified by media use, the more important will be the role that media play in the person's life and, therefore, the more
influence those media will have on that person. From a macroscopic, societal perspective, if more and more people become dependent on media, then the overall
influence of media will rise and media's role in society will become more central.
Thus, there should be a direct relationship between the amount of overall dependency and the degree of media influence or centrality at any given point in time.
Melvin DeFleur and Sandra Ball-Rokeach have provided a fuller explanation in
several assertions (1975, pp. 261–263). First, the *"basis of media influence lies in
the relationship between the larger social system, the media's role in that system, and
audience relationships to the media."* Effects occur, not because all-powerful media
or omnipotent sources will that occurrence, but because the media operate in a
given way in a given social system to meet given audience wants and needs.

Second, *"the degree of audience dependence on media information is the key variable in understanding when and why media messages alter audience beliefs, feelings,
or behavior."* The ultimate occurrence and shape of media effects rests with the audience members and is related to how necessary a given medium or media message is to them. The uses people make of media determine their influence.

Third, *"in our industrial society, we are becoming increasingly dependent on the
media (a) to understand the social world, (b) to act meaningfully and effectively in
society, and (c) for fantasy and escape."* As our world becomes more complex, we
not only need the media to a greater degree to help us make sense, to help us understand what our best responses might be, and to help us relax and cope, but
also we ultimately come to know that world largely through those media. Note
the emphasis on sensemaking (Chapter 10) in this assertion. As we use media to
make sense of the social world, we permit media to shape our expectations.

Finally, fourth, *"the greater the need and consequently the stronger the dependency . . . the greater the likelihood"* that the media and their messages will have an effect. Not everyone will be equally influenced by media. Those who have greater needs and thus greater dependency on media will be most influenced.

If we remember our discussion of what constitutes an active audience (Chapter 10), we know that the best way to think of activity is to think of it as existing on a continuum, from completely inactive media consumers to very active ones. DeFleur and Ball-Rokeach, because they tied audience activity to audience dependence, described media dependency in just that way. Moreover, they explained that an individual's (or society's) level of dependency is a function of (a) *"the number and centrality (importance) of the specific information-delivery functions served by a medium"* and (b) *the degree of change and conflict present in society.*

These assertions can be illustrated by an example involving media use during a crisis. Think of your own media use the last time you found yourself in a natural crisis, in other words, in a time of change or conflict (earthquake, tornado, hurricane, or serious rain or snow storm). Or think about your media use on September 11, 2001. You probably spent more time watching television news than you did watching comedy shows. But consider what would have happened if the electricity had failed during your crisis. Then, the "number and centrality of television's information delivery functions" instantly would be reduced to a level below that of your portable radio. So radio and radio news might become your medium and content of choice, respectively. And no doubt, if the crises deepened, your dependence would increase. So also might your attentiveness and willingness to respond as "directed" by that medium and its messages.

DeFleur and Ball-Rokeach refined and expanded their media system dependency theory a number of times (1989, for example) to account for such "system change," but their thesis never varied much beyond their initial assertion that media can and do have powerful effects. Media dependency has been measured in a variety of ways, and each has its drawbacks. It has not yet been conclusively demonstrated that the experience of media dependency by average people is strongly related to a broad range of effects. Can we be dependent on media without experiencing dependency? Can we experience dependency when we are actually quite independent? If so, maybe we should measure dependency with behavioral rather than attitudinal measures of dependency. Is this theory better at explaining the consequences of short-term, situationally induced dependency (that is, reaction to a crisis) rather than long-term, chronic dependency? Finally, the theory doesn't directly address the question of whether there is some ideal level of media dependency. Are Americans currently too dependent on media or too independent? Is the trend toward increased or decreased dependency? Will new media increase our dependency or make us more independent? How will

---

Instant Access

Dependency Theory

Strengths	Weaknesses
1 Is elegant and descriptive	**1** Is difficult to empirically verify
2 Allows for systems orientation	**2** Meaning and power of dependency are unclear
3 Integrates microscopic and macroscopic theory	**3** Lacks power in explaining long-term effects
4 Explains role of media during crisis and social change	

---

new, user-directed technologies like the Internet and 500-channel direct broadcast satellites reshape dependence and independence?

Cultivation Analysis

CULTIVATION ANALYSIS *Theory that television "cultivates" or creates a world view that, although possibly inaccurate, becomes the reality because people believe it to be so*

Cultivation analysis, a theory developed by George Gerbner during the 1970s and 1980s, addresses macroscopic questions about the media's role in society. This theory represents a hybrid that combines aspects of both macroscopic and microscopic cultural theories considered in Chapter 9. Some researchers regard it as a possible prototype for future research whereas others consider it a poor example of how to do research. In our view, this controversy was a pivotal one in the development of mass communication theory. It came when the limited effects paradigm was still strong but had begun to show signs of waning. Cultural analysis approaches were beginning to receive more serious attention from humanist scholars. The controversy reveals a great deal about various opposing perspectives, most of which are still widely held.

You can begin your own evaluation of cultivation analysis by answering three questions. (1) In any given week, what are the chances that you will be involved in some kind of violence, about 1 in 10 or about 1 in 100? In the actual world, about .41 violent crimes occur per 100 Americans, or, less than 1 in 200. In the world of prime-time television, though, more than 64 percent of all characters are involved in violence. Was your answer closer to the actual or to the television world? (2) What percentage of all working males in the United States toil in law enforcement and crime detection? One percent or 5 percent? The U.S. Census says 1 percent, television says 12 percent. What did you say?

Finally, (3) of all the crimes that occur in the United States in any year, what proportion is violent crime like murder, rape, robbery, and assault? Would you guess 15 or 25 percent? If you hold the television view, you chose the higher number. On television, 77 percent of all major characters who commit crimes commit the violent kind. The *Statistical Abstract of the United States* reports that, in actuality, only 10 percent of all crime in the country is violent crime.

These questions come from Gerbner and his colleagues who founded and popularized cultivation theory. But their point was much more complex than simply stating that those who watch more television give answers that are more similar to the "TV answer" than to what official government data would suggest is correct. Their central argument is that television "cultivates" or creates a world view that, although possibly inaccurate, becomes the reality simply because we, as a people, believe it to be the reality and base our judgments about our own, everyday worlds on that "reality."

You'll remember from Chapter 8 that during the 1960s and early 1970s, interest in television as a social force, especially the medium's relationship to increasing individual and societal violence, reached its zenith. Two very important national examinations of the media, again especially television, were undertaken. The first was the National Commission on the Causes and Prevention of Violence, held in 1967 and 1968, and the second was the 1972 Surgeon General's Scientific Advisory Committee on Television and Social Behavior. One scientist involved in both efforts was Gerbner.

VIOLENCE INDEX
Annual content analysis of a sample week of network television prime-time fare demonstrating how much violence is present

His initial task was apparently simple enough: to produce a yearly **Violence Index**, essentially an annual content analysis of a sample week of network television prime-time fare that would demonstrate, from season to season, how much violence was actually present in that programming. The Index, however, was not without critics, and serious controversy developed around it. *TV Guide* magazine even called it the "million dollar mistake."

Debate raged about the definition of violence. How was "television violence" defined? Was verbal aggression really violence? Were two teenagers playfully scuffling violence? Other issues were raised. Why examine only network prime time? After school, early evening, and weekends are particularly heavy viewing times for most children. Why count only violence? Why not racism and sexism? Nonetheless, Gerbner and his associates attempted to meet the demands of their critics and each year refined their definitional and reporting schemes. But regardless of the attacks on their work, one thing did not change: Year in, year out, violence still appeared on prime-time television to a degree unmatched in the "real world," and it was violence of a nature unlike that found in that "real world." If television was truly a mirror of society or if that medium did simply reinforce the status quo, this video mirror, the Violence Index seemed to say, was more like one found in a fun house than in a home. In their 1982 analysis of television violence, for example, Gerbner and his colleagues discovered that "crime in prime time is at least 10 times as rampant as in the real world (and) an average of five to six acts of overt physical violence per hour involves over half of all major characters" (Gerbner, Gross, Morgan, & Signorielli, 1982, p. 106).

But the single most important criticism of the annual Violence Index ("So what?") remained to be answered. Still absent was the demonstration of any causal link between the fluctuating levels of annual televised mayhem and viewer aggressive behavior. The Gerbner team eventually addressed that challenge. In 1973, moving beyond the Violence Index, the group redefined its work as the **Cultural Indicators Project**, in which they conducted regular, periodic examinations of television programming and the "conceptions of social reality that viewing cultivates in child and adult audiences" (Gerbner & Gross, 1976, p. 174). Now they were looking at the "so what" and, in doing so, extended their research to issues well beyond violence.

CULTURAL INDICATORS PROJECT *In cultivation analysis, periodic examinations of television programming and the conceptions of social reality cultivated by viewing*

The Cultural Indicators research made five assumptions that were still being questioned in the early 1970s. These were first, that *television is essentially and fundamentally different from other forms of mass media.* Television is in more than 98 percent of all American homes. It does not require literacy, as do newspapers, magazines, and books. Unlike the movies, it's free (if you don't count the cost of advertising added to the products you buy). It combines pictures and sound, unlike radio. It requires no mobility, as do churches, movies, and theaters. Television is the only medium in history with which people can interact at the earliest and latest years of life, not to mention all those years in between.

Because of television's accessibility and availability to everyone, the second assumption of the Cultural Indicators Project is that *the medium is the "central cultural arm" of American society;* it is, as Gerbner and his colleagues (1978, p. 178) argued, "the chief creator of synthetic cultural patterns (entertainment and information) for the most heterogeneous mass publics in history, including large groups that have never shared in any common public message systems."

The third assumption flows logically from this shared reality: "the *substance* of the consciousness cultivated by TV is not so much specific attitudes and opinions as more basic assumptions about the 'facts' of life and standards of judgment on which conclusions are based" (Gerbner & Gross, 1976, p. 175).

Because most television stations and networks target the same audiences, and because they depend on relatively generic, formulaic, cyclical, repetitive forms of programs and stories, the fourth Cultural Indicators assumption became *television's major cultural function is to stabilize social patterns, to cultivate resistance to change;* it is a medium of socialization and enculturation. Again, Gerbner and his cohorts said it well (1978, p. 178): "The repetitive pattern of television's mass-produced messages and images forms the mainstream of the common symbolic environment that cultivates the most widely shared conceptions of reality. We live in terms of the stories we tell—stories about what things exist, stories about how things work, and stories about what to do—and television tells them all through news, drama, and advertising to almost everybody most of the time." If you're reading closely, you can hear not only the echoes of social construction of reality and symbolic interaction, but also the call to understand television as a ritual, rather than transmissional medium.

In adopting this more ritualistic view, however, the Cultural Indicators researchers' fifth assumption—that *the observable, measurable, independent contributions of television to the culture are relatively small*—caused additional controversy. In explaining this position, Gerbner used his **ice-age analogy**: "But just as an average temperature shift of a few degrees can lead to an ice age or the outcomes of elections can be determined by slight margins, so too can a relatively small but pervasive influence make a crucial difference. The 'size' of an 'effect' is far less critical than the direction of its steady contribution" (Gerbner et al., 1980, p. 14). Their argument was not that television's impact was inconsequential. Rather, they argued that although television's measurable, observable, independent effect on the culture at any point in time might be small, that impact was, nonetheless, present and significant. Put somewhat differently, television's impact on our collective sense of reality is real and important, even though that effect might be beyond clear-cut scientific measurement, might defy easy observation, and might be inextricably bound to other factors in the culture.

ICE-AGE ANALOGY
In cultivation analysis, idea that the size of television's influence is less critical than the direction of its steady contribution

The Controversy

Throughout this text, we have introduced you to various controversies, camps, and antagonistic perspectives. The debate (as well as its intensity) that surrounded cultivation analysis, then, should come as no surprise, especially because, if nothing else, the Gerbner work attempted to use traditional social scientific research methods to examine very large-scale humanistic questions. In other words, Gerbner and his colleagues used tools of inquiry most often identified with the transmissional perspective and limited effects findings to examine questions most often identified with the ritual view. Horace Newcomb (1978, p. 265), for example, wrote, "More than any other research effort in the area of television studies the work of Gerbner and Gross and their associates sits squarely at the juncture of the social sciences and the humanities." This, more than anything, is what fueled so much debate. By asserting effects that were beyond the apparent control of most audience members, the Cultural Indicators Project offended those humanists who felt that their turf had been improperly appropriated and misinterpreted. In asserting significant but possibly unmeasurable, unobservable effects, the project challenged the work, if not the belief system of the many social scientists who still adhered to the limited effects paradigm. Actually, the Gerbner group dismissed virtually all existing attitude change research, all television violence research conducted in laboratories, all television research that looked at *change* as the only measure of the medium's effect, and all research that employed an individual program or one particular type of program; in essence, almost all extant television effects research was deemed of small value.

We will let Newcomb speak for the humanists. He claimed that "the question, 'What does it all mean?' is, essentially, a humanistic question" (1978, p. 266). Then he accused Gerbner and his colleagues of misapplying the values of humanism. First, he argued, *television's ideas and the symbols that express them on that medium are not created there.* Those symbols have a history and meaning in the culture that existed long before now and apart from television. Violence, for example, has many meanings and has always had many meanings for Americans.

Second, he argued that the Cultural Indicators Project *ignored the wide variety of "organization and expression of these ideas in the world of television."* In other words, violence, for example, is not presented as uniformly on television as Cultural Indicators would have us believe.

Finally, his most serious complaint about the Gerbner research was that it *did not permit the possibility that individual members of the television audience can apply different, individual meanings to what they see on television.* Newcomb summarized his humanist objections this way, "It may be that all the messages of television speak with a single intent and are ruled by a single dominant symbol whose meaning is clear to a mass audience, or to that part of the audience heavily involved with those messages. But I have yet to see evidence sufficient to warrant such a reductive view of human experience in America" (1978, p. 281).

The assumptions of the Cultural Indicators approach are clearly imbedded in Gerbner and Gross' reply (1979). As for Newcomb's first challenge, they argued that those ideas and symbols must be learned *somewhere,* "we are born into and grow up in a symbolic environment of which television is now the mainstream that *cultivates* stable images after some of its own patterns" (p. 228). As to the second humanistic criticism, Gerbner and Gross responded, "We consider most television plays assembly-line drama rather than works of unique craftsmanship. The patterns that the corporate assembly-line imparts to its products becomes the aggregate and repetitive terms of common exposure and usage" (p. 223). And, finally, they asserted that regardless of whether or not individual audience members can apply their own interpretations to what they see on the screen, the

> fact is that heavy viewers overestimate their chances of involvement in violence and their general vulnerability (compared to light viewers in the same social groups) *however defined.* Newcomb's big question, 'what does violence mean to the respondents' is not only irrelevant but distracting. We study what

exposure to violence-laden television contributes to their conceptions of the realities of their own lives. (p. 227)

Attack also came from social scientists who were as disturbed by Gerbner's research methods as they were by his dismissal of their results. The exchange between Gerbner and Gross and their prime nemesis, Paul Hirsch, is indicative. Hirsch charged the Cultural Indicators group with employing poor definitions of amounts of viewing, of improperly combining groups of viewers in their survey samples, of selectively reporting only results that fit their theory, of failure to employ traditional demographic controls, and of developing explanations after the fact for results that did not match their hypotheses. In addressing these claims, Gerbner and his colleagues mockingly labeled Hirsch's analysis of their work "a brilliant scholarly surprise attack making mincemeat out of a plodding band of academic poachers," and sarcastically added, Hirsch's

> masterful "reanalysis" of selected data not only demolishes cumulative results of a decade of fairly massive cooperative research and theory building, along with substantial independent confirmation; it also demonstrates that the research is both worthless and stubbornly wrong-headed. Unlikely as that dramatic coup for pure science might be we intend to demonstrate that Hirsch's analysis is flawed, incomplete, and tendentious. (1981, p. 39)

And from there, things got unfriendly.

Yet Newcomb, called "one of the first" cultivation critics by Michael Morgan and Nancy Signorielli, wrote of the Gerbner group,

> Their foresight to collect data on a systematic, long-term basis, to move out of the laboratory and away from the closed experimental model, will enable other researchers to avoid costly mistakes. Their material holds a wealth of information. The violence topic provides only one of many symbol clusters to be examined. As they move into new areas, and hopefully retrieve more, and more complex information from audiences, we should see whole new sets of questions and answers emerging to aid us in explaining television's role in our culture. (Newcomb, 1978, p. 281)

What exactly were the conclusions drawn initially by the Violence Index, then ultimately by Cultural Indicators that generated so much disagreement, that so inflamed what we generally think of as scientific objectivity?

The Products of Cultivation Analysis

To scientifically demonstrate their view of television as a culturally influential medium, cultivation researchers depended on a four-step process. The first they

MESSAGE SYSTEM
ANALYSIS *In cultiva-*
tion analysis, de-
tailed content
analyses of televi-
sion programming
to assess recurring
and consistent
presentations of
images, themes,
values, and por-
trayals

called **message system analysis,** detailed content analyses of television programming to assess its most recurring and consistent presentations of images, themes, values, and portrayals. The second step is the *formulation of questions about viewers' social realities.* Remember the earlier questions about crime? Those were drawn from a cultivation study. The third step is to *survey the audience,* posing the questions from step two to its members and asking them about their amount of television consumption. Finally, step four entails *comparing the social realities of light and heavy viewers.* The product, as stated by Morgan and Signorielli (1990, p. 20), should not be surprising:

> The questions posed to respondents do not mention television, and the respondents' awareness of the source of their information is seen as irrelevant. The resulting relationships . . . between amount of viewing and the tendency to respond to these questions in the terms of the dominant and repetitive facts, values, and ideologies of the world of television . . . illuminate television's contribution to viewers' conceptions of social reality.

CULTIVATION *In*
cultivation analysis,
television's contri-
bution to the cre-
ation of a culture's
frameworks or
knowledge and
underlying general
concepts

MAINSTREAMING *In*
cultivation analysis,
the process, espe-
cially for heavier
viewers, by which
television's symbols
monopolize and
dominate other
sources of informa-
tion and ideas
about the world

RESONANCE *In*
cultivation analysis,
when viewers see
things on television
that are congruent
with their own
everyday realities

What is television's contribution? Cultivation theorists argue that its major contribution is **cultivation,** a cultural process relating "to coherent frameworks or knowledge and to underlying general concepts . . . cultivated by exposure to the total and organically related world of television rather than exposure to individual programs and selections" (Gerbner, 1990, p. 255).

This cultivation occurs in two ways. The first is **mainstreaming,** where, especially for heavier viewers, television's symbols monopolize and dominate other sources of information and ideas about the world. People's internalized social realities eventually move toward the mainstream, not a mainstream in any political sense, but a culturally dominant reality that is more closely aligned with television's reality than with any objective reality. Is the criminal judicial system failing us? It is if we think it is.

The second way cultivation manifests itself is through **resonance,** when viewers see things on television that are most congruent with their own everyday realities. In essence, these people get a "double dose" of cultivation because what they see on the screen resonates with their actual lives. Some city dwellers, for example, might see the violent world of television resonated in their deteriorating neighborhoods.

The Mean World Index

A particularly instructive example of cultivation is the **Mean World Index,** a series of three questions:

Instant Access

Cultivation Analysis

Strengths	Weaknesses
1 Combines macro- and micro-level theories	1 Is methodologically troubling to many
2 Provides detailed explanation of television's unique role	2 Assumes homogeneity of television content
3 Applies empirical study to widely-held humanistic assumptions	3 Focuses on heavy users of television
4 Redefines *effect* as more than observable behavior change	4 Is difficult to apply to media used less heavily than television
5 Applies to wide variety of effects issues	
6 Provides basis for social change	

MEAN WORLD INDEX *In cultivation analysis, a series of questions about the incidence of crime and violence, the answers to which can be used to differentiate heavy and light viewers*

1 Do you believe that most people are just looking out for themselves?

2 Do you think that you can't be too careful in dealing with people?

3 Do you think that most people would take advantage of you if they got the chance?

Of course, the television perspective on each of these assertions is obvious. But would light and heavy viewers give differing responses? Would the amount of television consumed erase individual distinctions like income and education? Gerbner and his colleagues (1980) found the answer to these questions to be "yes." Heavy viewers were much more likely to see the world as a mean place than were light viewers. Better educated, financially better-off viewers in general saw the world as less mean than did those with less education and income, but heavy viewers from the better educated, better-off groups saw the world as just as dangerous as did low income and less educated people. In other words, heavy viewers held a "mainstreamed" perception of the world as a mean place.

A Final Note on Cultivation

Researchers have employed cultivation analysis to investigate the impact of television content on issues beyond violence and crime. It has been used in examinations of people's perceptions of the justice system (Choi, Massey, & Baran, 1988), fear of victimization (Sparks & Ogles, 1990), affluence, divorce, and working women (Potter, 1991), materialism (Reimer & Rosengren, 1990), values (Potter, 1990), attitudes toward racism (Allen & Hatchett, 1986), feelings of alienation (Signorielli, 1990), environmental concern (Shanahan, Morgan, & Stenbjerre, 1997), work (Signorielli & Kahlenberg, 2001), social stereotypes (Tan, 1982), civil liberties (Carlson, 1983), and anxiety (Zillman & Wakshlag, 1985). The assumptions of cultivation are supported throughout, though the strength of findings and the quality of the research vary greatly. These consistent results led the theory's creator, Gerbner, to identify what he called the **3 Bs of television**. Television

3 Bs OF TELEVISION
In cultivation analysis, the idea that television blurs, blends, and bends reality

1 *Blurs* traditional distinctions of people's views of their world.

2 *Blends* their realities into television's cultural mainstream.

3 *Bends* that mainstream to the institutional interests of television and its sponsors.

He added,

> The historical circumstances in which we find ourselves have taken the magic of human life—living in a universe erected by culture—out of the hands of families and small communities. What has been a richly diverse hand-crafted process has become—for better or worse, or both—a complex manufacturing and mass-distribution enterprise. This has abolished much of the provincialism and parochialism, as well as some of the elitism, of the pretelevision era. It has enriched parochial cultural horizons. It also gave increasingly massive industrial conglomerates the right to conjure up much of what we think about, know, and do in common. (Gerbner, 1990, p. 261)

Clearly, Gerbner does not seem to think that this is a particularly fair trade-off and, as such, he places cultivation analysis in the realm of critical theory. Others do the same. James Shanahan and Vicki Jones, for example, state,

> Cultivation is sometimes taken as a return to a strong "powerful effects" view of mass media. This view isn't completely incorrect, but it misses the point that cultivation was originally conceived as a *critical* theory, which happens to address media issues precisely and only because the mass media (especially television) serve the function of storytelling . . . (T)elevision is the dominant medium for distributing messages from cultural, social and economic elites . . . Cultivation is more than just an analysis of effects from a specific medium; it is an analysis of the *institution* of television and its social role. (1999, p. 32)

Throughout the development of cultivation theory and the growing body of research based on it, Gerbner was able to retain control over essential elements of the theory despite ongoing arguments in favor of various changes. One of the most controversial elements of the theory is the focus on heavy users of television, with no regard for the specific programs that individuals were viewing. Cultivation, it was claimed, ignored the need to identify heavy users of specific types of programs—news users, sit-com users, soap opera users, and so on. James Potter (1993), for example, argued that cultivation's conceptualization of exposure to television is too global. Recently, Kahlor, Gorham, and Gilligan (1999) argued that cultivation theory will never have broad application unless it is revised to accommodate more specific measures of exposure.

Media as Culture Industries: The Commodification of Culture

COMMODIFICATION OF CULTURE *The study of what happens when culture is mass produced and distributed in direct competition with locally based cultures*

One of the most intriguing and challenging perspectives to emerge from critical cultural studies is the **commodification of culture**, the study of what happens when culture is mass produced and distributed in direct competition with locally based cultures (Enzensberger, 1974; Hay, 1989; Jhally, 1987). According to this viewpoint, media are industries specializing in the production and distribution of cultural commodities. As with other modern industries, they have grown at the expense of small, local producers, and the consequences of this displacement have been and continue to be disruptive to people's lives.

In earlier social orders such as medieval kingdoms, everyday life culture was created and controlled by geographically and socially isolated communities. Though kings and lords might dominate an overall social order and have their own culture, it was often totally separate from and had relatively little influence over the folk cultures structuring the everyday experience of average people. Only in modern social orders have elites begun to develop subversive forms of mass culture capable of intruding into and disrupting everyday life culture, say commodification of culture theorists. These new forms can function as very subtle but effective ideologies, leading people to misinterpret their experiences and then act against their own self-interests.

Elites are able to disrupt everyday cultures by using a rather insidious and ingenious strategy. They take bits and pieces of folk culture, weave them together to create attractive mass culture content, and then market it as a substitute for everyday forms of folk culture. Thus, not only are elites able to subvert legitimate local cultures but also they earn profits doing so. People actually subsidize the subversion of their everyday culture. As we've seen, one early and particularly tragic example of this was Nazi Germany where a pseudo-folk culture was created and used to transform daily life.

This strategy has been especially successful in the United States where, unlike Nazi Germany, media entrepreneurs have remained relatively independent from political institutions. Mass culture gained steadily in popularity, spawning huge industries that successfully competed for the attention and interest of most Americans. Within the United States, criticism of mass culture was muted. Most

Americans accepted the cultural commodities emerging from New York and Hollywood as somehow their own. But these same commodities aroused considerable controversy when U.S. media entrepreneurs exported them to other nations. The power of these commodities to reshape daily life was quite obvious in most Third World nations, and even more disruptive.

In *The Media Are American* (1977), Jeremy Tunstall provided a cogent description of how American media entrepreneurs developed their strategy for creating universally attractive cultural commodities. He also traced how they succeeded internationally against strong competition from France and Britain. In the late nineteenth and early twentieth centuries, American entrepreneurs had access to powerful new communications technology but no clear notion of how it could be used to make profits. Most big industrialists regarded media as no more than minor and highly speculative enterprises. Few were willing to invest the money necessary to create viable industries. How could messages broadcast through the air or crude, black and white, moving images on a movie screen be used to earn profits? Would people really pay to see or hear these things? How should industries be organized to manufacture and market cultural products? Most early attempts to answer these questions failed, but through trial and effort, a successful strategy was developed.

According to Tunstall, Tin Pan Alley in New York City provided the model that was later emulated by other U.S. media industries. The authors of popular music specialized in taking melodies from folk music and transforming them into short, attractive songs. These were easily marketed to mass audiences who didn't have the time or the aesthetic training to appreciate longer, more sophisticated forms of music. In its early days, Tin Pan Alley was a musical sweatshop in which songwriters were ill-paid and overworked while sheet music and recording company entrepreneurs reaped huge profits. By keeping production and distribution costs quite low, rapid expansion was possible and profits grew accordingly. Inevitably, expansion carried the entrepreneurs beyond the United States. Because many were first generation European immigrants, they knew how to return and gain a foothold in Europe. The Second World War provided an ideal opportunity to additionally subvert European culture. The American military demanded and received permission to import massive quantities of U.S.-style popular culture into Europe where it proved popular. American Armed Forces Radio was especially influential in its broadcasts of popular music and entertainment shows.

What are the consequences of lifting bits of everyday life culture out of their context, repackaging, and then marketing them back to people? Critical theorists have provided many intriguing answers to this question.

1 **When elements of everyday culture are selected for repackaging, only a very limited range is chosen, and important elements are overlooked or consciously ignored.** For example, elements of culture important for structuring the experi-

ence of small minority groups are likely to be ignored while culture practiced by large segments of the population will be emphasized. For a good illustration of this, watch some situation comedies from the 1960s like *Father Knows Best* and *Leave It to Beaver.* During this era, these programs provided a very homogeneous and idealized picture of American family life. They might make you wonder whether there were any poor people, working women, or ethnic groups living in the United States in 1965.

2 **The repackaging process involves dramatization of those elements of culture that have been selected.** Certain forms of action are highlighted, their importance is exaggerated, and others are ignored. Such dramatization makes the final commodity attractive to as large an audience as possible. Potentially boring, controversial, or offensive elements are removed. Features are added that are known to appeal to large audience segments. Thus, attention-getting and emotion-arousing actions, for example sex and violence, are routinely featured. This is a major reason that car chases, gun fights, and verbal conflict dominate prime-time television and Hollywood movies, but casual conversations between friends are rare (unless they include a joke every fifteen seconds—then you have comedy).

3 **The marketing of cultural commodities is done in a way that maximizes the likelihood that they will intrude into and ultimately disrupt everyday life.** The success of the media industries depends on marketing as much content as possible to as many people as possible with no consideration for how this content will actually be used or what its long-term consequences will be. An analogy can be made to pollution of the physical environment caused by food packaging. The packaging adds nothing to the nutritional value of the food but is merely a marketing device—it moves the product off the shelf. Pollution results when we carelessly dispose of this packaging or when there is so much of it that there is no place to put it. Unlike trash, media commodities are less tangible and their packaging is completely integrated into the cultural content. There are no recycling bins for cultural packaging. When we consume the product, we consume the packaging. It intrudes and disrupts.

4 **The elites who operate the cultural industries generally are ignorant of the consequences of their work.** This ignorance is based partly on their alienation from the people who consume their products. They live in Hollywood or New York City, not in typical neighborhoods. Ignorance is maintained partly through strategic avoidance or denial of evidence about consequences in much the same way that the tobacco industry has concealed and lied about research documenting the negative effects of smoking. Media industries have developed formal mechanisms for rationalizing their impact and explaining away consequences. One involves supporting empirical social research and the limited effects findings that it produces.

Instant Access

Commodification of Culture

Strengths	Weaknesses
1 Provides basis for social change	1 Argues for, but does not empirically demonstrate effects
2 Identifies problems created by repackaging of cultural content	2 Has overly pessimistic view of media influence and average people

---

Another involves professionalization. Although this can have positive benefits (see Chapter 5), media practitioners can also use it to justify routine production practices while they reject potentially useful innovations.

5   **Disruption of everyday life takes many forms—some are obviously linked to consumption of especially deleterious content, but other forms of disruption are very subtle and occur over long periods.** Disruption ranges from propagation of misconceptions about the social world—like those cultivation analysis has examined—to disruption of social institutions. Consequences can be both microscopic and macroscopic and take many different forms. For example, Joshua Meyrowitz (1985) argued that media have deprived us of a sense of place. Neil Postman (1985) believes that media focus too much on entertainment, with serious long-term consequences. He as also examined media disruption in books entitled *The Disappearance of Childhood* (1994) and *The End of Education* (1996). Kathleen Jamieson lamented the decline of political speechmaking brought about by electronic media (1988) and, with Karlyn Campbell, media's corruption of the meaning of citizen action (1997). Michael Parenti (1992), in *Make-Believe Media: The Politics of Entertainment*, also explores this theme.

Researchers who are attempting to study globalization of media are increasingly adopting commodification of cultural theory. It provides for them a way to understand how Western media content, especially television programs and movies, may intrude into and disrupt indigenous cultures around the world. More on this in the next chapter.

Advertising: The Ultimate Cultural Commodity

Not surprisingly, critical cultural studies researchers have directed their most devastating criticism toward advertising. Advertising is viewed as the ultimate cultural commodity (Hay, 1989; Jhally, 1987). Advertising packages promotional messages so that they will be attended to and acted on by people who often have little interest in and no real need for most of the advertised products or services. Consumption of specific products is routinely portrayed as the best way to construct a worthwhile personal identity, have fun, make friends and influence people, or solve problems (often ones you never knew you had). Be all you can be. You deserve a break today. Just do it.

Compared with other forms of mass media content, advertising comes closest to fitting older Marxist notions of ideology. It is intended to encourage consumption that serves the interest of product manufacturers but may not be in the interest of individual consumers. Advertising is clearly designed to intrude into and disrupt routine buying habits and purchase decisions. It attempts to stimulate and reinforce consumption even if it might be detrimental to the long-term health of individuals. For some products, such as cigarettes and alcohol, successful advertising campaigns induce people to engage in self-destructive actions. In many cases, we are simply encouraged to consume things that serve little real purpose for us or serve only the purposes that advertising itself creates. One obvious example is when we buy specific brands of clothing because their advertising has promoted them as status symbols. The clothing does provide basic protection for our bodies, but used clothing from a thrift store could provide the same protection.

News Production Research

During the past three decades, several studies have been done on the production and consumption of news content (Crouse, 1973; Epstein, 1973; Fishman, 1980; Gans, 1979; Gitlin, 1980; Tuchman, 1978). Most of the research we discuss in this section was conducted by British and American sociologists during the 1970s and 1980s. Their purpose was to critically analyze how journalists routinely cover news. Most of this research supports theories about the intrusion of media into politics as well as cultural commodification theories.

NEWS PRODUCTION RESEARCH *The study of how the institutional routines of news production inevitably produce distorted or biased content*

W. Lance Bennett (1988) surveyed **news production research** literature and summarized four ways in which current news production practices distort or bias news content:

1 **Personalized News:** Most people relate better to individuals than to groups or institutions, so most news stories center around people. According to Bennett, "The focus on individual actors who are easy to identify with positively or negatively invites members of the news audience to project their own private feelings and fantasies directly onto public life" (1988, p. 27). Thus, personalization helps people

relate to and find relevance in remote events. It does this, however, at a cost—it risks transforming the larger social world into a gigantic soap opera. For example, even as all Americans had their lives disrupted by the September 11 terrorist attacks, and as U.S. diplomats sought accommodations from the Afghanistan government, and as U.S. Special Forces were being ferried to the Middle East, the *Boston Globe* of September 22, 2001, offered readers this headline summarizing the ongoing conflict, BUSH-TALIBAN STALEMATE GROWS.

2 **Dramatized News:** Like all media commodities, news must be attractively packaged, and a primary means of doing this involves dramatization. Edward Jay Epstein provided the following quotation from a policy memorandum written by a network television news producer:

> Every news story should, without any sacrifice of probity or responsibility, display the attributes of fiction, of drama. It should have structure and conflict, problem and denouement, rising action and falling action, a beginning, a middle, and an end. These are not only the essentials of drama; they are the essentials of narrative. (1973, pp. 4–5)

Bennett and Murray Edelman (1985) argued that this type of narrative is very limiting and inherently biased toward supporting the status quo. They have called for development of more innovative narrative structures as one means of reforming the news industry.

3 **Fragmented News:** The typical newspaper and news broadcast is made up of brief, capsulized reports of events—snapshots of the social world. By constructing news in this way, journalists attempt to fulfill their norm of objectivity. Events are treated in isolation with little effort to interconnect them. Connection requires putting them into a broader context, and this would require making speculative, sometimes controversial linkages. Is there a link between three isolated plane crashes, or between three separate toxic waste spills? By compartmentalizing events, news reports make it difficult for news consumers to make their own connections. Bennett argued that when journalists attempt to do analysis, they create a collage. They assemble evidence and viewpoints from conflicting sources and then juxtapose these pieces in a manner that defies interpretation, especially by news consumers who lack interest or background knowledge. These stories might meet the norm of being "balanced" but they don't assist the reader in making sense of things.

4 **Normalized News:** Stories about disasters or about social movements tend to "normalize" these potential threats to the status quo. Elite sources are allowed to explain disasters and to challenge movement members. Elites are presented as authoritative, rational, knowledgeable people who are effectively coping with threats. They can be trusted to bring things back to normal. If there is a problem

with aircraft technology, it will be repaired—the FAA has the flight recorder and will pinpoint the cause of the crash as soon as possible. If movements make legitimate demands, they will be satisfied—the governor has announced that he is forming a blue ribbon commission to study the problem.

OBJECTIVITY RITUALS
In news production research, the term for professional practices designed to ensure objectivity that are implicitly biased toward support of the status quo

Gaye Tuchman (1978) provides a good example of news production research. She studied how the values held by journalists influence news even when considerable effort is made to guard against that influence. She observed journalists as they covered social movements and concluded that production practices were implicitly biased toward support of the status quo. She found that reporters engage in **objectivity rituals**—they have set procedures for producing unbiased news stories that actually introduce bias. For example, when leaders of a controversial movement were interviewed, their statements were never allowed to stand alone. Journalists routinely attempted to "balance" these statements by reporting the views of authorities who opposed the movements. Reporters frequently selected the most unusual or controversial statements made by movement leaders and contrasted these with the more conventional views of mainstream group leaders. Reporters made little effort to understand the overall philosophy of the movement. Lacking understanding, they inevitably took statements out of context and misrepresented movement ideals. Thus, though reporters never explicitly expressed negative views about these groups, their lack of understanding, their casual methods for selecting quotes, and their use of elite sources led to stories that were harmful to the movements they covered. Tuchman's arguments have been collaborated by Mark Fishman (1980) and Todd Gitlin (1980).

John Stauber and Sheldon Rampton use environmental news as their example of how these objectivity rituals routinely support the status quo. Whereas the world scientific community overwhelmingly believes in global warming and the greenhouse effect, with some estimates as high as 95 percent of all scientists working in climatology, astronomy, and meteorology accepting these phenomena as scientific fact, when they are covered in the popular press, the issue is presented as one scientist says this and another says that. Reporters, in their efforts to be "fair" and "objective" seek out spokespeople from both sides, often turning to groups like The Global Climate Coalition, a public relations creation of the world's leading chemical companies (1995, pp. 123–142). In a 30-second television news spot that presents two experts, the logical audience reading is that this issue is in some scientific dispute.

News production research remains a significant focus for researchers. In *Framing Public Life: Perspectives on Media and Our Understanding of the Social World,* Steve Reese, Oscar Gandy, and August Grant (2001) have included studies of news production along with framing studies that look at media content or audience reception. Their book demonstrates the importance of news production research as

Instant Access

News Production Research

Strengths	Weaknesses
1 Provides recommendations for potentially useful changes in news production practices	1 Focuses on news production practices but has not empirically demonstrated their effect
2 Raises important questions about routine news production practices	2 Has pessimistic view of journalists and their social role
3 Can be used to study production of many different types of news	3 Has been ignored and rejected as impractical by practicing journalists

part of any comprehensive effort to probe the way that public understanding of news events develops. News production research is also an important aspect of current research on risk communication. News stories about threats to public health and safety can produce widely varying levels of public concern depending on how these threats are described and the context in which they are presented. The profound and widespread public fear that followed news coverage of the terrorist attacks on September 11th demonstrated what happens when threats are highlighted. This event has provoked considerable debate within the news industry concerning news production practices.

Media Intrusion Theory

MEDIA INTRUSION THEORY *Idea that media have intruded into and taken over politics to the degree that politics have become subverted*

Dennis Davis (1990) labeled this body of recent research dealing with political communications **media intrusion theory.** This theory can be regarded as a contemporary variant of elite pluralism, especially the work of a political scientist, V. O. Key (see Chapter 7). It assumes that politics operate best when they are hierarchically structured, when a political elite mediates between the public and its elected leaders. This elite has a grassroots base. Leaders work their way into positions of power through their involvement in local, regional, and national social organizations—from local parent teacher groups to the national Red Cross. Political parties serve as umbrella organizations in which the leaders of various groups broker power. Most members of this elite don't hold political office but work behind the scenes serving the interests of the groups that they lead. Some theorists are concerned because many social groups are losing membership and influence. Media are blamed for this because many people stay home to watch television rather than participate in local groups. Ironically, when political elites can no longer rely on local groups to support them, they are forced to turn to political consultants who advise them on how to use media to rally support. But the televised political advertising and dramatic news coverage required to rally apathetic supporters have a high price. Elites must spend precious time raising money and then spend it on questionable forms of campaign communication. Television stations reap windfall profits from this advertising, but broadcast journalists express frustration about the way that political consultants manipulate news coverage.

The decline of political parties has been well documented as has been the drop in political affiliation and voting (Entman, 1989). These changes occurred at the same time that television became the dominant medium for news. A linkage between these events is plausible but has proved hard to establish empirically. Media intrusion theorists typically argue that television has subverted politics by undermining political party control over elections. Some even argue that television has replaced parties in the election process (Patterson, 1980). Candidates no longer need party support—some actively avoid it. Instead, candidates hire political consultants to guide their media use. Candidates are often advised to avoid all mention of their political party. Campaigns promote candidates, not parties.

Media intrusion theorists frequently cite the findings of the news production researchers to support their positions. These theorists claim that political reports are too personalized, too dramatized, and too fragmented. Politics is often reported as a game between opposing teams with the major politicians viewed as star players. Stories focus on media-hyped spectacles (Edelman, 1988)—on big plays, on life and death struggles to score points. These reports don't help news consumers develop useful understandings of politics. Rather, they encourage consumers to become political spectators, content to sit on the sidelines while the stars play the game.

Some journalists reject the media intrusion argument by asserting that they have little control over elections. They don't intrude into politics. Instead, their reporting efforts are being disrupted by political consultants. These journalists point out that the political parties chose to give up control over presidential nominations when they decided to permit primary elections to be held across the nation. As the power of political parties has declined and the influence of political consultants has increased, manipulation of media by politicians has increased. Political consultants have developed very effective strategies for obtaining favorable news coverage for their candidates (Davis, 1990). During campaigns, journalists rely on particular production practices for gathering and generating news stories. Consultants are very knowledgeable about these practices and are skilled

Box 11b Media Intrusion, Then and Now

Media practitioners, too, are concerned with media intrusion into politics. Carl Bernstein, best known for his coverage of the Watergate scandal, said the following about the American media's contemporary performance and their intrusion into politics.

"The America rendered today in the American media is illusionary and delusionary—disfigured, unreal, disconnected from the true contexts of our lives. In covering real American life the media—weekly, daily, hourly—breaks new ground in getting it wrong. The coverage is distorted by celebrity; by the reduction of news to gossip; by sensationalism, which is always turning away from a society's real condition; and by a political and social discourse that we—the press, the media, the politicians, *and* the people—are turning into a sewer."

He offered this example, "'All right, was it really the best sex you ever had?' Those were the words of Diane Sawyer, in an interview of Marla Maples on *Prime Time Live*, a broadcast of ABC News (where 'more Americans get their news than any other source'). Those words marked a new low. For more than 15 years we

have been moving away from real journalism toward the creation of a sleazoid info-tainment culture in which the lines between Oprah and Geraldo and Diane, between the New York *Post* and *Newsday* are too often indistinguishable. In this new culture of journalistic titillation, we teach readers and viewers that the trivial is significant, that the lurid and the loopy are more important than real news" (Bernstein, 1992, p. C4).

Recall media coverage of the Special Prosecutor, President Clinton, Monica Lewinsky crisis that engulfed the United States in 1998 and 1999. Given your estimation of how the events surrounding this upheaval were handled by the media, do you think many of Bernstein's colleagues took his words to heart? Media critic Steven Brill (1998, p. 123) labeled "the media's performance a true scandal, a true example of an institution corrupted to its core." What possible abuses or failures could have moved him to such a harsh evaluation? What could he have meant when he said, "The abuses that were Watergate spawned great reporting. The Lewinsky story has reversed the process"?

at supplying useful information and convenient events. These "anticipated" events make it very easy to cover the candidate as the consultant wants and hard for journalists to find material for alternate stories. (Not all journalists dispute media intrusion theory, as you can see in Box 11b.)

For example, one recent news management strategy is to limit what a candidate says each day. By repeating the same terse comment over and over, the candidate hopes to force broadcast reporters to pick up and use the "sound bite of the day." The candidate avoids talking candidly to reporters because statements could be used to construct alternate stories. Journalists pride themselves on covering, not making news, so they find it hard to break out of the limitations imposed by shrewd consultants.

Instant Access

Media Intrusion Theory

Strengths	Weaknesses
1 Provides basis for social change	1 Focuses on operation of news media but has not empirically demonstrated its effect
2 Raises important questions about operation of news media organizations	2 Has overly pessimistic view of news media and their social role
	3 Focuses too much on intrusion into politics
	4 Is based on elite pluralism assumptions

There are no easy answers to the questions posed by media intrusion theory. Thomas Patterson (1994) summarized findings from his research during the previous 20 years, presenting a devastating analysis of the deterioration of presidential campaign communication. The best solution that he can offer is to shorten the campaigns. This he believes would return some power to the political parties and lessen the likelihood that overdramatized news coverage of trivial campaign happenings will determine who gets elected. Robert Entman (1989) argues that a solution can be reached only if politicians, journalists, and the public change their behavior. Politicians must stop relying on manipulative and expensive strategies, journalists must cover issues rather than spectacles, and the public must give serious attention to issues, not campaign spectacles and personalities. But how likely is it that such solutions can actually be implemented? Politicians and journalists are reluctant to change patterns of behavior that serve their immediate purposes—getting elected to office and attracting audiences to campaign coverage. And after every election campaign in recent years, private foundations have sponsored major conferences at which politicians and journalists have pledged to improve the quality of campaign communication. But the same mistakes are continually repeated in campaign after campaign. An increasingly alienated public seems unlikely to suddenly develop an interest in issues even if they become bored with political spectacles. The 2000 presidential election fiasco that ended in the U.S. Supreme Court may further reinforce public cynicism about elections.

Summary

The theories reviewed in this chapter are quite diverse but provide a surprisingly coherent and complementary vision of contemporary American society. This vision is troubling. It argues that media influence is far more powerful and pervasive than limited effects theories imply. Media might be capable of turning culture into a commodity with serious consequences. What we know about public issues, the terms we use to define issues, and the importance we assign to various issues all might be strongly influenced by media. Defenders of limited effects theory have questioned this "return to a powerful effects perspective on media." In their view, the theories we have reviewed in this chapter are too speculative and not sufficiently grounded in empirical research. These defenders point out that there still is no convincing evidence that media ever have the power to alter attitudes on a large scale, especially if these attitudes are well established and associated with strong emotions. Audiences are too "obstinate" to permit such manipulation.

But if media can't cause instant conversion of vast audiences to new ideologies, then just how powerful can they be? We can answer this question by expanding and extending the mantra of agenda-setting theory to encompass the other theories reviewed in this chapter. Agenda-setting theory states that media don't tell people *what to think* (that is, media don't directly influence attitudes), but media do tell people what to think about—they can and do affect the importance that we assign to various public issues. If we take this a little further, we can argue that media also tell people *how to think about* issues specifically and the social world generally—the media frame issues for us and cultivate our perceptions of the social world so that we are more likely to make sense of things in some ways rather than others. If we expect to see a "mean world," we will find our expectations constantly confirmed by television violence and on televised news. Media might also tell people *what to talk about* (spiral of silence) when they discuss issues with others. Finally, media can have a profound influence on the *accessibility and quality of information* we use as we try to think, talk, and act in our social world. If the only information we can easily access is the information provided in infotainment or political spectacle, there will be many important things we never learn about from the media. Moreover, our impressions of the things that we *do* learn about might be strongly affected by the "packaging" of the information.

Another way of summarizing these arguments is through the following five assumptions:

- Electronic media are fundamentally different from the print media that have preceded them.
- Electronic media constitute a culture industry that has become central to the formation, transmission, and maintenance of culture in American society.

- Electronic media cultivate a general consciousness or worldview on which many people's conclusions, judgments, and actions are based.

- Electronic media's major cultural influence is to stabilize social patterns, preserve the status quo, and allow power to be increasingly centralized.

- The measurable, identifiable contributions of electronic media to the culture at any one time are relatively small. But, the overall, long-term influence is all-pervasive.

So how do you answer the questions raised about media by the theories in this chapter? Is McLuhan your guide, or are the cultivation or commodification of culture theorists? Are you optimistic or pessimistic concerning the role of media? Should media be striving to serve the purposes that libertarian thinkers assigned to them? Or were these purposes too idealistic given the necessity for media to earn profits in an increasingly competitive marketplace? Is it a problem if media act as a powerful agent for the status quo? To what extent do media shape your own view of your world?

Exploring Mass Communication Theory

 1 The Internet offers several interesting sites devoted to Marshall McLuhan and his ideas. Visit a few and determine for yourself what the contemporary take is on McLuhan and his ideas. Here are a couple sites to get you started.

> *The McLuhan Probes*
> http://www.mcluhan.ca/

> *Marshall McLuhan Links*
> http://www.law.pitt.edu/hibbitts/mcl.htm

 2 George Gerbner, as do other good critical theorists, uses his theory as the basis for social and political action. He is a founding member of the Cultural Environment Movement, a coalition of 150 independent organizations spread across 64 countries that are committed to the restoration of the balance of power between media industries and those who consume their products. Visit its Web site and identify the influence not only of cultivation analysis and commodification of culture in particular but also of critical theory in general.

> *Cultural Environment Movement*
> http://www.cemnet.org/

 3 Use **InfoTrac College Edition** to scan the tables of contents of recent editions of *Broadcasting & Cable* and *Editor & Publisher.* These are the primary trade publications

of the broadcasting and newspaper industries, respectively. Identify articles that deal with the issue of the possible cultural effects of these media. What is the prevailing view of each industry on its social and cultural impact? Now, use **InfoTrac College Edition** again, but go to *The Columbia Journalism Review*. This is a leading journal of commentary on media performance. Scan its table of contents to find articles that might (or might not) offer an alternative view on media's performance. Reconcile the differing views you uncover.

 4 Use **InfoTrac College Edition** to scan the table of contents of *Campaigns & Elections*. Identify articles that are based on social marketing theory. Read and analyze a few, preferably one that describes a social marketing effort and one that analyzes the effectiveness of such an effort.

Critical Thinking Questions

1 To what extent do you think media content fosters support for the status quo? If it does, is this necessarily a bad thing, as critical theorists contend? If it does not, should it? Defend your position.

2 Has your life been affected or disrupted by consumption of cultural commodities, including advertising? Can you think of any examples of misconceptions about yourself or the world that you got from media content? Could you have avoided making these mistakes? To what extent should media practitioners be held responsible for them?

3 Almost everyone thinks that U.S. politics needs reform. Do you agree with arguments that place considerable responsibility for this situation on the mass media? Could or should national politics and national political campaigns be reported differently?

4 How did news coverage of the September 11th terrorist attacks influence you and the people you know? Do you think that people became too fearful? Were children unnecessarily traumatized? Could or should the story have been handled differently? What about the way public officials reacted? What do you think of the recommendations offered in Box 11a?

5 Can you think of a situation in which you were reluctant to express your opinions on an issue because media reports indicated that these opinions were becoming less popular? In other words, have you been a victim of the spiral of silence? Are you afraid of becoming socially isolated when you express unpopular views on issues? If not, do you have friends and family (reference groups) who you can count on for support even if you express unpopular views?

6 Do you know any heavy users of television? If so, is Gerbner right? Do these people have views of the social world that are biased toward the way that medium portrays it? Are they more fearful of being victims of crime and more supportive of police power?

Significant People and Their Writing

DeFleur, Melvin L., and Sandra Ball-Rokeach (1975). *Theories of Mass Communication,* 3rd edition. New York: David McKay.

Gerbner, George, and Larry Gross (1972). "Living with Television: The Violence Profile." *Journal of Communication,* 26: 173–199.

Grosswiler, Paul. (1997). *Method in the Message: Rethinking McLuhan Through Critical Theory.* Montreal: Black Rose Books.

Jhally, Sut, ed., (1987). *The Codes of Advertising: Fetishism and the Political Economy of Meaning in the Consumer Society.* London: Frances Pinter.

McLuhan, Marshall (1951). *The Mechanical Bride.* New York: Vanguard.

———. (1964). *Understanding Media: The Extensions of Man.* New York: McGraw-Hill.

Newcomb, Horace M., and Paul M. Hirsch (1983). "Television as a Cultural Forum: Implications for Research." *Quarterly Review of Film,* 8: 45–55.

Noelle-Neumann, Elisabeth (1984). *The Spiral of Silence.* Chicago: University of Chicago Press.

Patterson, Thomas (1994). *Out of Order.* New York: Vintage.

Signorielli, Nancy, and Michael Morgan, eds., (1990). *Cultivation Analysis: New Directions in Media Effects Research.* Newbury Park, CA: Sage.

Tichenor, Phillip, George A. Donohue, and Clarice N. Olien (1980). *Community Conflict and the Press.* Beverly Hills, CA: Sage.

Tuchman, Gaye (1978). *Making News: A Study in the Construction of Reality.* New York: Free Press.

Tunstall, Jeremy (1977). *The Media Are American: Anglo-American Media in the World.* New York: Columbia University Press.

Chapter 12

Trends in Mass Communication Theory: Seeking Consensus, Facing Challenges

As you read these words, more than 800 communications satellites are circling the globe. By the year 2008, there will be 2,200 in orbit, providing instantaneous, worldwide telephone service, direct home and car reception of audio and video, and incredibly fast and expanded access to the Internet and the World Wide Web (Lo, 1998). Back on Earth, turn of the century media consumers are increasingly signing on for direct satellite television, rushing to buy DVD players and set up home theater systems, and growing more dependent on the services offered via the Internet. Several government agencies, including the FCC and the Department of Commerce's National Telecommunications and Information Administration, are busy working out rules and regulations to keep pace with and control this telecommunications revolution. As all this unfolds, the population of the United States is becoming more multicultural and pluralistic, with some demographers predicting that within a generation, there will be no one majority race or nationality in the United States.

Ours is an era not unlike that of the development of mass society theory, or that of the entrenchment of the limited effects perspective, or that which produced social cognitive theory and uses and gratifications. At each turn in mass communication theory, the introduction of new technologies, interest in and efforts at controlling them, and a concern that their use not conflict with democratic and pluralistic ideals (Chapter 1) have initiated and shaped emerging ideas about the role of media in the lives of individuals and in the cultures and societies they occupy. Contemporary mass communication theory must evolve—and is evolving—to accommodate these rapidly moving and powerful alterations in the audience/mass media relationship.

Overview

As we've seen throughout this text, mass communication research in the United States has undergone a profound transformation in the past forty years. Some changes were the result of the rise of critical and cultural theories and the challenge they posed to the limited effects paradigm. But change also came from within the limited effects paradigm as researchers moved away from a narrow focus on short-term, direct effects and developed active audience theories of mass communication. Still more change was initiated by researchers who argued that mass communication theory should be integrated with interpersonal communication theory to create comprehensive theories of communication (Hawkins, Wiemann, & Pingree, 1988).

Now, however, this ferment appears to be giving way to a growing consensus on mass communication scholarship. A dialogue has been established between scholars, and new, broader perspectives are being proposed. We first consider **communication science,** a perspective that unites researchers who prefer to base their inquiry on quantitative, empirical research methods. We then discuss recent critical and cultural studies scholarship and see that these scholars also are moving toward consensus. Recently, Klaus Bruhn Jensen, a Danish scholar, has offered **social semiotics theory** (Jensen, 1995) as a unifying framework for mass communication research.

These trends toward consensus within the field are likely to be challenged well into this century by external forces promising to confound media scholarship. We identify four forces that pose the most serious difficulties and discuss how contemporary mass communication theory might build on existing ideas while responding to these forces.

The most obvious of these external forces is the ongoing revolution in communications technology, one that shows no signs of weakening. This revolution is producing technologies and applications that fill every niche on the communications spectrum, ranging from the intrapersonal communication we carry on with ourselves to powerful forms of mass communication capable of simultaneously sending messages to every person on earth. Each of these new media is likely to play different roles in society and in our personal lives. Most will quickly disappear and a handful will succeed—often for unexpected reasons. Some older media will persist, but their roles will be greatly altered or diminished. This is what happened to radio after the rise of television in the 1960s. Others will disappear entirely, like weekly mass circulation magazines in th[...] searchers will struggle to keep pace with this rapidly changin[...]

The second force is closely related to the first. Since the en[...] a new world order has been emerging. One primary attribute o[...] is globalization. More and more social organizations are bein[...]

COMMUNICATION SCIENCE *A perspective on communication that unites a variety of perspectives and quantitative methodologies to assess the communication process in its entirety*

SOCIAL SEMIOTICS THEORY *A perspective on mass communication that unites the methods and beliefs of cultural theorists with those of critical theorists*

have worldwide scope. These include multinational governmental organizations such as the European Community, multinational corporations, and worldwide nongovernmental organizations (NGOs) (Smith, 1991). Powerful communications technologies, such as satellites and the Internet, enable these organizations to easily span space and time. As the power of these organizations expands, that of individual nation states tends to contract. There is growing hope that NGOs could play an especially important role in development of civil society in emerging democracies around the world. Research will be needed to assess this possibility and exploit whatever potential exists for NGOs to serve as buffers between national governments and multinational corporations.

The third force is less visible, but some futurists argue it is likely to be even more powerful than these first two in reshaping the social world. It involves a transition from modern forms of social order to postmodern forms. French theorists pioneered many intriguing notions about this transition. If they are right, we are on the verge of making the most significant changes in social organization since the thirteenth century. The resurgence of indigenous cultures worldwide is being seen as one aspect of this transformation.

Finally, rapidly expanding scientific insight into the powers and the limitations of the human organism will necessitate constant reformulation of media theories. In a variety of fields ranging from the biological sciences to cognitive psychology, research is likely to produce powerful understandings of the way we deal with and act on information from both the physical and social environment. Ironically, the more we come to understand the power of computers to emulate and take over human communication abilities, the more we come to understand ourselves.

We close this chapter with a discussion of media literacy, seen by many as not only necessitated by the rapid expansion and diffusion of new communication technologies, but also as one logical outcome of all these years of ferment in the field of mass communication theory.

Communication Science

By the 1980s, some empirical media researchers concluded that the constant ferment of competing ideas and research methods was impeding the development of a coherent approach to communications research. One result of this awareness was the creation of communication science, a perspective on research that integrates all research approaches that are grounded in quantitative, empirical, behavioral research methods. Communication science effectively unites limited effects research with active audience and **interpersonal communication** research. The development of communication science can be seen as an effort to rebuild the empirical research tradition within the field by breaking that tradition's strong asso-

INTERPERSONAL COMMUNICATION *Communication* *tween one or a* *eople*

ciation with limited effects and broadening it to address a much larger range of research questions and issues.

Communication science, *per se,* was initially defined in the late 1980s by researchers who wanted to eliminate unfruitful fragmentation and provide a defining core philosophy for the scientific study of all forms of communication. This is an effort to be inclusive rather than exclusive, to reject many of the outdated assumptions of the limited effects paradigm while retaining its strong empirical focus—to unify under a single banner empirical researchers working in all areas of communication.

Charles Berger and Steven Chaffee (1987b) not only promoted the movement, but also helped to reify it by titling their volume *Handbook of Communication Science.* In this book, they offered the following definition and explanation,

> Communication science seeks to understand the production, processing, and effects of symbol and signal systems by developing testable theories, containing lawful generalizations, that explain phenomena associated with production, processing, and effects. This definition is sufficiently general to embrace various communication contexts, including the production, processing, or effects of symbol or signal systems (including nonverbal) in interpersonal, organizational, mass, political, instructional or other contexts. (p. 17)

Although this definition is inclusive in certain respects, it also clearly excludes some types of theory and research from its domain. Theory should *explain* phenomena. Theory should consist of *lawful generalizations* that are *testable* using empirical research methods. These criteria exclude most forms of political economy and cultural studies scholarship. Thus, despite its claims to inclusiveness, communication science adheres to many of the definitions of social research initially formulated by Paul Lazarsfeld and his contemporaries. Communication science attempts to unify one group of scholars while excluding forms of scholarship that don't meet its criteria for scientific research. And, as you can see in Box 12a, this "discrimination" causes conflict even among the most respected mass communication theorists.

Two Views of Communication Science

Chaffee and Berger (1987) offered a restructuring of the scientific study of communication, one that ignored the usual narrow interest in specific aspects of the communication process as applied in individual circumstances or settings. Instead, it was based on the four levels at which communication phenomena occur:

1 *Intra-individual,* the analysis of communication that occurs within the individual

2 *Interpersonal,* the analysis of communication relationships between two or small groups of people

Box 12a   Where Have All the Milestones Gone?

Melvin DeFleur, whom you met in Chapter 11 as one of the creators of media systems dependency theory, has had a long and distinguished career as a mass communication theorist. Among the work for which he is best known is the book *Milestones in Mass Communication*, written with Shearon Lowery. Having appeared in numerous editions, this book presents the most important advances in mass communication theory through an examination of the research that signaled or initiated those changes. You should be familiar with many of the *milestones* DeFleur and Lowery describe—Cantril's research on *The War of the Worlds* radio broadcast, the Hovland/Yale Group's program of persuasion research, the Erie County voter studies of Lazarsfeld and his colleagues, the work of the uses and gratifications founders, Bandura's theory of modeling and social cognition, Rogers' diffusion of innovation research, McComb and Shaw's landmark study of media's agenda-setting power.

But, argues DeFleur in a controversial article entitled "Where Have All the Milestones Gone? The Decline of Significant Research on the Process and Effects of Mass Communication" (1998), since these seminal works, "few studies have made significant theoretical contributions" (p. 85) and, as a result, "the development of media theory seems stalled" (p. 88).

This is particularly surprising, he argues, because since what he sees as those earlier heydays of significant mass communication research:

- The media have expanded both in number and reach
- They have become more complex
- The number of people working in the media industries has increased dramatically
- Colleges and universities provide far more instruction on media and media issues

Admitting that many researchers will disagree with him because they believe they are doing important research or because he has ignored some important work (Gerbner's cultivation analysis or the research leading to the development of media-related quasi-systems theory, for example), he presents six reasons for the decrease in "the production of groundbreaking research" (p. 86). Five are practical—the move of many social scientists away from mass communication inquiry to other important research questions; the absence of long-term, programmatic research programs (like Hovland's work); the flight of talented mass communication researchers away from universities to higher paying industry research jobs; reductions in the amount of grant money for mass

3   *Network or organizational,* the analysis of larger groups of people and the contexts of their continuing relationships

4   *Macroscopic societal,* the analysis of the communication characteristics and activities of large social systems

Their argument is straightforward—all communication can be best understood on two or more of these levels rather than in isolation. Because all levels are necessarily interconnected, changes at one level must affect other levels. A simple exam-

Box 12a Where Have All the Milestones Gone? (*continued*)

communication research; and changes in the work environment for university professors (the rise in the number of part-time faculty places more work on full-time faculty, leaving them less time to conduct important research, and the pressure to earn tenure encourages quick, short-term research studies).

DeFleur's sixth reason for the drop off in important media scholarship—the shift to nonquantitative and critical research—is of particular interest to us as we ponder the future of mass communication theory because it relegates "to the sidelines" (p. 94) virtually all cultural, critical, political economy, and postmodern research.

Not all mass communication researchers and theorists accept DeFleur's view. Respected communication researcher and writer Samuel Becker offers a position diametrically opposed to DeFleur's:

The current ferment in the field is not due solely, if at all, to the limitations of our social science; much of it is attributable to the fact that there are so many exciting options available to young communication scholars today . . . It may well be this variety of riches that is making our choices so difficult and casting the field into ferment . . . How can anyone possibly argue for greater homogeneity in our ap-

proaches to communication scholarship than presently exists? We can, and should, argue for better *quality scholarship,* whatever its underlying philosophy or methodology, but not that our particular way is *the* right way. (1989, 127–128)

But what do you think? Of all the theories you've read, which seem to make the most sense to you? Which have been most valuable in helping you develop your own personally meaningful understandings of the role of media in your lives and in shaping your view of the world around you? Do you reject as interesting but relatively unimportant culturally or critically based theories such as McLuhan's ideas, social marketing theory, commodification of culture, news production research, media intrusion theory, frame analysis, social construction of reality, and symbolic interaction? Do neomarxist oriented scholars like those in the British cultural studies camp have nothing to tell us? Can any of this work, which seems to be gaining much contemporary interest, produce milestones that re-shape our understanding of the media and the mass communication process? DeFleur thinks not and has the courage (and standing in the discipline) to say so. But Becker relishes the ferment. In it, he sees strength. What about you?

ple should suffice. Investigations of the effects of television violence are generally associated with social cognitive or modeling theory, usually with mass communication, and usually with researchers trained as psychologists. But what individual factors, self-esteem for example, cause a person to favor violent media content (intra-individual level)? How does that person deal with conflict with his or her friends after consuming a steady diet of televised violence (interpersonal level)? What does the presence in our schools, for example, of people socialized by violent television stories imply for how teachers run their classrooms (organizational level)? And what do changes in the operation of our educational system, theoretically linked to alterations in school discipline and authority, mean for us as a society and as a people (macroscopic level)?

Viewing the major distinction in communication theory as between mass communication and interpersonal communication, Pingree, Wiemann, and Hawkins (1988, p. 11) suggested a communication science based on two distinct stages in communication processes: the first, *antecedents of communication*, would involve the study of "situations, personality traits, orientations, abilities, and so on that lead to communication behaviors," resulting in theories "about selection and control mechanisms, and the norms and schemas that bring them into play." The second stage, *consequences of communication*, would involve the study of the results or outcomes of communication and result in theories about the "necessary characteristics of communication, mechanisms of effect, and strength of effects." They believed that this communication science would render the mass versus interpersonal dichotomy obsolete (how, for example, can we understand the effects of televised violence without examining its effects between two or more people?). Thus, it would be obvious to communication scientists that although this antecedent-consequence division is one of convenience and somewhat artificial, it forces them to continuously integrate the two into better explanations and understandings.

An Example of Communication Science

It is still early, but communication science appears to be having the unifying impact on communication (and by extension, mass communication) theory desired by its proponents. This effort to revitalize empirical research was initially viewed by some critics as nothing more than an attempt to re-label and restore the limited effects paradigm. This criticism has faded. Proponents see it as an important effort to integrate existing scholarship, retain and even advance scientific standards, prioritize development of new empirical research methods, and ultimately broaden the scope of empirical research.

Jennings Bryant and Richard Street offer an example of communication science that is consciously imbedded in this approach (1988). They made an effort to unify, under the antecedents-of-communication umbrella, the discipline's understanding of the *active communicator* because both mass and interpersonal communication researchers and theorists have examined the idea of active versus passive communicators. Bryant and Street wrote,

> In the mass and interpersonal communication literatures alike, we read statement after statement claiming that today's message receivers have abundant message options and actively select from and act on these messages in such a

Instant Access	**Communication Science**	

Strengths

1 Unifies much disparate behavioral science-based theory and research

2 Integrates interpersonal and mass communication notions

3 Provides explanations at micro and macro levels

4 Offers testable generalizations

5 Respects abilities of audience members

Weaknesses

1 Excludes cultural, critical, and other non-empirically based research and theory

2 Might not be able to effectively integrate disparate theories

3 Tends to focus on micro-level and provide very limited explanations

4 Could provoke controversies with efforts to integrate theories

> way as to construct subjective meanings from the manifold symbols available to them . . . (T)he active communicator's choice-making and meaning construction are purposeful, strategic, and goal-directed. (1988, p. 162)

They argued, however, that despite the existence of a now-common view of an active communicator, mass and interpersonal communication scholars drew little from each other. This situation developed because of differences in their theoretical focus (receiver-oriented in mass communication, source-oriented in interpersonal communication), their different views of the communication process itself (mass communication seeing it as more directional, interpersonal as more interactive), and the outcomes or effects of communication (mass communication accepting receivers' behavior as more changeable, interpersonal communication judging it more stable).

Bryant and Street's implicit message is clear. The limited effects model that for so long dominated mass communication theory might have been less influential had mass communication theorists ignored these distinctions and paid more attention to what they had in common with interpersonal communication scholars: a shared interest in the mechanisms underlying individuals' choices of and exposure to specific messages and a mutual concern for explaining the nature of message perception and how messages are processed. Bryant and Street concluded,

> Today many of our leading communication scholars seem to recognize that most, but not all, human communicative behavior is purposeful and strategic,

and their newer hierarchical models are being equipped with branching arteries designed to accommodate the realities of automatic as well as controlled behavior. Such models would appear to give us the potential to construct theories of communicative behavior as complex and elegant as communication itself. All we need to do is to avoid another wrong turn at this critical junction. (1988, p. 185)

Although Bryant and Street summarized an impressive array of studies spanning mass and interpersonal research, they stopped short of incorporating cultural analysis or critical cultural studies, which would have meant expanding communication science beyond the boundaries of testable theory based on lawful generalizations. As we pointed out in Chapter 10, cultural research has devoted increasing attention to "audience activity." Cultural researchers recognize that individuals should not be regarded as social robots doomed to act out cultural scripts or elite ideologies. Instead, people should be understood as relatively autonomous, active seekers of meaning, capable of creating and shaping their experiences using cultural artifacts and practices. When artifacts and practices are too narrowly constrained, as in romance novels, people have the ability to reject simplistic interpretations and to engage in oppositional decoding that transcends the limitations of existing artifacts and practices. This is especially likely if people band together to form groups in which members help one another resist the "dominant reading" inherent in a text and develop an alternate reading.

Social Semiotics Theory

At the same time that communication science was being developed, critical and cultural studies researchers faced problems partly caused by their success. By the mid-1980s, strong cultural studies Ph.D. programs had been established at several universities. Graduate students from these programs were hired at other universities. The scholarship of these researchers stimulated work by many others who lacked training in cultural studies theory or research methods. In addition to mass communication, scholars in such diverse fields as literature, speech communication, sociology, and political science were attracted to cultural studies. The result was a meteoric rise in the amount of scholarship that was labeled cultural studies, but much of it lacked grounding in the theories and scholarly traditions central to this perspective's development in Europe. Purely descriptive research on popular culture was confused with true theory-based cultural scholarship.

Questions arose among critical and cultural studies scholars concerning the value of some of the research that was categorized as "cultural studies." These discussions were intensified by old debates between those who favored macroscopic, political economy approaches and those who preferred research grounded in ethnographic studies of audiences or the analysis of texts (Chapter 11). Scholars from these schools harshly criticized each others' work. Political economists blamed cultural studies researchers for unleashing a flood of marginal scholarship that served little purpose beyond providing engaging (and marketable) discussions of how people experience popular media content (Garnham, 1995).

Despite the attacks and counterattacks, there have been periodic calls to reconcile differences between the two schools of cultural scholarship and focus on their common concerns (Kellner, 1997; Meehan, Mosco, & Wasco, 1994; Murdock, 1989b). There are recent signs that this might be happening in the form of what Karl Jensen (1995) calls a social semiotics theory of mass communication. If successful, this theory could support critical cultural scholarship in much the same way that communication science has helped create consensus among empirical media researchers. Even if Jensen's social semiotics is unsuccessful, efforts to integrate the two dominant traditions of cultural scholarship will continue despite the fears of political economists that integration will imperil the political agenda of critical scholarship.

Jensen's social semiotics theory is intriguing for another reason. He wants to integrate communication science with critical and cultural studies theories. Jensen frequently cites communication science scholarship and has no problem finding a place for this research within the perspective he develops. He argues that communication science and cultural studies share a common focus on audience activity as well as a common desire to understand how audience members make sense of media messages. He argues that there is value to both quantitative and qualitative research traditions and that both yield useful insights.

In developing his theory, Jensen seeks a middle ground between older deterministic theories (that is, mass society theory) and naive assertions that audiences are completely free to interpret media content however they choose. His perspective owes much to James Carey's ritual definition of communication (Chapter 9). This debt is apparent in the way Jensen depicts the role of media in daily life:

> Increasingly, mass media serve to structure a day in the life of Western, urbanized societies, as they represent institutions in the political, economic, and cultural spheres of society as continuous points of reference for everyday routines. Thus, listening to news on a (clock) radio when waking up is a way of linking up with the temporal structure of, and the latest events in, community and nation. Next, a newspaper read over breakfast is, among other things, a guide to planning leisure activities later in the day. As one goes to work, a Walkman or a car radio may create a customized media environment which fills the gap between two well-defined contexts of home and work. In different work settings, media occur as continuous mood-setters canceling, in part, the reality of labor (music in offices or shops), as constitutive elements of an institution (economic news in the financial sector), or as cultural resources for a specific purpose (funnies during a lunch break, radio traffic reports for the

journey home). Shopping malls, department stores, and supermarkets, visited on the way home, offer a carefully structured sequence of experiences of merchandise, music, advertising, announcements, and more merchandise to complement and orient the sequence of purchases. The electronic household, cinemas, arcades, and entertainment centers offer occasions to reconsider and transcend some of the previous routines. In each case, mass media contribute to the process of semiosis which sustains the everyday of individuals and reproduces the institutions of the social collective. (1995, pp. 68–69)

SEMIOSIS *The process of interpreting and using signs*

SEMIOTICS *Sign systems*

SITUATED ACTIVITY *In social semiotics theory, activities that occur in specific social environments that shape and are shaped by our interpretation of signs*

A central argument in Jensen's theory is that much of everyday life is devoted to **semiosis**—the process of interpreting and using signs. Our ability to do this is based on our knowledge of **semiotics** (sign systems) that we have gained from past interpersonal and mass communication. Whenever we interpret sign systems during the course of daily life, this is a **situated activity**—it occurs in specific social environments, and these environments help *to shape and are shaped by* our interpretation of signs. This mutual shaping is *reflexive.* Jensen attributes this perspective on semiosis to American philosopher Charles Pierce who articulated a reflexive view of the relationship between sign systems and human communities. For example, the existence of sets of words defined in various ways allows us to label and make sense of action. The existence of these sign systems encourages certain actions and discourages others. If situations are sufficiently ambiguous, we might need to create new signs or apply existing signs in creative ways to interpret what is going on. Once these signs are created, however, they become the structure that determines future action. These notions are similar to and very consistent with symbolic interaction, social construction of reality, and frame analysis theories discussed in Chapter 10.

In addition to an active audience focus, Jensen shares the communication science desire to develop a perspective of mass communication that is comprehensive and covers all levels of analysis from individual to societal. He wrote,

Furthermore, I take as an initial premise, at the *theoretical* level of analysis, that societies come before media as generators of meaning. Meaning flows from existing social institutions and everyday contexts, via media professionals and audiences, to the mass media, not vice versa. For most people, most of the time, mass communication is hardly the factor determining their personal or social orientation and action. Meaning is ascribed to the discourses and practices of mass communication with reference to the social contexts which they represent and address. In sum, the center of mass communication, and of mass communication research, lies outside the mass media as such—within the discourses, practices, and institutions *in whose reproduction the media participate.* (1995, pp. 61–62)

In this quote, Jensen articulates a perspective of the relative power of media that comes close to a limited effects perspective and that is quite compatible with

Instant Access

Social Semiotics Theory

Strengths	Weaknesses
1 Differentiates between descriptive popular culture research and theory-based work	1 Is nonempirical (but parts could be empirically tested)
2 Provides explanations at micro and macro levels	2 Produces untestable generalizations
3 Can include empirically based communication science	3 Might be too optimistic in its reach
4 Unites various cultural, critical, and political economy theories	
5 Offers realistic assessment of audience's vulnerabilities and powers	

PRAGMATIST THEORY
Communication theory examining who participates in transforming communication into action, in which sectors and institutions of society, with what basis in everyday life, by what form of consensus concerning criteria and procedures, and with what consequences for the structure of society

theories popular among communication science advocates. Meaning is generated within human communities and then flows through media. Media participate in reproducing social practices and institutions, but they don't determine or control these practices or institutions. To properly understand the role and power of mass media, researchers need to understand how media *facilitate and bias the "reproduction" of discourses, practices, and institutions.* Several theories at home in communication science are consistent with this perspective. For example, agenda-setting theory argues that media don't have the power to tell people what to think (that is, determine their personal or social orientation and action), but media do have the power to constrain thought—to limit it to the agenda of issues that are routinely featured in media content.

Just what does Jensen's perspective add to existing theories of mass communication? He summarizes the central questions about media that arise from earlier social behavioral and normative theories of communication. These questions will sound familiar because we have considered many of them in earlier chapters of this book. Jensen contrasts these questions with his approach, which he describes as a **pragmatist theory**, writing,

Whereas basic communications theories such as Lasswell (1948/1966) and Jakobson (1960/1981) address questions of who, says what, in which medium and code, to whom, in what context, and with what effects, the normative theories of communication ask who is permitted to communicate, about what, with whom, in which medium, to what extent, emphasizing rights rather than results. A pragmatist theory of communication would want to examine, in addition, who participates in transforming communication into action, in which sectors and institutions of society, with what basis in everyday life, by what form of consensus concerning criteria and procedures, and with what consequences for the structuration of society. In the perspective of "communication rights" these questions represent a *minimalist* conception of communication: the making of discursive and interpretive difference is an enabling condition of making a social difference, which may ensure that other social rights are enacted in practice. Communication is a semiotic means to a social end. (1995, p. 192)

Can a single theoretical perspective effectively address all of these questions? It will be interesting to see if Jensen's perspective can create consensus among critical and cultural researchers.

The Communications Revolution

Throughout this book, we have considered the sometimes-radical changes that have taken place in communication technology and the consequent alterations in the media industries. Although few people question the importance of these transformations, there are serious disputes about where today's advances will lead us. One of the most important challenges to media theory is how to conceptualize new communication media and conduct research that can assess the role of these media for society and for individuals. In addressing this challenge, media scholars don't get much help from the people who are leading this technological revolution or their critics. These folks have radically different visions of where technological change is taking us. Consider the following quotes:

From Microsoft founder Bill Gates:

The revolution in communications is just beginning. It will take place over several decades, and will be driven by new "applications"—new tools, often meeting currently unforeseen needs . . . one of the most remarkable aspects of this new communications technology is that it will eliminate distance. It won't matter if someone you're contacting is in the next room or on another continent, because this highly mediated network will be unconstrained by miles and kilometers.

A different metaphor [from the Information Superhighway] that I think comes closer to describing a lot of the activities that will take place is that of the ultimate market. Markets from trading floors to malls are fundamental to human society, and I believe this new one will eventually be the world's central department store. It will be where we social animals will sell, trade, invest, haggle, pick stuff up, argue, meet new people, and hang out. Think of the hustle and bustle of the New York Stock Exchange or a farmers' market or of a bookstore full of people looking for fascinating stories and information. All manner of human activity takes place, from billion-dollar deals to flirtations. The highway will enable capabilities that seem magical when they are described, but represent technology at work to make our lives easier and better. (1995, p.6)

From Liss Jeffrey, Senior Research Associate at the McLuhan Program in Culture and Technology at the University of Toronto:

Two-way interactive media present new opportunities. The ability of the user to actively request information on demand to meet knowledge needs departs from a conventional broadcast model. Training in the new literacies required for genuine access should form part of a comprehensive strategy for a new information society. Libraries, community centres, and educational institutions should be supported in their efforts to supply services to those who lack home equipment.

Systems designed for ease of use will facilitate access. The current transition shifts from a one-way limited choice broadcasting system, to a two way capacity, and the ability to design your own selection guide through the use of personal programming agents. The consumer can become an entrepreneur and producer, if system access is open and monopolies of knowledge are prevented. The audience is both citizen and consumer, and a public (library) model must be evolved to counterbalance a market (mall) model. The success of the Internet, and failure of bureaucrat- and telco-driven initiatives . . . indicates that the public wants to drive the system, not have it imposed. (1995, p. 6)

From Canadian artist Robert Adrian:

We could call our era the "Telephone Era" or the 20th century the "Telephone Century" without much exaggeration. The telephone was, and still is, the only generally available, unprogrammed, participatory, personal and interactive communications medium—aside from face-to-face contact. Programmed broadcasting media like radio and television are universally available via satellite, microwave, or cable networks but they are one-way systems in which a commodity—information, entertainment, services—is distributed to a consuming, or potentially consuming, public. Feedback from these systems is in the form of the "body count" of viewers/listeners or in the analyses of sales figures for the advertised products. With the telephone, on the other hand, it is the service itself which is the commodity and the user supplies his or her own content: users communicate in a two-way exchange between equal partners. In this sense the telephone network is a public space, a meeting place open to all who have telephone access.

In this age of property-fetishism, the odd thing about "telephone space" is that nobody owns it—not the telephone companies, because they only provide the service, not governments, which merely meddle, snoop and regulate, nor the users, who simply take it for granted—like rain or electricity. And here lies the problem: Public utilities or spaces are not amenable to policies of profit maximization. In a low-cost/low-quality two-way communications system like the telephone, value-added services are extremely limited and growth, in a saturated market like North America or Western Europe, has become sluggish. Most telephone users just want to talk to each other and send a few faxes back and forth. The cake is too small and, since de-regulation, the cake-eaters too many. The answer appears to be: increase bandwidth! Increased bandwidth allows telephone space to be appropriated for commercial propaganda; occupied by infotainment commodities; turned into a shopping mall. Increased bandwidth is not very interesting for those who simply want to talk to each other—and people who just want to talk to each other are even less interesting to the new telecom corporations whose profits will come mostly from the products and services they sell or rent online. What these corporations really want is interactive cable TV—with the interactivity restricted to online shopping, video games and pay-to-view movies—with the telephone thrown in as a give-away because it requires almost no space on the cable. The Infobahn in this definition is little more than a catalogue of products, services, information and entertainment that can be ordered or purchased and consumed online. Mr. Gore's Superhighway is really an electronic "Golden Mile," there to be cruised like any suburban shopping strip, for entertainment, sex, fun and consumables. (1995, online)

So, who's right? Should we welcome or fear the "ultimate market" predicted by Bill Gates? Do we need public policies to protect us from this marketplace? What about the "ultimate library?" Is that something we need? Even if we need it, are we willing to pay for it? Even if we had it, would we work to develop the information literacy skills needed to make effective use of it? And what about the "ultimate telephone?" What would we do with it that we aren't already doing with our current low-tech phones? What would you do with a videophone system that could simultaneously link you to 200 other people? Which is the right vision for us? Would the success of the "ultimate market" doom the "ultimate library" and the "ultimate telephone?" Are these visions mutually exclusive, or could they all be realized? If they were all realized, would it lead to a very disconnected society in which some of us form communities grouped around the library and others network via the telephone while still others seek thrills and sex in Bill Gates' marketplace?

Questions like these are at the heart of the very serious debates about the future that are beginning to take place around the world. But despite all the news media attention to the Internet and other forms of new media, these telecommunications policy discussions go on in relative obscurity. If these debates are to be resolved in useful ways, many more of us will need to participate in them. Media theory and research will need to be developed and used to address these issues.

If you look carefully at the questions surrounding the emerging communication technologies, they are not so different from those historically raised whenever a new communication technology has appeared. Is the current revolution different? Some futurists argue that it is indeed. They believe this revolution is so radical that the only comparable change is nothing less than the invention of the printing press. But, are they right? Or should we trust Bill Gates who seems to think this technology is a simple (but nevertheless magical) extension of the status quo? Where do you want to spend your future—at the shopping mall, the library, or on the telephone?

The End of Mass Communication

In 1999, a few days before his untimely death, Steve Chaffee lectured on the subject of "the end of mass communication." That talk became the basis of an article cowritten with Miriam Metzger (2001). In it, the authors explore this topic at length. Their essential argument is that new media are bringing an end to mass communication and fundamentally altering how media will be structured, used, and conceptualized in the 21st century. Here are some of their observations concerning the impact of these changes on research:

> One of the assumptions of empirical studies of media content has been that the media are limited (in number), identifiable, and therefore, knowable through quantitative research. This is changing . . . (T)he amount of material available from the new media is vast, which makes studies of media content more difficult than ever before. In fact, Internet content is literally unbounded . . . To exacerbate this problem, each individual user's experience with content may differ in the new media environment, as interactive technologies allow for users to select a subset of the available content on, for example, an entire Web site.
>
> Studies of media audiences may suffer the same fate as audiences become harder to identify and monitor in the new media environment . . . Media effects studies, too, may be more difficult with audiences that are not as well assembled or accessible to researchers as they once were. In addition, mass communication law and policy will have to change dramatically.
>
> Mass communication is typified by television, whereas video games and Web sites may be considered the archetypes of media communication. User motivation also changes as communication moves from mass to media.
>
> In the mass communication environment, social control is maintained through laws (e.g., content regulation), professional ethics, and public education. In the new media environment, technical devices and monitoring are used to keep people in line. (pp. 371–373)

Chaffee and Metzger also discuss the impact of new media on theory. They point out that some theories like agenda setting and cultivation are based on the assumption that audiences use a finite number of media regularly and routinely for news and entertainment. Such theories will become harder to apply and may need to be fundamentally revised. Critical theory and cultural studies may need less alteration. With the emergence of dominant Internet content providers like

AOL-Time Warner, old concerns about media concentration have continued relevance in the new media environment. Concerns about access to media will remain important as we confront the "digital divide" between those with easy access to new media and those without access.

Globalization and Media

Beginning in 1945, the United States and the Soviet Union effectively carved the world into two warring camps. The United States led the Western bloc of nations and the Soviets led the East. Their battleground in this Cold War was the Third World, a group of nonaligned nations whose allegiance was sought by both superpowers. The Russians and the Americans poured millions of rubles and dollars in economic and military aid into the Third World in an often-desperate effort to prop up sympathetic foreign regimes and win over the hearts and minds of average citizens. A bipolar world order was established that persisted until the Cold War ended in the late 1980s with the dissolution of the Soviet Union and the fall of the Berlin Wall.

Since the end of the Cold War, a new world order has begun to emerge. It is based on international capitalism and the unrestricted cross-border flow of capital and information. This flow is essential to the operation of multinational companies, but it also permits development of many other multinational organizations. Unlike the previous world order, the new order is being imposed through a quiet revolution that is widely referred to as **globalization.** Globalization is proceeding very rapidly in certain areas. For example, a global framework for business is being created by many different multinational organizations such as the World Bank and the International Monetary Union. In most cases, globalization involves the spread of Western social institutions into all the regions previously dominated by the East. In rare cases, Eastern institutions are expanding into the West.

GLOBALIZATION
The establishment of social organizations that span geographic, political, and cultural boundaries

Many different types of multinational social organizations are developing and exerting influence. Three of the most important types of organizations are multinational governmental organizations, multinational corporations, and worldwide nongovernmental organizations (NGOs). In general, multinational governmental organizations, from the United Nations to various regional alliances, seek to strengthen and stabilize international relations so that other multinational organizations can operate freely. Multinational corporations, from McDonalds to Siemans, work to earn profits for shareholders by producing and distributing commodities. Increasingly, large companies regard globalization as essential to their efficient operation and long-term survival. The recent merger of Chrysler with Mercedes-Benz and those of several large oil companies illustrate this trend. Corporations that operate in several nations are thought to have many competitive advantages over those that operate only locally. Among other things, multinationals can produce goods wherever it is cheapest to do so and market them wherever the profit margin is highest. This is especially important when information commodities are being produced and distributed because these can be made anywhere and instantly distributed everywhere. Finally, NGOs, from the Red Cross to Greenpeace, seek to provide a broad range of human services that restore, sustain, or improve the quality of life. By spanning international boundaries, NGOs move resources and skills to places where they are most needed.

All these multinational organizations depend heavily on communications technology. As new technologies are introduced, the power of these organizations is likely to grow. Today, multinational corporations can continuously monitor all aspects of their operations in all parts of the world. Financial data flow freely across national boundaries and into computers in regional and international headquarters. At the same time, however, multinational governmental organizations and NGOs monitor the activity of these corporations. For example, if corporations exploit workers in Third World nations, their activities can be publicized internationally with important consequences for their businesses.

Some of the most prominent multinational corporations specialize in communications commodities that they distribute to audiences around the world. Ted Turner (CNN), Rupert Murdoch (FOX), and Michael Eisner (Disney) have led the way in developing multinational communications corporations (Smith, 1991). Their companies are experimenting with many new strategies for producing and distributing cultural materials. The Cable News Network gathers news from bureaus and independent reporters around the world, packages it in Atlanta for regional audiences, and then distributes these content packages to these regions. Currently, many multinational communications companies are American, and they produce much of their content in the United States. However, we can expect to see more and more production done in places where it can be done cheaply. American media might eventually have a significant amount of foreign-produced content that is brought to us by U.S.-based multinational corporations.

Globalization Problems

Although globalization has many benefits, it is also widely criticized. Small nations argue that their power is challenged and undermined by multinational corporations or by foreign media content that promotes alien norms and values. The airwaves of many small nations are flooded with U.S.-produced content because it is sold to broadcasters at prices far below what it would cost to produce locally. Multinational corporations often drive hard bargains with small nations, threatening to move their operations elsewhere if laws are passed that restrict their freedom or increase their operating costs. Local cultures everywhere are said to be under siege by mass culture produced in Hollywood. The evidence for this is mixed at best. In *Jihad vs. Mc-World*, Benjamin R. Barber (1995) argues that globalization of business has actually fueled the rise of traditional ethnic and cultural social movements. Samuel Huntington (1996) echoes these views in *The Clash of Civilizations*. Both Barber and Huntington argue that efforts to establish a favorable climate for global business have ignited a backlash from traditional cultures. For example, fundamentalist Islamic groups are gaining power in many Middle Eastern nations by arousing local resentment against global organizations. This movement ultimately led to the September 11th attacks on the World Trade Center and Pentagon. At the same time, long-suppressed ethnic minorities and indigenous peoples are demanding the right to practice their traditional cultures from Scotland and Wales to the Balkans, Africa, and India.

Other critics of globalization trends wonder where individuals will find an identity in a world that seems to be simultaneously imploding and exploding (Morley & Robins, 1995) and where national boundaries are increasingly irrelevant. During the past century, mass media played an important role in creating and reinforcing national identities. But if new media are everywhere and simultaneously promoting many different cultural and social identities, how will people choose among them? This question is likely to be less important for Americans but will be central for people in smaller nation states that are being absorbed into larger international communities.

Role of Media in Globalization

Mass media and new media are essential to both globalization and the social movements that react against it. Multinational corporations and nongovernmental organizations rely on many different media to carry out their day-to-day operations. Local or regional groups that resist or subvert global organizations also turn to media as an essential tool. One of the first places in the world to demonstrate this was Iran in the late 1970s. The Shah "globalized" Iran by allowing Western nations to freely set up branches of their companies and distribute mass media content. But the Ayatollah Khomeini led a successful revolt against the Shah, partly by distributing audiocassette recordings of the Ayatollah's speeches. Big Media met Small Media, and in this case, small media proved more powerful.

Often the outcome of such confrontations is mixed. One of the more visible multinational media corporations is Music Television (MTV). This corporation is so conscious of its role that it coined the phrase "think global, act local." MTV argues that we all need to be globally aware but remember to take action locally.

Presumably this is what MTV is doing as it sets up a global music production and distribution system. In many nations and regions, MTV has sparked the creation of competing companies that are more successful than MTV in "thinking local." These companies challenge MTV by featuring local artists and regional ethnic music. The influence of MTV can still be found because these local artists often blend western-style music with local music to create songs that have strong appeal to younger audiences. India currently provides some of the best examples of this phenomenon. In the future, we are likely to see many similar examples. Is local culture being globalized or is global culture being localized?

Globalization is clearly a much more complex phenomenon than was the effort to spread capitalist and communist ideologies during the Cold War. Global capitalists are primarily interested in producing and distributing commodities so they can earn profits. Globalized businesses generally don't work to convert locals to their beliefs. They are satisfied if they are allowed to conduct their business operations without interference. Communications media allow these worldwide companies to move information and capital anywhere around the globe at the touch of a button. Big media corporations like those run by Murdoch are happy if their movies sell well and their news and entertainment commodities earn profits. Local resistance to the products is tolerated. In some cases, local controversies can actually increase sales for foreign content.

Mass media and new media can be used by NGOs to promote local cultures. Social movements can use videocassettes and the Internet to organize and mobilize their members. In many parts of the world, national governments have relinquished their control of broadcasting. Radio and television stations that reflect local cultures and ethnic groups are flourishing alongside stations that carry foreign programming. In nations like India or those that made up the former Soviet Union, cultural diversity at the local level poses serious problems for national governments. Government-controlled media must compete with private media to try to reach local audiences.

Where will all of this lead? Can there be a creative tension between trends toward centralization of power in the hands of international organizations and trends toward localized cultural identities? Will we disintegrate into an endless array of local cultures or be absorbed into a homogeneous mass culture? Will international business and global media corporations dominate global culture? These questions will challenge media theorists for some time.

An optimistic answer to these questions can be found in a new theory of cultural hybidity. This theory argues that in many situations there can be useful new forms of culture generated out of the confrontation of global and local culture. The confrontation can produce a hybrid culture that has advantages over the cultures that gave rise to it. Researchers have begun to explore this theory in many locations around the world (Kraidy, 1999). The role of mass communication theory in this beneficial shift, according to Dutch media researcher Cees Hamelink (2001), will be to answer several vexing questions:

1 How can media provide global access to information?

2 How can global censorship be best minimized?

3 Can the media be something more than a global billboard?

4 What is the best forum for the governance of global communication?

5 How can global risk (terrorism, environmental degradation, warfare) be minimized?

DEVELOPMENT COM-
MUNICATION THEORY
*The strategic and
intentional use of
communication to
advance socially
beneficial goals.*

One emerging perspective, **development communication theory**, offers possible avenues toward answering these questions. Broadly defined as "a process of strategic intervention toward social change initiated by institutions and communities," it calls for "the intentional use of communication technologies and processes to advance socially beneficial goals, focusing on the use of communication for development." It should be no surprise to readers of this chapter that this new theory was developed in response to "emerging digital and convergent communication technologies" and "the global expansion of private investment in communications industries" (Wilkins & Mody, 2001, p. 385). Already, development communication theory has been applied to AIDS education, fertility practices, and improved conditions for women in developing nations.

Postmodern Criticism of Modernity

POSTMODERNISM
*Theory that modern
social orders are
not sustainable and
will inevitably
bring about their
own destruction*

MODERNITY *Forms
of social organiza-
tion and culture
that have become
dominant in the
West since the
fourteenth century*

Mass media can be regarded as one of the most powerful expressions of the "spirit" of our age. Although there have been many achievements of science during this and the last centuries, few touch our daily lives so frequently as media. Bill Gates is right when he uses "magical" to describe the new media of today, but in previous decades, the telegraph, the telephone, radio, television, and movies were equally magical. As we have seen, many troubling questions can be asked about these magical devices and their power to span time and space. Since the end of the Second World War, a group of European philosophers and social thinkers has expressed increasing skepticism concerning the value of science and the power to control the physical and social world. According to these **postmodern** theorists, there is a dark side to **modernity**, to the forms of social organization and culture that have become dominant in the West since the fourteenth century. Postmodern theorists believe that such things as large-scale, mechanized warfare, holocausts, and widespread destruction of the environment are as "modern" as the great achievements of science and technology. Mass communication theory cannot ignore this perspective.

The term *postmodern* derives from the central assumption of all these theorists: Modern social orders cannot be sustained, and they will inevitably bring about their own destruction. Postmodernists differ widely about how modernity will end. Some argue that radically different forms of culture and social order have already emerged and will increasingly dominate during the next few centuries. These theorists point to new social movements that are more concerned about personal identity and local culture than with larger questions of social injustice or old-fashioned forms of political power. These movements are said to have abandoned a modernist desire to impose order by creating social institutions that order society. Rather, contemporary social movements seek to build spaces in which communities can create and consume culture. Others believe that modern social orders will not permit these new movements to succeed without a struggle. These theorists foresee an apocalyptic end to modernity that will take the form of a nuclear war, a biological plague, or a worldwide economic collapse.

Some postmodernists argue that the worldview of average people isn't all that far removed from the worldview of premodern European peasants. These theorists believe that modernity—with its faith in progress and its desire to use science and technology to control the physical and social world—was an elitist rather than a popular vision. After all, scientists are rarely revered in popular culture but, instead, are frequently stereotyped as socially inept nerds or as mad scientists like Doctors Strangelove or Frankenstein. Even as scientific achievements mount, more people read books about religion, the occult, and the supernatural than read scientific texts. Can you name a television show about science that has achieved the popularity of the *X-Files?* Magic remains a popular fascination even as science seeks to debunk it. Thousands will pay to see David Copperfield perform his prestidigitation, but nobody buys tickets to see scientists perform experiments.

Some social theorists accept the postmodern argument that many forms of modernity are ending, but they don't expect a sudden end. These theorists regard the present era as a transition period in which important opportunities for constructive social change are appearing (Giddens, 1991). As older ways of doing things are rejected or fail, new possibilities for action are created. Anthony Giddens argues that modernity assigned great importance to individuality and reflective thought. In modern social orders, individuals are encouraged to reflect on their lives and define themselves as having an identity that is to some extent independent of the communities in which they live and the culture that they share with others. This gives individuals an ability to make interpretations and decisions that are to some extent independent of culture and community.

But the power to reflect carries with it the power to worry about who we are and what our place should be in the social world. It is possible for individuals and for groups to make wrong decisions and interpretations. We can worry too much. Our sense of individualism can become a source of isolation and estrangement. Unlike Giddens, who thinks reflective thought is beneficial, many postmodernists are pessimistic about the value of individualism and reflective thought. They argue that our ever-growing capacity to reflect on our own abilities and potentialities has been accompanied by trends toward self-deception, violence, and a willingness to tolerate injustice or prejudice. If we have trouble defining ourselves and understanding our place in an ambiguous social world, we might blame others and join hate groups as a way of dealing with our anxieties.

Avoiding the Dreams of Modernity

METANARRATIVES *In postmodernism, myths that rationalize courses of action that would otherwise be interpreted as insane or incoherent*

One interesting argument advanced by postmodernists is that modernity fostered and was sustained by many myths or **metanarratives**. These stories allowed people to rationalize courses of action that would otherwise have been interpreted as insane or incoherent. Hitler's theory of a "master race" or Marxist notions about a "revolutionary proletariat led by a vanguard party" are only two of the many modern myths that have achieved historical prominence.

Mass media provide an important means of propagating modern metanarratives. One common theme in many of these mediated myths is the inevitability of progress. Every scientific finding, every technological innovation is regarded as one more step along the way toward a bright and shining future. With the use of scientific methods and technology, the physical world can be mastered and turned into an earthly paradise. Industrialization can produce untold material wealth for more and more people. Civilization and High Culture will continue to develop. Human beings will reach their true potential, unfettered by poverty, ignorance, and disease. If rationally controlled development can be maintained, it will lead inevitably to a world of peace and prosperity.

These are noble and ambitious goals, and they form an optimistic and comforting metanarrative. But they are dangerous when pursued without sufficient concern for long-term consequences for the environment or a sufficient understanding of human limitations. These powerful metanarratives marginalized criticism. They provided a pretext and legitimization for large-scale warfare, genocide, and many other atrocities.

After World War II, despite the threats posed and contradictions implied by the Cold War, dreams of modernity were sustained. The Cold War actually might have heightened commitment to these dreams and reduced awareness of their dangers. For example, in 1954, Lyman Bryson articulated a renewed vision of worldwide modernization led by communication media:

> The communications revolution, working in our present condition of welfare and freedom, has made it possible to move our general discontent to higher levels of aspiration and to escape the rigidities of peasant thinking. It can also become the tool by which we build a community of ideas of world scope. The schemes for world organization which now engage the efforts of so many generous men and women are plans for bringing all of the world's population within one system of communication . . . There are no mechanical difficulties that would keep us from speaking to practically all the inhabitants of the earth with one voice, if a wise enough voice could be found. It would not cost too much. There is, of course, no world language, and that may check the growth of a world public opinion and a world spirit for a long time . . . English, the speech of business, is spreading over the world as business spreads. The language problem may be solved.
>
> The real problem remains, what voices are wise enough to speak to all men? The community of ideas in our own country is in the making. Can it be the preparation and the example for a community of ideas for the world? (pp. 89–90)

These are brave ideas indeed, uttered at a time when the rapid expansion of Communist influence around the world appeared to make it more likely that the "one system of communication" would be controlled from Moscow rather than Washington. To men like Bryson, the United States was obligated to nurture the "one voice" that might lead the world forward. If that voice arose from the Soviet Bloc, progress (as we knew it) would cease. Thus, it was important that we develop communication technology and encourage the spread of English as a world language. Eventually, our voice would link the world in a "community of ideas." Today, Bryson's words seem naive, elitist, and more than a little chauvinistic, a dream of modernity as problematic in its own way as those being formulated in Moscow, Beijing, or Hanoi.

Postmodern theory poses important questions for media theorists. It asks how we can be sure that our theories are not just more "dreams of modernity"—unwitting pretexts for more death and destruction. If we believe that new media technology can be so useful, how can we be certain that its power won't be turned against ourselves? Bill Gates foresees the ultimate market—is this a liberating vision or something that locks us into social practices that are limiting rather than enriching?

Postmodern theorists provide a second challenge for media theorists. Postmodernism argues that mass media are at the center of the rapid disintegration of modernism. To the extent that we have become dependent on media for stimuli that help us structure and make sense of everyday experience, we are open to media influence. Postmodernists argue that a vicious cycle has been established in which media distribute more and more content that undermines our capacity

Instant Access	*Postmodernism*	
Strengths		**Weaknesses**
1 Challenges widely held modernist beliefs		1 Doesn't recognize strengths of modern social institutions
2 Raises critical questions about the impact of technology on society		2 Challenges many core beliefs of both technophiles and media researchers (might have difficulty attracting scholarly attention)
3 Permits both optimistic and pessimistic assessments of technology and audiences		3 Offers no constructive alternative to modernity

to maintain a unified experience of reality. As this capacity is undermined, our use of media changes in ways that encourage media to provide content that is even more destabilizing. For example, television advertising has become increasingly "postmodern" as advertisers try to draw our attention to individual ads by flooding the screen with diverse sounds and visual images. Ads often have no narrative, just juxtaposed sequences of images and sounds that form a fascinating collage. These ads might be successful in attracting attention and increasing sales for individual products, but if every ad becomes a cryptic collage, collage ads might be even less effective than the ads they displaced.

Challenges from Cognitive Psychology and Biological Science

It is possible to argue that we stand on the threshold of a revolution in our understanding of ourselves as biological organisms (Anderson, 1990; Gardner, 1985). As a result, mass communication theory will have to accommodate these new understandings.

We now possess the scientific methods to probe the depths of human physiology, including the most complex organ—the brain. Within the next generation, we can expect to catalog the human genome and begin to use this knowledge to "re-engineer" the human body. Researchers already manipulate the genes of fetuses before birth in an effort to avoid genetic defects. Although postmodernists warn that this knowledge will lead to even more social instability, these scientific advances appear unstoppable.

As biologists work to understand the operation of the human body, cognitive psychologists are probing the operation of the human mind. We touched on their research in Chapter 10 in our discussion of information processing theory. The goal of much of this research is to understand how the mind can accomplish the many tasks it is able to achieve, and researchers often approach the brain as a sort of biological computer. Compared with electronic computers, the mind performs much more complex tasks and requires far less space or energy. But researchers are also finding that the brain has some important limitations.

Humans appear to have limited ability to take in and process new sensory information about changes going on around them (Lang, Newhagen, & Reeves, 1996). To make up for these limitations, we have developed many strategies for determining what information to pay attention to and what to ignore. Most of these strategies are "hard-wired" into lower level cognitive processes. Our conscious mind does not and cannot influence these processes (Shiffrin & Schneider, 1977). These lower-level processes deal with incoming information in ways that appear to improve our chances of survival in a hostile physical environment. This is why we are so sensitive to sudden changes in external stimuli (for example, sudden movements against a static background, shifts in the intensity of sound), but why we usually fail to notice subtle changes that go on at the same time that these more powerful changes are taking place. And these extreme changes also tend to release a flood of adrenaline so that we are ready to fight or run away from danger. But today, this "fight or flight response" is more likely to occur in response to an action adventure or horror film than in response to a real threat (Lang, Newhagen, & Reeves, 1996). The movie producer is exploiting the way lower-level cognitive processes deal with new information and taking advantage of the fact that most people enjoy an "adrenaline high."

MASTER COGNITIVE PROCESS *Operation of the conscious mind that takes, organizes, and uses information conveyed to it from a vast number of lower level processes (sometimes called* meta cognitive process)

Although lower-level cognitive processes are important, consciousness itself is truly fascinating. The conscious mind can be viewed as a **master** or **meta cognitive process** that somehow manages to take, organize, and then use information conveyed to it from a vast number of low-level processes. For example, lower-level processes create a low-quality representation of the external environment in our brains, but consciousness scans this representation and determines how to make sense of it so that learning takes place (Schank & Abelson, 1977).

Sociobiologists and an increasing number of cognitive psychologists argue that consciousness emerged as our early human ancestors struggled for survival in a hostile and ever changing physical environment. Although most animal species survive through adaptation of their physical bodies, human beings developed a very different strategy. They survived by evolving (a) cognitive processes (lower-level processes and then consciousness) and (b) structured social practices (culture). The powerful combination of cognition and culture enabled humans to deal with threats from predators, disease, and weather. Thus, specific cognitive processes and specific social practices might be mutually interdependent, having evolved together over time. As cognitive processes evolved, individuals who possessed them had an improved ability to engage in specific social practices. These individuals had a better chance of personal survival, and the communities in which they lived were more likely to survive.

But this scenario doesn't necessarily account for consciousness. In fact, it could be argued that consciousness is actually a threat to survival in environments that require fast action in response to life or death threats. For example, a stalking predator might not allow us time to think about how to deal with it. In the time it takes us to think of a response, we will be killed. Consciousness constantly monitors and gathers information from lower level cognitive processes. We must then process this information, make sense of it, and then determine a course of action. This simply takes too long in many situations. Or consider a more likely example. Great athletes don't succeed by having an intellect that allows them to carefully consider and then consciously guide the bodily movements necessary to hit a golf ball or catch a rolling and breaking wave. Consciousness might play a role in practicing these actions, but when the game is on the line, successful athletes don't spend much time thinking about what they are doing. In fact, we talk about individuals being "natural athletes" and "in the zone"—a recognition that their ability to control their bodies seems more "hard-wired" than learned.

It can be argued that the most important thing that consciousness does for us is that it enables us to live in communities that are bound together by a shared culture. This might not seem important, or it might seem like simple common sense. Our ability to understand and relate to other people is so much a part of daily life that we take it for granted and assume it must be easy to accomplish. It is as natural as breathing. But like breathing, this process is quite complex. Cognitive psychologists estimate we devote most of our conscious thought to trying to understand other people and plan our actions in relation to them. If you doubt the importance of this, consider what happens to autistic people whose conscious mind doesn't work properly. Persons with severe forms of autism are "mind blind"—that is, they can't conceive of the existence of other minds like their own. They live in a world where the only consciousness is their own. The consequences are devastating. Loving parents struggle to develop a relationship with autistic children and can't. Autistic people often have enormous talents for music or mathematics, but those talents are usually wasted because autists can't develop and use them within a community. Because they can't plan their actions to coordinate with others, it is extremely difficult for others to relate to them. Most are ostracized from society and live in a private world where others can't and won't intrude (Baron-Cohen, 1995).

The findings from research in biology and psychology will have many important implications for media scholars—especially with the emergence of so many different forms of new media. This is because, as McLuhan asserted, media are extensions of our senses (Chapter 11). New media allow us—possibly even compel us—to extend our senses in new ways. Nevertheless, as McLuhan also observed, when we extend one sense, we might create an imbalance. This could happen because we prioritize certain lower-level processes and not others. McLuhan offered interesting speculation about the consequences of these imbalances. For example, he argued that the strong association highly literate people have between linear thought and rationality stems from the fact that written words are necessarily written down in a linear fashion. We come to associate sequentially with rationality. But in the hyperlinked world of the Internet, we can surf from one site to the next, backward and forward, up and down. We make connections and meanings in a very nonlinear network. Will this lead us to develop a nonlinear form of rationality?

As individuals we differ greatly in how we experience the way different media extend our senses. Consider your own relationship to media. Are you drawn to certain media that allow you to develop and sustain certain experiences? People who achieve high levels of traditional literacy find reading books to be one of the most enjoyable activities in their lives. Often as children, they are drawn to reading with the same compulsion that other children are drawn to visual images on a television or movie screen or to the auditory stimulation of music. But many, if not most, people don't share this attraction to reading. It is estimated that more than half the American population is functionally illiterate—they can't read well enough to use print media for even simple tasks. At best, these people can read warning signs posted on doors or along highways. Their experience of reading is vastly different from that of persons with high levels of literacy (Purcell-Gates, 1997).

Throughout much of the modern era, there has been a widely held assumption that most, if not all human beings are capable of achieving the same high levels of traditional literacy. This assumption underlies the American system of public education and our notions about democratic government. If everyone becomes equally literate and can effectively use print media, then everyone can participate as equals in self-government. Now cognitive psychologists are challenging this assumption. Research is showing that the lower-level cognitive processes that support traditional literacy vary greatly from one person to another. Each of us has unique combinations of these processes. Some of us have just the right combination so that literacy is attractive and easy. Others have the wrong combination. In still others, there are minor breakdowns in just one or two of these lower level processes, and these lead to learning disabilities that make reading a painful rather than a joyful experience.

If different media extend our senses in radically different ways, and we are entering an era in which many different forms of media are likely to develop, what are the possibilities and what are the likely problems? One optimistic possibility is that we each might be able to identify a set of media that are well matched to our cognitive strengths. If we have a learning disability that makes print media hard to use, but we are very good at processing visual images in certain ways, then we can locate media that fit these abilities and avoid print media. At an early age, children could have their cognitive skills tested, and their parents could be told which media will be harder or easier for them to use. But would this be either wise or practical? Can the same information be packaged and transmitted with equal effectiveness through various media? Or will children who aren't trained in traditional literacy be forever cut off from information that could enrich their lives?

The Media Literacy Movement

Implicitly or explicitly, communication scholars are responding to the twin realities of different media extending our senses in different ways and the development of many different forms of media. Communication scholars recognize that

- The audience is indeed active but not necessarily imperial (uses and gratifications).
- The audience's needs, opportunities, and choices are somehow constrained (critical cultural studies).
- Content can direct action (social cognitive theory; social semiotic theory).
- People must realistically assess how their interaction with media texts can determine the functions that interaction can serve for them in their environments (cultural theory).
- People have differing levels of cognitive processing ability (cognitive and biological sciences).

MEDIA LITERACY
The ability to access, analyze, evaluate, and communicate messages

As such, the best way to ensure functional (rather than dysfunctional) use of media is to increase individuals' media use skills. This is **media literacy.**

Anthropologists, sociologists, linguists, historians, communication scientists—virtually all disciplines that study how people and groups communicate to survive and prosper—have long understood that as humans moved from preliterate or oral culture to literate culture, they assumed greater control over their environments and lives. With writing came the ability to communicate across time and space. People no longer had to be in the presence of those with whom they wished to communicate (Eisenstein, 1979; Inglis, 1990; Innis, 1951).

The invention of the printing press in the mid-1400s infinitely expanded the importance and reach of the written word and power began to shift from those who were born into it to those who could make the best use of communication. If literacy—traditionally understood to mean the ability to read and write—increases people's control over their environments and lives, it logically follows that an expanded literacy—one necessitated by a world in which so much "reading" and "writing" occurs in the mass media—should do the same. As critical theorist Stuart Ewen wrote, "Historically, links between literacy and democracy are inseparable from the notion of an informed populace, conversant with the issues that touch upon their lives, enabled with tools that allow them to participate actively in public deliberation and social change. Nineteenth-century struggles for literacy and education were never limited to the ability to read. They were also about learning to write and thus about expanding the number and variety of voices heard in published interchanges and debates. Literacy was about crossing the lines that had historically separated men of ideas from ordinary people, about the social enfranchisement of those who had been excluded from the compensation of citizenship" (2000, p. 448). As such, Ewen argued elsewhere (1996, p. 413), "In a society where instrumental images are employed to petition our affections at every turn—often without a word—educational curricula must . . . encourage the development of tools for critically analyzing images. For democracy to prevail, image making as a communicative activity must be undertaken by ordinary citizens as well. The aesthetic realm—and the enigmatic ties linking aesthetic, social, economic, political, and ethical values—must be brought down to earth as a subject of study."

Alan Rubin (1998, p. 3) offered three definitions of media literacy: From the National Leadership Conference on Media Literacy—*the ability to access, analyze, evaluate, and communicate messages.* From media scholar Paul Messaris—*knowledge about how media function in society.* From mass communication researchers Justin Lewis and Sut Jhally—*understanding cultural, economic, political, and technological constraints on the creation, production, and transmission of messages.* Rubin added,

> All definitions emphasize specific knowledge, awareness, and rationality, that is, cognitive processing of information. Most focus on critical evaluations of messages, whereas some include the communication of messages. Media literacy, then, is about understanding the sources and technologies of communication, the codes that are used, the messages that are produced, and the selection, interpretation, and impact of those messages. (1998, p. 3)

Communication scholars William Christ and W. James Potter offered an additional overview of media literacy, writing,

> Most conceptualizations (of media literacy) include the following elements: Media are constructed and construct reality; media have commercial implications; media have ideological and political implications; form and content are related in each medium, each of which has a unique aesthetic, codes, and conventions; and receivers negotiate meaning in media. (1998, pp. 7–8)

A careful reader can easily find evidence in these two summations of all the audience- and culture-centered theories we've discussed in this book.

Two Views of Media Literacy

One of the first systematic efforts to place media literacy in audience- and culture-centered theory and to frame it as a skill that must and can be improved was provided by mass communication scholar Art Silverblatt. Silverblatt's core argument parallels the point we made earlier, "The traditional definition of *literacy* applies only to print: 'having a knowledge of letters; instructed; learned.' However, the principal channels of media now include print, photography, film, radio, and television. In light of the emergence of these other channels of mass communications, this definition of literacy must be expanded" (1995, pp. 1–2). As such, he identified five elements of media literacy (1995, pp. 2–3):

- An awareness of the impact of the media on the individual and society

- An understanding of the process of mass communication

- The development of strategies with which to analyze and discuss media messages

- An awareness of media content as a "text" that provides insight into our contemporary culture and ourselves

- The cultivation of an enhanced enjoyment, understanding, and appreciation of media content

Potter (1998) takes a slightly different approach, describing several foundational or bedrock ideas supporting media literacy:

1 *Media literacy is a continuum, not a category.* "Media literacy is not a categorical condition like being a high school graduate or being an American . . . Media literacy is best regarded as a continuum in which there are degrees . . . There is always room for improvement" (p. 6).

2 *Media literacy needs to be developed.* "As we reach higher levels of maturation intellectually, emotionally, and morally we are able to perceive more in media messages . . . Maturation raises our potential, but we must actively develop our skills and knowledge structures in order to deliver on that potential" (pp. 6–7).

3 *Media literacy is multidimensional.* Potter identifies four dimensions of media literacy. Each operates on a continuum. In other words, we interact with media messages in four ways and we do so with varying levels of awareness and skill. These dimensions are the following:

- The *cognitive domain* refers to mental processes and thinking

- The *emotional domain* is the dimension of feeling

- The *aesthetic domain* refers to the ability to enjoy, understand, and appreciate media content from an artistic point of view
- The *moral domain* refers to the ability to infer the values underlying the messages (p. 8)

4 *The purpose of media literacy is to give us more control over interpretations.* "All media messages are interpretations . . . A key to media literacy is not to engage in the impossible quest for truthful or objective messages. They don't exist" (p. 9).

Thirty-four states now mandate media literacy in their primary and secondary school curricula. *The Journal of Communication* devoted a special issue to the subject (Media Literacy Symposium, 1998). Scores of sites on the World Wide Web are expressly devoted to helping individuals improve their media literacy skills. And although many observers see the media literacy movement as the natural product of mass communication theory's long journey to its present state, others see it as even another factor that, if ever fully realized, will cause even more ferment because new theories will have to be developed to account for its impact on the audience/media relationship.

Summary

Two encouraging efforts are being made to reduce the level of ferment in mass communication theory. The first is communication science, a perspective that integrates all research approaches grounded in quantitative, empirical, behavioral research methods. In joining limited effects ideas, active audience theories, and research on interpersonal communication, communication science includes most forms of quantitative, empirical research and the theories it supports. Communication science does, however, exclude cultural, critical, and political economic theories.

Social semiotics theory, the integration of communication science and critical and cultural studies focusing on audience activity to understand how audience members make sense of media messages, is the second effort to bring some unity to thinking about mass communication. Social semiotics is a more inclusive theory, but many observers believe its acceptance of work rooted in nonempirical inquiry keeps it outside communication science. This theory is only one of several being proposed as a means of integrating critical and cultural theories.

As proponents of both theories work to integrate the disparate views within and between their perspectives, several forces promise to reshape mass communication theory even more. The first is the communications revolution. A flood of new communication technologies and their uses are changing the audience/media relationship in ways that we can only speculate about. The second is that globalization of the media requires that mass communication theory itself become more global and expansive. If mass communication knows no borders, neither should the theories that purport to explain it.

The third is the rise of postmodern thinking, with its calls for caution in our rush toward ever more attractive and powerful applications of communication technology. This rejection of modernism influences mass communication theory in two ways—by dampening the optimism of theorists' predictions and by suggesting a study of media's contribution to modernism's endurance because modernism's values are maintained in the culture's metanarratives.

The fourth force that will reshape contemporary mass communication theory is advances in our understanding of how people process sensory information and learn. Mass communication theorists must accommodate new knowledge of how individuals interact with, process, and use media content.

Future theories will need to address the full spectrum of mediated communication—from cell phones to the Internet. These theories must assess how mediation takes place, the social context and social implications of using various media, the cognitive processes and skills necessary to encode and decode various types of messages from one type of media as opposed to another, and how individuals can take more control of the media they use to send and receive messages.

The media literacy movement is designed to do just that—improve individuals' control over the media they use to send and receive messages. Media literacy is seen as a skill that can be improved and one that exists on a continuum—we are not equally media literate in all situations, all the time, and with all media.

Despite the challenges facing media theory, this is likely to be an exciting and productive era. It might be decades, if not centuries, before theorists ever again have the opportunity to witness and try to understand the rise of entirely new media systems. Media theorists have never had available to them the powerful conceptual tools we now possess. As you seek to address these challenges, remember the advice of Professor Waterhouse (Chapter 2): "Thinking is asking questions. Thinking well is asking good questions."

Exploring Mass Communication Theory

1   Media literacy is not only the province of mass communication scholars. More than 30 states require media literacy instruction as part of their elementary and secondary school curricula and dozens of public interest groups now focus their efforts on teaching media literacy. Go online and search *media literacy* to see some of the different approaches. Here are a few sites to get you started.

Alliance for a Media Literate America
http://www.amlainfo.org

Association for Media Literacy
http://www.aml.ca/

Center for Media Literacy
http://www.medialit.org

Media Education
http://www.mediaeducation.com

Media Education Foundation
http://www.igc.org/mef

Media Literacy
http://www.medialiteracy.com

Media Literacy Clearing House
http://www.med.sc.edu:1081/

Media Workshop
http://www.mediaworkshop.org

2   Postmodernism generates much contentious comment on the Web. Two sites, in particular, are indicative. The first, from Links2Go, provides a chat room as well as links to sites dealing with postmodernism. Here you can find an array of opinion and commentary. The Council for Human Secularism offers a specific take on the theory.

Links2Go
http://www.links2go.com/channel/Postmodernism

Council for Secular Humanism
http://www.secularhumanism.org/

3   Use **InfoTrac College Edition** to scan educational journals such as *Educational Leadership, Childhood Education,* and *Exceptional Children.* Identify articles that discuss children's differing cognitive strategies and teaching techniques that cater to these various ways of learning. Choose one or two that focus on media use to meet different learning needs, and discuss the match between the specific technology and individual way of learning.

4   The Internet and the World Wide Web are the heart of the communications revolution. Use **InfoTrac College Edition** to review the tables of contents of new technology-based publications such as *Information Technology and Libraries, Online, PC Magazine, PC Week,* and *PC/Computing. The Futurist* is worth checking as well. Identify articles that deal specifically with technology's impact on all forms of communication. If you can, find one that offers an optimistic assessment of technology's impact and one that is less so. Compare the arguments in both.

Critical Thinking Questions

1 Where would you place yourself along a media literacy continuum that runs from clueless to completely in control of interpretation? Defend your answer.

2 Are you a new communication technology optimist or a new technology pessimist? Do you think the rapid and sometimes amazing advances we are seeing in how we can interact with one another and our environments will produce a more humane culture or one that leaves us separated and isolated? Support your answer, using evidence from your current media use if you can.

3 Good or bad, societal and cultural change will inevitably follow advances in communication technology. But who should direct or shape that change? If "the market" is to provide that direction, will some groups be served more than others will? Will some groups benefit and some be disadvantaged more than others will? Identify the winners and losers in the communication revolution should the market rule.

4 Should government or some other technocracy (Chapter 5), presumably with the best interests of all in mind, regulate the new communication technologies? Defend your answer.

5 Maybe the market should direct the social and cultural change that follows advances in communication technology. Maybe the government should, but what of the public? Media literacy advocates believe that people—if they are sufficiently media literate—will do the best job. After all, their lives and their worlds will be affected. Do you think this view of people's willingness and ability to actively participate in the mass communication process is too optimistic? Defend your answer, using examples from your own media use if you can.

6 What do you think about the spread of Western popular culture around the world? What are the strengths and the limitations of the vision of the social world that are inherent in this culture? How willing are you to seek out and learn from social perspectives offered by movies and television programs coming from other countries? When was the last time you saw a foreign film or television program (other than one from Britain)? Do you find foreign films boring and if so why do you think you react to them that way?

7 For better or worse, the horrific events of September 11, 2001, put globalization right at the top of most people's agendas. At that time, did the anti-American sentiment that seemed to permeate much of the world's public opinion surprise you? What about now? Can you explain the antagonism toward the United States in terms of America's domination of globalization, as do many globalization critics? How do American media figure into the problem?

Significant People and Their Writing

Berger, Charles R., and Stephen H. Chaffee, eds., (1987). *Handbook of Communication Sciences.* Newbury Park, CA: Sage.

Bryant, James, and Richard L. Street (1988). "From Reactivity to Activity and Action: An Evolving Concept and *Weltanschauung* in Mass and Interpersonal Communication." In R. P. Hawkins, J. M. Wiemann, and S. Pingree, eds., *Advancing Communication Science: Merging Mass and Interpersonal Processes.* Newbury Park, CA: Sage.

Hawkins, Robert P., John M. Wiemann, and Susan Pingree, eds. (1988). *Advancing Communication Science: Merging Mass and Interpersonal Processes.* Newbury Park, CA: Sage.

Jensen, Karl Bruhn (1995). *The Social Semiotics of Mass Communication.* Thousand Oaks, CA: Sage.

Potter, W. James (1998). *Media Literacy.* Thousand Oaks, CA: Sage.

Silverblatt, Art. (1995). *Media Literacy: Keys to Interpreting Media Messages.* Westport, CT: Praeger.

References

Adorno, T., and M. Horkheimer (1972). *Dialectic of Enlightenment.* New York: Herder and Herder.

Adrian, R. (1995). "Infobahn Blues." *CTHEORY,* article 21 (http://www. ctheory.com/a-infobahn _blues.html).

Alasuutari, P. (1999). "Introduction: Three Phases of Reception Studies." In P. Alasuutari, ed., *Rethinking the Media Audience.*Thousand Oaks, CA: Sage.

Albiniak, P. (2000). "Violent Media, Violent Kids?" *Broadcasting & Cable,* July 31: 14.

Allen, R. L., and S. Hatchett (1986). "The Media and Social Reality Effects: Self and System Orientations of Blacks." *Communication Research,* 13: 97–123.

Allport, G. W. (1967). "Attitudes." In M. Fishbein, ed., *Readings in Attitude Theory and Measurement.* New York: John Wiley.

Allport, G. W., and L. J. Postman (1945). "The Basic Psychology of Rumor." *Transactions of the New York Academy of Sciences,* 8: 61–81.

Alterman, E. (1998). "The News from Quinn-Broderville." *The Nation,* 14 December, p. 10.

Altschull, J. H. (1990). *From Milton to McLuhan: The Ideas Behind American Journalism.* New York: Longman.

Anderson, D. R., and E. P. Lorch (1983). "Looking at Television: Action or Reaction?" In J. Bryant and D. R. Anderson, eds., *Children's Understanding of Television: Research on Attention and Comprehension.* New York: Academic.

Anderson, J. R. (1990). *Cognitive Psychology and Its Implications,* 3rd ed. New York: W. H. Freeman.

Andison, F. S. (1977). "TV Violence and Viewer Aggression: A Culmination of Study Results 1956–1976." *Public Opinion Quarterly,* 41: 314–331.

Arato, A., and E. Gebhardt, eds. (1978). *The Essential Frankfurt School Reader.* New York: Urizen.

Arnett, E. C. (1999). "Plugged-in Kids Worry Experts." *San José Mercury News,* November 18: 1A, cont. 14A.

Bagdikian, B. H. (1992). *The Media Monopoly,* 4th ed. Boston: Beacon.

Bailey, K. D. (1982). *Methods of Social Research.* New York: Free Press.

Baker, R. K., and S. J. Ball (1969). *Violence and the Media: A Staff Report to the National Commission on the Causes and Prevention of Violence, Volume 9A.* Washington: U.S. Government.

Ball-Rokeach, S. J. (2001). "The Politics of Studying Media Violence: Reflections 30 Years After the Violence Commission." *Mass Communication & Society,* 4: 3–18.

Bandura, A. (1994). "Social Cognitive Theory of Mass Communication." In J. Bryant and D. Zillman, eds., *Media Effects: Advances in Theory and Research.* Hillsdale, NJ: Erlbaum.

———. (1971). *Psychological Modeling: Conflicting Theories.* Chicago: Aldine Atherton.

———. (1965). "Influence of Models' Reinforcement Contingencies on the Acquisition of Imitative Responses." *Journal of Personality and Social Psychology,* 1: 589–595.

Bandura, A., D. Ross, and S. A. Ross (1963). "Imitation of Film-Mediated Aggressive Models." *Journal of Abnormal Social Psychology,* 66: 3–11.

Baran, S. J., and V. J. Blasko (1984). "Social Perceptions and the By-Products of Advertising." *Journal of Communication,* 34: 12–20.

Baran, S. J., and T. P. Meyer (1974). "Imitation and Identification: Two Compatible Approaches to Social Learning from the Electronic Media." *AV Communication Review,* 22: 167–179.

Barber, B. R. (1995). *Jihad vs. McWorld.* New York: Times.

Barnouw, E. (1966). *A History of Broadcasting in the United States: A Tower in Babel,* Vol. I. New York: Oxford University Press.

Baron-Cohen, S. (1995). *Mindblindness: An Essay on Autism and Theory of Mind.* Cambridge, MA: MIT Press.

Barrow, J. D. (1998). *Impossibility: The Limits of Science and the Science of Limits.* New York: Oxford University Press.

Bates, S. (2001). *Realigning Journalism with Democracy: The Hutchins Commission, Its Times, and Ours.* Online: http://www.annenberg.nwu.edu.

Bauer, R. A., and A. H. Bauer (1960). "America, Mass Society and Mass Media." *Journal of Social Issues,* 10: 3–66.

Becker, S. (1989). "Communication Studies: Visions of the Future." In B. Dervin, L. Grossberg, B. J. O'Keefe, and E. Wartella, eds., *Rethinking Communication: Volume 2, Paradigm Exemplars.* Newbury Park, CA: Sage.

Belkin, L. (2000). "The Making of an 8-Year-Old Woman." *New York Times Magazine,* December 24: 38–43.

Bennett, W. L. (1988). *News: The Politics of Illusion,* 2nd ed. New York: Longman.

Bennett, W. L., and M. Edelman (1985). "Toward a New Political Narrative." *Journal of Communication,* 35: 128–138.

Berelson, B. (1961). "The Great Debate on Cultural Democracy." In D. N. Barrett, ed., *Values in America.* Notre Dame, IN: University of Notre Dame Press.

———. (1959). "The State of Communication Research." *Public Opinion Quarterly,* 23: 1–6.

———. (1949). "What 'Missing the Newspaper' Means." In P. F. Lazarsfeld and F. N. Stanton, eds., *Communications Research, 1948–1949.* New York: Harper.

Berelson, B., P. F. Lazarsfeld, and W. N. McPhee (1954). *Voting: A Study of Opinion Formation in a Presidential Campaign.* Chicago: University of Chicago Press.

Berger, C. R., and S. H. Chaffee (1987a). "The Study of Communication as a Science." In C. R. Berger and S. H. Chaffee, eds., *Handbook of Communication Sciences.* Newbury Park, CA: Sage.

———., eds. (1987b). *Handbook of Communication Science.* Newbury Park, CA: Sage.

Berger, P. L., and T. Luckmann (1966). *The Social Construction of Reality: A Treatise in the Sociology of Knowledge.* Garden City, NY: Doubleday.

Berkowitz, L. (1965). "Some Aspects of Observed Aggression." *Journal of Personality and Social Psychology,* 2: 359–369.

Berkowitz, L., and R. G. Geen (1966). "Film Violence and the Cue Properties of Available Targets."

Journal of Personality and Social Psychology, 3: 525–530.

Bernstein, C. (1992). "Feeding the Idiot Culture." *San José Mercury News,* June 21: C4.

Bloom, A. D. (1987). *The Closing of the American Mind: How Higher Education Has Failed Democracy and Impoverished the Souls of Today's Students.* New York: Simon & Schuster.

Blumer, H. (1969). *Symbolic Interactionism.* Englewood Cliffs, NJ: Prentice-Hall.

Blumler, J. G. (1979). "The Role of Theory in Uses and Gratifications Studies." *Communication Research,* 6: 9–36.

Blumler, J. G., M. Gurevitch, and E. Katz (1985). "Reaching Out: A Future for Gratifications Research." In K. E. Rosengren, L. A. Wenner, and P. Palmgreen, eds., *Media Gratifications Research: Current Perspectives.* Beverly Hills, CA: Sage.

Blumler, J. G., and E. Katz, eds. (1974). *The Uses of Mass Communications: Current Perspectives on Gratifications Research.* Beverly Hills, CA: Sage.

Boneva, B., R. Kraut, and D. Frohlich (2001). "Using E-mail for Personal Relationships: The Difference Gender Makes." *American Behavioral Scientist,* 45: 530–550.

Bowers, J. W., and J. A. Courtright (1984). *Communication Research Methods.* Glenview, IL: Scott, Foresman.

Brantlinger, P. (1983). *Bread and Circuses: Theories of Mass Culture as Social Decay.* Ithaca, NY: Cornell University Press.

Brill, S. (1998). "Pressgate." *Brill's Content,* August, 122–151.

Bronfenbrenner, U. (1970). *Two Worlds of Childhood: U.S. and U.S.S.R.* New York: Sage.

Brooks, D. (2002). "Looking Back on Tomorrow." *Atlantic Monthly,* April, 20–22.

Brownell, B. A. (1983). "Interpretations of Twentieth-Century Urban Progressive Reform." In D. R. Colburn and G. E. Pozzetta, eds., *Reform and*

Reformers in the Progressive Era. Westport, CT: Greenwood.

Brunsdon, C., and D. Morley (1981). "'Crossroads': Notes on Soap Opera." *Screen,* 22: 327.

———. (1978). *Everyday Television: 'Nationwide.'* London: British Film Institute.

Bryant, J., and D. R. Anderson (1983). *Children's Understanding of Television: Research on Attention and Comprehension.* New York: Academic.

Bryant, J., and R. L. Street (1988). "From Reactivity to Activity and Action: An Evolving Concept and *Weltanschauung* in Mass and Interpersonal Communication." In R. P. Hawkins, J. M. Wiemann, and S. Pingree, eds., *Advancing Communication Science: Merging Mass and Interpersonal Processes.* Newbury Park, CA: Sage.

Bryson, L. (1954). *The Drive Toward Reason: In the Service of a Free People.* New York: Harper.

Buckley, W. (1967). *Sociology and Modern Systems Theory.* Englewood Cliffs, NJ: Prentice-Hall.

Campbell, A., P. W. Converse, W. E. Miller, and D. E. Stokes (1960). *The American Voter.* New York: Wiley.

Cantril, H., H. Gaudet, and H. Herzog (1940). *Invasion from Mars.* Princeton, NJ: Princeton University Press.

Carey, J. (1989). *Communication as Culture: Essays on Media and Society.* Winchester, MA: Unwin Hyman.

———. (1977). "Mass Communication Research and Cultural Studies: An American View." In J. Curran, M. Gurevitch, J. Woollacott, J. Marriott, and C. Roberts, eds., *Mass Communication and Society.* London: Open University Press.

———. (1975a). "Culture and Communications." *Communication Research,* 2: 173–191.

———. (1975b). *Sociology and Public Affairs: The Chicago School.* Beverly Hills, CA: Sage.

Carlson, J. M. (1983). "Crime Show Viewing by Preadults: The Impact on Attitudes Toward Civil Liberties." *Communication Research,* 10: 529–552.

Carlson, M. (1990). "Presumed Innocent." *Time,* January 22, pp. 10–14.

Chaffee, S. H., and C. R. Berger (1987). "What Communication Scientists Do." In C. R. Berger and S. H. Chaffee, eds., *Handbook of Communication Sciences.* Newbury Park, CA: Sage.

Chaffee, S. H. and M. J. Metzger. (2001). "The End of Mass Communication?" *Mass Communication & Society,* 4: 365–379.

Choi, Y. S., K. K. Massey, and S. J. Baran (1988, May). "Cultivating the Perception of an Unjust World: Media Portrayals of the Criminal Justice System." Paper presented to the Annual Convention of the International Communication Association, San Francisco, CA.

Chomsky, N. (1991). *Deterring Democracy.* New York: Verso.

———. (1969). *American Power and the New Mandarins.* New York: Pantheon.

Christ, W. G., and W. J. Potter (1998). "Media Literacy, Media Education, and the Academy." *Journal of Communication,* 48: 5–15.

Christians, C. G., J. P. Ferre, and P. M. Fackler. (1993). *Good News: Social Ethics and the Press.* New York: Oxford University Press.

Cohen, B. C. (1963). *The Press and Foreign Policy.* Princeton, NJ: Princeton University Press.

Comstock, G. (1991). *Television and the American Child.* San Diego: Academic.

Crouse, T. (1973). *The Boys on the Bus.* New York: Random House.

Crowley, D. J., and P. Heyer (1991). *Communication in History: Technology, Culture, Society.* New York: Longman.

Cultural Environment Movement. (1996). "Viewers' Declaration of Independence." *Cultural Environment Monitor,* 1: 1.

Dalton, T. A. (1997). "Reporting on Race: A Tale of Two Cities." *Columbia Journalism Review,* 36, September/October: 54–57.

Daly, J. A. "Colloquy: Getting Older and Getting Better: Challenges for Communication Research." *Human Communication Research,* 26: 331–338.

Davis, D. K. (1990). "News and Politics." In D. L. Swanson and D. Nimmo, eds., *New Directions in Political Communication.* Newbury Park, CA: Sage.

Davis, D. K., and S. J. Baran (1981). *Mass Communication and Everyday Life: A Perspective on Theory and Effects.* Belmont, CA: Wadsworth.

Davis, D. K., and J. P. Robinson (1989). "Newsflow and Democratic Society in an Age of Electronic Media." In G. Comstock, ed., *Public Communication and Behavior,* Vol. 3. New York: Academic.

Davis, R. E. (1976). *Response to Innovation: A Study of Popular Argument About New Mass Media.* New York: Arno.

DeFleur, M. L. (1998). "Where Have All the Milestones Gone? The Decline of Significant Research on the Process and Effects of Mass Communication." *Mass Communication & Society,* 1: 85–98.

———. (1970). *Theories of Mass Communication.* New York: David McKay.

DeFleur, M. L., and S. Ball-Rokeach (1989). *Theories of Mass Communication,* 5th ed. New York: David McKay.

———. (1975). *Theories of Mass Communication,* 3rd edition. New York: David McKay.

DeFleur, M. L., and O. N. Larsen (1958). *The Flow of Information.* New York: Harper.

Delia, J. (1987). "Communication Research: A History." In C. Berger and S. Chaffee, eds., *Handbook of Communication Science.* Beverly Hills, CA: Sage.

Dervin, B. (1989). "Changing Conceptions of the Audience." In R. E. Rice and C. Atkin, eds., *Public Communication Campaigns,* 2nd ed. Beverly Hills, CA: Sage.

Deutschmann, P. J., and W. A. Danielson (1960). "Diffusion of Knowledge of the Major News Story." *Journalism Quarterly,* 37: 345–355.

Dewey, J. (1927). *The Public and Its Problems.* New York: Holt.

Dimmick, J., S. Patterson, and J. Sikand. (1996). "Personal Telephone Networks: A Typology and Two Empirical Studies." *Journal of Broadcasting and Electronic Media,* 40: 45–59.

Dimmick, J. W., J. Sikand, and S. J. Patterson. (1994). "Gratifications of the Household Telephone: Sociability, Instrumentality, and Reassurance." *Communication Research,* 21: 643–663.

Donohue, G. A., P. J. Tichenor, and C. N. Olien (1986). "Metro Daily Pullback and Knowledge Gaps, Within and Between Communities." *Communication Research,* 13: 453–471.

"Drug War Is Failing—It's Time to Give Treatment a Chance." (1998). *San José Mercury News,* 25 November: 6B.

Durkheim, É. (1951). *Suicide: étude de sociologie.* New York: Free Press

Edelman, M. (1988). *Constructing the Political Spectacle.* Chicago: University of Chicago Press.

Effron, S. (1997). "The North Carolina Experiment." *Columbia Journalism Review,* 35, January/February: 12–14.

Eisenstein, E. L. (1979). *The Printing Press as an Agent of Change: Communications and Cultural Transformations in Early-Modern Europe.* Cambridge: Cambridge University Press.

Elms, A. C. (1972). *Social Psychology and Social Relevance.* Boston: Little, Brown.

Entman, R. M. (1989). *Democracy Without Citizens: Media and the Decay of American Politics.* New York: Oxford University Press.

Enzensberger, H. M. (1974). *The Consciousness Industry.* New York: Seabury.

Epstein, E. J. (1973). *News from Nowhere: Television and the News.* New York: Random House.

Evangelista, B. (2001). "Mystery Links." *San Francisco Chronicle,* July 30: D1, cont. D3.

Ewen, S. (2000). "Memoirs of a Commodity Fetishist." *Mass Communication & Society,* 3: 439–452.

———. (1996). *PR! A Social History of Spin.* New York: Basic Books.

FAIR. (2000). "Pre-Convention Coverage Whitewashes Police Violence, Distorts Activists' Agenda." July 25: Online, FAIR-L@listserv .american.edu.

Faules, D. F., and D. C. Alexander (1978). *Communication and Social Behavior: A Symbolic Interaction Perspective.* Reading, MA: Addison-Wesley.

"Fear Factor." (2001). *Broadcasting & Cable,* July 9: 54.

"Ferment in the Field" (1983). *Journal of Communication* (Special Issue): 33.

Feshbach, S. (1961). "The Stimulating versus Cathartic Effects of a Vicarious Aggressive Activity." *Journal of Abnormal and Social Psychology,* 63: 381–385.

Feshbach, S., and R. D. Singer (1971). *Television and Aggression: An Experimental Field Study.* San Francisco: Jossey-Bass.

Festinger, L. (1962). "Cognitive Dissonance." *Scientific American,* 207: 93.

Fisher, D. E., and M. J. Fisher (1996). *Tube: The Invention of Television.* Washington, DC: Counterpoint.

Fishman, M. (1980). *Manufacturing the News.* Austin: University of Texas Press.

Flavell, J. H. (1992). "Cognitive Development: Past, Present, and Future." *Developmental Psychology,* 28: 998–1005.

Freedman, L. Z. (1961). "Daydream in a Vacuum Tube: A Psychiatrist's Comment on the Effects of Television." In W. Schramm, J. Lyle, and E. B. Parker, eds., *Television in the Lives of Our Children.* Stanford, CA: Stanford University Press.

Friedrich, C. J. (1943). "Principles of Informational Strategy." *Public Opinion Quarterly,* 7: 77–89.

Frost, R., and J. Stauffer (1987). "The Effects of Social Class, Gender, and Personality on Psychological Responses to Filmed Violence." *Journal of Communication,* 37: 29–45.

Fukuyama, F. (1999). "The Great Disruption: Human Nature and the Reconstruction of Social Order." *Atlantic Monthly*, May: 55–80.

Funkhouser, G., and M. McCombs (1971). "The Rise and Fall of News Diffusion." *Public Opinion Quarterly*, 50: 107–113.

Gans, H. (1979). *Deciding What's News*. New York: Pantheon.

Gardner, H. (1985). *The Mind's New Science*. New York: Basic.

Garnham, N. (1995). "Political Economy and Cultural Studies: Reconciliation or Divorce?" *Critical Studies in Mass Communication*, 12: 95–100.

Gary, B. (1996). "Communication Research, the Rockefeller Foundation, and Mobilization for the War on Words, 1938–1944." *Journal of Communication*, 46: 124–147.

Gates, W. (1995). *The Road Ahead*. New York: Viking.

Gerbner, G. (2001). "The Cultural Arm of the Corporate Establishment: Reflections on the Work of Herb Schiller." *Journal of Broadcasting & Electronic Media*, 45: 186–190.

———. (1990). "Epilogue: Advancing on the Path of Righteousness (Maybe)." In N. Signorielli and M. Morgan, eds., *Cultivation Analysis: New Directions in Media Effects Research*. Newbury Park, CA: Sage.

Gerbner, G., and L. Gross. (1979). "Editorial Response: A Reply to Newcomb's 'Humanistic Critique.'" *Communication Research*, 6: 223–230.

———. (1976). "Living with Television: The Violence Profile." *Journal of Communication*, 26: 173–199.

Gerbner, G., L. Gross, M. Jackson-Beeck, S. Jeffries-Fox, and N. Signorielli (1978). "Cultural Indicators: Violence Profile No. 9." *Journal of Communication*, 28: 176–206.

Gerbner, G., L. Gross, M. Morgan, and N. Signorielli. (1982). "Charting the Mainstream: Television's Contributions to Political Orientations." *Journal of Communication*, 32: 100–127.

———. (1981). "A Curious Journey into the Scary World of Paul Hirsch." *Communication Research*, 8: 39–72.

———. (1980). "The 'Mainstreaming' of America: Violence Profile No. 11." *Journal of Communication*, 30: 10–29.

Gibbs, N. (1994). "Death and Deceit." *Time*, November 14: 42–48.

Giddens, A. (1991). *Modernity and Self-Identity: Self and Society in the Late Modern Age*. Stanford, CA: Stanford University Press.

Gillmor, D. M. and Barron, J. A. (1974). Mass Communication Law: Cases and Comments. St. Paul, MN: West.

Gitlin, T. (1980). *The Whole World Is Watching: Mass Media in the Making and Unmaking of the New Left*. Berkeley: University of California Press.

Glasgow University Media Group, eds. (1980). *More Bad News*. London: Routledge and Kegan Paul.

———., eds. (1976). *Bad News*. London: Routledge and Kegan Paul.

Gleick, J. (1987). *Chaos: Making a New Science*. New York: Viking.

Glynn, C. J., and J. M. McLeod (1985). "Implications of the Spiral of Silence Theory for Communication and Public Opinion Research." In K. R. Sanders, L. L. Kaid, and D. D. Nimmo, eds., *Political Communication Yearbook, 1984*. Carbondale: Southern Illinois University Press.

Goffman, E. (1979). *Gender Advertisements*. New York: Harper Colophon.

———. (1974). *Frame Analysis: An Essay on the Organization of Experience*. New York: Harper & Row.

Goldberg, M. E., M. Fishbein, and S. E. Middlestadt, eds. (1997). *Social Marketing: Theoretical and Practical Perspectives*. Hillsdale, NJ: Erlbaum.

Gould, J. (1972). "TV Violence Held Unharmful to Youth." *New York Times*, January 11: 27.

Gould, S. J. (2000). *The Lying Stones of Marrakech: Penultimate Reflections in Natural History.* New York: Harmony Books.

Graber, D. (1987). *Processing the News,* 2nd ed. New York: Longman.

Greenberg, B., and E. Parker, eds. (1965). *The Kennedy Assassination and the American Public.* Stanford, CA: Stanford University Press.

Griffin, E. M. (1994). *A First Look at Communication Theory.* New York: McGraw-Hill.

Grossberg, L. (1989). "The Circulation of Cultural Studies." *Critical Studies in Mass Communication,* 6: 413–421.

———. (1983). "Cultural Studies Revisited and Revised." In M. S. Mander, ed., *Communications in Transition.* New York: Praeger.

Grossberg, L., and C. Nelson (1988). "Introduction: The Territory of Marxism." In C. Nelson and L. Grossberg, eds., *Marxism and the Interpretation of Culture.* Urbana: University of Illinois Press.

Grossberg, L., C. Nelson, and P. Treichler (1992). *Cultural Studies.* London: Routledge.

Grosswiler, Paul. (1997). *Method in the Message: Rethinking McLuhan Through Critical Theory.* Montreal: Black Rose Books.

Gunaratne, S. A. (1998). "Old Wine in a New Bottle: Public Journalism, Developmental Journalism, and Social Responsibility." In M. E. Roloff, ed., *Communication Yearbook 21.* Thousand Oaks, CA: Sage.

Gunter, B. (1987). *Poor Reception: Misunderstanding and Forgetting Broadcast News.* Hillsdale, NJ: Erlbaum.

Habermas, J. (1989). *The Structural Transformation of the Public Sphere.* Cambridge, MA: MIT Press.

———. (1971). *Knowledge and Human Interest.* Boston: Beacon.

Hachten, W. A. (1992). *The World News Prism.* Ames: Iowa State University Press.

Hall, S. (1982). "The Rediscovery of 'Ideology': Return of the Repressed in Media Studies." In M. Gure-vitch, T. Bennett, J. Curran, and J. Woollacott, eds., *Culture, Society and the Media.* New York: Methuen.

———. (1981a). "Notes on Deconstructing 'The Popular.'" In R. Samuel, ed., *People's History and Socialist Theory.* London: Routledge.

———. (1981b). "The Whites of Their Eyes: Racist Ideologies and the Media." In G. Bridges & R. Brundt, eds., *Silver Linings.* London: Lawrence and Wishart.

———. (1980a). "Encoding and Decoding in the Television Discourse." In S. Hall, ed., *Culture, Media, Language.* London: Hutchinson.

———. (1980b). "Cultural Studies: Two Paradigms." *Media, Culture and Society,* 2: 57–72.

———. (1973). *Encoding and Decoding in the Television Discourse.* CCCS Stencilled Paper 7, University of Birmingham.

Hall, S., D. Hobson, A. Lowe, and P. Willis, eds. (1982). *Culture, Media, Language.* London: Hutchinson.

Halloran, J. D. (1964/65). "Television and Violence." *The Twentieth Century,* Winter: 61–72.

Hamelink, C. J. (2001). "Considering Communication Issues and Problems Around the Globe." *ICA News,* November: 8–9.

Hardt, H. (1999). "Shifting Paradigms: Decentering the Discourse of Mass Communication Research." *Mass Communication & Society,* 2: 175–183.

Hart, P., and J. Naureckas. (2001). "Feminist Rap 'Indecent,' Says FCC." *Extra! Update,* August: 4.

Hawkins, R. P., J. M. Wiemann, and S. Pingree, eds. (1988). *Advancing Communication Science: Merging Mass and Interpersonal Processes.* Newbury Park, CA: Sage.

Hay, J. (1989). "Advertising as a Cultural Text (Rethinking Message Analysis in a Recombinant Culture)." In B. Dervin, L. Grossberg, B. J. O'Keefe, and E. Wartella, eds., *Rethinking Communication: Volume 2, Paradigm Exemplars.* Newbury Park, CA: Sage.

Herman, E. S. (1996). "The Propaganda Model Revisited." *Monthly Review,* July–August: 115–128.

Herman, E. S., and N. Chomsky, (1988). *Manufacturing Consent*. New York: Pantheon.

Herzog, B. (2000). *States of Mind*. Winston-Salem, NC: John F. Blair.

Herzog, H. (1944). "Motivations and Gratifications of Daily Serial Listeners." In P. F. Lazarsfeld and F. N. Stanton, eds., *Radio Research, 1942–1943*. New York: Duell, Sloan and Pearce.

Herzstein, R. E. (1978). *The War That Hitler Won*. New York: Putnam.

Hirsch, P. M. (1981). "On Not Learning from One's Own Mistakes: A Reanalysis of Gerbner et al.'s Findings on Cultivation Analysis, Part II" *Communication Research*, 8: 3–37.

Hitler, A. (1933). *Mein Kampf: Zwe Bände in Enemband*. München: F. Eher.

Hobson, D. (1982). *Crossroads: The Drama of a Soap Opera*. London: Methuen.

Hovland, C. I., I. L. Janis, and H. H. Kelley (1953). *Communication and Persuasion*. New Haven, CT: Yale University Press.

Hovland, C. I., A. A. Lumsdaine, and F. D. Sheffield (1949). *Experiments on Mass Communication*. Princeton, NJ: Princeton University Press.

Huntington, S. P. (1996). *The Clash of Civilizations and the Remaking of World Order*. New York: Simon & Schuster.

Huston, A. C., E. Donnerstein, H. Fairchild, N. D. Feshbach, P. A. Katz, J. P. Murray, E. A. Rubenstein, B. L. Wilcox, and D. Zuckerman (1992). *Big World, Small Screen*. Lincoln: University of Nebraska Press.

Inglis, F. (1990). *Media Theory: An Introduction*. Oxford: Basil Blackwell.

Innis, H. A. (1951). *The Bias of Communication*. Toronto: University of Toronto Press.

————. (1950). *Empire and Communication*. Toronto: University of Toronto Press.

Iyengar, S. (1991). *Is Anyone Responsible? How Television Frames Political Issues*. Chicago: University of Chicago Press.

Iyengar, S., and D. R. Kinder (1987). *News That Matters: Television and American Opinion*. Chicago: University of Chicago Press.

————. (1986). "More Than Meets the Eye: TV News, Priming, and Public Evaluations of the President." In G. Comstock, ed., *Public Communication and Behavior*, Vol. 1. New York: Academic.

Jacobs, J. (1998). "Big Brother Just Wants Us to Be Happy." *San José Mercury News*, 13 August, p. 9B.

Jamieson, K. H. (1988). *Eloquence in an Electronic Age: The Transformation of Political Speechmaking*. New York: Oxford University Press.

Jamieson, K. H., and K. K. Campbell (1997). *The Interplay of Influence: News, Advertising, Politics, and the Mass Media*. Belmont, CA: Wadsworth.

Jamieson, K. H., and M. E. P. Seligman (2001). "Six Rules for Government and Press on Terrorism: Undercutting Fear Itself." Unpublished report prepared for government officials and journalists based on a workshop of experts on countering fear, panic, and terror and administrators on large U.S. corporations, Philadelphia, November.

Jeffrey, L. (1995). *Report Submitted to the Canadian Radio and Television Commission by The McLuhan Program in Culture and Technology at the University of Toronto*. Toronto: Canadian Radio and Television Commission.

Jensen, K. B. (1995). *The Social Semiotics of Mass Communication*. Thousand Oaks, CA: Sage.

————. (1990). "Television Futures: A Social Action Methodology for Studying Interpretive Communities." *Critical Studies in Mass Communication*, 7: 129–146.

Jhally, S., ed. (1987). *The Codes of Advertising: Fetishism and the Political Economy of Meaning in the Consumer Society*. New York: St. Martin's.

Jo, E. and L. Berkowitz (1994). "A Priming Effect Analysis of Media Influences: An Update." In J. Bryant and D. Zillman, eds., *Media Effects: Advances in Theory and Research*. Hillsdale, NJ: Erlbaum.

Johnson, J. D., L. A. Jackson, and L. Gatto (1995). "Violent Attitudes and Deferred Academic Aspirations: Deleterious Effects of Exposure to Rap Music." *Basic and Applied Social Psychology,* 16: 27–41.

Jordan, Amy B. (1996). *The State of Children's Television: An Examination of Quantity, Quality, and Industry Beliefs.* Philadelphia: Annenberg Public Policy Center.

Kahlor, L., B.W. Gorham, and E. Gilligan. (1999). "A Reconceptualization of Cultivation as a 'Good Theory' with Help from the 'Thin Ideal.'" Paper presented to the Annual Conference of the Association for Education in Journalism and Mass Communication, New Orleans.

Katz, E. (1983). "Publicity and Pluralistic Ignorance: Notes on 'The Spiral of Silence.'" In E. Wartella and D. C. Whitney, eds., *Mass Communication Review Yearbook 4.* Beverly Hills, CA: Sage.

Katz, E., J. G. Blumler, and M. Gurevitch (1974). "Utilization of Mass Communication by the Individual." In J. G. Blumler and E. Katz, eds., *The Uses of Mass Communications: Current Perspectives on Gratifications Research.* Beverly Hills, CA: Sage.

Katz, E., and P. F. Lazarsfeld (1955). *Personal Influence: The Part Played by People in the Flow of Communications.* New York: Free Press.

Keane, J. (1991). *The Media and Democracy.* Cambridge, UK: Polity Press.

Kellner, D. (1997). "Overcoming the Divide: Cultural Studies and Political Economy." In M. Ferguson and P. Golding, eds., *Cultural Studies in Question.* Thousand Oaks, CA: Sage.

Kerlinger, F. N. (1986). *Foundations of Behavioral Research.* New York: Holt, Rinehart, & Winston.

Key, V. O. (1961). *Public Opinion and American Democracy.* New York: Knopf.

Kirkpatrick, D. D. (2001). "Jewelry Ad Gets Novel Placement." *Providence Journal,* September 4: A2.

Klapper, J. T. (1960). *The Effects of Mass Communication.* New York: Free Press.

———. (1949). *The Effects of Mass Media.* New York: Columbia University Bureau of Applied Social Research.

Kornhauser, A., and P. F. Lazarsfeld (1935). "The Technique of Market Research from the Standpoint of a Psychologist." *Institute of Management,* 16: 3–15, 19–21.

Kornhauser, W. (1959). *The Politics of Mass Society.* New York: Free Press.

Kraidy, M. (1999). "The Global, the Local, and the Hybrid: A Native Ethnography of Globalization." *Critical Studies in Mass Communication,* 16: 456–476.

Kreiling, A. (1984). "Television in American Ideological Hopes and Fears." In W. D. Rowland, Jr. and B. Watkins, eds., *Interpreting Television: Current Research Perspectives.* Beverly Hills, CA: Sage.

Krippendorf, K. (1986). *Information Theory: Structural Models for Qualitative Data.* Newbury Park, CA: Sage.

Kuhn, T. (1970). *The Structure of Scientific Revolutions,* 2nd ed. Chicago: University of Chicago Press.

Lacayo, R. (1994). "Strangers in the Shadows." *Time,* November 14: 46–47.

Laitinen, R. E., and R. F. Rakos (1997). "Corporate Control of Media and Propaganda: A Behavior Analysis." In P. A. Lamal, ed., *Cultural Contingencies: Behavior Analytic Perspectives on Cultural Practices.* Westport, CT: Praeger.

Lang, A. (1990). "Involuntary Attention and Physiological Arousal Evoked by Structural Features and Mild Emotion in TV Commercials." *Communication Research,* 17: 275–299.

Lang, A., J. Newhagen, and B. Reeves (1996). "Negative Video as Structure: Emotion, Attention, Capacity and Memory." *Journal of Broadcasting and Electronic Media,* 40(4): 460–478.

Lang, K., and G. E. Lang (1983). *The Battle for Public Opinion: The President, the Press, and the Polls During Watergate.* New York: Columbia University Press.

Lasswell, H. D. (1949). "The Structure and Function of Communication in Society." In W. S. Schramm, ed., *Mass Communication.* Urbana: University of Illinois Press.

————. (1948). "The Structure and Function of Communication in Society." In L. Bryson, ed., *The Communication of Ideas*. New York: Harper.

————. (1934). *World Politics and Personal Insecurity*. Chicago: University of Chicago Press.

————. (1927). *Propaganda Technique in the World War*. New York: Knopf.

Lavey, W. G. (1993). "Inconsistencies in Applications of Economics at the Federal Communications Commission." *Federal Communications Law Journal*, 45: 437–490.

Lazarsfeld, P. F. (1969). "An Episode in the History of Social Research: A Memoir." In D. Fleming and B. Bailyn, eds., *The Intellectual Migration: Europe and America, 1930–1960*. Cambridge, MA: Belknap Press of Harvard University.

————. (1941). "Remarks on Administrative and Critical Communication Research." *Studies in Philosophy and Social Science*, 9: 2–16.

Lazarsfeld, P. F., B. Berelson, and H. Gaudet (1944). *The People's Choice: How the Voter Makes Up His Mind in a Presidential Campaign*. New York: Duell, Sloan & Pearce.

Lazarsfeld, P., and F. N. Stanton, eds. (1942). *Radio Research, 1941*. New York: Duell, Sloan & Pearce.

Leedy, P. D. (1997). *Practical Research: Planning and Design*. New York: Macmillan.

Levy, M., and S. Windahl (1985). "The Concept of Audience Activity." In K. E. Rosengren, L. A. Wenner, and P. Palmgreen, eds., *Media Gratifications Research: Current Perspectives*. Beverly Hills, CA: Sage.

Liebert, Robert M., and Joyce N. Sprafkin. (1988). *The Early Window: Effects of Television on Children and Youth*. New York: Pergamon.

Lind, R. A. and N. Rockler, (2001). "Competing Ethos: Reliance on Profit versus Social Responsibility by Laypeople Planning a Television Newscast." *Journal of Broadcasting & Electronic Media*, 45: 118–134.

Lippmann, W. (1922). *Public Opinion*. New York: Macmillan.

Littlejohn, S. W. (1996). *Theories of Human Communication*. Belmont, CA: Wadsworth.

Lo, C. (1998). "Space Jam." *Wired*, October: 142–143.

Long, E. (1989). "Feminism and Cultural Studies." *Critical Studies in Mass Communication*, 6: 427–435.

Lowery, S. A., and M. L. DeFleur (1995). *Milestones in Mass Communication Research*, 3rd ed. White Plains, NY: Longman.

Lovell, T. (1981). "Ideology and 'Coronation Street.'" In R. Dyer, C. Geraghty, M. Jordan, T. Lovell, R. Paterson and J. Stewart, eds., *Coronation Street*. London: British Film Institute.

Manners, J. (2000). "Plug Away." *Brill's Content*, June: 39.

Marcuse, H. (1978). *An Essay on Liberation*. Boston: Beacon.

————. (1969). *The Aesthetic Dimension*. Boston: Beacon.

————. (1941). "Some Social Implications of Modern Technology." In A. Arato and E. Gebhardt, eds., (1978). *The Essential Frankfurt School Reader*. New York: Urizen.

Martin-Barbero, J. (1993). *Communication, Culture and Hegemony: From the Media to Mediations*. (trans. by E. Fox and R. A. White). Newbury Park, CA: Sage.

Martindale, D. (1960). *The Nature and Types of Sociological Theory*. Boston: Houghton-Mifflin.

Mast, G., and B. F. Kawin (1996). *A Short History of the Movies*. Boston: Allyn & Bacon.

Matson, F. M. (1964). *The Broken Image: Man, Science and Society*. New York: Braziller.

Mayne, J. (1993). *Cinema and Spectatorship*. London: Routledge.

McChesney, R. W. (1997). *Corporate Media and the Threat to Democracy*. New York: Seven Stories.

McCombs, M. E. (1981). "The Agenda-Setting Approach." In D. D. Nimmo and K. R. Sanders, eds., *Handbook of Political Communication.* Beverly Hills, CA: Sage.

McCombs, M. and S. I. Ghanem (2001). "The Convergence of Agenda Setting and Framing." In S. D. Reese, O. H. Gandy, and A. E. Grant, eds. (2001). *Framing Public Life: Perspectives on Media and Our Understanding of the Social World.* Mahwah, NJ: Erlbaum.

McCombs, M. E., and D. L. Shaw (1972). "The Agenda-Setting Function of Mass Media." *Public Opinion Quarterly,* 36: 176–187.

McConnell, B. (2001). "FCC Hip-Hop Deep in #@!*" *Broadcasting & Cable,* July 9: 28.

McIntyre, J. S. (1987). "Repositioning a Landmark: The Hutchins Commission and Freedom of the Press." *Critical Studies in Mass Communication,* 4: 95–135.

McLuhan, M. (1964). *Understanding Media: The Extensions of Man.* New York: McGraw-Hill.

———. (1951). *The Mechanical Bride.* New York: Vanguard.

McQuail, D. (1994). *Mass Communication Theory: An Introduction,* 4th ed. Beverly Hills, CA: Sage.

———. (1987). *Mass Communication Theory: An Introduction,* 2nd ed. Beverly Hills, CA: Sage.

McRobbie, A. (1984). "Settling Accounts with Subcultures: A Feminist Critique." *Screen Education,* 34: 37–49.

Mead, G. H. (1934). *Mind, Self and Society.* Chicago: University of Chicago Press.

Media Literacy Symposium (1998). *Journal of Communication,* Vol. 48.

Medved, M. (1992). *Hollywood vs. America: Popular Culture and the War on Traditional Values.* New York: HarperCollins.

Meehan, E. R., V. Mosco, and J. Wasco (1994). "Rethinking Political Economy: Change and Continuity." In M. Levy and M. Gurevitch, eds. *Defining Media Studies: Reflections on the Future of the Field.* New York: Oxford University Press.

Mendelsohn, H. (1966). *Mass Entertainment.* New Haven, CT: College and University Press.

Merten, K. (1984). "Some Silence in the Spiral of Silence." In K. R. Sanders, L. L. Kaid, and D. D. Nimmo, eds., *Political Communication Yearbook, 1984.* Carbondale: Southern Illinois University Press.

Merton, R. K. (1967). *On Theoretical Sociology.* New York: Free Press.

———. (1949). *Social Theory and Social Structure.* Glencoe, IL: Free Press.

Meyrowitz, J. (1985). *No Sense of Place: The Impact of Electronic Media on Social Behavior.* New York: Oxford University Press.

Miller, G. R., and M. Burgoon (1978). "Persuasion Research: Review and Commentary." In B. D. Ruben, ed., *Communication Yearbook 2.* New Brunswick, NJ: Transaction.

Miller, K. (2002). *Communication Theories: Perspectives, Processes, and Contexts.* Boston, McGraw-Hill.

Miller, N. E., and J. Dollard (1941). *Social Learning and Imitation.* New Haven, CT: Yale University Press.

Mills, C. W. (1959). *The Sociological Imagination.* New York: Oxford University Press.

Mills, C. Wright (1957). *The Power Elite.* New York: Oxford University Press.

Moerman, M. (1992). "Life After C.A.: An Ethnographer's Autobiography." In G. Watson and R. M. Seiler, eds. *Text in Context: Contributions to Ethnomethodology.* Newbury Park, CA: Sage.

Moores, S. (1993). *Interpreting Audiences: The Ethnography of Media Consumption.* Thousand Oaks, CA: Sage.

Morgan, M., and N. Signorielli (1990). "Cultivation Analysis: Conceptualization and Methodology." In N. Signorielli and M. Morgan, eds., *Cultivation Analysis: New Directions in Media Effects Research.* Newbury Park, CA: Sage.

Morley, D. (1980). *The "Nationwide" Audience: Structure and Decoding.* London: British Film Institute.

Morley, D., and K. Robins (1995). *Spaces of Identity: Global Media, Electronic Landscapes, and Cultural Boundaries.* London: Routledge.

Mosco, V., and A. Herman (1981). "Critical Theory and Electronic Media." *Theory and Society,* 10: 869–896.

Mott, F. L. (1941). *American Journalism.* New York: Macmillan.

Moy, P., D. Domke, and K. Stamm (2001). "The Spiral of Silence and Public Opinion of Affirmative Action." *Journalism & Mass Communication Quarterly,* 78: 7–25.

Moyers, B. (2001). "Journalism & Democracy: On the Importance of Being a 'Public Nuisance.'" *The Nation,* May 7: 11–17.

Mumford, L. (1975). *Findings and Keepings: Analects for an Autobiography.* New York: Harcourt, Brace, Jovanovich.

Murdock, G. (1989a). "Critical Activity and Audience Activity." In B. Dervin, L. Grossberg, B. J. O'Keefe, and E. Wartella, eds., *Rethinking Communication: Volume 2, Paradigm Exemplars.* Newbury Park, CA: Sage.

———. (1989b). "Critical Studies: Missing Links." *Critical Studies in Mass Communication,* 6: 436–440.

Napoli, P. M. (1999). "The Marketplace of Ideas Metaphor in Communications Regulation." *Journal of Communication,* 49: 151–169.

Nelson, C., and L. Grossberg (1988). *Marxism and the Interpretation of Culture.* Chicago: University of Illinois Press.

Newcomb, H. (2000). *Television: The Critical View.* New York: Oxford University Press.

———. (1994). *Television: The Critical View.* New York: Oxford University Press.

———. (1978). "Assessing the Violence Profile Studies of Gerbner and Gross: A Humanistic Critique and Suggestion." *Communication Research,* 5: 264–283.

———. (1974). *TV: The Most Popular Art.* New York: Oxford University Press.

Newcomb, H., and P. M. Hirsch (1983). "Television as a Cultural Forum: Implications for Research." *Quarterly Review of Film,* 8: 45–55.

Ninety-Second Congress. (1972). *Hearings Before the Subcommittee on Communications on the Surgeon General's Report by the Scientific Advisory Committee on Television and Social Behavior.* Washington, DC: U.S. Government.

Noelle-Neumann, E. (1985). "The Spiral of Silence: A Response." In K. R. Sanders, L. L. Kaid, and D. D. Nimmo, eds., *Political Communication Yearbook, 1984.* Carbondale: Southern Illinois University Press.

———. (1984). *The Spiral of Silence—Our Social Skin.* Chicago: University of Chicago Press.

———. (1973). "Return to the Concept of the Powerful Mass Media." *Studies of Broadcasting,* 9: 68–105.

O'Connor, A. (1989). "The Problem of American Cultural Studies." *Critical Studies in Mass Communication,* 6: 405–413.

O'Leary, E. K. (2001). "A Great Injustice to College Students." *Providence Journal,* September 14: 2001, p. B7.

Orwell, G. (1960). *1984.* New York: Signet Books. (Reprint of Harcourt Brace Jovanovich, 1949).

Palmgreen, P., L. A. Wenner, and K. E. Rosengren (1985). "Uses and Gratifications Research: The Past Ten Years." In K. E. Rosengren, L. A. Wenner, and P. Palmgreen, eds., *Media Gratifications Research: Current Perspectives.* Beverly Hills, CA: Sage.

Parenti, M. (1992). *Make-Believe Media: The Politics of Entertainment.* New York: St. Martin's.

Patterson, T. E. (1994). *Out of Order.* New York: Vintage.

———. (1980). *The Mass Media Election: How Americans Choose Their President.* New York: Praeger.

Paul, B., M. B. Salwen, and M. Dupagne (2000). "The Third-Person Effect: A Meta-Analysis of the Perceptual Hypothesis." *Mass Communication & Society,* 3: 57–85.

Peirce, C. (1955). In J. Buchler, ed., *Philosophical Writings of Peirce*. New York: Dover.

Peterson, D. L., and K. S. Pfost (1989). "Influence of Rock Videos on Attitudes of Violence Against Women." *Psychological Reports,* 64: 319–322.

Pingree, S., J. M. Wiemann, and R. P. Hawkins (1988). "Editors' Introduction: Toward Conceptual Synthesis." In R. P. Hawkins, J. M. Wiemann, and S. Pingree, eds., *Advancing Communication Science: Merging Mass and Interpersonal Processes.* Newbury Park, CA: Sage.

Postman, N. (1996). *The End of Education.* New York: Vintage.

———. (1994). *The Disappearance of Childhood.* New York: Vintage.

———. (1985). *Amusing Ourselves to Death: Public Discourse in the Age of Show Business.* New York: Penguin.

Potter, D. (2001). "News for Sale." *American Journalism Review,* September: 68.

Potter, W. J. (1998). *Media Literacy.* Thousand Oaks, CA: Sage.

———. (1997). "The Problem of Indexing Risk of Viewing Television Aggression." *Critical Studies in Mass Communication,* 14: 228–248.

———. (1993). "Cultivation Theory and Research: A Conceptual Critique." *Human Communication Research,* 19: 564–601.

———. (1991). "The Relationships Between First and Second Order Measures of Cultivation." *Human Communication Research,* 18: 92–113.

———. (1990). "Adolescents' Perceptions of the Primary Values of Television Programming." *Journalism and Mass Communication Quarterly,* 67: 843–851.

Pratkanis, A. R. and E. Aronson (1992). *Age of Propaganda: The Everyday Use and Abuse of Persuasion.* New York: W.H. Freeman.

Protess, D. L., F. L. Cook, J. C. Doppelt, J. S. Ettema, M. T. Gordon, D. R. Leff, and P. Miller (1991). *The Journalism of Outrage.* New York: Guilford.

Purcell-Gates, V. (1997). *Other People's Words: The Cycle of Low Literacy.* Cambridge, MA: Harvard University Press.

Radio-Television News Directors Association. (2000). "Code of Ethics and Professional Conduct." Online: http://www.rtnda.org/ethics/coe.shtml.

Radway, J. (1986). "Identifying Ideological Seams: Mass Culture, Analytical Method, and Political Practice." *Communication* 9: 93–123.

———. (1984). *Reading the Romance: Women, Patriarchy, and Popular Literature.* Chapel Hill: University of North Carolina Press.

Reese, S. D., O. H. Gandy, and A. E. Grant, eds. (2001). *Framing Public Life: Perspectives on Media and Our Understanding of the Social World.* Mahwah, NJ: Erlbaum.

Reimer, B., and K. E. Rosengren (1990). "Cultivated Viewers and Readers: A Life-Style Perspective." In N. Signorielli and M. Morgan, eds., *Cultivation Analysis: New Directions in Media Effects Research.* Newbury Park, CA: Sage.

Rice, R. E., and C. Atkin (1989). *Public Communication Campaigns,* 2nd ed. Beverly Hills, CA: Sage.

Ritzer, G. (1983). *Sociological Theory.* New York: Knopf.

Robinson, J. P., and D. K. Davis (1990). "Television News and the Informed Public: Not the Main Source." *Journal of Communication,* 40: 106–119.

Robinson, J. P., and M. Levy, with D. K. Davis, eds. (1986). *The Main Source: Learning from Television News.* Newbury Park, CA: Sage.

Rogers, E. M. (2000). "The Extensions of Men: The Correspondence of Marshall McLuhan and Edward T. Hall." *Mass Communication & Society,* 3: 117–135.

———. (1986). "History of Communication Science." In E. M. Rogers, ed., *Communication Technology: The New Media in Society.* New York: Free Press.

Rogers, Everett M. (1983). *Diffusion of Innovations,* 3rd ed. New York: Free Press.

————. (1962). *Diffusion of Innovations*. New York: Free Press.

Rogers, E. M., J. W. Dearing, and D. Bergman (1993). "The Anatomy of Agenda-Setting Research." *Journal of Communication,* 43: 68–84.

Rosnow, R. L., and E. J. Robinson (1967). *Experiments in Persuasion*. New York: Academic.

Rubin, A. M. (1998). "Editor's Note: Media Literacy." *Journal of Communication,* 48: 3–4.

————. (1994). "Media Uses and Effects: A Uses-and-Gratifications Perspective." In J. Bryant and D. Zillman, eds., *Media Effects: Advances in Theory and Research*. Hillsdale, NJ: Erlbaum.

Rubin, A. M., and P. M. Haridakis (2001). "Mass Communication Research at the Dawn of the 21st Century." In W. B. Gudykunst, ed., *Communication Yearbook 24*. Thousand Oaks, CA: Sage.

Ruggiero, T. E. (2000). "Uses and Gratifications Theory in the 21st Century." *Mass Communication & Society,* 3: 3–37.

Salmon, C. T., and F. G. Kline (1985). "The Spiral of Silence Ten Years Later: An Examination and Evaluation." In K. R. Sanders, L. L. Kaid, and D. D. Nimmo, ed., *Political Communication Yearbook, 1984*. Carbondale: Southern Illinois University Press.

Schank, R. C., and R. P. Abelson (1977). *Scripts, Plans, Goals and Understanding: An Inquiry Into Human Knowledge Structures*. Hillsdale, NJ: Erlbaum.

Scheufele, D. A. (2000). "Agenda-Setting, Priming, and Framing Revisited: Another Look at Cognitive Effects of Political Communication." *Mass Communication & Society,* 3: 297–316.

Schiller, H. I. (2000). *Living in the Number One Country: Reflections from a Critic of American Empire*. New York: Seven Stories Press.

————. (1989). *Culture, Inc. : The Corporate Takeover of Public Expression*. New York: Oxford University Press.

————. (1973). *The Mind Managers*. Boston: Beacon.

Schramm, W. (1960). *Mass Communication,* 2nd ed. Urbana: University of Illinois Press.

————. (1954). *The Process and Effects of Mass Communication*. Urbana: University of Illinois Press.

Schramm, W., J. Lyle, and E. Parker (1961). *Television in the Lives of Our Children*. Stanford, CA: Stanford University Press.

Schutz, A. (1970). *On Phenomenology and Social Relations*. Chicago: University of Chicago Press.

————. (1967). *The Phenomenology of the Social World*. Evanston, IL: Northwestern University Press.

Scruton, R. (2000). *An Intelligent Person's Guide to Modern Culture*. South Bend, IN: St. Augustine's Press.

Shanahan, J., and V. Jones (1999). "Cultivation and Social Control." In D. Demers and K. Viswanath, eds., *Mass Media, Social Control and Social Change*. Ames: Iowa State University Press.

Shanahan, J., M. Morgan, and M. Stenbjerre (1997). "Green or Brown? Television and the Cultivation of Environmental Concern." *Journal of Broadcasting & Electronic Media,* 45: 118–134.

Shannon, C., and W. Weaver (1949). *The Mathematical Theory of Communication*. Urbana: University of Illinois Press.

Shiffrin, R. S., and W. Schneider (1977). "Controlled and Automatic Human Information Processing II: Perceptual Learning, Automatic Attending and a General Theory." *Psychological Review,* 84: 127–190.

Siebert, F. S., T. Peterson, and W. Schramm (1956). *Four Theories of the Press*. Urbana: University of Illinois Press.

Signorielli, N. (1990). "Television's Mean and Dangerous World: A Continuation of the Cultural Indicators Perspective." In N. Signorielli and M. Morgan, eds., *Cultivation Analysis: New Directions in Media Effects Research*. Newbury Park, CA: Sage.

Signorielli, N., and M. Morgan, eds., (1990). *Cultivation Analysis: New Directions in Media Effects Research*. Newbury Park, CA: Sage.

Signorielli, N., and S. Kahlenberg (2001). "Television's World of Work in the Nineties." *Journal of Broadcasting & Electronic Media,* 41: 305–323.

Silverblatt, A. (1995). *Media Literacy: Keys to Interpreting Media Messages.* Westport, CT: Praeger.

Simon, H. A. (1981). *The Sciences of the Artificial.* Cambridge, MA: MIT Press.

Simon, T., T. Atwater, and R. Alexander (1988). "FCC Broadcast Content Regulation: Policymaking in a Vacuum." Paper presented at the annual meeting of the Association for Education in Journalism and Mass Communication, Portland, OR, August.

Singer, J. L., and D. G. Singer (1983). "Implications of Childhood Television Viewing for Cognition, Imagination, and Emotion." In J. Bryant and D. R. Anderson, eds., *Children's Understanding of Television: Research on Attention and Comprehension.* New York: Academic.

Smith, A. (1991). *The Age of Behemoths: The Globalization of Mass Media Firms.* New York: Priority.

Solomon, M. R. (1983). "The Role of Products as Social Stimuli: A Symbolic Interactionism Perspective." *Journal of Consumer Research,* 10: 319–329.

Sparks, G. G., and R. M. Ogles (1990). "The Difference Between Fear of Victimization and Probability of Being Victimized: Implications for Cultivation." *Journal of Broadcasting & Electronic Media,* 34: 351–358.

Sproule, J. M. (1997). *Propaganda and Democracy: The American Experience of Media and Mass Persuasion.* New York: Cambridge University Press.

———. (1994). *Channels of Propaganda.* Bloomington, IN: EDINFO.

Stafford, L., S. L. Kline, and J. Dimmick (1999). "Home E-mail: Relational Maintenance and Gratification Opportunities." *Journal of Broadcasting & Electronic Media,* 43: 659–669.

Stauber, J. C., and S. Rampton (1995). *Toxic Sludge Is Good for You: Lies, Damn Lies and the Public Relations Industry.* Monroe, ME: Common Courage.

Steiner, L. (1988). "Oppositional Decoding as an Act of Resistance." *Critical Studies in Mass Communication,* 5: 1–15.

Stevenson, R. L. (1994). *Global Communication in the Twenty-First Century.* New York: Longman.

Stouffer, S. A., E. A. Suchman, L. C. DeVinney, S. A. Star, and R. M. Williams (1949). *The American Soldier: Adjustment During Army Life,* Vol. I. Princeton, NJ: Princeton University Press.

Tan, A. S. (1982). "Television Use and Social Stereotypes." *Journalism Quarterly,* 59: 119–122.

Thomson, O. (1977). *Mass Persuasion in History.* Edinburgh, UK: Paul Harris.

Tichenor, P. J., G. A. Donohue, and C. N. Olien (1980). *Community Conflict and the Press.* Beverly Hills, CA: Sage.

———. (1970). "Mass Media Flow and Differential Growth of Knowledge." *Public Opinion Quarterly,* 34: 159–170.

Trench, M. (1990). *Cyberpunk.* Mystic Fire Videos. New York: Intercon.

Tuchman, G. (1978). *Making News: A Study in the Construction of Reality.* New York: Free Press.

Tunstall, J. (1983). "The Trouble with U. S. Communication Research." *Journal of Communication,* 33: 2–95.

———. (1977). *The Media Are American: Anglo-American Media in the World.* New York: Columbia University Press.

Turner, J. H. (1998). *The Structure of Sociological Theory,* 6th edition. Belmont, CA: Wadsworth.

Vander Neut, T. (1999). "Do Violent Images Cause Violent Behavior?" *Risk & Insurance,* November: 38–40.

Wartella, E. (1979). "The Developmental Perspective." In E. Wartella, ed., *Children Communicating: Media and Development of Thought, Speech, and Understanding.* Beverly Hills, CA: Sage.

Wartella, E. (1997). *The Context of Television Violence.* Boston: Allyn & Bacon.

Wartella, E., and B. Reeves (1985). "Historical Trends in Research on Children and the Media 1900–1960." *Journal of Communication*, 35: 118–133.

Westley, B. H., and M. MacLean (1957). "A Conceptual Model for Mass Communication Research." *Journalism Quarterly*, 34: 31–38.

White, R. W. (1972). *The Enterprise of Living: Growth and Organization in Personality.* New York: Holt, Rinehart & Winston.

Wiener, N. (1961). *Cybernetics*, 2nd ed. Cambridge, MA: MIT Press.

———. (1954). *The Human Use of Human Beings: Cybernetics and Society.* Garden City, NY: Doubleday Anchor.

Wilkins, K. G., and B. Mody (2001). "Reshaping Development Communication: Developing Communication and Communicating Development." *Communication Theory*, 11: 385–396.

Williams, F., R. E. Rice, and E. M. Rogers (1988). *Research Methods and the New Media.* New York: Free Press.

Williams, R. (1974). *Television: Technology and Cultural Form.* London: Fontana.

———. (1967). *Communications.* New York: Barnes and Noble.

Windahl, S. (1981). "Uses and Gratifications at the Crossroads." In G. C. Wilhoit and H. De Bock, eds., *Mass Communication Review Yearbook.* Beverly Hills, CA: Sage.

Wolf, G. (1996). "The Wisdom of Saint Marshall, the Holy Fool." *Wired*, 4 (January): 122–125, 182–187.

Wood, G., and T. McBride (1997). "Origins of Orienting and Defensive Responses: An Evolutionary Perspective." In P. J. Lang, R. F. Simons, and M. Balaban, eds., *Attention and Orienting: Sensory and Motivational Processes.* Hillsdale, NJ: Erlbaum.

"World-Class Tax Dodger!" (1998). *Mother Jones Extra*, September/October, p. 3.

World War II, The Propaganda Battle, Walk Through the 20th Century. (1982). New York: PBS Video.

Wright, C. R. (1986). *Mass Communication: A Sociological Perspective*, 3rd ed. New York: Random House.

———. (1974). "Functional Analysis and Mass Communication Revisited." In J. G. Blumler and E. Katz, eds., *The Uses of Mass Communications: Current Perspectives on Gratifications Research.* Beverly Hills, CA: Sage.

———. (1959). *Mass Communication: A Sociological Perspective*, 1st ed. New York: Random House.

Zillman, D., and J. Wakshlag (1985). "Fear of Victimization and the Appeal of Crime Drama." In D. Zillman and J. Bryant eds., *Selective Exposure to Communication.* Hillsdale, NJ: Erlbaum.

Zimbardo, P. G., and A. L. Weber (1997). *Psychology.* New York: Longman.

Zoll, D. (1999). "Spin City." *San Francisco Bay Guardian*, May 19: 12.

Index

Note: Page numbers in *italics* indicate Instant Access summaries.